IMMIGRATION REFORM AND AMERICA'S UNCHOSEN FUTURE

✶ ✶ ✶

Otis L. Graham, Jr.

authorHOUSE®

AuthorHouse™
1663 Liberty Drive, Suite 200
Bloomington, IN 47403
www.authorhouse.com
Phone: 1-800-839-8640

First published by AuthorHouse 11/21/2008

ISBN: 978-1-4389-0997-4 (e)
ISBN: 978-1-4389-0995-0 (sc)
ISBN: 978-1-4389-0996-7 (hc)

Library of Congress Control Number: 2008910469

Printed in the United States of America
Bloomington, Indiana

This book is printed on acid-free paper.

Contents

PART IV: Still Losing Ground: The Nineties

PART V: The Hinge of History: Across Open Borders, America's Enemies Enter and Attack

Introduction

The vantage point of this memoir is the internal history, as this writer saw and experienced it, of a social movement that grew up to challenge the mass immigration era that began in the 1960s. The unwelcome demographic and cultural future brought by this sustained mass immigration was chosen in public but not chosen publicly, as most citizens were most of the time not paying attention, lacked information and understanding, and were steeped by America's educational institutions in disabling myths and misunderstandings. Some of the American public did awaken, slowly, then mobilized in a social movement to reduce immigration. This book is my reconstruction of that ongoing reform effort based on memory and files gathered along the way.

While our reform movement is stronger than ever, as I write, we have been losing in the struggle to shape immigration policy. Current demographic trends, driven by immigration, will continue to carry us and our descendants to a place where the American people do not want to go—a destination they were never asked or allowed by their ruling elites and their enfeebled political system to choose or reject for themselves. Immigration carries the American nation toward a more globe-resembling population in its cultural multiplicity. Some welcome this for a variety of reasons including the prospect of enhanced world leadership. Some foresee the possibility of the weakening of social cohesion, mounting class and ethnoracial division, and even regional separatism. More predictable and harmful results from the population growth path are the inevitable crowding and congestion, the degradation of the nation's ecological underpinnings, intensifying energy, water, and other resource shortages, just at the time the nation enters the unprecedented crisis brought on by global warming and the "peak oil" transition when petroleum demand outstrips global supply.

The mix of these elements cannot be predicted, but taken in the large perspective, it will not be welcomed by our descendants, who will ask history who was responsible, and who resisted.

This book is my account of the Americans who resisted.

The people who put us on this road and kept us there against mounting objections and complaints from a slowly-awakening public have been America's political, economic, and social elites, as well as foreign immigrants surging into the country, legally and illegally, in a mass immigration that began in the 1960s at the invitation of the federal government and which now appears to have unstoppable momentum and at least another half century to run. The elites chose this societal future in pursuit of their own short-term economic or political gains, because of a misguided moralism and sentimentality combined with demographic and environmental ignorance. History will treat them harshly, though in recent years they have basked in the conviction that they occupy the moral high ground.

The immigrants to America, perhaps even the illegal ones, will likely continue to be seen in a more forgiving light, given the immigrant origins of all of us if you go back far enough, and the benign intentions of almost all of them. In the words of UCLA astronomer Ben Zuckerman (who suspects he heard it from Dick Lamm, who thinks he probably remembered and slightly modified it from Polish writer Stanislaw Jerzy Lec): "In an avalanche, each individual, unique snowflake pleads not guilty."

Otis L. Graham, Jr.
Chapel Hill, North Carolina

PART I:
PATHS TO IMMIGRATION
REFORM

Chapter One:
Into the Sixties and Social Movement Time

*There is simply nothing so important to a people and its
government as how many of them there are, whether their
number is growing or declining...and...which way these
numbers are moving.* — Daniel Patrick Moynihan

I arrived at immigration reform through the familiar social
movements of the sixties. One must, of course, start earlier. In the
late forties, I spent many Saturdays in the downtown Nashville public
library, reading historical novels. One day, wandering the cool marble
corridors and taking a wrong turn away from the shelves of my favorite
books, I happened on two unusual books that told, in different ways,
an unnerving story about how something unprecedented had evolved
quickly out of the past and threatened the human future. The books
were Fairfield Osborne's, *Our Plundered Planet* (1948) and William
Vogt's, *Road to Survival* (1948). From these pioneering books (somehow
my browsing missed the real pioneer, George Perkins Marsh, *Man and
Nature*, published in 1864), I became aware of a way of viewing and
assessing the human situation that transcended the clichéd categories
of the Cold War era I had grown up in. These books presented a new,
and (to me) profoundly unsettling argument that the world I knew, one
of dazzling postwar progress, appeared in reality to be headed toward
serious environmental and resource troubles, due to population growth
and the mounting abuses of nature.

Vogt, in particular, was blunt about population growth, saying, "We
Americans are probably now overpopulated."

Some years later, I realized that these books overdid the Malthusian gloom, as writers will do when attempting to catch the attention of an ignorant and apathetic public. However, I was young and naturally interested in the forces that were shaping the future. Here were authors who seemed to have aligned their sights along some basic, and to me and most Americans, unpondered trend lines—the trajectories of human numbers and their implications for resource depletion and environmental degradation.

These authors' anticipation of a global ecocrisis, to use later terminology, made a connection to my boyhood experience in the hills south of Nashville. Here I had early developed my own local environmental worries and a sense of the unwelcome side of the growth all my elders seemed to uncritically welcome. My younger brother, Hugh, and I had somehow as young boys become strong environmentalists— without using or knowing the word. We and a couple of pals felt ourselves friends, observers and protectors of the rabbits, minnows, and turtles inhabiting the bottomland and Brown's Creek running below our home on the southern outskirts of Nashville, Tennessee. We were never so happy as when hiking on a Saturday around the edges of wildfowl-decorated, civilization untouched Radnor Lake, nestled in the Harpeth Hills south of town (owned by a railroad, Radnor Lake was a hunting preserve). We worried about that lake habitat, as suburban homes and new roads were pushed by bulldozers up the rising ground toward the forest line and the lake. Brown's Creek was a daily playground, but the meadows alongside it were relentlessly subdivided by the developers' stakes, followed by housing tracts on treeless lots. People's trashy ways were everywhere.

"The world is turning to broken glass," Hugh ruefully complained on the day we found shards of beer bottles thrown with other trash from a bridge over our creek.

As boys, we spent our free time hiking in the Harpeth Hills, or camping at Fall Creek Falls State Park, or paddling to overnight camps along the Caney Fork River. When developers staked out house plots in "the Bottoms" along Brown's Creek, we ripped them out each evening, until the police were called, and the developers won—as they have every day of my life.

* * *

Social movements? At Yale, in the 1950s, they hadn't arrived, in the sense of card tables in student gathering places urging some sort of signing up and local action. Rosa Parks, I knew, refused to give up her bus seat in Montgomery, Alabama in the middle of my junior year; Martin Luther King, Jr. formed an organization to push for enlarged civil rights that spring. I sympathized with King against the southern whites who ran the South I had come from, but these seemed distant events in Alabama, Georgia, and Mississippi to a kid sentenced to New Haven for four years. Al Lowenstein, then a Yale law school student, often showed up in the wrestling room in Payne Whitney gym and talked to those of us who would listen about a world stirring with the revolt against racial injustice and the importance of finding a personal place in that crusade. I was sympathetic and aligned with the cause Al described, but I felt confined to New Haven, with summers commanded by the U. S. Navy, in accord with the terms of my NROTC scholarship.

* * *

Then the 1960s came. After three years as an artillery officer in the Marines, I entered a U.S. history PhD program at Columbia University in New York, taught history at a small women's college in Washington, D.C., from 1962-65, and watched the black horse accompany John F. Kennedy's coffin across the bridge to his burial site in Virginia. My wife, daughter, and I moved to California in 1965, where I taught history for one year at a new campus of the state college system located at Hayward in the East Bay, then took a position on the faculty of the University of California, Santa Barbara.

It was social movement time. The struggle for racial equality was located in the South at first, but Berkeley was not far behind. An NAACP membership card became my first dues-paying, organizational social reform affiliation. I later attended meetings in the Palo Alto chapter when I lived there in 1965, and in the Santa Barbara NAACP offices at the corner of Ortega and Salsipuedes. When Martin Luther King, Jr. was assassinated, my wife and I went with other white friends to a black church in Santa Barbara to mourn, and show solidarity.

However, more than race relations in America urgently needed fixing in the sixties. Despite my background as a Marine officer from 1957 to 1960, I was troubled by American military intervention in Vietnam. I devoted months of intense reading to understand the situation in Southeast Asia, and in time joined another social movement—the effort to end the war and make joining or starting such wars a little harder. A small band of professors at my campus, the University of California at Santa Barbara, formed the campus anti-war caucus. I attended their second meeting, and they named me treasurer, handing me a can with twelve dollars inside. We marched downtown, held "teach-ins," and worried about how to harness and redirect the students' (and some of our own) sometimes unconstructive impulses.

In the fifties, the civil rights crusade was called "The Movement"— first, largest, and most important. Then at some point it became a habit to say (and express by dress, facial hair, and/or lifestyle) that one was "in The Movement," and that meant an involvement in or at least sympathy with a cluster of causes thought to be kindred—civil rights, anti-war, environment, women's rights, Indian's rights, and an expanding range of protests against the treatment of this or that group by the older (i.e. white male) America.

* * *

Choosing Your Main Social Movement

Environmental protection, however, seemed to me the societal reform that would require a longer effort and more fundamental re-thinking of society's assumptions than the others, and would meet more fierce opposition even than that thrown up by the Southern Bull Connors and the Military Industrial complex. For we Greens were challenging the most awesome opponent, the Growth idea and commitment, entwined with the American story of unlimited resources and endless frontiers, and defended by formidable organized lobbies of interest. Getting off the Growth Path as we knew it and onto a path toward sustainability became my main "social activist" issue. Exactly what that meant was still a bit unclear to me and the like-minded others I began to encounter. However, that population growth ought to end at the earliest possible moment was obvious. I endorsed the phrase somebody later came up with—"Whatever your cause, it's a lost cause without population limitation."

I was quite late in coming to this. It escaped my notice that President Eisenhower in the mid-fifties commissioned a report by William F. Draper that linked rapid population growth with growing global poverty and thus to the spread of communism. While the president rejected the proposal for federal birth control programs abroad, he later reversed himself and agreed to become an honorary vice-chair (with Harry Truman) of Planned Parenthood World Federation. By the sixties, I was following such developments, and understood that the idea that human population growth was a massive problem in places like India and Bangladesh expanded to include an overcrowding United States. John F. Kennedy's Secretary of the Interior, Stewart Udall, closed his influential 1963 book on environmental problems, *The Quiet Crisis*, with a warning that further population growth was incompatible with the nation's environmental goals. In a later printing of the book he noted how widespread was this sentiment in the sixties. Udall recalled that the Sierra Club's dynamic executive director, David Brower, expressed in the mid-1960s "the consensus of the environmental movement" when he said, 'We feel you don't have a conservation policy unless you have a population policy.'" A Stanford University biologist specializing in butterflies was so shocked by what he saw of human misery on a trip to India that he wrote a little polemic entitled *The Population Bomb*. Published in 1967, it catapulted Paul Ehrlich onto the best-seller lists and into media fame, including interviews in such popular magazines as *Mademoiselle* and *Playboy*. Other mass circulation magazines—*Life*, and *Parents Magazine*—ran featured articles on "Smaller Families: A National Imperative," or linking overpopulation with traffic problems. Organizers of the first Earth Day celebrations on April 22, 1970, stressed the importance of including in these events the necessity to curb and end population growth. Religious groups in the late sixties passed resolutions urging the government to endorse population stabilization, and President Richard Nixon in 1970 appointed the first national Commission on Population Growth and the American Future.

By the seventies, this expanding concern over world and United States population growth had become a growing social movement taking the form of membership-based lobbying group organization around the issue. Some of the established environmental organizations, such as Audubon and the Sierra Club, appointed population committees to integrate the issue into these group's educational and lobbying efforts, and the problem fit well within the outlook of Planned Parenthood. President Anthony Wayne Smith of the National Parks and Conservation Association wrote an editorial in the group's magazine arguing that "the pressures of a steadily rising population preclude adequate long-term solutions to conservation issues," and in 1978, the NPCA took the lead in forming a coalition of environmental and labor groups to press for measures to curb illegal immigration. Ehrlich and others in 1968 formed Zero Population Growth (ZPG), a new organization with only one issue—population growth, global and within the U.S.

We who had these concerns did not seem to have a name for ourselves. In addition to being environmentalists, were we also "Populationists"? No particular label stuck to the environmentalists who understood the demographic dimension of their tasks.

I joined ZPG quite early, but it was not clear what we Populationists should be doing, beyond encouraging small families, which meant support for the federal government's exploratory efforts (under Kennedy and Johnson) to launch programs to make birth control information and technology widely available.

* * *

California was bursting with growth when I arrived (thus contributing to it). The lemon groves and eucalyptus trees were going down before the homebuilders, the traffic was thickening, the beaches fouled, the air browning. Those who found this unacceptable joined groups where a shoulder could be put to the wheel of resistance to growth. In Santa Barbara there was GOO (Get Oil Out), which urged limits on offshore oil exploration and transport. I joined the brushfires of resistance to developers' plans for dense housing on places like the historic open space at More Mesa and governmental plans for the importation of growth-inducing water from the state north-south aqueduct. There were regional efforts to protect the coastline from oil infrastructure and enclosures by high-end developers, statewide growth-control and mildly populationist groups such as California Tomorrow. All had in common the conviction that the private forces driving growth and the environmental damage that it always brought were pushing community, region, and nation in the wrong basic directions. How to get a different future? The tools, conventional wisdom held, were public education and then "planning," a word every growth opponent used frequently.

Immigration reform? We are almost there, though you may not have noticed it coming.

* * *

We All Were Lefties

At this point, my thinking and behavior was in the mainstream of 1960s and post-sixties reformism. Of course, a university and a university town, especially on the "left coast," are not what could be called normal places. Yet every place and time has its mainstream, and it seemed that almost all my friends and people I interacted with on and off campus were, like myself, hooked up with one or more social reform movements, and were invariably sympathetic to the whole cluster—civil rights, feminism, environmentalism and growth control, end the war and curb the nuclear arms race. For my part, I was an FDR Democrat evolving toward the left as I lived through the Sixties. In 1968, the students for Robert Kennedy for President asked me to serve as their faculty advisor, which I did, though they needed no advice. Most of us mobilized by the causes of the sixties were expecting to change the world, soon.

We would have agreed with the British author C. P. Snow, when he was asked by a crowd of American college students in the late sixties, "What is the cause?"

Sensing that they wanted a short answer, Snow shouted, "Peace! Food! No more people than the Earth can take!"

No more people than the earth can take. He consensually anchored his advice on that at the end, and the audience responded with enthusiasm. Me, too, if I had been there.

Chapter Two:
The Seventies: Population Stabilization—A Goal Won and Then Lost

We have concluded that, in the long run, no substantial benefits will result from further growth of the Nation's population, rather that the gradual stabilization of our population would contribute significantly to the Nation's ability to solve its problems.
— Report of the Commission on Population Growth and the American Future (1972)

I have recounted the buildup of social movements in the sixties in order to locate population limitation among them, and therefore to make a place for the immigration restrictionist's sentiment that logically followed from it.

In a very short time, the cause of population stabilization went from being the most successful to the least successful social movement of that era. It emerged in the 1950s, and by the 1970s, it appeared to be in danger of disappearing due to its own success.

* * *

Of all the social reformers of that era, we Populationists had a simple goal. Compared to the radical dream of "social equality" for descendants of slaves, or permanent peace on Earth, we wanted population growth globally, and in America, to stop. Then it would be possible to move toward ecologically sustainable economies and civilizations, with America leading the way. As I discovered and aligned with this goal, the nation's natural demographic evolution was favorable to our hopes. Friends would say to me that there was really no need for any sort of social campaign for slower and then stabilized population growth. American fertility rates after the end of the "Baby Boom" in the mid-1960s had been precipitously declining, and the magic number of a fertility rate of 2.1 per woman—the rate that would in time produce a stable population—was reached in the mid-1970s. A stable or even declining population was just two generations away. We Populationists could not claim much credit for this, and were glad to accord the credit to American women, exercising (in some cases motivated by the educational efforts of Planned Parenthood, ZPG, and other "birth control" groups) free choice in reproductive matters.

As the goal of a stabilized population size approached, we expected to intensify our discussion of what population size seemed to be in the national interest, and how to get there. The historic cresting of population growth would allow societies to discuss their carrying capacity populations, and how to reach those totals. That second part, we knew, would be a bit complicated, but the historic end to human population growth seemed to have arrived in the United States—if fertility rates reached by the mid-1970s would hold. If fertility rates dropped below 2.1 (they did), then the stabilization of the American population would come more quickly. The most important (in my view) of the social movements had virtually achieved success by the end of the sixties, at least in the U. S. What other social movement could claim this?

Defeat Snatched From the Jaws of Victory

In 1972, there was more good news—at first glance. A national commission, the President's Commission on Population Growth and the American Future (named the Rockefeller Commission after its Chair, John D. Rockefeller III), issued a report endorsing we Populationists' analysis and hopes. The Commission recommended that, considering resources, environmental, and other social problems, "the nation welcome and plan for a stabilized population" which "would contribute significantly to the nation's ability to solve its problems."

This seemed the highest possible governmental endorsement for our cause. More important, the American people appeared to agree on small families and below replacement fertility. National demographic trends as summarized by the Commission amounted to a declaration of victory for those welcoming an end to the growth of the American population. Or, at least, impending victory. With stunning swiftness, the nation was approaching the end of its long demographic upward growth curve. Our population had increased from 76 million in 1900 to 205 million in 1970, but over that time the birthrate had been steadily declining, and population momentum slowing. True, an unexpected "Baby Boom" began in 1946, and reversed the fertility decline. This unexpected blip proved to be a brief aberration. Fertility rates resumed their decline in 1964, responding to the deeper forces at work which were changing the preferences of American women, and (presumably) their partners, with respect to family size. So rapid was the decline that resumed in the sixties that, by the early 1970s, the national media was reporting a "baby bust," meaning rapid fertility declines toward the "replacement level" rate of 2.1 live births per woman—and possibly below it!

A replacement level fertility rate of 2.1 children per woman of childbearing age was reached in 1976. Many people, misled by the media, misunderstood this to mean that population growth was over. To the more educated, it meant that an end to population growth was in sight. After "population momentum" lasting two generations had run its course, the population of the United States would stop growing.

To we Populationists, the end of U.S. population growth (the same trends were observable in all Western democracies) was an epochal success for humanity and all the creatures attempting to share the planet with us. Without government coercion of any kind, American women had chosen this demographic future, which was the key to so much else. With this demographic shift, our environmental protection goals would soon not seem like goalposts being constantly moved back by expanding populations. A protected ecosystem sustaining human economies now seemed attainable, if we did many other additional things having to do with ways of living on the planet. No wonder we Populationists were optimists, in those days.

We were also in for a rude awakening.

* * *

From Abroad, a Cancellation of Our American Success

Even as this demographic scenario was widely publicized in the 1970s, we learned in the same Rockefeller report, to our dismay, that another demographic force external to the U. S. was canceling it out—rising levels of immigration.

It seems that almost nobody saw this coming. There had been a little-noticed and poorly attended series of hearings on global demographic trends, i.e., on the alarming growth of human populations, in the House of Representatives in 1961-62, as part of the preparation for the reform of American immigration policy which was then far down the list of the president's legislative priorities. Demographers at those hearings warned that overcrowded and underdeveloped countries could be expected to export more and more people toward the U.S. and other western countries.

Few paid attention to what was said in poorly attended hearings on the world demographic background for considering immigration reform. Indeed, few had paid much attention to immigration at all since the late 1920s. The topic had slipped from the forefront of politics and the media in the 1920s when new restrictions combined with depression and war reduced immigration to a trickle. Spasmodic refugee flows from Hungary and Cuba in the 1950s were taken as isolated incidents. Immigration was a non-subject for most Americans in the 1960s; a piece of the past. After the 1920s, the country had been doing quite well with small amounts of it.

Notwithstanding, immigration policy in the sixties found its way to the table. No, that is too passive. It was *put* on the table by a handful of immigration expansionist reformers who had convinced John Kennedy to add immigration policy revision to his New Frontier agenda. Kennedy had allowed these reformers to write a book for his signature, *A Nation of Immigrants*, and had made cautious comments endorsing immigration reform. He was killed before he judged the political timing promising. Lyndon Johnson listened to those reformers, who made an eloquent and passionate case that the existing National

14

Origins Quota system was built on racial discrimination, and in the climate of the civil rights movement could no longer be tolerated. LBJ saw this connection at once, and another—that an America attempting to win the Cold War struggle for global hearts and minds seemed ill-served by an immigration policy that favored Europeans, blocked Asians, and proudly wore the label given it in the 1920s—the National Origins Quota system. Inaugurated in 1924 and modified in 1952, this immigration regime gave preference to those foreigners whose nationality matched the dominant groups in the U.S. as measured by the 1920 census. This was popular with the American people in general, as it seemed to shape immigration so as to be "a mirror of America" coming in on each incoming boatload, and there were not too many boatloads in any event. Aided by the Great Depression and World War II, these new restrictions substantially curbed immigration and allowed it to fade from public discussion—until the civil rights era began. Then a small but intense chorus of criticism focused on U. S. immigration law, claiming that it was akin to racial discrimination and should be replaced by a system of selection that "did not ask," in Lyndon Johnson's words, "what country you were born in."

On signing the Immigration Act of 1965, Johnson promised that the new law would make little difference except that discrimination on the basis of nationality would be removed from the immigrant selection process. No increase in numbers was expected. Indeed, administration officials repeatedly denied such a possibility. This policy change was not much noticed by the general public. I confess that I do not recall even noticing its discussion or passage, though I lived in Washington, D.C. at the time and taught American history at a local college.

Nevertheless, something large had happened. This unheralded reform law, coming at a time when international migration pressures were mounting and Mexican-Central American population doubling times were in the range of twenty to twenty-five years,ushered in a new era of mass immigration after the 1920s to 1960s lull. American immigration totals doubled in the 1970s; their demographic impact augmented by rising levels of illegal entry over the Mexican border.

The demographic implications of falling domestic fertility rates and rising levels of immigration were largely ignored until the report of the Rockefeller Population Commission of 1972. It pointed out that, if fertility rates and immigration levels were not changed, immigration would contribute 25 percent of U.S. population growth in the years ahead, and that did not account for illegal immigration. Upon discovering this from its staff and from research reports, the Rockefeller Commission blinked, and "were left floundering" by this "surprise" for which they were "unprepared," according to the words of an account of their deliberations published by Charles Keeley in *International Migration Review* in late 1972. The Commission's main concern was to end population growth, but it had unexpectedly collided with the crucial importance of immigration levels, and that was historically a sensitive subject. The Commission was "deeply split" and could agree only on two recommendations. Illegal immigration should be ended by sanctions on U.S. employers. As for legal immigration, while some commissioners wanted a reduction of 10 percent a year for five years, they could only agree on a recommendation that the numbers must not be increased in the future, lest it prevent the Commission's chief goal—population stabilization.

* * *

The implications of the Rockefeller report were stunning, yet hard to absorb. It told us that an essential goal pursued by the environmental movement—population stabilization—had been endorsed after extensive study by a distinguished national panel, and indeed seemed within our grasp by the early 1970s. No government programs were required. It was happening; an expression of American freedom, and especially more freedom for women.

Then we discovered that the federal government's immigration policies were moving the goal out of reach, though no branch or part of government had debated or authorized it.

An irony deepened our depression. President Nixon had not only refused to endorse the Rockefeller Report but had attacked its recommendations on abortion. He was silent while other critics of the report insisted that the federal government must never become involved in a population policy. However, we learned from the report that the Immigration Act of 1965 *was* population policy! Congress, with that law, had enacted a statute negating population stabilization aimed at unending expansion! So much for Nixon's stern promise that government must stay out of questions like American population size.

* * *

I shared the dismay of other Populationists at the 1972-73 discovery that immigration had become a driver of U.S. population growth, after the decisions of American citizens had pushed our fertility rates onto a path of stabilization and then decline. What was one to make of the cynical spectacle of a government denouncing the idea of a national population policy while covertly putting in place a major and sustained program of population expansion, but hiding it as immigration reform? In addition, what was one to make of a news media and public so ignorant or distracted that there was almost no comment or critique?

I had no remedial idea for this dismaying turn of events, and heard none from anyone else. The realization of the growing intrusion of the immigration factor into the national demographic future had been unexpected and sobering. Immigration was now a central problem for we environmentalists, whether we acknowledged it or not. This sudden intrusion of the immigration issue into the cause of environmentalism caught me, and all other Populationists known to me, unprepared. What was at stake, however, was brought home to me in lecture tours (arranged by USIA) that took me in the 1970s and 1980s to India, South Korea, Mexico, Colombia, and Argentina. In Old and New Delhi and elsewhere in India, I saw what the term "over-population" looked like in Third World streets. In rural villages in southern Mexico, I saw poor children standing in the doorways of cardboard huts clad only in T-shirts labeled "Dallas Cowboys," evidence that they knew that a journey to *El Norte* might put them into unknown luxury.

In South Korea during the daily noontime riot between university students and police, I asked where the other half of the student body was, and they told me, "In the library, studying. They plan to move to the U.S."

I began to sense the gathering of a human avalanche moving toward America and the rest of the West, ready to radically alter our national future.

Chapter Three:
We Growth Opponents Lower Our Sights

What is the cause? Peace. Food. No more people than the earth can take. — C. P. Snow

The discovery in the early 1970s of the power of the immigration factor to defeat the aspirations of the entire environmental movement produced among some of my friends a grumbling series of questions about immigration history: "How did this happen, this sudden immigration boom?" This was invariably embarrassing to me, an historian of modern U.S. who was expected to know a little something about recent immigration policy.

What I knew was more "little" than "something." My graduate education in U.S. history at Columbia University had been superb, but much was left out. For example, there was no environmental history in that (or any other) history department in the 1960s, and no women's history. As for immigration history, it was a small sub-field, with most history departments containing not even one such specialist. What immigration historians wrote was not expected to be a part of our qualifying or final exams. I began my graduate study in 1960 when Oscar Handlin at Harvard was just about the only historian of immigration whose work (invariably one book, *The Uprooted*) we might be expected to have read. At Columbia, Robert Cross, in an eclectic seminar on social history, had us read the dense classic, Florian and Znanieki, *The Polish Peasant in the United States*. It seemed that every graduate student I encountered had read John Higham's brilliant *Strangers in the Land: Patterns of American Nativism, 1860-1925*, a seminal work published in 1954. I had not gone beyond that smattering of information, as immigration history did not particularly interest me. It seemed to me a filiopietistic area that was intellectually moribund, taken up with stories of how our heroic ancestors had come here from Ireland, Italy, or Poland, "and built this country."

In the 1960s, I became a certified PhD carrying historian. When the sudden, unanticipated return of large-scale immigration conflicted with my social movement goals, I was unprepared to tell my friends where it had come from or how long it would run.

In the early 1970s, we environmentalists who were therefore also Populationists, acted initially as if the return of large-scale immigration could be ignored. There was available to we growth-controllers an uncontroversial alternative direction for our thoughts and activism. This was the fast-emerging idea that a solution to growth problems could be found by unifying a range of existing and newly imagined federal (and state/local) policies for building upon the basis of the existing zoning framework a system of measures for "controlling growth" to achieve both environmental and social equity goals. Considerable energy and enthusiasm flowed toward what was being called a National Growth Policy, nurtured in the 1970s by liberal Democrats such as Senator Hubert Humphrey and Morris Udall. I was caught up in this in my own back-bench way. I began to write a book which folded it into the evolution of the national planning idea. Stronger land use controls at the local level, guided by national infrastructure investment strategies would end bad growth and bring us good growth. Bad growth was "sprawl" invading prime agricultural land and wildlife habitat, and decaying industrial cities, both leading to metropolitan areas visualized as doughnuts, black-brown inner cores ringed by white and informally segregated perimeters. Good growth would be steered by local land use policies guided by regional planning goals within a national policy framework. The result would be more compact, nature respecting and racially mixed settlement patterns.

For a time I was drawn to this vision of an America bringing an end to the era of unquestioned growth guided only by developers' profit calculations, especially after attending a 1978 White House Conference on National Growth. Locally, I participated in the Santa Barbara version of "managing" growth by joining County Supervisor David Yager's citizens' advisory committee. We struggled to design stronger land use controls to curb growth in our water famished area. This in effect meant pushing the growth somewhere else in the county or region. While we urged regional planning, it was obvious (to a few of us locals) that national population growth had to be curbed for growth management to become more than just a "Not In My Backyard" enterprise. When some of us raised the question of who/what would control national population growth, we were told that declining fertility rates would take care of that. The growth control movement of the 1970s used the term "national" a lot, but their hearts were not in it. Local fights against "unwise" and "unplanned" development were our daily fare.

Thus the 1972 Rockefeller Report on the problems associated with further population growth had run the immigration issue up the flagpole, beneath the larger banner of a national policy to stabilize growth. The Rockefellers did not leave it at that. The Rockefeller Brothers Fund financed a task force of sixty-three environmental scientists and leaders who would "set an agenda." A blue ribbon panel of experts from universities and organizations such as the Conservation Foundation, Resources for the Future, and the Sierra Club Legal Defense Club, brought together a "consensus report" published in 1977 as Gerald Barney, ed., *The Unfinished Agenda*. The immigration connection to environmental defense held its place on the agenda—: America should "gradually reduce and stabilize quotas for legal immigration. Illegal entry into the U.S. should…be ended, and legal immigration reduced to a level approximating emigration."

* * *

Ending population growth and the immigration policy component of this mission, then, had been run up the policy discussion flagpole in the 1970s. Astonishingly, they both came down together. The Populationist impulse itself, within the environmentalist movement, where it had so quickly taken root, moved to the far margins of discussion. This was not so much an internal weakening as it was a retreat under intense, organized pressure. It is now clear, after the publication in 2002 of a pioneering essay-memoir by Roy Beck and Leon Kolankiewicz ("The Environmental Movement's Retreat from Advocating U.S. Population

Stabilization, 1978-1998," in Otis L. Graham, Jr., ed., *Environmental Politics and Policy, 1960s-1990s*), that the population issue itself came under fierce attack from a strange combination of forces—political conservatives mobilized against abortion, the Vatican, and some elements of the radical left and the black leadership of the civil rights movement.

This is another story, but it meant that as America's population from 1970 to the end of the century grew by 33 percent, or 70 million people, with most of the growth due to immigration (immigrants plus their children). There was almost no discussion of the costs of the growth or its major source—immigration. Over these years, one by one the environmental groups, including the Sierra Club, abandoned the populationist theme. By the end of the century, environmental protection and repair were expected to come through the familiar tools of governmental regulation and public education, but not ever or anywhere by population limits. The Populationist moment had passed. There were brief sightings in the unread pages of President Carter's *Global 2000 Report* (1980), President Clinton's 1996 report on sustainability, and as an insurrection within the ranks of the Sierra Club in the 1990s. These were flare-ups, and could gain no permanent traction.

Then, in 1978, somebody called and invited me to join a social movement to revive the insights of the Rockefeller report, and pursue their logic.

PART II:
ORGANIZING THE LAST
SIXTIES SOCIAL MOVEMENT

Chapter Four: A Liberal Think Tank and the Revival of Immigration Reform

I never particularly liked the population issue.
— Robert Maynard Hutchins

Actually, that 1978 phone call would not have come, but for a chain of events going back at least two years. It was September, 1976, as I recall. Democrats such as myself had the not unreasonable sense that our political enterprise was on the way up. The Democratic nominee for president, upstart Democratic Governor of Georgia, Jimmy Carter, turned out to be an intelligent man who spoke in paragraphs and had an attractive populist identity. He held a small lead in the polls over President Gerald Ford, and might have been on the way to sweeping Ford Republicans and Nixon holdovers out of the executive branch. In Santa Barbara, the Democratic party was then fairly cohesive, holding fund-raisers and social gatherings where I had become acquainted with Harry Ashmore. He was the South Carolinian who had shared a Pulitzer Prize with his newspaper as executive editor of the *Arkansas Gazette* during the desegregation of Little Rock High School. Harry's writing on school integration brought him to the attention of former president of the University of Chicago, Robert Maynard Hutchins, who added Ashmore to the board of the New York-based Fund for the Republic. In 1959, the Fund dissolved and Hutchins took the remaining money to Santa Barbara, where he established a new institution—the Center for the Study of Democratic Institutions—on a forty-two acre estate in Montecito on the south edge of town. Ashmore came with Hutchins, and became an associate of the Center. White-haired, courtly, smiling, and with a nice turn of phrase, Harry was often seen about town at

Democratic Party gatherings, or due to his celebrity status, introduced visiting lecturers. I met him in those circles and we became somewhat friendlier than just fellow Democrats, since both of us were (and he sounded like it) Southerners. His publisher boss at the *Arkansas Gazette* had been my cousin, Hugh Baskin Patterson.

Harry called me at home one weekday evening in 1975, and asked if I could meet him and Hutchins for lunch. This was mysterious, but then Hutchins and the Center had long been a bit mysterious to the other residents of Santa Barbara. The University of California at Santa Barbara was about twelve miles up the coast from the Center's sprawling white hilltop estate, but there was virtually no contact between the two institutions. In my first decade in Santa Barbara, I knew of no faculty member (or anyone else) who had been invited to the Center. Their writer-intellectuals—including, for various terms of residency, notables such as Alduous Huxley, William O. Douglas, Gunnar and Alva Myrdal, Mortimer Adler, Clifton Fadiman, and Harvey Wheeler— could only be seen if one were at the right Montecito cocktail parties. We assumed this detachment meant that Hutchins did not take us seriously out at the fairly new campus of the University of California, which was probably true. Nevertheless, we should not have taken it personally. As I later understood, Hutchins had given up on universities in general after years of trying to establish at the University of Chicago a real intellectual community and a core humanities curriculum built around "the Great Books" of the western canon.

He stated the purpose of the Center in these terms, "What is needed above everything else is for some group or institution that can try to do for our own time what the universities used to do—to formulate, state, clarify and advance the ideas that underlie our civilization."

That was elevating, but left much to the imagination. The Center published *The Center Magazine* beginning in 1960, and one could become a member, read the magazine, and get a sense of what went on in their daily meetings around "the big table." Hutchins' Center steered generally left of center, looking with a worried air into matters such as freedom of press and speech, the need for institutions for global peace and arms control, advancement of civil rights, and Constitutional questions interesting to Hutchins which usually meant civil liberties,

26

and, always, higher education. There was something high-minded and visionary about all this.

I would later learn that Hutchins' favorite bit of poetry was a line from Walt Whitman, "Solitary, singing in the West, I strike up for a new world."

I did not find room in our family budget in those days to subscribe to the magazine. Still, driving to the luncheon at the Biltmore Hotel, I had the advantage of knowing what Hutchins looked like. I had been one of the few UCSB faculty members invited to attend one of the Center sessions. This rare invitation came early in the 1970s from Center Associate Rexford Guy Tugwell, economist and a member of Franklin Roosevelt's "Brains Trust," who had read some of my writing on the New Deal. Tugwell invited me to visit and (silently) observe one of their daily 11:00 a.m. to 12:30 p.m. sessions in a large oval room where the members sat around a huge table. It was a session devoted to the presidency, and Harvard's Frank Freidel gave a paper on how FDR had tried to institutionalize planning. A few other visitors sat, as I did, in chairs against the wall. Hutchins, a tall, elegant and commanding figure, genially presided but had little to say. We visitors joined the group for lunch. That visit gave me no real sense of what the Center was up to, and Ashmore had not told me why I had been called to lunch with the great man himself. It was known in Santa Barbara, however, that the Center had entered a period of faltering finances, and the local press had carried stories as early as 1970 on reorganizations and downsizing of the ranks of resident Associates and some staff.

I soon learned that financial troubles had forced yet another drastic reorganization. The Center would now terminate all salaried Associates, yet continue what was called "the Dialogue" of daily meetings and produce occasional publications. The core "great minds" would be the small group of those Associates willing to accept early retirement and still come to the table. The Center now needed outside brain power. The University of California, they conceded, was a nearby pool of talent. I was a full professor at the nearby UC campus west of Santa Barbara, presumably knew the entire UCSB faculty, and had access to the other campuses. Would I come on board as Program Director, with the additional assignment of recruiting UC faculty from all eight campuses to join specific projects or sessions and write for *The Center Magazine*?

The Center would compensate me for taking a semester's unpaid leave, and after that I would be a paid consultant.

* * *

Joining The Center

I didn't hesitate, and soon occupied an office down the long, cool, marble-floored hall from Hutchins. The sprawling white mansion was half empty, the resident Associates were gone, and a reduced publications and administrative staff were scattered about. Lunch was served each day, and once or twice a week someone read a paper or led a discussion at the sounding of the 11:00 a.m. bell. Hutchins and I agreed that I would read through the program files for the last ten years, and make a judgment as to what parts of the Center's recent work still seemed like unfinished and important business, and which should for various reasons be closed out and replaced with new inquiries. I would then meet with him to discuss how to proceed. Some twelve to fifteen large blue boxes were brought to me, and I read through letters, memos, and essays on the Center's past and recent preoccupations—the *Pacem in Terris* conferences on world peace and disarmament, race relations including the new concept of affirmative action, the state of American education, the Constitutional issues involved in "exclusionary zoning," freedom of the press, and other issues touching upon the role of public information in a democracy, the role of corporations, and much else. One of these boxes leads into our story—the one marked "Population Problems."

Aldous Huxley, it seemed, had pressed the Center to think and worry much about global population, and some Dialogue sessions and occasional publications resulted. To this day, I recall vividly a session in which UN environmental official Maurice Strong delivered a vivid and brilliant update on the global ecological crisis, which he knew to be driven by unprecedented population growth. Was there a new direction in which the Center might take this inquiry? This was one of my keen interests in which I had no technical training. The files told me that the Center, relying mostly upon Associate and UC demographer Kingsley Davis (whom I met there), had sounded the alarm about world population growth in an informed and responsible way, without adding anything particularly new. What next?

I re-read the Rockefeller Commission report, and became curious about the fate of the discovery revealed there that rising levels of immigration had become a population-driving and therefore problematic element in the American future. I was surprised and intrigued by what I found and didn't find, as I prepared for my next bi-weekly meeting with Hutchins.

When I got around to the Population box, I gave Hutchins my view that the Center should continue programming on the population cluster of issues, and that the area most in need of attention was the demographic and other effects of recent immigration trends. The Center should engage this rising immigration topic, for it was beginning to determine the demographic future of the United States. I had little to say about the economic and social impacts of rising immigration levels, for I knew little about them. For me, it was the numbers that begged discussion. They spelled defeat for my central social cause. The illegality of much current immigration, I thought, should also interest a lawyer and former law school dean.

Robert Hutchins (I called him Bob, reluctantly and later) slowly sat back in his chair, and said with some seriousness, "I have never particularly liked the population issue. Aldous pressured us to do it, with encouragement from the Myrdals. So we did, but it wasn't fun. I especially don't like the immigration issue."

To this day, I cannot account for my reaction. This forty-one-year-old professor of no national reputation or importance was sitting in the office of the former Dean of Yale Law School, the former president of the University of Chicago, author, and foundation executive who had known and influenced many of the most distinguished educators, writers, and statesmen of the twentieth Century. The youngish professor had just been told that a programmatic suggestion he had made wasn't to the president's liking. Why didn't I move on to the next agenda item? What possessed me to continue the argument?

I will never know. The very building we were in, an aging, down-at-the-heels but hilltop-splendid estate built by the shirt magnate, George

Foster Peabody, was constructed around a courtyard opening onto the oval room with the big table. Here, I had been told, inquiries into complex social issues were unfettered, and intellectual freedom reigned, even if it did not occur in every corner of the nearby university. I must have been intoxicated by my four to six weeks of prowling down the halls of this place devoted to open inquiry.

For whatever reason, I did not nod and move on and out, but countered, "I thought the Center was founded to give voice to unpopular, even suppressed ideas and inquiries. Well, I can tell you that the inquiry I have recommended, into the impacts of current immigration upon America's demographic and social future, especially given the illegality of much of it, is stifled by something, because the discussion is not taking place. People seem afraid to explore this important issue. I thought that was where our mission began."

Hutchins' eyebrows rose, and he sat back, pausing.

"Are you *sure?*"

It was not the response I expected. We had been meeting for over an hour, and I had an instinct that it was time for brevity.

"Yes."

Another pause.

"Very well. Organize programs in that area, as you wish."

He never suggested limits or directions.

* * *

An Immigration Focus for the Center?

How would I accomplish this? None of the remaining elderly Associates—ten to twelve men and one woman, Elisabeth Mann Borgese, all living in the area and available for daily meetings—had any demographic expertise or interests. This inquiry had to be done by outside talent, although invited Associates might comment. I had a small, vaguely defined budget to pay writers to produce a paper, or merely (for less money) to come to a meeting to add to the discussion. Sessions were always taped, and thus allowed *The Center Magazine*, when it wished, to present several voices. It was for me to find the writers and presenters.

On a sprawling topic like immigration, however, we could hardly have one of our routine morning sessions. I hoped for at least an all-day conference with visitors who had some expertise, and I had a stroke of luck. One of the Center's directors was El Paso lawyer George McAlmon, who happened to be on friendly terms with another El Paso barrister, Leonel Castillo, whom President-elect Jimmy Carter had just appointed as the first Hispanic[1] to head the Immigration and Naturalization Service (INS). Socializing with George at the end of a board meeting, I raised the possibility of bringing Castillo to Santa Barbara for a day or more of meetings in which he could be briefed on immigration—a subject about which (George assured me) Castillo knew nothing. McAlmon's gift of several thousand dollars allowed me to bring Leonel Castillo to Santa Barbara, along with fifteen or so experts and others, for more than one day's attention. Now I had a different problem—lining up people to write position papers, or at least speak knowledgeably to major aspects of the issue.

My education accelerated from ground zero. I had told Hutchins that the demographic impacts of rising levels of immigration were subjects that the media and universities were avoiding, and perhaps even stifling. Authorized to make a quick reconnaissance of the subject to get acquainted with writers and the state of the public discussion, I was dismayed to find that the situation was worse, and also more complicated, than I had suspected.

Immigration received very brief mention in the *Rockefeller Report* of 1972, and only as a contributor of one-quarter of current national population growth. Rising levels of illegal entries across the southern border with Mexico began to receive considerable media coverage in the mid-1970s, most sensationally an October, 1976 piece in the *Reader's Digest* by Leonard Chapman, Commissioner of the Immigration and

---

[1] Terminology here is unsettled and somewhat contested. The Census Bureau in 1980 chose the word "Hispanic" to refer to people in the U. S. whose origins were Mexico, Puerto Rico, Cuba, i.e. all Spanish-speaking countries. This term suits many, though not those who object to lumping all these nationalities together and prefer Mejicanos, Cubanos, and so on. On the far left, the term "Latino" is preferred. I will use these terms interchangeably.

Naturalization Service (INS). Chapman, a former Commandant of the Marine Corps, warned of a "vast and silent invasion of illegal immigrants across our borders…fast reaching the proportions of a national disaster." He estimated the annual illegal flow between 250,000 to 500,000, the resident illegal population at 8 million, and the costs to the nation reaching $8 billion a year in welfare benefits, public services, and job loss to natives, especially black teenagers. Such complaints had generated two congressional initiatives—one for sanctions on employers of illegal immigrants, and another a guest worker program for agriculture—both stalled. President Ford appointed a task force to study the problem. Then he yielded office to Jimmy Carter who recognized a stalemate on this difficult issue where the basic facts were entangled in dispute. In the year I persuaded Hutchins to explore the issue, a national "Select Commission on Immigration Reform" was in the planning stages, with Father Theodore Hesburgh, president of Notre Dame, as Chair.

In reading the studies conducted by the Ford and Carter administrations, it took me little time to see that this was a policy failure that deserved attention. An illegal Mexican labor force had been filtering northward into southwestern agriculture since at least the 1920s, and it was legalized during World War II by the Bracero Program. I knew that the scholarship on that program was harshly critical of this government subsidy to western growers, and that ending it had been one of the wiser policy reforms of the Kennedy administration. Americans, I believed, should do their own work—even the hard work of stoop agriculture—and they would do it if market forces drove wages and working conditions upward toward decent standards. I did not want to eat vegetables picked by desperate and exploited workers overnighting in filthy quarters without running water, otherwise permanently in the shadows of our national life. Let Americans do that and all other work under American conditions, and let we consumers pay the difference. Legal immigration? Probably there were problems there, too, but I knew little about it. It seemed wise to focus on what was self-evidently wrong in immigration matters.

Even on the problem of expanding flows of illegal workers, there was plenty of controversy for a "think tank" to aspire to clarify. Against Chapman's views were the opinions of people who denied there was a problem, who argued that "undocumented" laborers—the term they insisted upon—were a seasonal event, since many and perhaps most, returned home below the border at the end of picking season. In any event, nothing could be done to stop this flow of needed labor to available jobs.

If there were no reliable measures of the *net* movement of illegal workers into the U.S., a vast change did seem to be taking place at the border. Border Patrol arrests for illegal entry rose from 110,000 in 1965 to 760,000 in 1975. The major source countries were Mexico and Central America, with smaller components from Jamaica, the Dominican Republic, Haiti, the Philippines, and Korea. The Los Angeles County Board of Supervisors called illegal immigration "one of the most important social issues in our society today." One official estimated that medical expenses for care given to illegals in Los Angeles public hospitals ran to fifty million dollars a year. New York city officials complained of the fiscal burden of the city's estimated two million illegals. Several states, including California, had passed laws penalizing employers who hired illegal workers. Enforcement was minimal, but the public irritation was sufficient to prompt the House of Representatives to pass an employer sanctions bill twice in the early 1970s. Both were bottled up in the senate by a southern senator (James Eastland, Dem.-Miss.) who was a large agricultural labor employer and believed in nothing so strongly as cheap workers—foreign, illegal, or otherwise.

The Ford administration's Domestic Council produced a special report on illegal immigration in early 1975, and it became my basic textbook. This new issue, or piece of the larger immigration issue, had legs. Jimmy Carter, in the year I began my review, appointed a cabinet task force on illegal immigration. The issue had forced itself onto the agenda of two successive presidents.

Had I misled Hutchins when I reported that immigration problems were being ignored in contemporary America? Yes and no. The avoidance of the issue among the nation's policy cognoscenti and the news media was real enough, and rooted in fear of the topic. Yet the problem of illegal immigration had not been successfully suppressed, and had somehow broken through to reach the political agendas of Ford and Carter. Still, the nation's intellectuals, university scholars, and public-issue pundits seemed to me to be saying little. Some were dismissive of the public's agitation over border-ignoring foreigners as "just more nativism"—

whatever that meant. General Chapman's talk about "invasion" seemed to invite such dismissals, as did his way of estimating the size of the problem. He told a congressional committee in 1974 that the resident illegal population numbered four to five million. Where did he get that number? Well, he had heard one to two million on the low side, and eight to ten million on the high side. So he split the difference, though he cited the high figure in his *Reader's Digest* article.

The level of discussion needed to be raised. I found a tough-minded 1975 report by David North and Marion Houstoun, *The Characteristics and Role of Illegal Aliens in the U.S. Labor Market*, but most of the thin "research" on the dimensions of the problem of illegal entry emphasized what wasn't known, and depicted the northward labor flow as a natural and desirable economic adjustment.

Even less was being said on legal immigration, which deserved scrutiny for many reasons beyond its demographic effects. American law and practice on refugees and asylum seekers were in disarray, the annual numbers recently driven upward by spasms of fleeing Haitians, Cubans, Central Americans, admitted under a constitutionally dubious "parole authority" of the president. Overall, the very thing that the system-reformers of 1965 had disavowed was rapidly happening— rising numbers of legal immigrants, and a profound shift in countries of origin. Nobody seemed much interested in this slow but possibly nation-changing development.

Yet it was illegal immigration in large and increasing numbers that was becoming the most visible problem generated by the immigration system. If anything is central to the American social system and performance, it is the rule of law. Sustained violation of it ought to attract keen scrutiny. It also seemed almost certain to me that infusion of Third World labor had a downward effect on American workers' wages and working conditions, at least in some places. Another reason for the Center to open a forum.

My hasty research was reinforced as time went on by something that made a deeper impression—my phone calls to "experts" on immigration, both for information, and in some cases, to invite the person to participate. I needed to surround our table with writers expressing several points of view from different angles of vision, but found in the public record only a light sprinkle of discussion—most of it on illegal immigration and dismissive of the problem. Soon I discovered that, if I focused on only illegal immigration, I could tap into two opposing schools. Telephone calls to persons gainfully employed in refugee and immigrant aid NGOs, especially if they were Latinos (overwhelmingly the case), would produce aggressive denials that illegal immigration was a problem worthy of attention; that we really didn't know anything reliable about it, and by the way, the term should be "undocumented entry." Calls to persons gainfully employed in the law enforcement side, especially the Border Patrol, elicited the Chapman view that the border was "out of control" and the situation was steadily worsening.

We could hardly explore the issue in a thoughtful way with only these polarized, and to some extent ideologically-based institutionalized responses, though they needed to be part of the discussion. What I found harder to round up were professors who wrote on the topic, or talented journalists and general writers who had done research and could bring both fact and considered opinion—from several angles. I found a few professors and government or foundation-based "experts" who had published on technical aspects of immigration, especially the hot topic of illegal immigration. Invariably, when they heard that I intended to cast the conference as dealing with illegal immigration, several agreed to come to a conference, but stated they wouldn't write or even present a position paper. A professor of industrial relations from UCLA, Walter Fogel, candidly admitted that his university colleagues had not appreciated his recent paper on illegal immigrant welfare costs, since he had hinted that further research might find them substantial. His liberal friends, which meant virtually all of them, disliked a research topic that might link an immigrant with some sort of social harm. He would come to the conference and present a paper suggesting making it a criminal offense to employ illegal immigrants. He was the only academic I could find who would write a discussion paper, though I easily signed up three professors teaching in what was being called "Chicano Studies," to give general comments about a highly politicized new field. They would argue that illegal immigration was not a problem and really shouldn't be illegal. A staff member from Zero Population Growth in Washington, Melanie Wirken, was well-informed on immigration and, as a Populationist, felt indignant about the demographic effects of the substantial and rising combined total of both legal and illegal immigration. However, some members of her organization's board and Washington staff were beginning to grumble that the organization's recent pronouncements about immigration as part of the population problem was running the risk of earning ZPG a reputation for blaming foreigners. She agreed to come to a meeting, but told me that she wouldn't take the lead in presenting a paper offering the critical assessment of U.S. policy on illegal entry that she had given me over the phone.

* * *

The conference on "Illegal Immigration and National Policy" was scheduled for March, 1977, and I had a problem. I had enlisted an INS official from Los Angeles who I expected to present the law enforcement "point of view," though his remarks turned out to be a bureaucratic "We're doing the best we can" report. The widely-known UC Santa Barbara biologist and writer, Garrett Hardin, came to speak his mind, which everybody knew would be a stern Populationist view that there was no more room in the lifeboat. The several Latinos, welfare administrators, and immigrant-aid organization staffers and four professors, agreed to say what they had told me over the phone, that, however you looked at it, there was no real problem with "undocumented workers." Leonel Castillo was coming, and expected to mostly ask questions and take notes. Actor Paul Newman showed up, as he had a right to do as a generous Center donor. He sat along the wall and revealed nothing of what went on behind those crystal blue eyes.

Who would present a broad overview of the debate over illegal immigration, summarizing the argument that it was a social problem imposing high costs, along with the counter-arguments? I could find no one qualified and willing. So, a week before the meeting, I wrote that central discussion paper.

The conference came and went, and produced no really memorable moments, and was not intended to reach any conclusion. I gave the lead paper, which was based substantially on the December, 1976 report of the Ford Domestic Council.

I noted the push and pull factors accounting for rising levels of illegal immigration, and concluded that "the range of objections" to the illegal flow "is impressive," including wage competition with some Americans, many of them black and brown. I summarized the leading "social issues" raised by critics—illegal immigration, apart from widening a zone in society of condoned law breaking, also contributed to a growing U.S. population (illegal combined with legal immigration constituted not 25 percent, as the Rockefeller Commission had stated, but 50 percent of U.S. population growth.) In addition, it sharpened racial and ethnic conflicts over jobs and community space, stimulated the establishment of smuggling rings, and the growth of a shadowy, underground population not fully integrated into society. I devoted only a paragraph to the environmental impacts of immigration-driven population growth, and nobody else brought it up or commented on the linkage.

I reviewed the proposals for control, including "a new national work card," summarized both conservative and liberal objections to serious control efforts, and offered tentative thoughts on why public outcry was not louder and policy reform seemed so distant and even unlikely.

Nobody responded at all to this grumpy question I posed to the Mexican government, "By what right do you permit population growth of 3.5 percent a year...and the export of your "surplus" people to your neighbors, while your elites still hold to their comfortable ways?"

I ended by quoting economist Ray Marshall's words, "We have stored up another underclass," and, perhaps thinking of the Center's overwhelmingly liberal constituency, wondered if some liberals might not gravitate toward "an exclusionary position" on the grounds that "by shutting off the recruitment of an underclass we can, for the first time in our history, force society to accord menial labor the reward it deserves"—to the benefit of America's lower rung workers—black, brown, yellow and white.

Castillo said little, asking questions from time to time that tended to sound like skepticism about illegal immigration's costs and the large numbers of illegals in the U.S. All the other Latinos disagreed with the thrust of my paper, i.e., that there was a large and growing problem here to be dealt with by firmer public policy. Without exception, they made what I thought to be unsupportable arguments that Mexico deserved to be a special case and Mexicans should be exempt from U.S. immigration laws because of the two nations' "historic relationship," by which they meant the U.S. had economically exploited Mexico for a long time, and of course had stolen a huge part of the country. One of the law enforcement officials caught my attention when he described how western agricultural growers had complained in 1965 that the end of the Bracero Program would ruin them, but in quick order they made investments in different crops and harvesting technology, and there was no problem. Everybody was cordial, and no one called anyone any bad names.

My paper, "Illegal Immigration: The Problem That Will Not Go Away," was published in the July/August 1977 issue of *The Center Magazine,* which then had a circulation of about 75,000.

Hutchins thanked me for arranging an interesting meeting (he never said a word during the discussions), and indicated that he might tolerate one more. I secured a grant from the California Council on the Humanities to hold another meeting on the ethics of immigration restriction, which we held in December, 1977. That meeting resulted in the publication of conference proceedings in the Center's periodical, *World Issues* (February/March 1978). The noted immigration historian from Johns Hopkins, John Higham, came out for that session, and I recall that he and one or two other people from the frigid East, especially, luxuriated in the large spaces of the white mansion on the hill with the view from the sunny patio across the drained swimming pool and down the Carpinteria Valley. A few tried to chat with Paul Newman, who had little to say, but rewarded our guests with blazing blue eyes that suggested wisdom. At one break, a few of us drove a short distance down the hill, took off our shoes and walked on the beach. On that walk, John Higham and I began to build what became a close friendship, which was important to my ongoing education.

* * *

After that conference, I pulled my thoughts together on the larger topic of appropriate U.S. policy in the mounting disarray in the area of immigration, and it appeared in *The Center Magazine* (May-June 1979), as "Illegal Immigration and the New Restrictionism." I argued that immigration reform toward lower numbers, differently selected, and an end of illegal entry should now be embraced by all American ethnic groups and certainly by liberals. As Cesar Chavez had emphasized, Mexican labor flows harmed Mexican-American workers most, and must be curbed.

"The enemy ought to be the [American] exploiter," I wrote, not these "ragged volunteer laborers worse off even than our own unemployed." I had by this time developed a home-grown distaste for we white Californians' growing addiction to illegal labor from Mexico, ignoring the wider social costs shifted from U.S. employers to society as a whole. The work got done cheaply, but that workforce developed American expectations, and more foreigners had to be imported. It was an indefensible way to get America's work done. An example. The Center's gardener was "Ted" Ibarra, a friendly, hard-working man who gave me cuttings from a small nursery below the parking lot. He also maintained there a secret second family, a wife and two sons, presumably not known to the official family he kept in a small house just off De La Guerra Street. Some people call this "family values," meaning among other things that Mexican men take pride in the number of children sired. Center staff told me that Ted might not be a citizen (his second wife admittedly was not), but he certainly did the estate's hard outdoor labor cheerfully. His two second-home sons, however, were surly teenagers born in America, and attended (sporadically) the local junior high school along with my own children; the lot of them unwilling to do the hard work of brush cutting on the Center's hillsides. What kind of solution to our "menial labor" problem had it been to permit Ted to live and work in Santa Barbara and his second and illegal "wife" to deliver two children who lived outside his official family of a wife and four kids? Forget the double family and the total fertility rate of six, his male offspring displayed the same feeble work ethic as my own kids and their friends. Would each wave of illegals then produce a generation of American teenagers who slouched through the malls, dropped out of high school, which required another wave of people who still had the work ethic—from southern Mexico and Central America, or from more distant and impoverished countries?

* * *

So we had our two conferences, and that seemed to be the end of it—for the Center, and for me. I had no plans to continue thinking and writing in this area.

Nevertheless, plans do not command the future. Without intending to be drawn into this controversy, I had published three essays on immigration in a magazine with a substantial national reputation. As it turned out, this was only the end of my own beginning.

Chapter Five:
Getting Organized

*I have looked you up, and... as a Presbyterian, you are supposed
to tithe. But I imagine that you don't tithe. So I am calling to
make it possible for you to tithe by giving of your time, in the line
of public service.* — Dr. John Tanton

The Michigan Doctor Calls

The phone rang one weekday evening in late summer, 1978.

"I would like to speak to professor Otis Graham."

"Speaking."

"My name is Dr. John Tanton from Petoskey, Michigan."

I remember cupping the receiver so that I could say to my wife,
"These doctors are getting desperate. They not only advertise; this one
is calling me from Michigan."

Tanton continued, "I have just read your article on illegal immigration
in The Center Magazine. We have a lot in common with your concerns.
I have looked you up, and you are the son of a Presbyterian minister. As
a Presbyterian, you are supposed to tithe, but I imagine you do not tithe.
So I am calling to make it possible for you to tithe by giving of your
time, in the line of public service. I'm forming a national organization
based in Washington, that will work toward immigration reform, both
the curbing of illegal immigration, and the reconsideration and revision
of both the numbers and the selection criteria for legal immigration.

Would you join us, on the board of directors, or in an advisory capacity? Your expenses for any trips to Washington will be paid."

I have never forgotten that volley of sentences, and the tone of quiet authority. I well remember my astonishment. He was right that I didn't tithe. The guilt card was expertly played. I asked some questions—mostly, as I recall, about the other people who would be involved. They were described as a long-time New York activist working on population issues for Planned Parenthood in New York (Sherry Barnes), a young environmental attorney from Grand Rapids who had agreed to become our first director (Roger Conner), and Tanton—who described himself as a Michigan M.D. and practicing ophthalmologist who was also an environmental activist. He promised to write, and a letter dated August 28 told me much more.

Tanton, I learned from this letter (and, years later, from his oral history), was a vigorous outdoorsman and hiker (usually with his wife, Mary Lou) who had been an environmental activist since the late 1950s. He joined the Wilderness Society to work on the Wilderness Act of 1964, and even earlier perceived the population driver behind environmental troubles. He had read the publications of the Population Reference Bureau, and served as a physician in the birth control clinic at Denver General Hospital while an intern there in the late 1950s.

From the outset, he displayed a certain strategic, organization-building talent. He either joined or founded his local Sierra Club and Audubon chapters in or around lightly-populated Petoskey, formed groups such as the Little Traverse Conservancy and the Hartwick Pines Natural History Association. Influenced by Paul Ehrlich's *The Population Bomb*, he joined Zero Population Growth (ZPG) in 1969, the year after it was founded. Elected to the national board in 1973, John tried to turn some of the organization's attention to the immigration source of American population growth.

He met with some success at first, supported by committed allies on the board like the resourceful Californian Judith Kunofsky. He chaired an Immigration Study Committee that produced discussion papers, sponsored a ZPG policy document endorsing immigration reform with a goal of reducing the national totals to 200,000, and successfully pushed for the hiring of a full-time lobbyist (Melanie Wirken, who had attended our Center conference in March). Tanton later told me that we had met at a ZPG national meeting in Rochester where I had given a talk on national planning, but I did not remember him. Elected president of ZPG for 1975-77, Tanton met with the leadership of two other environmental groups who shared the immigration concern—the Environmental Fund, and the National Parks and Conservation Association, led by the fearless Anthony Wayne Smith who had already testified before Congress that immigration must be curbed. The three agreed that no existing organization could adequately address the complex immigration issue.

The ZPG experience taught Dr. Tanton some hard lessons, later to be repeated in struggles to engage the Sierra Club with the immigration issue. Immigration was indeed connected to ZPG's mission, and for a time, the board appeared open to this reality. However, immigration reform proved to be a taboo-draped, technically formidable and politically divisive sideline. Some of ZPG's liberal staff began to make it clear that they were politically uncomfortable becoming known as critics of immigration, which to them sounded like they were critics of non-whites in some general way. Immigration "was a forbidden topic" in Washington circles, John recalled. He was also finding some potential donors to immigration reform uncomfortable with ZPG's "population control" image.

There seemed to be a need for "a new single purpose umbrella organization." By summer, 1978, Tanton was ready to form a new group. The ZPG board was supportive (some of them also relieved), agreeing that ZPG would hold funds for an organization Tanton proposed to call FAIR (Federation for American Immigration Reform) until the group's independent tax status 501 (©) (3) (tax exempt) was established.

* * *

Shortly after Tanton's phone call and letter, I met my colleague, Garrett Hardin as he slowly entered a UCSB library elevator on his crutches. I asked if he knew Tanton. Indeed he did. Tanton was an impressive doctor from upper Michigan who was active nationally in ZPG.

"What are his politics?"

Garrett paused, looking puzzled, and then said, "I don't think he has any politics...in the partisan sense."

A few months later, I gained a sense of Tanton's political inclinations, after reading a draft version of, "Proposal for a New Immigration Organization" that he circulated. It read, "Politically, it [FAIR] will seek a middle-of-the-road stance, eschewing the far right."

I agreed to join the FAIR board. No other environmental group of national size ever made me such an offer. What was to be my main social movement had called me out.

* * *

Founding FAIR

However, what was FAIR? Tanton had already consulted on this with many people, and used the weekend of the ZPG board meeting in October to clarify the new group's aims and procedures. I was allowed some early input, writing from Santa Barbara. In late October, he circulated several thoughts about organizational issues, along with a draft mission statement where some of my language had found its way:

"'Our Goal: To end illegal immigration into the U.S., and to reform policies governing immigration, conforming them to today's demographic, resource, political and social realities.'" The environmentalist/populationist emphasis came first. Other elements in the October "Statement of Principles of FAIR" doubtless owed something to the extensive deliberations within ZPG, reflecting the liberal ethos of inside-the-beltway Washington. "We wish to project an image of environmental concern, fairness, deliberateness, humaneness, rationality, unselfishness, middle-of-the-road, and a restrictionist (as opposed to exclusionist) point of view. We don't want to project an image of racism, jingoism, xenophobia, chauvinism or isolationism." I was happy to see this sentiment, though it seemed a bit defensive. At the end came a statement that was pure Tanton, and was derived from his 1975 essay which had taken second place in the Mitchell Prize contest:

"The age of mass international migration as a solution to national problems, and of mass migration to the U.S. should be brought to a close." ZPG's 1974 "Policy on U.S. Immigration" had the same Tanton stamp: "Legal immigration should be reduced to a level approximating emigration, bringing to a close the era of demographically significant immigration into the United States. Illegal entry into the U.S. should be ended."

* * *

The first board meeting of FAIR was scheduled for early February, 1979, but my records and memory tell me that I stopped off in Petoskey on an East Coast trip in December. Tanton and Conner were engaged in a week of brainstorming, and I spent an evening and left after breakfast. I found them to have warm personalities, intelligence, and they were animated, given to wit and laughter. This was reassuring, though I'm not sure just what else I was expecting. Conner, a graduate of Oberlin (a champion debater there) and the University of Michigan Law School, for five years had run the tiny West Michigan Environmental Action Council in Grand Rapids. They had a $90,000 budget, and Roger's salary was $16,000 a year. He turned out to have qualities of mind and character that only time would bring me to fully appreciate. Below average height, animated and articulate, sporting an outlandish mutton-chop set of sideburns connecting to his moustache, he was a young provincial headed for the deeper, shark-filled waters of Washington, D.C., known to him only through his recent few months as a ZPG board member. Very informed about environmental law and Michigan politics, Roger was struggling (as I was also) to master the lingo and political geography of national immigration policy. He proved to be a quick study. More important, he set a tone. A person of humane and decent instincts, he would would not authorize no language that could be said to even hint at ethnic dislike. The targets of our criticism were Americans—the politicians, pundits and lobbyists who had shaped and now defended the existing mass immigration system.

Tanton was impressive from the start. Handsome, trim, athletic, and apparently tireless, he seemed like three people, if not five. A successful eye surgeon, husband, and father of two, he was also an active Presbyterian who met with a public issues discussion group at the church on Thursday mornings (though I never heard him speak about his own religious beliefs). He was founder or activist with his wife, Mary Lou, in perhaps a dozen Michigan environmental groups, was currently national president of ZPG, a beekeeper whose honey regularly won local prizes, a tireless traveler to rugged national parks and historic sites; a man who played the piano, studied German, and could bend over from the waist and put his palms flat upon the floor. No ordinary man, Dr. John Tanton.

He won my special regard by believing that history had much to teach us. He had already sent me an essay ("full of lessons for us," he wrote on the cover) by immigration historian, William S. Bernard, on how a quickly formed Citizens Committee on Displaced Persons had in 1946-47 guided through Congress an unprecedented law allowing the special admission of European refugees. John also called my attention to a magisterial historical essay on "The Migrations of Human Populations" (*Scientific American* (September ,1974) by Kingsley Davis, which pronounced that mass migrations were a poor way to solve societal problems now that the globe was filled with people.

Tanton and Conner, I now knew, would be talented and congenial companions. I had not met the future board, or the others who might yet be a part of this restrictionist enterprise as staff or advisors. Before leaving for the first board meeting in February, I read or re-read several books on earlier immigration reform episodes, paying close attention to John Higham's *Strangers in the Land*, whose subtitle was "Patterns of American Nativism, 1860-1925." Tanton had written to me that he valued my historical perspective, but I had little historical knowledge or perspective on immigration. I needed some post-graduate work. What an education it has been.

Chapter Six:
What is a New Restrictionist?

We lack entirely a working term for citizens defending their community interest when immigrants, wittingly or unwittingly, put them at risk. —Chilton Williamson, Jr.

As we began organizing to become immigration reformers, I knew only a small amount about the history of such efforts. But that history, mis-remembered, would burden us from the first. Immigration reform in the 1970s and forward had, of course, precursors more than a century earlier. The long campaign to curb the "First Great Wave" of mass immigration that began after the Civil War was originally seen by historians (correctly, I believe) as one of the several social reform movements considered as part of the progressive era. Historians writing in the first half of the twentieth century had folded the immigration restrictionists into the progressive reform narrative. This was appropriate, since, along with the reformers aiming to dismantle monopoly power, end child labor, prohibit consumption of alcoholic beverages, or clean up the slums, the immigration restrictionists wanted to bring under governmental control the forces unleashed by capitalist energies—in this case, mass importation of cheap foreign labor. Progressive reformers such as Teddy Roosevelt, E. A. Ross, Hiram Johnson, and Samuel Gompers had added immigration restriction to their agendas. Early historians generally sympathized with that broad reform agenda, and saw regulation of immigration as akin to regulation of railroad rates, food and drugs, and corporate behavior, in that democratically elected governments had stepped in to regulate powerful and rampaging private forces.

The historians writing in the civil rights era, the 1950s and later, were at best uneasy with a story that placed the immigration reformers as part of the family of progressive mobilizations. They detected open racism and some anti-Semitism among (some of) the restrictionists, and the main job of today's historians, we all thought (I began teaching U.S. history in 1962), was to relentlessly discover and denounce racism wherever it could be found in America's past. The immigration restrictionists, or some of them, seemed to think in racial terms when deciding who should be admitted into America.

The historian who would gather these new race-sensitive impulses together and put forward a compelling new interpretation of immigration restriction was John Higham, who spent most of his career at Johns Hopkins. In the 1950s, young Higham was an outspoken and activist supporter of (black) civil rights who would march with Martin Luther King at Selma. *Strangers in the Land* (1954) was his first book, and remains the single most influential account of the immigration restrictionist impulse of the late nineteenth and early twentieth centuries. Earlier historians of immigration reform, when they gave it any attention at all, had presented that effort as part of the progressive reform family—a movement aimed at real problems in the American city and industrial workplaces, though here and there marred by xenophobia. Higham positioned the immigration reformers outside the "progressive" tradition entirely, and was relentlessly critical of those reformers (some of them) for their frequent invidious and sometimes openly racialist stigmatization of (some) foreigners. He depicted the progressive era immigration reformers as the heirs to the anti-Catholic "Know Nothing" Party of the 1850s—a political effort that had drawn the first use of the term "nativist," meant as a derogatory term for those prejudiced against immigrants in general and Catholics in particular. Whether organized as the American Protection Association or the Immigration Restriction League, two groups formed in the 1890s, expressing themselves from pamphlet, pulpit or platform. The restrictionists of the years before and just after World War I were depicted by Higham, often in their own words, as anti-foreigner racists who (some of them) ranked various peoples on a scale beginning at most inferior and running upward to most superior. To them, the "new immigration," the flow of inferior peoples from central and eastern Europe, southern Italy, and Asia, must be curbed. The implication seemed inescapable. Their enterprise must be condemned.

Any reader of *Strangers* would have come away with this message, so compelling was the exposition. The reviews of the book were all laudatory. All immigration reformers, not just the "Know Nothings" of the 1850s, now had their label—nativists—and a prominent, unenviable place in history. This became the story that historians told of the immigration restrictionist impulse of a century earlier, and was the story I encountered in graduate school at Columbia in the early 1960s. John Higham was not the first to emphasize the dark side of this part of the American reform tradition. I was exposed in graduate school to similar themes through the writings of Ray Allen Billington, Oscar Handlin, Eric Goldman, and my own doctoral advisor, Richard Hofstadter. Higham's eloquent book enjoyed a long popularity in paperback editions, and sold almost half a million copies.

Readers of *Strangers* thus took away a vivid impression that restrictionists were on a bigot's errand, and that was pretty much the essence of it.

That wasn't what Higham had intended to convey. We later learned, those of us who read his subsequent essays and gave them the attention they merited, that Higham's assessment of the restrictionist reform effort wasn't so simple as the term and denotation of the term "nativist" that his book's title suggested. As early as 1958, Higham wrote (in an obscure scholarly journal, the *Catholic Historical Review*) that "nativism now looks less adequate as a vehicle for studying the struggles of nationalities in America than my earlier report of it. The nativist theme, as defined and developed to date, is imaginatively exhausted." As a concept, it directs our attention too much to "subjective, irrational motives" and neglects and even screens out "the objective realities of ethnic relations" and "the structure of society." If he were writing the book again, he said in 1963, he would "take more account of aspects of the immigration restriction movement that cannot be sufficiently explained in terms of nativism." It was "a bad habit," he said in another place, "to label as nativist any kind of unfriendliness toward immigrants." He later explicitly endorsed the overall restrictionist effort to end uncontrolled immigration, and offered his judgment that it would have been better for the country had some limitations been put in place long before the 1920s. Higham himself was a restrictionist!

Since this Johns Hopkins historian, whose picture had been taken in locked-arm interracial marching down the hostile streets of Selma, Alabama, was manifestly not a nativist, immigration restriction and nativism were not synonymous, and the first could and did exist without the second.

Depending what you meant by nativism.

Fifteen years after I read Higham's book on nativism I opened several dictionaries, and found that "nativism" generally had three meanings—one from philosophy having to do with "innate ideas," and one from anthropology dealing with revivalist movements among indigenous peoples, neither of which I could fathom, And yet another definition ran this way: (nativism is) "the policy of protecting the interests of native inhabitants against those of immigrants." That definition left room for a prejudicial concern *only* for the interests of citizens and disregard for the interests and rights of immigrants, which is, in a mild way, the nasty definition some Americans in the 1850s gave to members of the Know Nothing Party and that historians like Higham turned into irrational xenophobia that haunted American history. It left room also for favoring citizens over immigrants *when and if their interests conflicted.* In those circumstances, as with job and wage competition or important cultural differences, a nativist could be called a patriot, a defender of the community and of posterity. I brought this up at an early meeting, and suggested that we deal with the ugly nativist label by claiming it for ourselves by teaching Americans this patriotic connotation. I was hooted into silence. Over the years, we were sometimes called nativists, and while we indignantly rebuffed the slur, I kept to myself my growing conviction, as I met and worked with more restrictionists, that we were indeed nativists in a forgotten meaning of that term.

* * *

Higham's Second Thoughts

I thus returned to Higham's work on the eve of my trip to Washington for the first FAIR board meeting, not only to refresh my memory of the history of immigration policy, but also because I remembered that there was another, almost hidden side to the story he told about immigration and its restriction. Labor leaders such as Terrance Powderly and Samuel Gompers—himself an immigrant—joined the effort to restrict immigration in order to protect American workers from the downward wage pressure and anti-union uses of cheap foreign labor. This was hardly mere xenophobia, an irrational fear of foreigners for their foreign-ness. I knew that the Socialist Party had always had a strong restrictionist element within it, based on something as thoroughly rational and justified as concern for American workers' wages and standards. Black leaders Fredrick Douglass and Booker T. Washington had urged the American business community not to turn to foreign labor as America industrialized, but to open those jobs to Blacks. Those voices were reminders that mass immigration brought real costs, and firm public control of it was good public policy.

* * *

Then what would it mean to espouse immigration restrictionism in 1978?

In our historical experience with large-scale immigration in the 1830s-40s and the 1880s-1920s, there were two restrictionist models to choose from. One focused on real social costs imposed by unregulated large-scale immigration from culturally different societies, and was located in the center-left of American politics. The other model, working on the center-right, occasionally spoke of real social costs to American workers and communities, but aimed most of its complaints against incoming millions of cultural inferiors who either would not or could not assimilate to higher American norms.

In my first writing on this subject, the Center conference paper, I had urged contemporary restrictionists to choose the first model, since the country had (thankfully) greatly changed, and issues of cultural difference would not only get little traction but would surely generate

51

disabling attacks. However, before the Center conference, I had never met a modern restrictionist—someone who thought that there was now too much immigration and much of it irrationally selected, and I didn't know where on the political spectrum they might be found.

What was an immigration restrictionist in the late 1970s? At our Center conference, that bright, engaging ZPGer, Melanie Wirken, spoke consistently as a critic of current immigration patterns. There wasn't a trace of hate or ethnic disparagement in Melanie's discourse during hours of discussion, both formal and informal. I scanned the rest of the cohort who seemed to regard illegal immigration as a problem to be fixed. Border Patrol and INS officials at the meeting were law enforcement people, and their restrictionism was a matter of carrying out professional obligations to uphold laws enacted by others. I could not detect in them any particular political or ideological coloration. Indeed, they appeared to have no views at all on legal immigration, but focused on combating illegal entry. Biologist Garrett Hardin was, as expected of the populationist author of the essay "Lifeboat Ethics," an unflinching restrictionist. However, Garrett, a complicated man, was a smiling, intellectual adventurer with no "racial" or ethnic emphases that I could find. For him, immigration was a population-expanding phenomenon, and therefore it should be looked at with suspicion. UCLA professor Walter Fogel, whose writing on immigration came to my attention, proved to be a restrictionist because of his concern with the vulnerability of the American labor force to sustained downward wage pressures from Third World labor. Historian John Higham thought restriction of some sort in 1978 was wise, though he gently warned against the mistakes of a century earlier (as did I). None of those people seemed the slightest bit "anti-immigrant" to me, and there wasn't a whiff of concern about what country the immigrants were coming from, i.e., their cultural or ethnoracial baggage (Garrett might be an exception here, but I am not sure; all I ever recall him saying about nationality was that we should look into the knapsack of each incoming immigrant and inspect an item called "culture." If it contained patriarchal, female subordination elements, count that against admitting him or her). The participants thought the system was broken, and that mass immigration, much of it illegal, was not good public policy for the U.S. in the 1970s or for any foreseeable future. They didn't think or talk like the more strident nativists in the history books. In an article published in 1978 in *The Center Magazine*, I called this new cluster of concerns "the New Restrictionism." We termed ourselves Restrictionists from there on, though several of us complained that it was an over-aged word with distorting baggage. In retrospect, I should have tried harder to come up with another term.

Chapter Seven: Building FAIR

Today, social movements which lack new-class support seldom coalesce and if they do get off the ground, they usually do not travel far. —Katherine Betts, *The Great Division*

Who was Tanton, and these people he was gathering together in Washington in 1978-79 to start an organization?

I had met him and Roger Conner in December, and found them intelligent and congenial people. Their reasons for opposition to uncontrolled immigration originated where mine did—in environmentalist-populationist concerns. This new organization, however, would have a board and staff I hadn't met, and we were planning to be a membership organization that would enroll thousands of Americans, some of them presumably living in the border states and quite angry at the "silent invasion" their government permitted. What I knew of the history of restrictionism led me to worry about who might march to the flag when we ran it up the pole.

I recall sitting in a window seat on the plane over Iowa, headed for Dulles airport and the February 1979 meeting of whoever I was meeting with, asking myself, "Who *are* these people?"

* * *

Meeting These People

We met on a crisply cool Friday morning in Washington. Roger, who had been working for a month out of spare basement offices on New Hampshire Avenue, led me, Melanie Wirken, her soon-to-be husband, David McClintock, and another man named David Yeres, who was, as I recall, the former director of Carter's Interagency Task Force on Immigration, on a visit to the offices of a Justice-State-Labor Department immigration task force, and then to the Capitol Hill offices of liberal philanthropist Stewart Mott, who we hoped would lend financial support. Immigration expert David North met us at the FAIR office. The conversation was animated, and very liberal in tone. We talked about immigrant labor competition with blacks, and how to build a coalition in that direction. In addition, we talked of how to interest foundations in our new and unusual cause.

The next day the small FAIR board convened—John; Sherry Barnes, the sparkling, quick-minded redhead insurance executive from Brooklyn and many Planned Parenthood wars; myself; writer and agronomist William Paddock and his wife Liz, Roger, and a staff member. This was a tiny board and skeleton staff, a diminutive group for such large reform ideas.

We soon learned that Tanton had gathered, in his two years of work on this project, an impressive list of people around the country who saw immigration as a broken system, as we did, and were ready to help in one way or another. They included liberal philanthropist Stewart Mott, Cornell economist Vernon Briggs, immigration specialist David North, Ford Foundation officer and demographer Michael Teitlebaum, foreign service officer Lindsey Grant, U.S. Senator from California S. I. Hayakawa, Duke sociologist Jacqueline Jackson, and others. It was a small group that met in those basement rooms on New Hampshire Avenue, but a larger (still small) group seemed available for a reform effort if one could be launched.

We were quite aware of the Caucasian character of our initial group, and pleased to learn that John had made contact with two non-Caucasians, Jackson and Hayakawa. I expressed hope about the participation of Hispanics, based on our assumption that those American workers most injured by the flow of Mexican and other low-skilled labor would be recent immigrant citizens from Mexico and further south. My optimism about allies here was also based on one recent experience. I had been invited after the Center conference to give a paper on illegal immigration at a meeting at the D. H. Lawrence Ranch in New Mexico. Most participants didn't agree with my argument that controlling illegal entry should be a high priority, though Melanie Wirken and David North were there to lend me support. During a break, I walked outside to gaze down a long mountain canyon, and up walked one of the Latino participants, Professor Carlos Cortes of U. C. Riverside, as I recall.

"I agree with you," he said in a soft voice, and walked quickly away.

I was encouraged by this apparent Latino opening. Later, discouragement took the upper hand, though there were fine individual Latino allies on the road ahead.

John had raised just enough money to get started—putting in his prize money from the Mitchell Prize, and gaining a pledge from philanthropist Jay Harris, former president of ZPG, for $100,000 for a five year start-up period. From that first meeting, money was a problem in that there never seemed to be enough of it to fight on all fronts adequately, but never a problem in that donors attempted to dictate, gently or forcefully, what the organization would do, say, and be.

What *would* the organization say or become?

"We need a brochure, a brochure," John repeated, an initial statement of purpose, of how we saw the task.

Roger recalls, in his oral history, that I said, "We had to invent a new language," one that expressed the need for regulatory reform of immigration in center-left terms, as the language of a century ago was too riddled with ethnoracial bias. We should focus upon economic costs to American labor and taxpayer, population growth with attendant environmental degradation, and we should avoid cultural differences. If I said this, it was hardly a novel idea; everyone brought that orientation to the occasion. What I didn't perceive at the time was the issue of "emotion" in this "new language" that we would hope to develop in the cause of restriction. If we felt indignation or alarm, then against whom would it be aimed? We agreed very early on that U.S. national policymakers should be the target of condemnation, and not the immigrants. Crafting a "new language" was more challenging than we initially suspected, as our opposition dredged up from the past, and endlessly repeated the old language to discredit and stereotype us.

I was deputized to write something overnight based on our conversations. I came in subsequently with three pages that contained several phrases and ideas we built upon—that the issue was not race or ethnicity, but numbers, and that out-of-control immigration inflicted multiple harms on the national interest; that legal immigration should be conformed to modern realities, and illegal immigration ended. In practice, we decided to focus on illegal immigration first, where the case for "doing something about it" was building strength in the society as a whole.

After the meeting the group and a few augmenting friends went to Roger and his wife Asta's small rented house in Arlington for dinner. The talk was spirited. We felt a certain exuberance at being, for the first time in most cases, among people who had already figured out the importance to the national well-being and future of lower levels of immigration. That evening, we didn't have to explain or defend this unconventional and often suspect position, that immigration to America was now bringing more bad than good. All present had come to that conclusion independently, and by a similar path. Toward the end of the evening, John began to play hymns on the piano, and we sang the words from memory—"Amazing Grace," "Work for the Night is Coming," and "Abide With Me." I made a mental note that the protestants had gathered, at least the white ones. This had been the core restrictionist constituency earlier in the century, as reform gained momentum. America could no longer be called "a Christian country," let alone Protestant. Just to imagine a winning coalition in its religious dimension, we would need black protestants very soon, along with Catholics, and Jews. The FAIR staff, within a year, contained all of these. It proved harder to "rainbow" the board and membership, though we never stopped trying.

* * *

"This Might Take Five or Ten Years"

What I most remember about this coming together in 1979 was the collective sense of optimism. I was the sole doubter that our restrictionist project was poised to turn the tide, promptly bringing to an end the mass immigration that was now entering a second decade.

I couldn't formulate at that time the reasons for my relative pessimism, and initially kept my half-formed doubts to myself. One should not join a collective enterprise, and then sap group spirits from within. The group as a whole, and those who joined as the years went by, saw themselves as launching, or at least providing, a national organizational voice for a small but nation-changing social movement. There was a general sense that our moment as players on the stage had come, that history ran our way. In my files I found a memo John had sent to us that winter.

"The time is right for the resolution of the immigration dilemmas facing the United States."

He itemized the reasons for his optimism. Public opinion polls repeatedly recorded strong majorities against the large-scale immigration status quo; the media reported rising public anger at the loss of border control; President Carter had studied the issue and proposed reforms; a Select Commission on Immigration and Refugee Policy was meeting under the chairmanship of Father Theodore Hesburgh of Notre Dame, and was due to report in 1980 and sure to recommend change. All that seemed required for substantial reform to come out of this merging of forces was an organization "to represent the national interest around which the dominant public opinion could coalesce...We will provide the organizational structure for the voiceless..."

John's timetable expressed the prevailing optimism. "This will be a very expensive campaign that will take at least five to ten years to put through."

* * *

At this distance, three decades later, that early optimism, the conviction that an historic policy change toward a smaller and better selected immigration stream was now possible, was sadly mistaken.

The central theme of this book is we reformers' progressive discovery, from the 1970s forward, that the American policy system had become hopelessly irrational and disabled on immigration (and many other) matters, and could not free itself from the rule of organized elites and factions. Several complex changes within American society combined with structural change in the political system to marginalize and frustrate our efforts. To report that I was the only early pessimist among the new restrictionist reformers suggests a depth of understanding I did not have in 1979. Acquiring an education about political and cultural realities and trends in the late twentieth century and early twenty-first century America is the main theme of this book. In forming FAIR, which we assumed would be a central player in a new and eventually successful social movement, all of us had embarked on a journey of exploration into the political, cultural and intellectual transformation of the United States.

If I was the leading and probably only pessimist in our founding group, it was not because this historian of the United States understood his country much better than the ophthalmologist, the Prudential insurance executive, the retired CEO of Shell Oil, the writer/agronomist, or the environmental lawyer. Years later, I recognize that my professional training and research-writing experience equipped me reasonably well (let others judge) for historical work on an earlier America, but not for contemporary policy battles in the America after the 1960s—a very different place. To anticipate what lay ahead, I needed, and was about to get, a second "graduate school" education in contemporary American politics and society. My own early pessimism had a flimsy and largely unexamined base. I was an historian of what we now call "the Long Progressive Era"—the years of industrialization and state building from the 1880s through the 1920s forward through the New Deal to the 1960s. Immigration restriction was one of those progressive reforms like women's suffrage, anti-monopoly law, child labor reform, and regulation of railroads, that equipped the modern state to bring under regulation some of the large forces that seemed to threaten social progress. In this era, social movements mobilized majorities for beneficial governmental intervention to produce desirable change. Presidents, from time to time, provided crucial leadership to overcome entrenched special interests. All social reform movements during this era believed in social mobilization within the rule of law and leading to desirable change. All I knew about the earlier immigration reform was that it had apparently reined in a big problem after four decades of effort, which suggested that the status quo to be reformed, unregulated immigration, had some formidable friends and might have them still. I also knew that at my university, and at all American universities after the 1960s, to raise the subject of immigration as a potential or actual problem was to generate frowns, at best. That was the basis of my skepticism when others talked about fixing the illegal immigration problem in five to ten years. The more I learned about this post-60s America that no one had ever seen, the less optimistic I became.

* * *

In retrospect, I am grateful for our innocence and optimism, for without it we might not have started, which would have deprived me of many fine comrades, and much education. The wide-minded economist Albert O. Hirschman, in his book, *Development Projects Observed* (1967), tells us that underestimation of the difficulties ahead is present at the birth of every enterprise to make large changes in society. It seems there is a "hiding hand" that invariably conceals from the view of those contemplating great ventures, public or private, the real price to be paid and the heavy odds against success. Without that hiding hand, Hirschman writes, much of human achievement would never have been undertaken. During that winter of 1978-79, and for some time to come, we New Restrictionists were accompanied by a "hiding hand" between ourselves and the monumental built-in resistance to the re-thinking of America's immigration myths and pieties, along with revising her policies. Good. It allowed us to go forward.

* * *

Our Steep Learning Curve

I had never seen a Washington-based, public policy engaged organization created, let alone operate. More important, neither had our new executive director. Roger had brains, energy, and five years as head of a struggling environmental law center. He would prove to have many talents, but no experience in Washington policy struggles or in the immigration issue. All we had to guide us was John's experience on the ZPG board, and Sherry's with Planned Parenthood. John had already decided that FAIR would engage in issue advocacy with the media and public, lobbying Congress, and possibly the administrative agencies when we got up to speed on the legislative agenda (and could hire a lobbyist), doing enough research to write position papers on issues, and developing a newsletter to rally the members. To support these familiar policy-changing and organization-building tools, the board had to help Roger raise funds from foundations and individuals, possibly through the relatively new technique of direct mail—a tool we did not fully understand. FAIR would, at least initially, have a small board, since John and Sherry were appalled by the complexities of decision-making with boards of thirty to forty people.

Who elected the board? John did, at first, and then the board itself, under bylaws we amateurs had to craft. If not at the first meeting, John soon added to the board, writer Bill Paddock, which meant that Liz Paddock would usually be sitting in (and she later spelled him on the board). Both were fluent in Spanish, and committed to the civil rights movement—liberals, for want of a better word. Doubtless thinking as much about establishing a centrist image as about board member wealth, John and Sherry persuaded former Gulf Oil president Sidney Swensrud, astonishingly enough a long-time population activist, to join. Sidney was not your usual corporate executive. He had concluded as a young man (in the 1920s) that world population growth was a serious problem, and he had been a population activist in the ranks of those who knew and supported Margaret Sanger and Planned Parenthood. This was frowned on by his business associates, but Sidney wasn't a man to be intimidated by other people's prejudices. In the 1980 election, however, Sidney acted in a predictable way, for a Republican. He voted enthusiastically for Ronald Reagan. Before he had given advice or written a check, Sidney's presence on the board rescued us from an undesirable political imbalance toward the left of center.

FAIR, we quickly agreed (this had been John's early thinking), would be an organization with a membership, but without membership control of the board. Initial planning documents spoke of "grass roots organizing," though we were fuzzy and uneasy in our thinking about what to do with or how to build this "base" out in the country. The "grass roots" matter would be a vexing and complex issue—more interesting to me than writing by-laws or sorting out the pros and cons of direct mail. I was, by then, entirely comfortable with FAIR's board, staff, and attached friends. However, who were these grassroots members? Might not some of them be a bit over-excited, lack our commitment to centrism in politics, hard facts, and moderation? Would they alter our agenda, goals, and tone? We developed computerized lists of our members, and sent them a newsletter and renewal notices, hoping to establishy a clearer sense of our mutual relationship.

* * *

The first thing that struck me in our early communications was the tone that John and Roger had already chosen when I was invited to participate. Centrism and moderation were the tone and thus part of the message.

"FAIR is dedicated to open and rational discussion of these [immigration] problems, feeling that this is the best way to avoid the ugly nativist and racial passions that have marked past immigration debates," John had written to environmentalist Hazel Henderson in August, 1979.

To me, a year earlier, he wrote, "I'm convinced that if reasonable people don't soon produce some solutions to the immigration dilemmas we face, then the less reasonable elements of our society will do so…"

In one of my letters, I replied that I had tilted a bit left of that. "A leading concern with me is to bring into FAIR strong representation from people and groups of liberal, progressive disposition." So that "immigration reform…is socially responsible, entirely non-racist, and not stupidly nationalistic."

Roger used similar language from the first: "We have learned from history that the discussion of immigration must not function as an excuse to arouse ugly nativist passions and racial animosity."

It was part of the language he used in one of our first fundraising letters. Roger had read *Strangers In The Land* at Oberlin.

* * *

Tilting Center-Left

How do you explain this center-liberal and slightly defensive tilt in our early internal conversations and subsequent self-definitions? Part of the answer comes from noting that three of the four of us who drafted the early phrasing had substantial liberal identification and roots, since John drew his early partners from environmentalist precincts, where his own activist roots were. Perhaps more important, looking back, was our collective understanding of the "world of ideas" that pervaded U.S. public policymaking. We knew we were preparing materials to introduce this new organization and enterprise to funders, the media, and other important players in the world of policymaking as the 1970s yielded to the 1980s. This world of policy players was a liberal world. We didn't, yet, see this as a large problem, but simply as a given. Reaganism was just then gathering strength and soon would enter the White House, but the Reaganites' experience confirmed our assumption that the world that any agents of change confronted in Washington, D.C. was a world dominated by liberal institutions, ideas, values, and vocabulary.

Beyond the pervasiveness of the broad liberal ethos in American public life at the national level, we assumed without debating it, that everybody in the nation's policy-influencing institutions had absorbed two simple and simplistic memories from the American past with respect to immigration. The first was the centrality and overwhelmingly positive image of immigration in the nation's experience and achievements, embodied in the symbolism that had evolved (rather, had been constructed) around the Statue of Liberty, and in the misleading but deathless slogan, "America is a nation of immigrants." We were stepping

64

forward as critics of an aspect of the national story that had been thoroughly romanticized into an invariably painless nation builder, and we would have to salute that mythologized tradition as we made the argument that this great force had in our own time turned negative in important respects and now required modification.

The second historical residue we expected to encounter among the educated classes was that the earlier critics of immigration who had restricted and attempted to re-shape the flow in the 1920s were moved by dark motives, and their project was unnecessary if not harmful. This might be called the Higham history lesson—a simplification against which Higham had unsuccessfully struggled for years. We had no time to wonder how this image of the earlier restrictionism had percolated from *Strangers In the Land* (and other books of like message but smaller readership) into college and high school history textbooks, and from there into the brains and emotions of the people who ran the country through government, media, voluntary associations, churches, foundations, and universities. We simply assumed that these two historian-crafted national memories were a fact of life, and that our effort would be prejudged in their light.

From the beginning, we sought to try to steer around the stereotype of nativist restrictionism, and to be New Restrictionists—moderate, balanced, appealing to no bigoted emotions, and relying upon the facts of current immigration's mounting costs. We greatly underestimated the difficulty of navigating around, or disarming, those historic associations.

* * *

Roger began to hire staff, but not many, given that our first year's budget was around $140,000. Two surprises came at once. If we nervously expected at least some eager applicants who wanted to keep all foreigners out of the country, we were pleasantly surprised. "Our issue" did not attract qualified job applicants to our door, since people seeking jobs in Washington seemed ignorant of the issue. Applicants for our staff positions, especially inexperienced young people who responded to our low salaries, wanted to find work in some sector, any sector, of Washington's policy community. They usually had no particular feeling about immigration at all, and they knew nothing about this complex policy world. If we had been launching a policy reform organization in environmental protection, health care, highways, or space exploration, experienced people would have been available. FAIR had to be built out of people who had to learn about the topic on the job, from Roger Conner on down (and upward through the board).

I remember only a few names and faces of staffers from those early days. Gerda Bikales came from the National Parks and Conservation Association, and she at least knew how Washington worked (and would later begin one of her congressional testimonies in French, to demonstrate that immigration reformers were not anti-foreign provincials). Recent Harvard graduate Gary Imhoff was our first writer, and this Jewish left-wing youngster finished up a Master's Degree program taking night courses at Howard University in Black history. Our first receptionist was black. My fears were proving groundless. People would not walk into FAIR's Washington office and see a lily-white group of staffers who looked like the congressional staff of a Republican from Kansas. Roger hired rainbow. Later in the 1980s, as budgets permitted, Leon Ralph was hired to build bridges to his African-American contacts, and Richard Estrada and Luis Acle went on payroll in the Washington office and Ray Hernandez served in the field in Texas to explore openings to Hispanics. It helped with congressional offices when FAIR could send as our lobbyist a stunningly attractive Iranian-American, Simin Yazdgerdi. Our staff throughout FAIR's existence looked a lot like America, all to the good. The down side was that every new hire, until later when we started a border project and hired former Border Patrol people like Jim Dorcy from San Diego, came in the door knowing next to nothing about immigration. They required months and even years of on-the-job learning.

* * *

Welcome to the New Immigration Wars in Washington

If a busy eye surgeon from Michigan, a Prudential insurance executive from New York, a history professor from California, a retired oil company executive from Pittsburgh and a retired agronomist whose principal home was in Florida decided to start a new organization in Washington, D.C. to revise the immigration law and practice of the United States, and if the entire initial staff knew nothing about the subject, you must pray for a period of calm on the issue, while your group gets up to speed.

This we didn't get. In 1979, the FAIR staff and board felt hard-pressed as we wrote by-laws, our first brochure explaining our view of what was wrong and needed changing, and the first newsletter to go to the 600 members we had somehow enlisted, and contracted for a direct mail campaign. This organizational work alone made for long days, but a broken immigration system forced us into the eye of a growing storm. The immigration system was thrust into the news at the end of the 1970s as large refugee flows from Haiti arrived in Florida, and a growing "invasion" (the word used by the Ford administration's head of INS) of the southwestern border by the one million illegal crossers who were apprehended annually and the others (three times those apprehended?) who were not stopped on their voyage northward.

America's porous borders became an issue that the president couldn't dodge. Jimmy Carter proposed a reform package, which included sanctions on employers hiring illegal immigrants and an amnesty to quickly "solve the problem" of the embedded illegal population too numerous to deport in this liberal era. This was a package of law enforcement measures mixed with forgiveness of law-breaking, and it promised to entangle Congress in the most formidable conflicts. The legislators, predictably, steered between action and inaction by asking for further study. A stalling measure was the appointment of the Hesburgh Commission (Select Commission on Immigration and Refugee Policy, or SCIRP), which held hearings in 1980 pursuant to its report expected early in 1981, with congressional action, or at least legislative battles, sure to follow.

Immigration reform of some sort appeared to be moving along the tracks, and our fledgling organization, incredibly enough the only lobbying group organized solely around immigration reform, was now in the frying pan as it moved into the fire. Roger went to lunch with SCIRP director Lawrence Fuchs in 1980, and explained our mission. Fuchs, a liberal academic from Brandeis University, was blunt. He well knew (and had written some of) the history of immigration restriction, and accepted the standard academic view that SCIRP's predecessor, the Dillingham Commission of 1909-11, had recommended immigration restriction out of misguided and xenophobic impulses (which was less than half the story). Fuchs intended to be the director who took the second national immigration commission down in history as the body that recommended *more* legal immigration, not less, displaying the moral progress that Fuchs and the rest of America's governing elites had made since the restrictionist Dillingham Commission of 1911. Roger asked if the commission had considered the environmental damage done by large-scale immigration and the population growth it engendered. This was a new idea for Fuchs, and to inoculate the commission against its restrictionist potential, he subsequently hired the cornucopian lightning rod, Julian Simon of the University of Maryland (of whom more later), to tell the commission what he had just argued in his 1980 book, *The Ultimate Resource*, that more people in any country improved its environmental circumstances rather than aggravating them, world without end.

Fuchs had given clear notice that any reduction or substantial change in the composition of legal immigration would get a cold staff shoulder at the new commission. On the positive side, FAIR's director had been granted a luncheon appointment and a frank discussion with SCIRP's counterpart. Roger and I were invited to testify as the commission held hearings around the country. No Congressman asked me any questions, and they asked few of Roger. However, we New Restrictionists were at least in the conversation, forewarned by the influential commission staff director that our views were wrong and would not prevail. Somehow, that seemed on the whole to be a good start.

PART III:
AMERICA TAKEN
WHERE IT DOES NOT WANT
TO GO : THE EIGHTIES

Chapter Eight:
The Eighties Arrive: Immigration Problems and the Reform Window

Our support was broad and thin like the top, warm layer of the Atlantic Ocean. — Roger Conner

In the 1970s, two currents of foreign populations into the U.S. drove the growing sense of a crisis in the broken U.S. immigration system—mounting illegal entries over the southern border, and a spasm of large refugee admissions. Between 1975 and 1979, some 300,000 refugees from the former Indochina were "paroled" into (meaning they were admitted by the Attorney General under dubious authority) the U.S., exceeding by seven to ten times the quota of 17,500 annually that was written into the 1965 law. Public resentment ran high, and Congress produced the Refugee Act of 1980—again expanding legal immigration, something the national legislators did on every available occasion from 1965 to the present time. The "normal flow" of refugees was tripled to 50,000, and generous provision for public assistance in resettlement was provided—which of course helped build a more substantial refugee industry rooted in church and ethnic groups. Few gave thought to another murky area of immigration policy, asylum seekers, especially those who presented themselves on American soil and sought refugee status.

On April 22, 1980, a busload of Cuban critics of the regime of Fidel Castro forced their way into the Peruvian Embassy seeking asylum, and Castro announced that anyone wishing to leave Cuba could come to the

71

port of Mariel and would be allowed to leave. Over the next weeks an informal flotilla streamed toward Miami, and encouraged by President Carter's remark in May that "we will welcome them with open hearts and open arms," 130,000 Cubans eventually landed in Florida. Castro helped swell the numbers by releasing prisoners from Cuban jails, many of whom continued to be criminals when they reached the U.S. On nightly television, American immigration policy (as to refugees) slipped into chaos, and Roger Conner was thrust onto a larger stage.

The Mariel crisis exposed, again and most spectacularly, the inadequacy of U.S. asylum and refugee policy, and increased media requests for comment from the only lobbying organization devoted to immigration reform. The board and Roger had no blueprint for a new refugee system, which was a complex challenge that was even that year dividing and perplexing the Hesburgh Commission. Roger urged a real ceiling on refugees within the real ceiling on all immigration that FAIR had been advocating. I don't recall that it occurred to anyone to point out that this would have saved Carter from making his unpopular (and some would say, illegal) blunder of inviting an unlimited Cuban exodus to a nearby rich country with a welfare system awaiting them. Roger used every media opportunity to focus attention on the larger issues of immigration that had gone out of control, not just in Florida but along the 2,000 mile Mexican border. In 1980, he appeared on the Today Show hosted by Tom Brokaw, then went to Miami where on talk radio he again proved adept at enlarging the focus from Cubans to the larger disarray of U.S. immigration policy and border controls.

Governor Lamm, Out of the Blue

By the end of the year, this publicity had boosted FAIR's membership to over 6,000, and one of those new members was more important than all the others. Colorado's popular (and eventually three-term) Governor, Richard Lamm, had announced that his state would not welcome the thousands of Cubans that the administration wanted to send there, and the public response to this in Colorado had been overwhelmingly positive. Lamm then saw Roger on the Today Show, and phoned from Denver.

"I think what you said was terrific. I want to know what I can do to help."

Roger was not accustomed to phone calls from governors, but even in his excitement at such a call, he couldn't have imagined how much help Dick Lamm would be. Tall, handsome, and youthful under his white hair, Lamm was a liberal Democrat and no-growth environmentalist who was a fearless maverick in politics, repeatedly taking principled stands that appeared politically suicidal but turned out to be popular. He sensed an intense public rebellion against the collapse of border controls, and FAIR was the only vehicle he had discovered for mobilizing and directing that sentiment. Beginning in late 1981, FAIR had a friend in Dick Lamm whose phone calls would be answered in the White House, and all the way down the governmental pyramid.

The Colorado Governor began to take Roger where he could never have gone through his own efforts—to meet with editorial boards of the most influential print media—*Time*, *The New York Times*, and the *Washington Post*. The editorial boards had a keen interest in immigration issues, given recent refugee arrivals, rising levels of illegal entry, and the expected report of the Hesburgh Commission which was sure to make a mark on the news. The 1980 presidential election meant that the commission's report would go to the desk of a new president, Ronald Reagan. In 1981, FAIR wedged itself into the discussion again. Our lobbyist (the first) Barnaby Zall, had fortuitously discovered that Senator Walter Huddleston of Kentucky shared critical views of the immigration mess, and "Dee" Huddleston became FAIR's other friend in high places. Huddleston began giving speeches mostly written by our Gary Imhoff, citing or borrowing from FAIR for certain data, and language.

Huddleston, on the floor of the Senate, said: "We all agree that there has to be some ceiling. We all agree that the U.S. cannot accommodate the worldwide demand to be allowed to come to America."

Fifty-one senators signed a Huddleston-sponsored letter to the new president, Ronald Reagan, urging that he seize the leadership of the reform enterprise that SCIRP had been nurturing for more than a year.

* * *

The commission's report, *U.S. Immigration Policy and the National Interest*, arrived in March, urging "closing the back door" of illegal immigration in order to protect from public backlash the generous front door of legal immigration. To curb illegal entry, SCIRP endorsed the idea that had found favor with liberals in the early 1960s and had been one of Carter's proposals, "employer sanctions," a law holding employers liable for hiring illegal immigrants. That decision put on center stage the enforcement mechanisms to give teeth to the ban on illegal hiring, and here the commission faltered—a bad omen. It could not agree on a mechanism for determining legal status at the workplace, and Chairman Hesburgh could only advise Congress that his own preference was for a counterfeit-proof Social Security card as a national identification document that would be useful for many social purposes, including work eligibility.

This proposal for employer sanctions backed by an unspecified verification system came coupled with a large concession to those who wanted nothing at all done about illegal immigration. The commission recommended an amnesty, or "legalization," (their preferred word for the proposal to forgive lawbreaking for all those illegally here) for a specified time and with a substantial work record in the U.S. A guestworker program to provide the politically potent western growers with the cheap labor they had enjoyed under the Bracero Program launched in World War II had strong support on the commission, but Chairman Hesburgh transmitted the idea along with his own objection that it had not worked well when tried in Europe, and had created "a "a second class of aliens" in the country.

On legal immigration, SCIRP's report did as Fuchs intended—rejected any changes toward lower numbers, recommending "a modest increase" on the grounds that the commission had concluded that legal immigration brought considerable economic and spiritual benefits and no costs. We were appalled at this deliberate mis-reading of the evidence. The mounting proof of social service costs, wage displacement, acceleration of population growth and environmental effects had been dismissed in the report, though studies finding all of those negative impacts of mass-scale immigration were referenced throughout the commission's staff report. Little was said in the main report of other problems within the legal immigration system, such as the chaotic refugee and asylum procedures, or the need to shift from the nepotism-dominated system of preference categories to skills needed in the American economy. The commission failed by one vote to agree to recommend ending the fifth preference. Chairman Hesburgh, in his congressional testimony, denounced the "chain migration" this provision generated. Under current law, he noted, if you admitted a foreign born married couple, each with two siblings, and each couple with three children, when naturalized, this couple could bring in eighty-four persons! Hesburgh clearly wished that the commission would call this a bad policy in need of correction.

He also accepted the argument (ours) that immigrants competed with Americans for jobs at some level, writing to the *New York Times* in 1986 that, assuming the U.S. economy created 30 million new jobs in the next fifteen years, "Can we afford to set aside more than 20 percent of them for foreign workers? No. It would be a disservice to our poor and unfortunate."

Yet his commission recommended expanding legal immigration.

We immigration reformers were unhappy with the packaging of an amnesty with an employer penalty process that might—and might not—somewhat "demagnetize" the pull of jobs in America upon Third World labor. Why did the SCIRP report feel like progress to us? Because some serious reform proposals aimed at reducing illegal entry were on the table; because Chairman Hesburgh saw to it that the report expressed concern for American workers; and because our tiny new organization had arrived in time for this opportunity. We imagined bringing to bear in the congressional debates a vigorous lobbying effort, backed by public opinion which we knew to be strongly restrictionist, to put a structure in place that was capable of curbing illegal entry, and at the same time minimize the amnesty concessions and fight off the expected agricultural guestworker ideas.

In retrospect, which is the time when I am always wiser than average, our assessment of the policy landscape and political possibilities was naïve and wrong. I should have given more weight to Chairman Hesburgh's personal statement in Appendix B to SCIRP's Final Report, which stated:

"I know there are a great many people who believe that immigration threatens the U.S. That fear is as old as the country...feared...fear...

feared... I do not share these fears...[of those who] blame immigrants... try to stir up enmity...irrational fear and hostility...irrational fear...one must be careful of demaguery..."

It was a rant taken straight out of the history books on the "Know Nothing" movement of pre-Civil War days, identifying all those who would reform legal immigration as fearful demagogues and xenophobes. Whether Hesburgh wrote this or Larry Fuchs wrote it for him, it suggested the climate of opinion in which our reformist arguments would be heard.

* * *

Facing this struggle, Roger conceded later that he had arrived as a congenital optimist, perhaps even more so than the FAIR board. It is only fair to recall that this collective optimism was built on certain real foundations. There was solid evidence that the vast majority of the American people thought that immigration was too large, and the illegal part was intolerable. We all knew the results of recent opinion polls, in which the American public, however the questions were phrased, overwhelmingly denounced illegal immigration and voted against enlargement of legal immigration. The poll results never changed very much, from FAIR's founding in 1979 to the day you read this book. In a democracy, public opinion of this strength and durability ought to be decisive, if mobilized politically—we thought, or, hoped.

"I'm finally involved in an organization I think can succeed," Bill Paddock wrote to friends. "We had a concept, employer sanctions, that could solve the problem of illegal immigration, and...we were on the side of truth, right, justice, and the American way."

He had a lot of company.

"I really did believe," Roger recalled, "that we had a combination of an effective leader in Simpson, a reform idea that made sense...employer sanctions, and a growing immigration problem."

Roger's comment about "an effective leader" deserves emphasis. Alan Simpson (Rep., Wyo.) was new to Washington, and his outlook and talents seemed almost providentially matched with America's immigration crisis. A first-term Republican senator from a respected and well-known Wyoming family, Simpson was assigned to the Hesburgh Commission where he mastered the details of immigration policy. As he discovered the disarray and irrationality in it, he developed a sense of mission. After the report's completion and with Republican control of the senate, Simpson was named chair of the Senate Immigration Subcommittee of the Judiciary Committee. The path to legislative achievement was suddenly open to this novice senator, and he seized the moment.

"The American people are so fed up with being told—when they want immigration laws enacted which they believe will serve the national interest and when they also want the law enforced—that they are being cruel, mean-spirited, and racist. It's time to slow down, to reassess."

Simpson's frontier wit could be hilarious, and ease tensions. The tall, folksy westerner did his homework, kept his word, and was respected on the other side of the aisle. When Roger Conner said, "We had a leader," he meant Simpson. The Wyoming senator would have to compromise in order to salvage the historic turning point of effective laws against hiring illegal immigrants, and we accepted the necessity of such balancing in order to achieve anything at all. If one forgets this, it is difficult to understand why the little band of reformers persisted so long and stubbornly in their efforts to achieve restrictionist reform through years in which mounting compromises aimed the legislative process toward a profound disappointment.

* * *

There were, of course, early discouragements that challenged the hopeful outlook among we restrictionist reformers. When Senator Huddleston had the Congressional Research Service study the impact of illegal immigrant populations on the apportionment of states' seats in the House of Representatives, it showed that illegal immigration was being allowed to dilute the political power of certain American citizens merely on the grounds of the state in which they lived. Pennsylvania, for example, after the 1980 census, lost two seats to sunbelt states with large illegal numbers whom the Census Bureau counted for purposes of apportionment. That news aroused the ire of the Pennsylvania delegation. FAIR brought a lawsuit (dismissed later for lack of standing), and the expected national media coverage came. Roger appeared on the MacNeill-Lehrer show, and was interviewed by CBS.

"This is going to be big," he confidently declared.

However, the story went nowhere, along with Pennsylvania's indignation. At the urging of Dick Lamm and others, Roger paid for an ad to run in the *Wall Street Journal* and *The New York Times*, calling attention to this distortion of American political institutions by the growing illegal population, and invited donations to FAIR.

"This is going to be big," Roger said again.

It wasn't. We pushed our outrageous news into the public eye, with very little response.

"We had been wrong" to regard the opinion polls as proof of a mobilized or mobilizable constituency for reform.

Roger later concluded, "Our support was broad and thin like the top, warm layer of the Atlantic ocean."

We were learning.

* * *

The Hesburgh report received high praise in the editorial pages of *The New York Times*, the *Washington Post* and other influential papers, commending its proposals for firm and determined changes required to end illegal immigration. The commission's cautious and limited recommendations on legal immigration tended to be given little emphasis in the press. Commission and news media seemed agreed that the broken part of American immigration policy was porous borders, and the machinery of government seemed to be grinding toward a solution to it.

The new Reagan administration, which had zero interest in immigration, had no choice but to quickly establish a task force to study it and decide on Reagan's position. A letter from Roger Conner of FAIR is in that task force's files in the Reagan Library, along with some evidence that it, and others like it, strengthened the hand of those few in the White House who thought the president should join and lead the immigration reformers. But Reagan had no interest in the topic, and some of his staff and advisors did not like what they read of the Hesburgh committee's recommendation that the government should enlarge its authority through a law, and penalize employers for hiring illegal workers. Active, effective, business-regulating government was not Reaganite music.

In July 1981, the administration, internally divided, put forward its suggestions, which were correctly perceived as a far weaker response than that of SCIRP. The administration ignored legal immigration entirely. On the illegal problem, they recommended an amnesty to make it disappear, and employer sanctions without a "national identity card," as they called the idea of an identification system, required to make sanctions enforceable. A guestworker program in agriculture was thrown in to appease the southwestern growers. Reagan's heart was not (which meant that his head certainly was not) into immigration matters. For the next five years, the president and his administration remained on the periphery of the battle for immigration reform, though Reagan occasionally (when asked) endorsed the general idea of repairing the immigration system, and signed the measure in late 1986. The main arena would be Congress, where Senator Alan Simpson emerged as the central figure.

Brushing aside the Reagan administration's proposals, Simpson and the Chairman of the House Subcommittee on Immigration, Romano Mazolli, held joint hearings where Father Hesburgh delivered an impassioned plea for serious reform to regain control of immigration. Then they began hearings on a package of reforms of their own, and decided to focus on illegal immigration only. They launched legislation in early 1982. To us, John Tanton had created FAIR just in time to participate in these epochal events.

* * *

Anti-Reform Arguments—and Ours

It seemed that Roger was organized reform's only spokesman in those early days before the FAIR staff expanded and trained itself, and long before other groups formed. As he debated "the opposition" (a cluster of Hispanic lobbyists, usually Vilma Martinez of La Raza, in concert with business and agribusiness spokespeople) on television, radio, and public forums, and as board members visited newspaper editorial boards or encountered the counter-arguments our views elicited, we became familiar with the arguments on the other side.

First came the contest over vocabulary. Immigrants, legal or otherwise, must be called "undocumented workers." We continued to make the crucial distinction between the lawful and the unlawful, but the media caved in and almost universally used the term "undocumented," which was an early setback in a battle over media terminology that we would not win until the end of the century. A law forgiving previous law-breaking was not amnesty, but "legalization." Immigration reformers were "anti-immigrant," "population control groups" "scapegoating" immigrants for America's internal problems. Welcome to the dominant tropes of American immigration politics on the open border side, imported from post-modernist, universal human rights discourse that had conquered the commanding heights of American intellectual life.

This universalist ethical ideology came with the historical mythology, which had in recent decades, gained such a hold on the American memory. "History taught" that immigration restriction was an unnecessary and disreputable cause, because immigration was good for the country and always had been in all of its forms—the more the better, including illegal immigration, which was merely an inevitable flow of people to jobs. Those who do not share this view had a hidden and shameful motive. They were the familiar bigots we had heard about in the disreputable American past—xenophobes, thinly disguised—or as Simpson once complained about such language, it labels reformers as "cruel, mean-spirited, and racist." In the past, restrictionists had predicted great harm would come to America if immigration were not restricted, but the large-scale immigration they opposed a hundred years ago strengthened and diversified America. Wrong then, the restrictionists were wrong now. Immigration is "the meaning of America," the weariest phrase of all. Without constant rejuvenation by immigrants, America would lose its innovative, entrepreneurial energies, and certain basic jobs wouldn't get done. In any case, the northward flow of labor was an historical event that was inevitable, and not controllable without police state measures, if at all.

* * *

We initially thought that these intellectually flimsy propositions wrapped in sentimental views of the past and present could be challenged and substantially discredited by facts, but we came in time to respect their tenacity at a level below logic or fact. I was reminded of a comment by the writer Jonathan Swift, that it is impossible to reason someone out of something he didn't reason himself into in the first place. The core proposition among those defending the status quo against Hesburgh-Simpson-Mazolli was an historical argument—that immigration restriction in America had been a racist enterprise which was without rational justification in the historical era when it arose, and that this was still true.

To this history lesson our response was one that was almost never counter-argued—that whatever the accuracy (which we disputed) of the interpretation that was fastened upon the immigration reformers of a century earlier, things have changed. The world is increasingly crowded and on the move to the affluent north by jet plane and steamship. The costs of Third World mass immigration, whether legal or illegal, were substantial. Both types of immigration required corrective attention and a firm sense of limits. Apart from social costs, the America that had absorbed the mass immigration of a century earlier had changed into a multiculturalist haven whose assimilative capacities were considerably enfeebled from an earlier time. We began to make these arguments in FAIR position papers, sent out in their yellow covers to what must have been a small readership of those who were already convinced—mostly our own members.

An early sign that it would be hard to get the attention of elites or the general public came when Dick Lamm and Gary Imhoff collaborated on *The Immigration Time Bomb*. FAIR spent some of our scarce money for a book tour, but "it really didn't catch on," Roger recalled, possibly because "public interest in this subject wasn't as deep as we imagined it to be."

As for the racist part, it took time and practice before we could move from indignant denial, which didn't seem to fully meet the problem, to contemptuous ridicule. Sherry Barnes liked to tell the story of a matriarchal friend of hers from Planned Parenthood, who returned in tears from a luncheon talk in which, for the first time, she had said that immigration had become, on balance, a problem.

"They called me a racist!," the friend tearfully complained.

"But, Janette," Sherry responded, "you've been called a murderess many times, and it never bothered you!"

"I know," was the answer, "but today they called me a *racist!*"

It took awhile to see this for what it was—a brutally effective, at first, attempt to intimidate and silence the opposition, counting upon deep reservoirs of white guilt. I recall the ripple of shock that went through a gathering of FAIR's Advisory Board in Washington when I told them, in a talk on what was meant by the new term "political correctness," that if they hadn't been called a racist that month, they must not have been doing their job as educators and citizen activists. "Rejoice in that name calling," someone else urged our group. If they call you a racist it means that they are badly losing the argument and feel forced to reach deep into the slimy depths of their bag of arguments in a desperate last ditch effort to push you out of the debate. As Hannah Arendt wrote, a favorite tactic of the dictators of the 1930s was to turn every statement of fact into a question of motive.

* * *

The Open Borderists—Who Were They?

The anti-reform argument we were encountering in the early 1980s was shaped by intellectuals and policy pundits. Then it was repeated to the media and policymakers by lobbyist groups. We soon became familiar with their speakers and views. The most impassioned in resisting reform and rejecting the moral legitimacy of its arguments were the Hispanic organizations, such as MALDEF and La Raza, which were Ford Foundation-nourished non-member organizations with a flimsy social base. Less strident and more rooted in a constituency was LULAC, a membership group with real roots in communities of the southwest. LULAC had a history of having opposed illegal immigration from Mexico from the 1920s into the 1960s. Then their position began to shift, as younger leadership pushed forward. Those groups now regarded themselves and were regarded by funders and the media as civil rights organizations, carrying on the work of Martin Luther King, Jr. They took part-ownership of the moral high ground claimed by the black struggle for equality. Like the blacks, they were given wide latitude in naming the bigots they claimed to face in the fight for civil rights, which increasingly included the right to migrate across borders. Their lobbyists were quick to denounce immigration reformers with the vicious language of bigotry unburdened by evidence, and they never seemed to talk of the public or national interest. Alan Simpson could not entirely hide his distaste for the Latino lobbies, whom he held in the same high regard as he held the western growers, whose motives he simplified in one outburst: "Their greed knows no bounds."

As we joined the debate over immigration in the 1980s, the territory to the right of center was home for a body of ideas and a social movement called American "conservatism." It emerged ," in the 1950s and gave focus and a national political agenda when Barry Goldwater ran for president in 1964 and Ronald Reagan came to the presidency in 1980. Whatever post-war American conservatism was, it had no real record of thought or action about immigration policies, which were battles of long ago that ended in the 1920s. Reagan was a sort of sentimental open-border man who held the employers' view that low-cost workers were a good thing, always. It was one of the many issues Reagan simply did not and would not think about. When he filled his cabinet with "conservatives," it was not anticipated that they would turn out to be divided on this issue. The Immigration task force set up in March, 1981 to formulate the administration's response to the Hesburgh report was chaired by Attorney General William French Smith, a conservative in the sense of staunch support for law enforcement and thus a reformer, with Hesburgh, of the illegal immigration situation. Simpson, another conservative reformer of that type, discovered before FAIR did that there were other types of conservatives in the White House and in OMB—people like Martin Anderson and his wife, Annelise. For them, conservatism meant that they preferred law-breaking at the border to a government strong enough to prevent it.

This deep division, which Reagan never really resolved and may not have understood, meant that in the battle over immigration reform the conservative administration arriving in 1981 was neither a decisive nor a consistent factor in the debate. It was pulled in two directions—the law and order instinct, and the open-border inactive government ideology. However, one of those verities of conservatism was intellectually more robust and aggressive than the other.

A relatively new, right-leaning think tank, the Heritage Foundation, published not just one but two roadmaps for the Reagan administration's dismantling of the liberal establishment. It was also in the early 1980s the main home of two especially active intellectuals whose arguments were rolled out against immigration reformers. One was journalist, Ben Wattenberg, who praised the current regime of mass immigration, legal and illegal, for diversifying and invigorating the country, which otherwise would begin to shrink in numbers and lose its social vitality.

More influential was Julian Simon, a Midwestern marketing professor who moved to the Washington area at the end of the 1970s. From his post at the University of Maryland and at the Heritage Foundation, he turned himself into one of the most audacious and frequently quoted apologists for the benefits of unending population growth. His *The Ultimate Resource* (more people, always more people) was published as we arrived in Washington. Simon was skilled at displaying familiarity with a wide range of issues connected to the immigration debate—whether immigrants brought economic gain or costs (gains), the relation of population growth to environmental problems (a growing population helps solve environmental problems), the uses of welfare by immigrants (minimal; they come to work). He was a formidable antagonist through the 1980s and into the 1990s. It had never occurred to us that we would confront a full-time "expert" who read all the evidence to mean that the U.S. should beg for immigration without limit, relished media interviews and lecture tours. Despite his preposterous views, he somehow survived as an oft-quoted source on the entire range of immigration questions. Another lesson was that the American media seeks stories in which some event or assertion can be countered by an outrageous rebuttal by someone with plausible credentials.

Simon understood this, and was facile and available for comment when a reporter had some immigration news peg. Was immigration contributing to an intensifying population problem, imposing substantial and rising social costs, especially on American labor and taxpayers? As we and others attempted to document the case that it was, Simon indefatigably offered pithy and quotable assertions that the opposite was the case. In so doing, he risked intellectual marginality and eventually contempt, which came in the 1990s and undermined his influence. FAIR produced a devastating summary of the scholarly critique that had met Simon's writing and verbal claims over the years ("Behind the Curtain: Julian Simon's Manipulation of Immigration Studies" [1996]), and Simon himself, we learned in his posthumously published autobiography, *A Life Against the Grain* (2002), basically agreed.

When the eminent Harvard biologist E. O. Wilson referred to Simon as "a buffoon," Simon told a reporter, "Wilson is right."

But Simon's performance, the intellectual equivalent of Ronald Reagan's brimming temperamental optimism, retained credibility much longer than one would have predicted and provided Open Borderites at least one reliable scholarly supporter.

* * *

The Restrictionist Perspective

What about the arguments on our side? They evolved, the board's thoughts and memo-writings now interacting with the verbalized thinking of our active executive director. We certainly needed a language and emphasis quite different from the restrictionists' arguments of a century earlier, whose thoughts and language often contained judgments about national groups that contemporary Americans no longer felt or tolerated in public discourse. We reached an early consensus that we were "New Restrictionists," as I had titled my 1978 essay, building on the enduring wisdom of the impulse to regulate and limit immigration rather than leave our borders entirely open in an era of unprecedented global population growth. We shared the earlier concern that American workers should not be forced to compete in their communities with Third World labor. We had stronger environmental concerns. We understood, as early restrictionists had not, the multiple harms that population growth inflicted. We had no interest in immigrants' nationalities/cultures, so long as the numbers were small so that assimilation could do its unifying work. Consensus came on the major themes of the New Restrictionism at a board meeting in Ligonier, Pennsylvania, west of Pittsburgh, where Sidney Swensrud maintained a home.

The cornerstone for us was bringing down the numbers, and replacing a mass immigration era that commenced in the 1960s with a smaller flow differently selected. How small, or how large? Some suggested that we should resort to the historical averages, which we calculated at around 300,000. This was shaky history and a poor basis for modern policy. Annual immigration averages for some decades in U.S. history had been (estimated at) less than 25,000. However, they exceeded a million for several pre-World War I years, and were actually negative in 1932, when more Americans were leaving than foreigners were arriving (apparently). An average for the entire national experience of the U.S. was not a sound basis for future plans. What was the national need for immigrants? Some of us thought there was no need for any. More of us wished to compromise with the "heritage of immigration" sentiments while keeping the numbers low, and were drawn to the estimates of annual emigration—250,000 or 300,000 a year, yielding zero net immigration. This was close to the national average per year, and it was consistent with one of our core goals—neutralizing immigration as a growth factor in American life. Whatever the annual number, set it low enough to have no growth-generating impacts.

As for illegal immigration, it must be ended to the greatest degree possible, by employer sanctions backed by a secure worker identification system to cut off the job magnet.

We were eager to begin the argument over the desirable configurations of legal immigration, which we argued must conform to the changed realities of modern America. The nation was no longer in need of more population, and was almost never in need of an augmented labor force. The U.S. should select its smaller numbers of legal immigrants in light of national economic needs, while offering a limited refugee commitment. The current system was not designed to serve national economic needs, as nearly 90 percent of legal immigrants were chosen by recent immigrants on the grounds of nepotism (officially called "family reunification").

Our basic arguments in the area of illegal and legal immigration were taking shape. Always, there was the moderate tone, "We are alarmed, but not alarmists."

Roger and John were especially active in discovering and opening dialogue with writers who shared our general criticisms of the broken immigration system. In those early days, we read and welcomed Sloan Foundation official Michael Teitlebaum's article in the Fall 1980 issue of *Foreign Affairs*. He argued that critics of U.S. refugee and asylum policy had a legitimate case; demographer Leon Bouvier's *The Impact of Immigration on U.S. Population Size;* the writings of economists Ray Marshall and Phil Martin, making the case that supplying cheap agricultural labor was not only an unwarranted subsidy from the public to growers, but depressed wages and stifled agricultural innovation.

* * *

Seeking Out Our Natural Allies

An immediate need was allies in reform, and here the picture was not encouraging. The reform coalition a century earlier had consisted of an influential array of groups who didn't normally agree—organized labor, patriotic societies, Republican politicians like TR and Henry Cabot Lodge, elements of the intelligentsia, the black leadership. We found that coalition had long ago shattered and was perhaps impossible to reassemble. Roger reported that the American Legion and Veterans of Foreign Wars seemed concerned about current immigration patterns, but they were incompetent and without energy or respect on the Hill. The labor movement was in the process (this was clear only later) of gradually and without fanfare shifting its position from worker-protective restrictionism to an astonishing open border position that exposed their members to competition from Third World labor—a position that organized labor embraced in the late 1990s. In the early 1980s, we found union leadership formally committed to controlling illegal immigration at least, but unpredictable as a lobbying force. They were entangled in some sort of cross-currents inside organized labor that we didn't understand.

Every member of the FAIR board was to one degree or another an environmentalist. Our executive director started his career as head of an environmental lobby group there. We assumed that environmental groups would lend some support, when the link between large-scale immigration and population growth was understood. We were wrong. The Audubon Society leadership was supportive for a short time, but they kept us at arm's length. We found resistance and even some hostility when we approached other green groups for support. We didn't fully understand their resistance, though John and Sherry had seen similar objections to any discussion of immigration within ZPG. We assumed we could eventually bring many green groups around when we got their full attention focused on the basic dynamic, by which immigration contributed to environmental damage. Later, an Australian sociologist of rare insight, Katherine Betts, helped us understand the dynamics by which societal elites, in this case those in charge of environmental lobbying organizations, see themselves on a certain moral high ground where any discussion of immigration is impermissible. There is, further, a more crass, class interest. The environmentalist leadership we hoped to enlist in our connected enterprise were educated people, often with two incomes per family. They, therefore, wanted reliable nannies, cooks and gardeners. They, too, were employers, though on a small scale, and sought cheap labor that was reliable and not cheeky. For these and perhaps other reasons, such as reliance upon the funding decisions of foundation staffers who shared with them the two circumstances mentioned above, we never made any sort of alliance with any group claiming to protect the American environment.

* * *

What about the African-American part of America? They, we reasoned, would provide natural ally-country. Most had not moved up into the nanny and gardener-consuming upper middle class, but still competed with immigrant labor in the service and construction trades. We looked for an opportunity to make our case and open communication with the top black leadership in Washington. One came when I remembered that Harold Fleming, head of the civil rights-oriented Potomac Institute in Washington, was a board member at Hutchins' Center in Montecito and had well-earned friendships among the black leadership in Washington. Harold and I had hit it off well, as southern whites who had lined up (he earlier and far more substantially than I) behind the civil rights movement. I called, briefly described our group and its purpose, and asked if he would broker a meeting with top NAACP leadership.

He had little enthusiasm for this, but friends do favors for friends. Harold set up a meeting on a weekend afternoon in the large meeting room of the Potomac Institute. John, Roger and I entered from one end of the high-ceiling room, and a somber, suit-and-vest black delegation came from the other end, led by Clarence Mitchell. They weren't cordial, and never smiled. They heard us out, and then, without any commentary on what we had said, declared that the issue was a difficult one and they wanted no part of it. The rank-and-file in the NAACP sometimes raised complaints about foreign labor, they conceded. However, a decision had been made at the top echelon of black and Hispanic leadership that they would join in an unbreakable civil rights coalition and never allow differences to emerge and weaken the common front. Immigration was off the table, the Hispanics stipulated, and thus the NAACP managers would not argue the merits of our view that black Americans were paying a price for open borders. The conversation was over.

We never gave up trying to add significant parts of black America to our enterprise, never stopped believing that surely it could be done, and found success with some remarkable individuals like Frank Morris, but never with the black organizational hierarchy. A phone call came to FAIR from a wealthy builder from California, and he asked what the organization would do with a million dollars. Roger had plenty of ideas, but asked Larry Kates why the Californian cared this much.

"Blacks are becoming unemployable in California," he answered. "Everybody prefers immigrants, any immigrants, but especially Mexicans. They work harder, and don't complain like the blacks."

"But you're a builder," Roger responded. "Isn't this just what you want?" Kates answered: "In tolerating rising levels of illegal immigration, we governing classes in California and elsewhere were merely building up an ever-larger even if internally divided lower class. Their resentments fueled by the low wages and high unemployment produced by endless replacement flows of Third World third-world labor. The Mexicans, in their second generation, will lose their work ethic like the blacks and eventually follow them onto welfare, and this lumpenproletariat will drift into class warfare against people like me and my developer friends. To head this off, you guys need to reach out to blacks to help you cut immigration, and I will fund some expanded lobbying and any other good ideas you have."

With Kates' gift, sizeable but not in the end reaching a million dollars, Roger hired six lobbyists to form a congressional task force. One of them was a black Californian named Leon Ralph, who came to Washington. Not surprisingly, he failed to make any headway with the black leadership there.

Seeking allies among Hispanics produced slightly better results. Hispanic organizations were hopelessly tied to their liberal foundation funders and the ethnic expansionist ideology of their staffs, but individual Hispanics were a different matter. Recalling Cesar Chavez' opposition to the importation into America of Mexican labor, we hoped to find many more and bring about a visible browning of the FAIR staff, making connections to Latino organizations for coalition building. This hope was disappointed, but there were smaller benefits. It was a pleasure to know and work with tall, erudite, Mexican-born Luis Acle from California, with the buoyant union organizer from Texas, Ray Hernandez, and above all with the imposing Richard Estrada, eloquent in speech and on paper. Our mail was always sprinkled with letters from Americans like Lupe Morfin-Moreno of Santa Ana, California, and Susan Gonzalez of Mystic, New York, who thanked FAIR for its efforts to bring immigration into line with the law and the national interest. These courageous Americans strengthened our sense of how large-scale illegal immigration undermined the gains and prospects of Americans of Latino background.. They confirmed our intuition that Americans of Mexican and other Hispanic heritage were no friends of open borders, despite the positions taken by self-appointed Latino "leaders."

Their reinforcement emboldened Roger in 1983 to spend $40,000 of our scant resources to commission a poll of Hispanic opinion on immigration. Carried out by a team of one Republican and one Democratic pollster (Lance Tarrance, Peter Hart), the results "were exactly what we thought we'd find," Roger recalled—overwhelming support among Latinos for stronger border controls, employer sanctions to reduce illegal immigration, and on amnesty, a split in which only plurality favored it, and then only for people who had been in the country for a long time. The poll was widely publicized, and subsequent polls confirmed its general findings.

* * *

Enlisting Members

The opening salvos of the battle over the Simpson-Mazzoli reform legislation found FAIR one year old, essentially alone as the only organization devoted to restriction of both illegal and legal immigration. It was quite difficult to find or nurture substantial institutional allies. The organization was at the low end of small among Washington lobbying groups. Roger reported 6,000 members in 1980, rising to 25,000 members by the middle of the decade.

We, of course, wanted more members, and like all membership groups, we hoped to influence national policymaking, and resorted to direct mail campaigns.

This turned out to be tricky work. To write a letter that would arouse Americans against the mounting irrationalities and social costs of uncontrolled immigration, the managers of the direct mail firms we hired urged inflammatory letters, headed up by the latest outrage. Determined to establish and maintain a moderate tone in Washington, we were being advised (like all other groups seeking members and donations) to be a bit immoderate in our membership-oriented mail. This made Roger acutely uncomfortable, and he resisted it, not always successfully. On more than one occasion, the letters we sent to enlist and arouse our supporters found their way to the attention of some congressman whom we had categorized as an open border patsy for the growers' lobby or listed as one we had pressured into changing a vote. We then found we had aroused an influential politician at the cost of adding a handful of members.

Beyond this, the messages we sent through direct mail to recruit our members were shaping that membership in ways we had not anticipated. Analysis showed our membership by the mid-1980s as predominately older, many retirees, and tilting toward the politically conservative end. FAIR staff who met with members during travel confirmed this, and shared Roger's worry that some FAIR member—it would only take one—might someday get media attention with some inflammatory bit of "hate speech," in one evening undermining our efforts to built a responsible, moderate image.

"We were paranoid about that, perhaps," Roger conceded.

Our staff were young and mostly liberal, and uneasiness about our members was natural. Neither Roger nor the board made any effort to form chapters in the early days.

Yet contact with members could be invigorating as well as educational. At our first board meeting in California, in San Diego in 1981, the board invited west coast members who had been especially active by phone or mail, and asked them to tell us what brought them to the issue. It was "a magical moment," someone later recalled. A mill worker from Oregon told of jobs lost to illegal immigrants, a college president told of uneasiness that his campus was using foreign students as cheap labor and then finding that they didn't return to the home country. A businessman complained that he was ashamed of the low wages he offered to workers he knew to be illegal, but could not compete if he held to an "American wage." A pair of black teachers from Long Beach told of the difficulties facing educators whose classes were shifting toward majorities of the Spanish-speaking children of illiterate peasants from rural Mexico. It was a warm moment devoid of bigotry, where we learned that, if this were a representative group, our members "weren't a bunch of redneck racists."

However we saw ourselves, when the organization was noticed in the media, it was invariably identified as "an anti-immigrant group" or "a conservative group." This characterization blocked or biased our access to many congressional offices and journalists. Fortunately,

Senator Simpson, while not exactly an ally, came to regard FAIR as a legitimate participant in the march of legislation. This has to be credited to Roger Conner's moderate tone and reliability on the facts, as well as the presence of Dick Lamm in our front ranks. Simpson and Congressman Mazzoli addressed a conference FAIR held after the meeting in San Diego in 1981, confirming that we were players, if puny by comparison to the others.

Thus the immigration reform effort launched in 1978 had by 1981 established a small presence in Washington, just as a series of events took place across America's Florida coast and the southwestern borders, thrusting current immigration policy into a more intense scrutiny and set the stage for major legislative reform activity.

Chapter Nine:
The IRCA Fiasco, 1981-1986:
Reform's Maiden Voyage

The simple truth is that we've lost control of our borders, and no nation can do that and survive. — President Ronald Reagan

The Commission and task force examinations of immigration problems launched by Presidents Carter and Reagan finally nudged serious congressional deliberation. In 1982, Simpson and Mazzoli held separate hearings, both building upon the Hesburgh formula for controlling illegal immigration, which Simpson called "a three-legged stool"—border enforcement, employer sanctions, and an enforcement system based on a counterfeit-resistance identification system for workers. Simpson's central idea for reform on the legal immigration side was an end to fifth preference (for adult brothers and sisters of citizens and LRAs), the mechanism driving chain migration pyramids. Mazzoli's was a real ceiling of 450,000 legal immigrants per year. We cheered both of these policy directions, and stood ready to add other proposals.

Then political forces sorted themselves into a mine field that prevented legislative resolution for five years. Simpson was first forced to yield to the pressure of liberal Democrats led by Senator Ted Kennedy and also Hispanic lobbyists, and reluctantly put a bargaining element on the table—a limited amnesty for illegals who had been in the country for a specified time. The White House could have joined most congressional Republicans and the Attorney General, William French Smith, in rejecting an amnesty, changing the reform dynamic in ways hard to anticipate. Reagan accepted the amnesty idea from the beginning, though he expressed his concerns about the welfare costs. Simpson's bill passed the Senate in 1982 with employer sanctions and an amnesty. In the more liberal and Democratic controlled House, other restrictionist reform measures were cut away. Mazzoli and Simpson lost their cap of 450,000 on legal immigration. As 1982 came to a close, the Democratic House leadership decided that bitter divisions and controversy made a vote in the House unwise in a year in which they all faced the electorate. Immigration reform was shoved into the next Congress.

A narrative with somewhat different details but very similar results took place in the 1983-84 session. By now it was becoming conventional wisdom that a "reform" package built around employer sanctions must include a concession to large-immigration forces in the form of an amnesty on some scale. Roger was profoundly uneasy with this pairing, and I was one of the board members inclined to reject it from the outset. Employer sanctions might pass in emasculated, unenforceable forms, while amnesties always "worked," usually more expansively largely than intended. The result would be a bargain in which restrictions didn't work and expansions did; a very uneven trade. Roger took every occasion to argue that any amnesty ought to be delayed until, and conditional upon, hard evidence that the border was under reasonable control and the flow of illegals had been drastically reduced.

Nevertheless, it is easier to devise good social policy than to participate in the legislative process, as we reformers learned who had never done either. We opposed the amnesty in principle and urged that it not be considered until sanctions had greatly cut the illegal numbers. Yet, as the amnesty idea stayed as part of "the bargain," we found ourselves entangled in efforts to limit the amnesty's numbers and the government's responsibility for welfare and social services, which almost made us appear to be acting as architects of an amnesty. We were disgruntled that Simpson had agreed to some sort of amnesty for bargaining purposes, as it forced us, if we were to be players, to lobby for smaller rather than larger amnesties, when we didn't want one at all or at least not until at least three years of sanctions proved we had the illegal numbers in a steep decline. Simpson somewhat testily pointed out in his defense that any real reform of immigration was almost impossible to move through the legislative machinery when the President was not strongly behind enforceable limitations, and his wobbling course could be and was exploited by the Democrats in order to partisanize and sabotage various important turns in the road. Reagan's passive stance made Simpson's hand weaker. Did we want to play the real game, or let the best be the enemy of the good? What reputation did we want in Washington—rigid idealists, or pragmatic tough bargainers? In selecting Roger as director, we had already gone the second way, on the amnesty and on other matters.

Simpson's package passed the Senate again in 1984, containing an elaborate amnesty (which even he began calling "legalization") in trade for employer sanctions in the weak form of a fraud-inviting system of several easily counterfeited documents. The only reform moving ahead in 1984 began to look like a border opening measure. The FAIR staff, buoyed by any signs that we were indeed players, enjoyed telling the board how frequently the organization was able to become involved in the legislation through contacts with Hill staff. This was hard for the board to confirm. We often wondered aloud whether we should be on a ship that seemed headed toward expanded immigration numbers, though under the label of reform.

Mazzoli's House negotiations reflected many of the same controversies. There were in the House, to us, several promising efforts to strengthen the worker identification system, as through a call-in phone registry based on the Social Security number. Angry denunciations of "a national identity card" depleted the shallow reservoirs of civility and tilted the legislation in the House also toward toothlessness.

By a narrow margin of six votes, the House passed a bill in June, 1984, that probably no member fully understood. Employer sanctions was still the core of the legislation. It was the only real reform element and was marred by weak enforcement measures. To gain sanctions, the bill's managers had accepted an amnesty that might include three million illegals. Not only did few members understand the legislation, but almost none were enthusiastic about it, especially in a presidential election year. We reformers were still supporters of the overall package, mistaking (in retrospect) as its reform core the historic imposition of employer penalties that would be worth any number of compromises.

Ironically, opponents of sanctions also exaggerated its importance, and called in all their chips to head off the penalties on employers. As the conference committee wrangled in late 1984, the Hispanic Caucus and a group of Hispanic lobbyists went to Speaker O'Neill's office, and in an emotional encounter reminded him of their Democratic voting record, their status as mistreated minorities once again faced with the prospect of discrimination, and demanded that the bill be killed.

"They told me if this legislation were passed they'd all be required to wear dog tags," he later explained, "and I promised them it would not pass."

The civil rights movement was a Democratic Party trophy, and it had been invoked again to trump everything else. O'Neill instantly responded to a constituency conceded to be occupying "the moral high ground" by virtue of having ancestors, some of whom may have experienced racial or ethnic discrimination. Hispanic legislators and lobbyists claimed that bigotry was about to gain a new foothold when employers had to scrutinize new hires for their immigration status. O'Neill promised that there would be no time for House consideration of a conference report in 1984. One man halted the American political machinery at the end of three years of effort.

There was much public outcry over this when a *New York Times* reporter broke the story of O'Neill's boss tactics, since it seemed to confirm a growing sense that the Democratic Party was a tool of leftist special-interest groups spawned in the Sixties and whose language and outlook were devoid of the words and concept of the national interest. O'Neill retreated, claiming that he had only promised the Hispanics "a delay," and defended himself against the criticism by saying that "there is no constituency for this bill," beyond "environmentalists and population types." That was us. The conference committee could not complete its work in October, 1984 before adjournment, and immigration reform awaited another day.

* * *

As 1985 arrived, we pondered O'Neill's remark that "there is no constituency for this bill." He never changed his mind about this, and those sentiments were probably shared by Ronald Reagan and Walter

Mondale, who ignored immigration problems in their campaigns for president in 1984. For we immigration reformers, it was frustrating to move into Reagan's second term with no legislative achievements, but especially dismaying to read newspaper reports that the Speaker of the House had declared in a contemptuous tone that we represented no constituency. Worse, O'Neill's daily actions, and the votes and comments of others in this struggle, showed plainly that he and they believed that *defeating* any restrictionist reform did have a constituency; one too strong to be ignored—Hispanic lobbyists and voters, labor unions, large agricultural growers, some church groups.

Whether we liked O'Neill's assessment or not, he was the political professional, assessing where votes and money were located. Our job was to change his mind the old-fashioned way, by demonstrating influence—mobilizing a large membership, ideas and arguments, building coalitions, and maybe even raising political money. In the mid-1980s we didn't have the necessary membership, coalition, or money, even if we were beginning to gather durable ideas and arguments. Becoming influential was going to take more time than anticipated.

The sentiment I heard most frequently was that our effort had behind it what could surely be turned into an irresistible force. Public opinion was overwhelmingly on our side. A Gallup Poll in 1977 found 77 percent in favor of employer sanctions, and that level of support was sustained into the 1980s. Surely it was possible to turn that public anger at immigration disarray into political influence behind a decisive change.

We explored ways to embarrass the obstructionists in the Congress and White House during the 1984 presidential campaign and debates by trying simply to raise the question: "What is your position on immigration reform?" The public would then hear that one or both were not seriously interested in or behind the issue of controlling illegal immigration, and surely a political price would be paid.

It was easy to strategize about using public opinion on immigration to punish or reward politicians. I should have recalled Shakespeare's lines: "Well, I too can call upon the mighty deep. But when you call, does he then hear you?" We broke through the silence only once, and then with the help of a knowledgeable journalist who came to the topic from our angle of view, Georgie Anne Geyer. She was appointed to the panel of questioners for one of the presidential debates between President Reagan and Democrat Walter Mondale. Roger provided her with a memo suggesting ways to raise the immigration issue. "Gigi" took up the challenge at once, declared immigration a foreign policy issue, and asked both candidates what was their position on illegal immigration. Both floundered a bit. Mondale said he was "against it" and Reagan endorsed employer sanctions. Then the issue slipped back into political obscurity.

* * *

A determined Simpson saddled up again in May, 1985, submitting legislation with a vitally important new element. An amnesty would proceed only if a special commission concluded that the effort to control the borders had curtailed the flows. This had been part of the Hesburgh report and we were enthusiastic about it. However, Ted Kennedy and the Hispanic lobby had strong feelings the other way, and within months Simpson retreated to a guarantee that an amnesty would wait no longer than three years. We felt that this contingency provision was a critical part of a workable reform plan, and our hearts sank.

Then Senator Pete Wilson (Rep., CA) introduced an agricultural guestworker plan that allowed an unlimited number of foreign workers to enter sectors of U.S. agriculture and work for nine months, presumably returning to their native countries thereafter. We had done our homework on guestworker programs, the Bracero experience here in the U.S. and the European programs, and were stunned that the Senate would consider another one. The Hesburgh Commission had looked hard at guestworker programs, and firmly rejected the idea. Simpson, too, was angrily negative about Wilson's proposal. This "open-ended guest worker program" would "repeat the most serious errors we have ever made in immigration policy, and "is not immigration reform." Wilson was defeated on a close vote, and at once came back with a revised version allowing 350,000 workers annually over a three-year period, which squeaked through a Senate vote in September. These low-wage workers would be free at the end of their contract to migrate to cities, leaving room for 350,000 more, all of whom would have families in Mexico or elsewhere ready to migrate up the chain in their turn. This slipped through the Senate in September 1985; Simpson calling it "exploitation deluxe." Now, at a late hour, immigration reform legislation contained a new version of this perennially bad idea.

House maneuvers were complex and intense. The new guestworker issue further splintered any elusive majority that seemed momentarily to be forming, and forced the maneuvering deep into 1986. That summer, Congressman Charles Schumer Dem., N.Y.) put together the votes in the House for a new and double mistake—a Special Agricultural Worker program which was a combination of an amnesty for current farm workers and a replenishment program offering new visas for agricultural workers willing to work for a specified period, after which they could leave the fields and settle legally anywhere in America.

* * *

Is There a Pig in That Poke?

In July, the FAIR board met at Airlie House in rural Virginia. We had never met in that lovely setting before and wouldn't again, because John was tight with money. He soon had us meeting in a D.C. motel, even when the date fell in the city's sweltering summer. At Airlie, despite the countryside and old-inn setting, we were depressed and uncertain. I distinctly remember that the only pleasant, light moment came after dinner the first night, when new board member Janet Harte, from Corpus Christi, Texas, wiped out three male board members by throwing three straight bull's-eyes in darts. The rest of the meeting was difficult and tense. We had no illusions that our decisions in late summer, 1986 would decide the fate of IRCA, but we certainly were positioning the organization in the eyes of its membership, donors, and anybody in immigration policy circles who might be paying attention.

We had strongly opposed amnesty and guestworker programs from the beginning, and what looked like two amnesties and one or two guestworker programs moved forward with the only reform element that survived—employer sanctions in what was clearly an unenforceable form. Could Alan Simpson, if this mess ever got to conference, make at least the main amnesty conditional on border control, and eliminate the agricultural guestworker program now attached to this complex legislation? It did not seem likely, though he and Roger had talked directly over the summer and Simpson vowed to make a fighting effort. Had the time come to denounce the entire package as irredeemably flawed, or were we best advised to remain players and hope for victories in the conference committee? If we bailed out before the end, would Alan Simpson or any other legislative leader (or president) ever work with us again?

Arriving at Airlie, we learned that the FAIR staff was seriously split, and consumed with internal argument. Roger led the half that wished to remain players and stay behind IRCA even in its mangled, border-opening form. K. C. McAlpin, a smart young Texas businessman who had taken a cut in income to join the FAIR staff, spoke for the other half of our work force in Washington.

"Our knowledgeable members around the country," he said, "are already communicating outrage that we had not already denounced this smelly bag of compromises, branding it as unsalvageable and in anything like its current form deserving of defeat and a fresh start some other day."

Roger's rejoinder was that the Senate might slip into Democratic hands as a result of the November elections, making Ted Kennedy Chairman of the Immigration Subcommittee, and our window of opportunity would have slipped away.

The board closed the doors for executive session, and we found ourselves equally split. I leaned toward K.C.'s analysis, appalled by the amnesties (there were three in the bill). But we eventually came to see, with John's help, that another issue for us was the institutional risks we took if the board rejected the position of our executive director. When in doubt, as we certainly were, you stick with your leader, especially if you are not ready to fire him. We moved ahead on Roger's track, with deep misgivings. At stake wasn't the legislation, which we lacked the strength to derail, but our reputations—with the Washington policymaking establishment, as responsible players, and with our membership who wanted us to point them in a direction more forward than backward.

A bill passed the House in October with the Schumer amendment in it—a new agricultural guestworker program that had not even been scrutinized in hearings. The conference committee couldn't agree, and IRCA seemed fated to die on the runway, again. Then a change in Reagan's travel schedule overseas gave weary conference members more time to cobble together an agreement. Probably nobody, certainly not general manager Simpson, believed that this package of inconsistent compromises was defensible public policy, but increasingly it seemed to both parties that the American people wanted some sort of result. They might blame everyone concerned, or whoever seemed to be responsible, if the futility was extended. A conference report came together, cleared both houses in early November, and the president signed IRCA on the sixth in a small room in the White House chosen by staff opponents of the measure in order to minimize attendance and TV coverage. Reagan made a brief, shameless statement about how big and fine a reform it was.

* * *

Assessing IRCA

U.S. law now imposed penalties on employers who hired illegal immigrants, with a verification system accepting any two of a lengthy list of easily forged documents as proof of citizenship. For this fraud-inviting system, Congress had traded four amnesties, one for those in residence since January 1, 1982, another for illegal agricultural workers who had worked at least three months in 1985-86, one for a group of Cuban/Haitian refugees of the Mariel era and one by moving the "registry date" (after which the Attorney General could adjust the status of any foreigner) from 1942 to 1972. It had also included, as a trade for enforcing the law through a penalty on employers of those illegally in the country, a new agricultural guestworker program, which all knowledgeable people knew would increase illegal immigration and keep agricultural wages low. Some 3.1 million illegals were removed from that category by IRCA's amnesties; 70 percent were Mexicans with a seventh grade education. A mid-90s study by the congressionally-appointed Jordan Commission found that the two main amnesties of

1986 brought in an additional 8 million relatives living abroad—5.2 overseas relatives per amnestied alien.

We were stunned when the full extent of the expansionist features began to come into view, all traded for penalties on employers based on an unenforceable system of verification. When legislators are tired and confused, at least on immigration matters, we learned that the frenzy of trading at the end of the process gives the advantage to the openers of loopholes, not the closers. In the hectic last days, no one seems to have noticed or objected to Section 314, allocating by lottery 5,000 visas to "qualified immigrants" from the top thirty-six nations "adversely affected" by the 1965 law—meaning a country that had not used more than 25 percent of its 20,000 quota (some countries were ruled ineligible, i.e., the top ten sending countries throughout American history). Senator Ted Kennedy had in mind only the Irish, whose falling quotas over the years prompted him to add this element to IRCA. The State Department named the thirty-six countries, most from Africa and Europe, and the first lottery in 1987 produced 1.4 million applications in the first week. What did this have to do with the employment needs of the U.S., or with family reunification—the cornerstones of our system of selection? This irrational new visa category had strong ethnic support in Congress, which expanded the "Diversity Lottery" visa pool to 40,000 between 1990-1994, and reserved 40 percent of these to the Irish. Discriminatory national origins considerations had crept back into American immigration policy. When the reform train begins to move, strange cargo is smuggled aboard.

* * *

Illegal border-crossings along the U.S.-Mexican border, as measured by arrests, eased a bit for several months while potential migrants waited to see if the government of El Norte was serious about arresting them if they entered the U.S. Since it wasn't, the magnet of American jobs still pulled Third World labor, which resumed its flow northward after less than a year of lower pressures. Illegal immigration surged again, building momentum through the 1990s, reaching annual totals of 500,000 at the opening of the next century. The number of illegals in the country by 2002 was estimated at ten to eleven million. The problem had been made worse. Historian Reed Ueda correctly called IRCA "the most generous immigration law passed in U.S. history." This "generosity," a misleading word with a nice ring, was directed toward foreigners who had broken our laws to enter. They broke them every day they remained, butting in line in front of those at home on the waiting list for visas.

* * *

This was our maiden voyage as immigration reformers—we optimists who thought it might take five or even ten years to "turn this around."

How to assess what had happened?

A much-contested law had finally been signed after five years of political horse trading, and expectations seemed generally restrained. The media did not report any euphoria from the parties involved. Reagan signed the legislation quickly and without ceremony. He didn't invite Senator Simpson, Congressman Mazolli or anyone else from the Hill. Simpson, who was sought by the press, had almost nothing to say. Roger cautiously told reporters that time would tell. To me he wrote, quoting Churchill: "This is not the end. This is not even the beginning of the end. This is just the end of the beginning."

I don't know if there were huge parties on November 6, 1986 in the offices of Senator Ted Kennedy, over at La Raza, among the lobbyists who represented southwestern and southern growers, among immigration lawyers, and in the Mexican Embassy. There should have been. Celebratory parties were justified in those places where ethnic aggrandizement and cheap labor were the only goals, and "immigration reform and control" were exactly what was not wanted. The reform and control hopers, backed by a broad and thin public opinion, had taken a good run at the immigration status quo, and the status quo had not only fended off restriction, but rewarded law-breaking and expanded the incoming numbers through the same flawed system of selection. We at FAIR, who had stayed with the process to the last, received very little congratulatory communication from anyone, certainly not from our members, some of whom wrote us to complain that they had hoped for better, and wondered where better had gone.

A year or two later, it was obvious that, in a head to head encounter between American political institutions and a sustained peaceful but illegal human invasion across undefended borders, those institutions pardoned most of the lawbreakers and set up workplace checks that were an international joke. We reformers sometimes asked and were asked why we had not at some point gotten off that train with a public statement that it deserved to be derailed and a fresh start made.

This second-guessing deserves a second look. I have already pointed out that Alan Simpson's emergence from Hesburgh Commission member to Chair of the Senate Immigration Subcommittee appeared to open an unprecedented historic reform opportunity. His knowledge of the issue and his determination to bring improvement to a fundamental breakdown in a nation-shaping system of population replenishment had not been matched since "Pat" McCarran (another mountain state immigration reformer) shored up and improved the national origins system in the early 1950s. Simpson was both more talented and more congenial.

This helps account for how long our enthusiasm persisted, even into 1986 when so much bad policy had been woven into the package. In retrospect, Alan Simpson did not have the power to maneuver a restrictionist reform measure through our system in the 1980s. Our hope that he might pull this off reflected an immature understanding of the country's political system, culture, and the place of this issue within both. We moved slowly up a steep learning curve.

Roger later reflected that our choice was to struggle to the end as supporters or be pictured as one of the spoilers—though it might be countered that we were too insignificant to be awarded that dubious honor in the press. The Hispanic lobbies were the real spoilers who wanted to defeat everything and preserve a broken system, he pointed out, and we did not want that image.

"Did I get trapped," Roger mused in his memoir, by a desire to be "a Washington insider?"

Most of the staff felt so, he admitted, and perhaps they were right to a degree.

"We were swept up in the momentum of the public support we had created."

Roger returned to the role of Simpson. No one could have predicted that the senator and his chief aide, Dick Day, would become exhausted in the final hours of negotiations. Simpson failed to press hard for a list of improvements in important details of the legislation that we and others had discussed with him. The Wyoming senator has not published any memoir of these events, but surely he would point out that a passive and probably uncomprehending president in the White House allowed mixed signals to go out to the end. Attorney General Ed Meese refused to back Simpson on the crucial "legalization commission" empowered to decide if sanctions were working well enough to trigger the amnesty or not, even though INS Commissioner Alan Nelson supported this "conditional amnesty" provision. With the White House signaling that Simpson was on his own on this one, several Republican senators voted against the conditional amnesty, allowing the amnesty to proceed before sanctions had been tested. All of this happened very fast at the end. We gambled on Simpson in conference, and we were not sufficiently aware of the weak hand of cards he held.

* * *

Still, the view that nothing of real value came with IRCA, and that it was a mistake to go down to the end with it, may be too harsh on FAIR, the only organized lobby behind it. Employer sanctions in the final package rested upon a list of easily-counterfeited documents inviting massive fraud. The law provided what looked like a corrective mechanism. The president was empowered to sponsor pilot experiments in the states toward a single national identification document, a ladder of improvement upward. No one could know that Reagan, and after him, Bush and Clinton, would show no interest in this. They left this policy experimentation authorized by IRCA unexplored. The legislation outlined a path toward strengthening the sanctions, and who could have known that subsequent presidents would squander that opportunity.

It is also easy to forget important parts of the contemporary setting. The pressure on the government, and all the stakeholder groups, to reach agreement and pass some sort of immigration package, was enormous. A major theme in the policy discourse around this issue was the fear that government ineptitude at border control would unleash a wave of national hysteria against immigrants. Fuchs and Father Hesburgh spoke of this frequently, and with urgency. Cope with the illegal problem, they said, or face a backlash from the American public, which has, history tells us, even if contemporary evidence is lacking, a strong xenophobic streak just beneath the surface.

A lot of intelligent people shared this fear of a sudden outburst of popular "nativism." Immigration historian John Higham in 1984 wrote that at the beginning of the twentieth century, "the inescapable need for some rational control over the volume of immigration in an increasingly crowded world was plain to see, then as now" and he scolded the "unyielding resistance from the newer ethnic groups" along with business interests for blocking any reform. It allowed the problem to "fester and grow until a wave of national hysteria" seemed inevitable. Passing a deeply flawed reform law seemed preferable to deadlock and inaction—the apparent alternatives. Dick Lamm put together a public announcement in major newspapers in early 1986, signed by former Presidents Ford and Carter, among major political figures, urging all participants to salvage Simpson-Mazzoli. These political heavyweights thought there was an important opportunity for averting a popular backlash. Virtually every large newspaper in the country, led by *The New York Times* and the *Washington Post*, praised the legislation when it arrived on Reagan's desk. They urged him to sign it, and welcomed it as an improvement when it became law.

Recalling this context helps us to understand the widespread touching faith in the Simpson-Mazzoli experiment with employer sanctions that we reformers shared with others, even as the crippling compromises piled up.

* * *

The Positive Side of Defeat

Enough had been said about the verdicts of hindsight on this first inning of the game of immigration reform. Real reform had lost, but our team on the field for the first time in a century had been a "responsible player," giving the benefit of the doubt to the promises of legislators and administrators proposing the "Grand Bargain." When the government failed over the next two decades to carry out the promises of the bargainers, that "trust me" tactic was discredited, and Simpson's preference for "enforce first and verify" had many adherents in the critically important policy fights ahead of us in the Bush years, 2001-2009.

The expansionist results from IRCA's passage and implementation must be weighed against an institutional achievement not sufficiently appreciated. Our fledgling organization had taken up the restrictionist reform cause in 1978-79, after this cause had been dormant for more than half a century. The restrictionism of the late nineteenth and early twentieth centuries had by then been given by historians and the media a negative reputation as mostly bigots on an unnecessary mission. When we emerged in the latter 1970s the Expansionists at once branded us as re-emergent "nativists" and "anti-immigrationists," hoping with slurs pointing to bigoted motives to avoid engaging our arguments on the merits of the case. They may have expected and must have hoped that our language, arguments, and body English would cooperate, and confirm that the redneck racists had once again mobilized behind xenophobia in much the same way as some of the restrictionists one hundred years earlier. As important to us as helping to shape a law that offered a chance to control illegal immigration was developing a constructive, fact-based, moderate voice and reputation on this emotional issue so that we could exert influence on immigration policy far into the future.

When the IRCA marathon was over, two things were true. The national interest and we reformers had lost, as the law we had worked to shape almost immediately made things worse, and illegal immigration resumed at rising levels. Institutionally, we New Restrictionists were still in the game, still players, even if we were far behind after the first inning. For we restrictionists in the 1980s had not conformed to the ugly stereotypes many had attempted to fashion on us. FAIR's point of view was given wide attention through the entire IRCA battle—in congressional testimony, on Good Morning America, the big evening news shows, and McNeill-Lehrer, before the editorial boards of major newspapers. Alan Simpson spoke at FAIR gatherings repeatedly, as did Mazzoli, Senator Huddleston, historian John Higham, and Harvard ethnicity expert Nathan Glazer. Gatherings of acknowledged bigots are not visited by people of this stature. FAIR had from time to time endured a smear attack aimed to delegitimize its point of view on the grounds of hidden motives known only to right-thinking people. On the whole, this had not been successful. Some media and policymakers tried to marginalize the New Restrictionists by pontificating about their "real motives," but this tactic faced two obstacles that splintered its effect. One was the awkward fact that two-thirds to three-quarters of the American people were restrictionists, suggesting that media and policy elites might be prudent to regard this position as legitimate even if morally backward. A second problem with the tactic of name-calling and guilt-by-associating restrictionists into marginality and possibly a cowed silence was the absolute lack of evidence supporting the charge. Unlike the earlier restrictionist movement, there wasn't a whiff in our discourse of some of the sour themes of an earlier time—calling some immigrants "mongrels," open anti-Semitism, and no harping on immigrants' dual loyalties. With liberal and moderate language, we had played the immigration policy reform game through this first long IRCA inning. We testified before commissions and Congress, appeared on the evening news, and sometimes had our telephone calls answered on Capitol Hill and at the INS. The inning went badly, but we were expected to come out for the next one.

* * *

The credit for this must be broadly spread around. John insisted from the beginning on a moderate tone and image, and invented phrases such as "alarmed but not alarmists," and he hired the right messenger—Roger Conner. Much credit goes to the reform movement's first celebrity or recognized national figure, Colorado Governor Dick Lamm. This three-term, liberal-environmentalist Democrat courageously and at considerable personal career risk spent his own political capital to reach out for immigration reform allies in the higher political circles that none of us could contact. One example was the large-scale newspaper ads in which Lamm brought together former Presidents Ford and Carter, Father Hesburgh, and other Americans of stature to urge responsible action to curb illegal immigration. He joined the FAIR Board in 1982, his armed bodyguard sitting quietly in the hallway while we deliberated. Apart from his astute political and policy judgment, Dick Lamm's involvement opened doors and got phones answered, which built institutional strength even while we were handed a bad first-inning score.

Above all, in my view, the face and image of the new immigration restrictionist reform in the 1980s was shaped by Roger Conner. Our staff was small, mostly young, and without exception just learning the fine points of immigration policy and politics. When congressional testimony was needed, when the phone rang from a reporter or news organization, or when a think tank in Washington wanted a speaker or panelist from the restrictionist, reform perspective—it had to be Roger, for we had for several years no trained substitutes. The board created the language and arguments of FAIR, and insisted upon fact-based analysis, moderation, and a critical focus on fumbling American policymakers rather than immigrants who went on welfare or clogged hospital emergency rooms when they weren't working.

It was Roger who was seen and heard, and who became the messenger of this new voice—immigration reform. He might have been, despite the board's instructions, any number of unfortunate things—eloquent in complaining about immigrant behavior; a passionate advocate of border fortification; or a man with the body English of foreigner suspicion. Instead, he was affable and upbeat, a verbally adroit, quick-witted, fact-anchored critic of American government for allowing access to its sacred rights of citizenship to spin out of control, undermine the rule of law, and undercut the economic prospects of American workers. His tone and message were matters of comment in two major stories in 1983.

In a lengthy and influential essay, "Immigration," by respected journalist James Fallows and appearing in the venerable *The Atlantic Monthly* in November 1983, Roger was described as "a compact, sandy-haired lawyer, thirty-five years old, with a puckishly all-American look" whose mother had taken in ironing and did domestic work. Fallows reported Conner as committed to immigration limitation because "immigration was the biggest environmental question of all" in that it drove American population numbers relentlessly upward with no end in sight. Beyond this, "the victims of immigration are the marginal workers, with low education," most especially African-Americans—a point forcefully made by two other people associated with FAIR and quoted in the article, Cornell economist Vernon Briggs and T. Willard Fair, head of the Miami Urban League. In Fallow's survey of all the arguments and players in the rising battle over rising immigration, FAIR's Roger Conner projected an image of environmentalists with a keen sympathy for the lower rungs of the American workforce who were competing with cheap foreign labor.

A *Washington Post* story in November that year conveyed the same image. Speaking at Howard University in Washington, Roger told his black audience that Americans were losing jobs to immigrants, and "the applause was spirited. It was an effective performance Conner has repeated many times. Conner delivers his position in an envelope of traditionally liberal concerns."

Post writer Carlyle Murphy went on: "Conner...is known for his intelligence, enthusiasm, organizing abilities articulateness and earnestness."

A critic said that "Roger enjoys the restrictionism too much," and Arnold Torres, director of LULAC whom FAIR had called "a self-appointed leader" since the membership had never elected him, responded that "FAIR is a very dangerous organization."

Fallows and the *Post* writer had not conveyed that impression. Roger Conner and the New Restrictionists were speaking a language stripped of the occasional racial and we-they hostility of a century earlier.

Chapter Ten:
Building Reform Capability:
Institutions, Ideas, Talent

Every nation has an economic policy and a foreign policy. The time has come to speak more openly of a population policy. By this I mean not just the capping of growth when the population hits the wall, as in China and India, but a policy based on a rational solution of this problem; what, in the judgment of its informed citizenry, is the optimal population? — Edmund O. Wilson,
<u>The Diversity of Life</u>

The passage of IRCA brought only a brief pause in the combat over immigration. Legal immigration had received far less attention by the Hesburgh Commission than illegal, and their agenda for change in the legal side was skimpy and cautious. Yet their deliberations had exposed several serious shortcomings which made a deep impression on at least one member of the group—Senator Alan Simpson. Our system of selection, he (and many others, including us at FAIR) came to believe, over-emphasized kinship to the expense of skills useful in America. Admitting close to 90 percent of immigrants because they were related to recent immigrants generated "chain migration" of people chosen not by America's policymakers but by blood relations to recent immigrants. The commission also heard from critics of the existing system that annual immigration ought to be tied to the labor force needs of our economy and fluctuate with it—which it could not do if altered by Congress every twenty years or so.

Simpson had intended to take up these and other flaws in the legal system in 1981, but was soon forced to set aside that agenda and focus on illegal immigration. After IRCA, Simpson met in 1987 with Democratic leaders Ted Kennedy in the Senate and Charles Shumer in the House, laying plans for reform of legal immigration. The legislative process cranked up, and FAIR staff testified eight times before congressional committees that year. We were hopeful—again.

* * *

Becoming the nation's foremost organization dedicated to immigration analysis and reform was a formidable assignment for a small outfit less than a decade old. Board and staff of FAIR, mostly the latter, geared up, as the political opportunity arrived, to inform legislators and any interested part of the public of changes needed in the legal immigration regime to align it with the national interest. We built upon the reform ideas that had surfaced in the SCIRP deliberations, on the expertise of the handful of academics and researchers we had located and brain picked (such as Vernon Briggs (Cornell), Leon Bouvier (Population Reference Bureau), and Phil Martin (UC Davis), on Simpson and his staff, and on the writings of the board's more scholarly members, Dick Lamm and Garrett Hardin (and myself, if we are to believe Roger Conner's oral history).

These many years later, I am impressed at how well prepared we were for the next round in the reconsideration of America's legal immigration regime. My evidence is a three-page article in *Science* magazine in July, 1988. FAIR that summer convened in D.C. a conference on what an ideal legal immigration regime would look like, and what principles should guide it. The editors of the highly respected *Science* magazine had earlier decided that immigration was becoming a major nation-shaping force, and assigned one of their top public policy writers, Constance Holdren, to write a story on what remained to be done after IRCA had become the congressional answer to illegal immigration. She called Roger, heard of our conference, attended with her notepad, and wrote a lucid and wide-ranging article, calling FAIR "a restrictionist" group that is concerned with long-term economic, environmental, and demographic effects of immigration." Good start.

At the conference she heard the critiques of current legal immigration that we had pulled together over a decade—that immigration had reached a nation-changing scale that had never been intended by the authors of the major reforms of 1965; that 90 percent of new admissions were selected by "nepotism," or family reunification, yielding "an influx of low-skilled people." Our current immigration policy had been formed, Alan Simpson was fond of saying, of "equal parts of emotion, racism, guilt, and fear." Holdren added that a vague humanitarianism, along with wildly flawed assumptions about the expected consequences, had guided the 1965 architects. By the 1980s, it was plain that "immigration is a social policy which…is not based on any research or on any long-term vision of the country's values and needs." She heard us, loud and clear.

What should be done? Holdren's piece captured the leading ideas—annual immigration should be capped (refugee totals included) at a level permitting national population stabilization; selection should be shifted decisively away from family reunification and toward skills important to the U.S. economy/society. Her article made no mention of any interest in "national origins," as there had been none. It was all about numbers, and how to select the annual fewer. As for the future, would the problems analyzed at the meeting be dealt with in the legislation being put forward by Senators Simpson and Kennedy?

"It is difficult to imagine how rational, long-term decisions can be made in the absence of a larger vision about the future shape of the U.S. population," she concluded. "But population policy has never grabbed widespread interest."

* * *

Doing the intellectual work of understanding policy flaws and constructing promising alternatives had been very hard work, but the 1988 conference indicated that we had done that part of our work well. Lobbying came next, pushing ideas through the system, and this was more daunting than the intellectual work that must precede it. The staff, and to some extent the board, were immersed in daily tactics, in learning the policy terrain, lingo, and players. Organizations needed also to think about how to reach the goals so painstakingly constructed, especially organizations that have just endured a painful defeat. My experience at FAIR gave me some sympathy for boards of directors who wrestle with difficult and important daily issues of a tactical sort, and never get around to strategic considerations. FAIR was directed by a board whose members had full-time day jobs, or commitments, elsewhere. As the passage of a flawed IRCA brought an end to one cycle of effort, it gave way without much pause to a legislative wrestle over legal immigration. Who had the time or impulse to think strategically about the future of our effort? Day to day tactical problems seemed a large enough assignment. Staff, who were always day to day people, encouraged the board in this focus.

My own tactical rather than strategic focus was hard to defend. I had written a book about American national planning (*Toward a Planned Society*, Oxford University Press, 1976) and writing it gave me a modest education in the importance of long-range thinking in large organizations, including national governments. I knew that somebody needed to look away from daily battles to the longer term. However, strategic thinking about immigration reform wouldn't come from me. I was a fully engaged history professor in a university that stressed research and publication, and I was helping to raise our two children. Like the insurance company executive, the retired Shell Oil president and the writer from Iowa and the others, I came to board meetings ready to deal with an agenda set by someone else. We expected it to be about pressing tactical questions—which of course it was. The agenda was a staff-set agenda, i.e., Roger's, and it was always tactical.

Fortunately, someone came forward in the person of a busy ophthalmologist from Michigan who found time to set in place the institutional foundations of our effort in the first place. John wrote a memo for a board meeting in October, 1986—I seem to remember that it was entitled "Quo Vadis," and assessed our progress and our weaknesses, while suggesting some innovations.

The FAIR budget in 1979 had been $216,000. It crossed over the million mark ($1,269,000) in 1982, and reached $1,543,000 in 1985. The expansion of resources did notdidn't reflect a huge membership, which had reached 40-45,000 by 1986. Members' dues were set at a modest twenty-five dollars, barely enough to keep the office open and send the members a newsletter. We attracted support from a small number of foundations. The occasional liberal foundation such as that of Stewart Mott was soon outnumbered by others whose interests were generally labeled as "conservative" by the media. A $1.5 million budget in Washington got you an organization of fifteen or so staff members—a pygmy among D.C. lobbying institutions. We had to enlarge our sources of income, John wrote, as well as the income itself. "I would summarize our effort as under-capitalized" and Washington-based in outlook and focus. We tended to measure our success "in new laws passed."

Sidney Swensrud put forward an alternative, and forcefully insisted that our strenuous and to-date mostly losing battles in the corridors of Congress should now be matched by new ideas in the defense of our physical borders. This proposed border focus made some of us initially nervous. We liberals on the board warned against "a police image and focus." But Sidney, impassioned and indignant at this elemental collapse of the rule of law, was persuasive in arguing that we develop a program focused on how to secure the borders. When it came down to it, foreigners in a large and continuing stream were vaulting contemptuously over our borders, and it bothered all of us deeply, whatever our political leanings. This was certainly true of our members from California, who often wrote to urge us to make the integrity of our southern border the focus of attention. We hired one or two former Border Patrol veterans and began work on a border control project—a study of promising policy changes as well as physical structures on the southern border that the government had lacked the motivation or the courage to explore.

What came out of this project was a FAIR model of a series of structures and excavations that wasn't a wall and didn't look like one. Our new director, Dan Stein, had the model constructed on a large cardboard surface that could be folded in half and fit into the trunk of a car. FAIR staff took it up to Capitol Hill where a handful of congressmen were amused, and out to the southwestern border where BP officers thanked the organization for a new idea.

* * *

This was a sideline. FAIR needed a stronger Washington policy presence. To get the attention of the Tip O'Neill's of the policy world, and of the politicians who concluded with O'Neill that "there no constituency there" among the restrictionists, there must be a lobbying force with either campaign money, voters being mobilized, or both. FAIR was at that time the only organization lobbying for reform in a restrictionist direction, but dispensed no campaign money and couldn't be sure we were optimally mobilizing our 45,000 members. We needed more "raw political power," John wrote, which meant "work at the grassroots."

That was easier to say than accomplish. The FAIR staff were Washington people, and when they thought of "raw political power" they though of alliances with other, larger, older Washington organizations, reachable by a Metro ride. We had approached groups we knew to be negatively affected by the overall impact of mass immigration from the under-developed world—African American groups, organized labor, and environmental organizations. We directed Roger to continue to explore these alliances, and also to make common cause with "the patriotic societies" such as veterans and their descendants, groups that John and I knew had been at the center of the restrictionist coalition a century earlier. All of these efforts met with disappointing results.

Membership expansion was essential. The Sierra Club in 1986, according to the *Encyclopedia of Associations* (1986), had a membership of 350,000 and 185 staff; the National Rifle Association had three million members and 350 staff; the Audubon Society had a membership of 510,000 and 490 local chapters. FAIR came out of the IRCA battle counting 45,000 active donors, scattered across fifty states.

Thus the O'Neill's in Washington did not fear us or our members. Neither did local and state politicians and officials, whose role in immigration policymaking and enforcement we were just beginning to appreciate. We needed more members, and we needed them to be more active and visible, if we could somehow channel the activism. Our initial efforts in this direction were cautious and conventional. We asked our members to "write a letter to your congressman" on some upcoming vote—the most passive way of being active. Something better and additional was required.

* * *

Should We Organize the Grassroots?

Slowly, in the latter part of the 1980s, FAIR began experiments to fashion a larger and more engaged grassroots presence, without taking the step toward setting up local or regional "chapters." Events ran ahead of us. Some local chapters had already voluntarily formed, here and there, mostly in Texas and California. There was one in Santa Barbara when I moved back there in 1989 after a decade on the faculty of the University of North Carolina, Chapel Hill. Opening a FAIR Florida office had not worked out, but a one-person office was established in Los Angeles. After INS Commissioner Alan Nelson left the government he became FAIR's lobbying force in Sacramento for several years. Board member Janet Harte, a fluent Spanish speaker, had gathered mostly Anglo sprinkled with Latino friends into an immigration discussion group in Corpus Christi, Texas. Several of us went there to meet these aroused citizens, and were so reassured by their quality and judgment that we urged them to form a chapter as an experiment (we did not use that word with them) in grassroots mobilization. They did, and another FAIR chapter formed spontaneously in Austin. I think there may have been a few other local "chapters," and we held our first national membership meeting in Washington, D.C. in October, 1987. When these local activists asked us what they should be doing, we had no ready answer beyond "write to your congressman," or picket local businesses known to hire illegals. We had no materials to send them on activities they might pursue locally, and no staff trained in this sort of "field" management. FAIR cautiously began to move in these directions, unaware that, in California, a rebellion at the grassroots was brewing that would force us to get outside Washington and equip ourselves to engage, draw strength from and channel the energies and passions of an awakening among grassroots Americans.

* * *

Changing the Guard

Sometimes organizations that don't meet their goals change their leadership as well as re-think their strategies, tactics and structure. FAIR had not met its goals in the legislative war leading to IRCA. In retrospect, they were unreachable. The American political system in the 1980s could not generate and focus the political will to bring illegal immigration under control, though we continued to hope that the employer sanctions framework could in time be made the basis for movement in that direction. As for problems in legal immigration, Congress had essentially ignored them for a decade.

Arguably, however, FAIR had been reasonably successful in that it established an institutional presence, and had participated as a legitimate voice, sometimes applauded.

"In twenty-three years of covering international affairs," columnist Georgie Ann Geyer wrote, "I have never seen a more admirable American effort than immigration reform. " Praise is deserved by Senator Simpson," she went on, and "the remarkable citizens' group, FAIR," who "resisted any descent into demagoguery against the foreigner...and remained unfailingly rational, polite, just.

"FAIR has played a constructive and important role by bringing balanced and thoughtful research to the debate on this highly sensitive issue," Senator Simpson said.

"FAIR has worked in a reasonable and responsible manner to... present its case to the public and press," Congressman Tony Coelho stated for a FAIR brochure.

At the close of a history of "nativist" movements in American history (*The Party of Fear*, 1988) , historian David Bennett surveyed the debates over IRCA in the mid-Eighties, and concluded that "there is no major right-wing antialien effort calling for action in the name of the old nativism. Indeed, there is no "movement" at all. There is FAIR, an educational lobby." We were not happy that he found no (social) "movement," but it was some achievement to have created a New Restrictionism recognized as profoundly different from the old.

No one to my knowledge was anything but pleased with Roger Conner's leadership. However, change came, as his tenth year at FAIR approached. At the board's suggestion, he changed his title to president and devoted more time to fundraising and coalition building. Dan Stein, a FAIR staffer who had earned a law degree studying at night at George Washington law school, became executive director. Then Roger resigned and took a position with a non-profit working to strengthen the institutions of community in America. We feted him at a farewell dinner, where he was "roasted" by former Senator Eugene McCarthy, journalist Georgie Ann Geyer, and INS chief Alan Nelson, with an appreciative letter from Senator Simpson: "Should we have been more a grassroots movement?," Roger later mused in an oral history. Yet, worried about "redneck, racist sentiment..." he had provided a leadership style and tone that led away from emotion and resentment.

Chapter Eleven:
"A Skirmish in a Wider War"

My New York friends would never forgive me. No, you guys are right, but I can't go public on this. — Theodore H. White

John Tanton Looks to History for Ideas

John would sometimes phone in the evening when he knew I had finished work (which was about 11:00 p.m., his time), usually when his historical appetites were running high. He asked me a lot of questions about the immigration reform movement prior to World War I, about organizations like the Boston-based Immigration Reform League, the American Protective Association, and the role in the 1921-24 legislative struggles of an influential activist who had come to his attention, Col. John B. Trevor. He quickly exhausted what little I knew. Then one night in the mid-1980s he asked how another social movement, American conservatism, had managed to make a comeback from the debacle of the Goldwater presidential candidacy in 1964 and put Ronald Reagan in the White House by 1981, setting the stage for an historic reform turn in American public policy.

I knew something about this. My own explanation began with the errors and misjudgments of the liberals, but John was more interested in the positive side. He wanted to know how the anti-liberals had pulled themselves together and gained energy and direction through an intellectual offensive. We talked of a long battle of ideas, and of the crucial role of well-funded "conservative" or free market think tanks like Heritage, Cato, and the American Enterprise Institute, augmented by policy magazines like *Policy Review*, *The Public Interest*, and the long climb of Bill Buckley's *The National Review* into intellectual respectability and a significant audience. To change accepted ideas and challenge the status quo, new institutions had been essential. John seemed energized by these strategy sessions, which I knew were not limited to me.

He also asked me for readings on the origins and implications of two terms becoming increasingly heard in the 1980s. One was "political correctness" (PC), a new term for an ever-larger blanket of taboos draped over a growing number of topics and terms, stifling discussion. Of course, "immigration as a problem" was among them, a thoroughly taboo topic. Immigration as bringing in new Einsteins and Vietnamese high school valedictorians was wide open territory, but to find immigrant-related social costs was politically incorrect and fiercely condemned.

A second much heard term was "multiculturalism," a new and ill-defined label that had somehow emerged (one scholar found the term in forty newspaper articles in 1981 and 2,000 eleven years later, a fifty-fold increase) as an unchallenged ideal and aspiration for America and the world. At least this was true among the chattering classes, who edited and provided content for the media, ran the universities and national religious organizations, and increasingly, the corporations. The term means more than one thing, I wrote to him, but it may be called the conviction, among other things, that what America needed was more ethnoracial and cultural diversification away from the WASP norm and that our society should thus welcome and invite other cultures. This romantic sentiment and body of ideas, ultimately centrifugal in its thrust, was more a critique of American life and history than an affirmation of anything in particular beyond unfailing cultural tolerance. It had no goal but more diversity, and naturally welcomed the leaky immigration system launched in 1965, setting loose the great demographic engine of the multiculturalist project.

The readings I sent to John and the board reflected a mix of views, but through my commentary I tried to make it clear that these currents of thought and feeling created a hostile climate to our own efforts. As a university person I was especially aware of PC on university campuses and in American intellectual life generally. Too much of what I heard and saw in the academy had the ring of left-wing McCarthyism—a distressing stifling of the sort of free debate that had drawn me to the American university in the first place.

At one meeting, quickly packing his briefcase to catch a plane, John commented that as important as immigration reform was in shaping the future of America, "this is but a skirmish in a wider war."

At the next opportunity I asked for clarification of this remarkable statement.

"America is caught in a wide and deep cultural transformation," he responded, "as well as a demographic one. FAIR was formed to address one of these adverse changes. There are other battle fronts." Or so I remember his words.

He seemed to have reached a point in his thinking when he felt that the immigration reform movement should be engaged with other organized efforts to influence the larger social churning of ideas and values in what journalists were calling "the culture wars" over America's future.

I am perpetually in favor of broadening one's horizons and intellectually engaging the major social forces of the day. However, John's new interests posed an institutional problem at the very least, leaving aside the question of how much a man can do in this life. FAIR had its hands more than full as a lobbying and policy advocacy organization on one complex issue—immigration. To engage and explore these other topics meant that more organizational innovation was clearly needed, but who would do it? We at FAIR were up to our chins in immigration's complexities. Such problems defeat me easily. But not John Tanton. In a period of about five years through the mid-1980s, John launched or shared with others a mid-wife role in several new institutions—an organization (U. S. English) to promote the use of English as America's official language for conducting public business; a foundation (U.S. Foundation, often shortened to U.S., Inc.) to house John and Mary Lou Tanton's many Michigan-oriented conservation organizations; and a new journal (*The Social Contract*) and publishing house (The Social Contract Press) devoted to a cluster of population-environment-immigration-assimilation issues; and an annual meeting of writers (The Writers Workshop) interested in these topics.[2] He played

---

[2] For a full account of the Tantons' creative energies and the range of their interests, see Petoskey lawyer and close friend John F. Rohe's *Mary Lou and John Tanton: A Journey Into American Conservation* (2002).

a supportive, fund-raising role in the founding of a new research center, CIS—the Center for Immigration Studies.

* * *

"Launched several new institutions" was easy for me to type onto the screen.

It is not easy to do.

In the non-profit world, this means, at the least and in a condensed summary, conceiving and articulating an institutional need; raising money to make a beginning; working with others to devise effective organizational forms; locating and persuading new (or old) talent to take on new roles; and raising more money as the mission grows and matures.

By the end of the 1970s, John Tanton, a full-time practicing physician and father, had done this several times in Michigan.

By the end of the 1980s he had launched or helped nudge into life five or six new policy reform institutions operating at the national level, and began to correspond and meet with writers and activists in Europe, Australia, and Canada. To my knowledge.

I am undoubtedly leaving some things out, because I did not live in Petoskey, Michigan, and watch John at work on a daily basis. I know from many contacts, conversations, and our annual end-of-year letters, that he still had time to raise bees, hike with Mary Lou in the mountains of the desert southwest, climb the Matterhorn, join a weekly book discussion club at his local Presbyterian church, play the piano in the evening, and study German.

* * *

The first national organization John founded after the establishment of FAIR was (I think) U. S. English.

John had become convinced from years of conversations with ordinary people about large-scale immigration that the rawest nerve was not job competition or social welfare costs, certainly not population growth and environmental impacts, but social assimilation and national identity. The older America had insisted that immigrants become Americans at once, "shedding their European skins," in John Adams' phrase. This had been true until the 1960s and 1970s, when America, or large parts of it, became admirably more tolerant of "social difference" in general, and the culture moved toward minority racial and ethnic self-assertion as well as WASP guilt. By the 1980s, Americans were complaining (we heard this theme in our membership correspondence) that immigrants were no longer expected to learn English (or American history), but had their native languages reinforced by bi-lingual education classes. Again, John concluded that an organization was needed to focus that citizen concern. What would the organization do? Defend English as the sole language of the nation in conducting public business, however that could be done.

* * *

When I heard of this initiative in 1982, I was sympathetic, though puzzled as to how one would "defend English." I decided that it was not my sort of issue, and I did not follow it closely, or expect a great deal from it. In this I misjudged the dynamics of the language issue and its contribution to the awareness of immigration-brought problems. My wiser brother, Hugh Davis Graham, a distinguished American historian whose wife, Janet, taught English as a Second Language, soon joined the U.S. English board. John saw the defense of language effort as worth doing in its own right, but also as a way to educate people to see that a lot of worrisome trends were linked to mass immigration, and to produce volunteers for its reform. John convinced California Senator S. I. Hayakawa, a distinguished linguist and former president of San Francisco State University who had received national publicity by resisting student radicalism on his and other campuses, to join him. Other early board members were Gerda Bikales of the FAIR staff, a displaced person from post-war Europe who wrote an important position paper based on research conducted in Europe, and Leo Sorenson, a Danish immigrant. An advisory board included Walter Cronkite, Alistair Cooke, and Jacques Barzun.

The first direct mail solicitation by U. S. English was dropped in June, 1983, and produced stunningly successful results. The new organization vaulted to a membership of 300,000 in one year. Language was a hot button, and the defense of English movement was impressively growing. To me this all seemed for the good, but I was busy with other things.

Later, I learned that Roger Conner and Liz Paddock were increasingly alarmed by what they saw as John's willingness to tap into new sources of emotions in the effort to change immigration policy. Roger recalled the impact of reading John Higham's *Strangers In The Land*, and in his oral history drew the lessons he found there.

"If the only way to beat them was to turn to animosity toward the ethnically and racially different immigrants…I wasn't willing to do that. I thought that was the one thing that would do more harm to America than the continuing immigration."

To me, an organizational defense of English as the national language, however one did that, in an era of expanding bilingual education programs run as foreign language maintenance projects, was not a "turn to animosity toward the ethnically and racially different." U.S. English, to the best of my knowledge, attacked no foreigners, but only U.S. officials who were moving America toward an officially multilingual society. The best way to harm new immigrants, they argued, was to create language enclaves buffering new Americans from the healthy pressures to learn the language of upward mobility.

In retrospect, if not at the time, I can see that Roger and Liz correctly sensed that explicitly addressing the cultural issues that mass foreign immigration put into play was a new and risky emphasis for the immigration reform movement, which had focused first of all on illegal entry, and based its critique of legal immigration chiefly on economic, environmental and population arguments. They were cautious, and more impressed by the openings for criticism than the energies to be tapped in the cultural emphasis. Here they were expressing a fear of unleashed emotion that one frequently found in the public talk of American elites.

John saw this differently in those days, and I tended to come down on his side. I did not think Americans were on the verge of becoming raving "nativists," in the prevailing use of that term, just because some organization in Washington began to document and call attention to the costs and dysfunctions in the existing immigration status quo. In fact, the inflamed emotions, incivility and name-calling that many commentators predicted or claimed to hear from the restrictionist camp were in fact turning up mostly on the other side, among the Expansionists, and especially among the small number of Hispanics who were professional activists. We learned this first, perhaps, when John made a mistake in the early exploration of the cultural dimensions of the changes brought by mass immigration.

* * *

The mistake came in 1986. John was now identified not only as the founder of FAIR but as the principal organizer of the group—U. S. English—that had successfully won referenda in California in 1984 and 1986, and in 1988 in Arizona and Colorado. John and his allies were making a difference, and he attracted what was being called "oppositional research." Could dirt be dug up, or something that could be called dirt, and posted on the media? John wrote a long memo to those planning to attend the fourth Writers Workshop in May (still, in 1986, called by his whacky initial title, the Witan) in order to frame for discussion some of the "non-economic consequences of immigration to California" raised by Leon Bouvier's recent paper (written with Phil Martin), *Population Change and the Future of California*. We discussed culture, language, and demography—sensitive topics stifled under a general taboo in the freest country in the world. In the memo he asked a number of politically incorrect questions, among them: "Is apartheid in Southern California's future? Will Latin American migrants bring with them the tradition of the mordida, the lack of involvement in public affairs, etc.? What is the conservation ethic of the Asian and Latin American newcomers? Will they adopt ours or keep theirs? Will blacks be able to improve their lot in the face of the Latin onslaught? What exactly is it that holds a diverse society together? I think the answers to many of these questions depend on how well people assimilate."

Good questions, but he didn't leave it there. He spoke of differential fertility between ethnic or national groups, and then made an attempt at humor, as was his habit in meetings on heavy subjects.

"Is advice to limit one's family simply advice to move over and let someone else with greater reproductive powers occupy the space? Perhaps this is the first instance in which those with their pants up are going to get caught by those with their pants down!"

It never occurred to John that his correspondence to a small component of his large circle of friends and respected writers might fall into the wrong hands. This memo did come into the hands of freelance writer James Crawford, possibly (John thought) through the agency of a disgruntled employee just leaving FAIR. Crawford not only spread the memo upon the media, where it was selectively quoted, but read portions of it over the phone to Linda Chavez, then director of U. S. English. A brief uproar ensued, Chavez resigned, along with advisory board members Cronkite and Cooke. John was charged with racist words, when he thought his words were about cultural behavior and the question of assimilation. He hastily resigned from the board of U.S. English—a step he soon regretted, but too late.

* * *

An Annual Convocation

Another institution arising out of John's consultations and thoughts in the 1980s was an annual gathering of writers and intellectuals interested in immigration and the topics attached to it—assimilation, national cohesion, population growth and its environmental impacts. I missed the first of these meetings, a small gathering held under the auspices of Governor Lamm in Colorado in 1982. John and Roger were there, Michael Teitelbaum, and others. John called it "the Witan," short for the old English term Witanagemot, or National Council to the crown. He soon changed the title, fortunately, to The Writers Workshop, and it has been an intellectual feast for over two decades.

I was invited to the second (and all subsequent) Writers Workshop held in San Diego in 1983, bringing together twelve to fifteen writers on immigration or related themes, all of them Americans (subsequent Workshops would also include writers from Australia and Europe). The central event on this occasion was not our invigorating discussions, but a visit to the border in the Tijuana-San Diego sector, conducted by the Border Patrol.

It was, for all but John, a first visit, and vividly memorable. The southern border of the U.S. had experienced a startling increase in illegal traffic, as judged by one (incomplete) measure, apprehensions by the Border Patrol. Apprehensions in 1985 had jumped to 1.2 million, an 11 percent increase over the year before. Apprehensions ten years earlier, in 1975, had been 383,000. In 1985, in the busy San Diego sector, half a million came across, an estimated one in four of them apprehended. We were invited to watch one day's action there.

The Border Patrol briefed us late in the afternoon—how many illegal immigrants came over each day, where and how they came, how the BP officers arranged their forces to detect and arrest, what was done with those apprehended (brief incarceration, no effective database entries for individuals, then a bus trip back across the border, after a meal).

As evening approached, we rode south in Border Patrol vans to the Imperial Beach sector where we saw ten or twenty males walking north in the surf, chest-high, headed for San Diego. We then drove east to the center of activity—the "soccer field." We stood on a high ridge which sloped down to the border between Tijuana and the United States, hardly discernible as an intermittent fence giving way to a large level playground where Mexicans and OTMs, "Other Than Mexicans" from Guatemala and Honduras but also as far away as China, India and Pakistan, kicked soccer balls, cooked and ate tortillas, waiting for evening. By late afternoon, as my son who visited the site later, writer and historian Wade Graham, wrote in an essay ("Masters of the Game") in *Harper's*, the soccer field took on the appearance of a crowded outdoor sporting event, complete with vendors hawking tacos and drinks, counterfeit American documents, and the services of guides, called coyotes or *polleros*, after the *pollos*, or chickens, as the smugglers described their human cargo. As dusk fell the people would start coming, sometimes in small groups of twos and threes, sometimes in ranks of hundreds.

The night we were there was a cold one, and a large crowd almost entirely composed of young males warmed themselves around fires before starting the mass run northward. During our weekend there, BP officers arrested people from ninety-six foreign countries in the sector of the border—separating, in a map-making sense only, Mexico and the

U.S., Tijuana and San Diego, and reaching from the ocean eastward to the low mountains. That stretch of the border was a very busy *entrepot* for a global industry involved in human trafficking. We were bluntly told of the costs of this industry to the incoming illegal immigrants, some of them women and children, who were at the mercy of the rough, arid terrain and the "coyotes" who charged them fees. We all felt some shame to be citizens of a country that permitted, and was through its unregulated job market a partner, in such a vicious and unnecessary system.

It was an emotional moment for everyone on our tour who had not seen this before. The sunlight faded, and the large crowds of people just south of a flimsy fence on the north side of the soccer field began to stir, and then moved northward in ragged lines, breaking into a trot or a dead run, and veering into canyons leading northward. Some of us were given BP laser night vision glasses, and could watch the human flow as a stream of red fugitive figures. The BP told us that those they apprehended would probably be trying it again in twenty-four hours. From where we stood, the word "invasion" no longer seemed the inflammatory term of a former director of the INS. This *was* an invasion, though a distinctive one, by people not carrying weapons, and individually (with the usual human exceptions), intending no harm.

Around midnight we were bused back to our motel in San Diego, all of us somewhat shaken. What we had seen happened every night at the end of every 365 days of the year, was highly organized, growing in size annually, and brought to this sector of an essentially open American border people not only from Mexico and Central America, but from Asia, the Middle East, and a disintegrating Soviet empire. We all had a deep impression of national vulnerability and outright weakness—not because the Border Patrol officers were corrupt or incompetent, for they were impressive professionals. They were deeply frustrated that their efforts were part of an elaborate, government-sponsored game in which the alien almost always eventually got through if he kept trying, and was never punished even when caught. There were no disincentives—little if any detention time, a meal and a shower, and no reliable identification leading to punishment for repeat offenders. At the border, America wasn't a serious country, was in a sense and in that place contemptible, even though the enforcement professionals made admirable efforts with their puny tools. I was given a green BP cap with the words, *"Mas Migra, Protectores de la Frontera,"* and when I wore it one day in Santa Barbara it shocked and angered some of my friends, who spent the Sixties learning to call the police "pigs." I wore it as a token of support, but such reactions to that hat told me again that the road ahead was steep.

* * *

One writer at the meeting in San Diego was the remarkably successful journalist and historian Theodore White, author of many books, most notably a series of accounts of American presidential elections. Earlier in the day before that evening trip to the border between San Diego and Tijuana, White had spoken passionately in our meetings about the negative consequences of losing control of the border between a population-stabilizing developed country and a population-exploding Third World country sharing a 2,000 mile border. He, like the rest of us at the soccer field, was incredulous at this glimpse of a steady, daily-nightly flow of human beings from around the world, illegally joining the American adventure in flagrant violation of American law. After dinner the second night in San Diego, John asked White if he would "write a piece to help us with the cause." White recoiled, almost frightened.

"My New York friends would never forgive me. No, you guys are right, but I can't go public on this."

By this time, I was intimately familiar with the taboo on any discussion of immigration that had a critical sound, or that suggested that immigrants were responsible for some costs as well as some benefits. Hearing White's agitated response, I had my first glimpse of the especially intense emotional Jewish version of that taboo. His whole heritage, and his standing with all his Jewish friends, was imperiled (he was certain) if he went public with his worries about the state of immigration. I did not suspect it then, but this would become an important sub-theme of our experience as immigration reformers. American Jews were especially irrational about immigration for well known reasons. They were also formidable opponents, or allies, in any issue of public policy in America. Would it ever be possible to enlist some of this gifted

American minority in our movement? Fortunately we did. FAIR's staff was enhanced by several talented people of Jewish background—Dan Stein, Ira Mehlman, Gary Imhoff, Gerda Bikales, and this is a partial list. But American Jews have played a smaller role in the immigration reform movement than we wished.

I learned from John, years later, that White died shortly after our border visit, while writing a draft of a report on what he had seen and thought. His son finished the article, which was published in *Time*. In White's memoir, *In Search of History* (1978), he wrote, "The old English political culture had lost control over…the polyglot peoples of America [who] had no common heritage but only ideas to bind them together," and concluded his book with this:

> *What would be really at issue was whether America would be transformed, in the name of Opportunity, simply into a Place, a gathering of discretely defined and entitled groups, interests and heritages; or whether it could continue to be a nation, where all heritages joined under the same roof—ideas of communities within government.*

* * *

The Social Contract

At some point—I'm not sure I have these in order—John established a new journal, *The Social Contract*. The magazine's editorial offices were in Petoskey, where John had earlier set up a non-national organization to house his various enterprises—U.S., Inc. In 1978, when I had that phone call from this unknown Petoskey doctor and wondered what sort he was, I should have flown to visit the modest offices of U. S., Inc., in the remote place Tanton had placed it. In that attractive city overlooking Little Traverse Bay I would have met U. S., Inc. staffers Dorothy and Nikki, retired Presbyterian minister Bob Kyser, lawyer/environmentalist John Rohe, historian Wayne Lutton, and of course environmentalist Mary Lou Tanton—and would have quickly realized that this new acquaintance of mine, John Tanton, represented, and gathered about him, expanding circles of fine Americans.

Though Petoskey was, apparently, a fine place for John Tanton to practice medicine, raise a family—and, when he decided to launch social movements, start U. S. Inc. to house his activities—it was hardly an intellectual center where writers criss-crossed. Establish a new journal exploring national and international dimensions of population, immigration, and culture, somewhat enigmatically called *The Social Contract*, in Petoskey? John plunged ahead, served as publisher, and hired as editor the many-talented Bob Kyser, later adding to the editorial staff historian Wayne Lutton. The first issue, in Fall, 1990, somewhat vaguely announced that *TSC* would devote its attention to a cluster of issues—population growth, immigration, a common language, the balance between rights and responsibilities. Whatever one thought of *TSC,* there was (and is) nothing quite like it—a place where the taboo-enshrouded topic-cluster of the demographic and cultural transformation of America (and Western Europe and Australia) was robustly reported and analyzed. Each issue of the journal usually had a topical focus—the costs of immigration, the role of the churches in immigration discussion and refugee issues, international immigration flows and politics, immigration and free trade.

* * *

That was not quite the end of John's role in national institution building (to my knowledge). He scheduled one Writers' Workshop meeting in October, 1987, in Boston, to discuss two topics—ideas for omnibus legislation to reform legal immigration, and—here he goes again—"the wisdom of starting a new national organization to attempt to redress the balance that has grown up in our society between rights and responsibilities...individualism and community." To provide background for the second assignment, we read several recent books on this issue—Morris Janowitz's *The Reconstruction of Patriotism*, Bob Bellah's surprising best-seller, *Habits of the Heart*, Richard Morgan's *Disabling America: The Rights Industry in Our Time*, and a couple of essays by sociologist Amitai Etzioni, who attended the meeting and discussed the possibility of starting a new journal addressed to the growing concern for "radical individualism, me-isms, and the group attack on the commons." I remember that the discussion of the fragmenting of American culture was heady and stimulating, but it wasn't clear whether or how to set up a new organization to focus on this, which John gave the initial working title of *The American Civic Rights and Responsibilities Union* (ACRRU). Amitai, a brilliant and genial academic entrepreneur, eventually started his own organization and journal. John and Roger then established in 1988 a small organization called the American Association for Rights and Responsibilities, with Roger as director.

Immigration Think Tank?

In 1985, John was importantly involved in a collective effort to give life to another of the ideas he and I (and others) had discussed, that policy reform movements needed respected research institutions— think tanks—to produce policy literature and develop policy expertise for congressional testimony and public appearances. This was an area where I knew more than John Tanton the eye surgeon, and there were few if any others.

As the new era of mass immigration began in the 1960s, the nation's universities were producing little immigration policy scholarship of any kind. Their response to million-plus immigration levels from historically different source countries was sluggish. It took the form of a slowly growing body of research on the immigrants themselves— what were their countries of origin and characteristics? How were they assimilating? How did America "feel" toward the incoming Vietnamese, Russian Jews, and Mexican rural villagers? Their impacts on America and Americans received a much smaller amount of research attention, and only on those impacts assumed to be enriching—starting new small businesses in decaying center cities, serving as seven-day-a-week graduate students and lab assistants in science and engineering, providing a cheap labor supply in agriculture and low-wage urban services, supplying that Vietnamese-born merit scholar graduating at the top of a suburban high school in Palo Alto or Winnetka.

As we became familiar with the issue, it was clear that academic and social policy researchers, at my University of California and elsewhere, were refusing to pursue the immigration connection to any number of social problems intensifying in local life in all immigration-impacted states. It was known that American immigration policy (and non-enforcement of policy allowing a large illegal flow) produced what labor economist Phil Martin called an asymmetrical "hourglass effect" in terms of their social capital—a little bulge at the top of scientists and other professionals, a large bulge at the bottom of semi-literate unskilled people. We admitted the Vietnamese honor students and Taiwanese or Nigerian chemical engineers who brought—which is another way of saying, deprived their own nations by leaving with—considerable resources in social capital. The American media liked stories about these, while having no interest in stories about the cost to Vietnam and Taiwan of the loss of those skilled and successful professionals. Then there was the vast majority of immigrants to the U.S. at the bottom of this hourglass—especially the Mexican and Central American agricultural laborers with less than a sixth grade education, adding to America's povertied classes and social pathologies while performing much appreciated menial labor. What was the balance of gain and cost to America in all of this, and how might that balance be improved?

Marxist literature contains the phrase, "the social wage," meaning that component of working class livelihoods that came not from the wage paid by the employer but from society/taxpayers in the form of schools, hospital emergency rooms, and social services. Research on these costs of contemporary immigration flows was skimpy and almost entirely dismissive of significant problems. Media attention to such costs was meager, and reporters had little time or editorial encouragement to dig out the facts that academic researchers were ignoring. Did recent immigrants contribute to job displacement and downward pressure on wages? If so, where and with what labor market effects? What were the long-term trends in the levels of human capital immigrants brought to the U.S., especially when the Mexican illegal and legal rural labor flow rose to such a large proportion of foreign entrants? Were social service costs covered by taxes paid? What about immigration's connection to rising rates of TB and tropical diseases, or to gang formation being reported here and there in the country? The universities and social science research centers were not at all interested in such questions about the costs of immigration. If those costs were addressed, it was in order to conclude that they were far outweighed by the benefits.

Those of us at FAIR and around the reform movement were in touch with a handful of immigration researchers like David North, Phil Martin, and Vernon Briggs, who often complained to each other that the cost side was being ignored when not denied in the research reports coming out of the universities, and institutions such as RAND, Brookings, and the Urban Institute. There was in effect an informal taboo on research projects inquiring into immigrant labor market impacts on wages and standards, crime links, welfare, educational and criminal justice costs. The University of California established a new public policy institute in the early Nineties, and when I wrote to inquire if the costs of immigration was a fundable research area, I received a hostile letter from an administrator assuring me that this was out of bounds. This taboo created huge empty shelves in the market for information and ideas on the impacts of the remarkable mass immigration flows initiated in the 1960s.

There was, then, no taboo on immigration policy research, just on any negative impacts imputed to the immigrants themselves. A Center for Migration Studies (CSM) had been founded in New York in 1964, and its studies and annual conferences were entirely devoted to the U.S. structure and practice of immigration policy from the point of view of potential immigrants and asylum seekers, i.e., how to get more foreigners into the U.S. There was no need for more of this. Professor Wayne Cornelius of the University of California, San Diego established the Center for U.S.-Mexican Studies in 1979, which soon secured Ford Foundation funding and published papers on what parts of Mexico the northward migrants came from, their work, and travel routes in the U.S. From the beginning, Cornelius' center found problems only in the north American regulation of immigration. "The 'problem' is not the migrant himself, but his illegal status in the U.S." Open the borders.

* * *

In the period when John and I talked (among other things) about the importance of new, independent research institutions broadening the topics and sharpening the critical analysis of immigration research and public education, others, I know from conversations, had the same idea—David North, Vernon Briggs, Malcolm Lovell, and FAIR staffers Gary Imhoff and Patrick Burns, both of whom had a research bent. Why couldn't FAIR take this on, Roger Conner argued, and become what he (and his successor, Dan Stein) envisioned, a "full service institution?" Imhoff and Burns (and I, and some others) had a different view. We argued that, while advocacy institutions like FAIR needed in-house publications and a modest research capability, this did not meet the need for the volume and quality of independent policy research demanded by America's policy machinery.

John soon was persuaded. He either raised, or we had offered to us by somebody who had the same idea, $50,000 as seed money for an independent think tank. The money would go farther if it was protected by tax-exempt status, so FAIR held the money for a few months until the new institution received its 501(©)(3) certification. A former Foreign Service officer and environmental writer, Lindsey Grant, was asked to draw up a charter for such an institution, to focus the discussion. I chaired the Steering Committee (to become the founding board) of a new and independent Center for Immigration Studies (CIS), a name that may have been Lindsey's idea. FAIR did not, as some have said, "found" CIS, or have anything to do with it beyond establishing a bank account for a couple of months. I was chairman of the CIS board from its establishment, and nobody from FAIR said a word to me about the new institution, knowing we were charting our own path. John supported the idea of CIS but played no part in its organization, and was scrupulous in allowing the early core of researchers and writers to take charge of the design. I don't believe he has ever been in the CIS offices, over all these years. The new CIS board was expected to shape the institution, and it did, from the first meeting and forward.

I had objected that I should not be the chairman of the board of such an institution, given my lack of credentials in immigration research. John responded that this was a "*faut de mieux*" situation of lacking anyone better who was willing to lead. I had a PhD, and had published four or five articles on the history of immigration policy. This was not towering expertise on contemporary immigration, but John said something about the intellectual pleasures of working with a board of scholars who knew more than I did.

He was right about that. With the advice of a lot of people, I recruited a board in 1985—Cornell economist Vernon Briggs; Liz Paddock; demographer Leon Bouvier; Malcolm Lovell, a reform-minded manager at the Department of Labor; Frank Morris, then dean of graduate studies at Morgan State University and formerly director of the Congressional Black Caucus Foundation; Roger Conner; and George Grayson, a professor of Mexican politics based at William and Mary University.

CIS was also poor. In hiring as our first director, retired Foreign Service officer David Simcox (who had extensive experience in Latin America), we shamelessly took advantage of his pensioned status and D.C. domicile to offer our paltry salary. Simcox started work in the fall of 1985, and proved a superb choice, combining editorial and writing skills with State Department visa experience and Kentucky-born toughness and sense of humor. Our first publication made a strong impression, a (1987) paper by the respected University of California, Davis economist Philip Martin, describing how illegal immigrants in California "colonized" certain workplaces through kinship hiring, thus displacing American workers.

* * *

Tanton, M. D. and Historian

By this time I knew of John's deep engagement with history, at several levels. It was no surprise when he devoted an early issue of _TSC_ to the role of bad and misapplied history in impeding clear thought and policy revisionism in immigration. In truth, he had discovered the importance of history before discovering me. It was a matter of continuing astonishment to me that this eye surgeon from Michigan, busier with private life, profession, and public service activities than anyone I knew, somehow found intellectual room for a devotion to history in its several uses. He studied the history of earlier immigration restriction movements for lessons for our own efforts. He understood that bad history was one of our obstacles, and encouraged better history wherever the potential seemed to raise its head.

One day, to my astonishment, he told me that he wanted help with the preservation of FAIR's records so that scholars in the years ahead could write the story more fully and accurately. I know of no history department that archives its own records, and here was an eye surgeon taking the time to ask how to preserve the raw material of our efforts for users far down the road. He somehow had raised money to launch a FAIR history project in 1988. I still have his memo, proposing "to get better archiving and library procedures in FAIR's day-to-day life, so materials are not lost." The result was a FAIR oral history project, interviews with all founding board members and many subsequent ones, and an arrangement with the Gelman Library at George Washington University to receive, organize, and make available the records of FAIR. John wanted the full record of what we did, and why we did it, available to historians, journalists, and high school essayists—in short, for posterity.

* * *

More Work For History

John and I were not the only ones to feel the weight of the dead albatross of false historical analogies upon our efforts to argue that times had changed and required a new immigration policy. FAIR staff writer Gary Imhoff was a very smart Harvard grad who generally left work on Friday afternoons in the company of a swirl of black graduate students from Howard University, where Gary took classes. He proposed to me in a letter in 1986 that we collaborate on a new, revisionist history. We had occasionally "talked history," and he knew as well as I did that much of the American left/progressive leadership in the generation prior to World War I had criticized unregulated immigration for its downward pressure on native workers' wages and a range of other real social costs. Why not write a history, he proposed, that restored this dimension to the drive for immigration limitation by framing immigration restriction as one of the basic reforms of the progressive era? He was especially impressed that African-American leaders like Booker Washington, Frederick Douglass and A. Philip Randolph had been restrictionists and critics of mass immigration. Such a book could also emphasize the benefits of the four decade-long "breathing space" in permitting successful assimilation of the thirty million immigrants that had come.

I decided that my research priorities—established by a grant from the Twentieth Century Fund to work on the industrial policy question—would not make room for this. However, an article was manageable, on the vexing issue of the role of historical interpretation in immigration policy debate generally. In a 1986 essay in *The Public Historian*, I argued that flawed historical memories of and "history lessons" from the earlier mass immigration era distorted the contemporary policy debate.

The distortion took three main forms. The first might be called the Statue of Liberty Myth, which held that unlimited asylum for anyone in the world wishing to move to the U.S. had from the first been "the core meaning" of the American nation, and the national experiment would somehow end if it were questioned or altered. This was historically incorrect at several levels.

The other two flawed history lessons had to do with the character and contribution of the restrictionist reform movement and the system of regulation it finally put in place in the early 1920s. The restrictionists of the early part of the century were moved by a mixture of concerns. They objected to the substantial social costs of unlimited immigration as felt by American workers especially, mixing this with some worries about assimilation of such numbers from the new non-European sources, and some stubborn cultural and ethnic biases. Historians after mid-century altered that story, teaching the future governmental and media elites of modern America that restrictionism across our entire past had addressed no real problems, only psychological ones besetting racist bigots. In the 1960s and after, with the civil rights impulse running strongly and this history lesson the only one available, any proposal for restriction of immigration toward lower numbers and different selection criteria was automatically labeled as "nativist" and "anti-immigrant," which at once shifted the discussion from the merits of existing policy to the motives of the critics of that policy. A distorted history no longer contained recognition of the social costs of mass immigration, but turned advocacy of strictly regulated immigration into some sort of moral failing.

Further, the successful assimilation of the thirty million immigrants that came in the First Great Wave, I argued, did not "prove" that the restrictionists' concerns about assimilation had been misplaced. A more plausible interpretation would credit the breathing space brought by immigration restriction (and the global economic depression of the 1930s) for much of the successful assimilation that allowed the United States to enter World War II unimpaired by debilitating ethno racial divisions as an ignorant Adolph Hitler had predicted. In any event, what was needed in immigration policy was not mindless copying of whatever earlier Americans had thought or done on immigration, but responsiveness to new realities. "Our circumstances have changed," I argued, and borrowed a phrase from some forgotten French philosopher (Paul Valery?): "The future is not what it used to be."

* * *

We reformers, astonishing to admit, were still basically optimistic, after having been thoroughly beaten in the first round. I had more pessimistic moments than most of us, but we were an optimistic company, still persuaded that we would eventually win, which to us meant restoring a small immigration policy for the U.S.—because this is what the public wanted, and because it was best for a range of national interests and not harmful to any.

As time went by, we did seem better organized than before. Immigration reform organizations slowly multiplied, there was an immigation-centered journal of ideas, an annual writers' workshop (enlisting European and Australian guests) to explore linked topics of demography, cultural change, globalization, and national identity, and a think tank to work on immigration policy.

The issue that mobilized our social movement, mass immigration and its consequences, continued to force its way into a larger place in national discussion as immigration flows grew larger, including the illegal ones. Historian David Reimers, for example, discerned what he called a "turn against immigration" across the 1980s that he thought would surely have radical policy reform implications, and historian Roger Daniels wrote an article in 1986, stating as his "major if unstated premise was that a severe reduction in the volume of immigration was all but certain."

Both were later pleased to be quite wrong. Daniels, writing a few years later, asked: "Why was our vision so poor?"

I have the same question, for my vision was almost as poor as theirs.

PART IV:
STILL LOSING GROUND:
THE NINETIES

Chapter Twelve: 1990:
Another Round of Immigration Reform, Another Step Backward Toward Expansionism

I'm exhausted, worried, and anxious. — Dan Stein

Against the background of mounting predictions and expectations that public opinion was hardening against the mass immigration era inaugurated in the Sixties, a second round of immigration reform began just at the end of the 1980s. The reform direction was a surprise and shock for us. Congress expanded immigration again, as we exerted every effort to respond to public opinion and move the other way.

This expansion took the form of the Immigration Reform Law of 1990, paralleled by slowly collapsing enforcement of IRCA.

Alan Simpson in a sense initiated this second defeat when he and Senator Kennedy in 1988 agreed to launch an effort to "reform legal immigration." The Wyoming senator meant restrictionist reform on the principles of the untouched agenda of reforms of legal immigration put forward by the Hesburgh Commission. That he so badly misjudged the political prospects for that agenda should comfort those of us farther from the centers of power who also thought it a good time for Congress to take up the repair of flaws in the legal immigration system.

* * *

Simpson's agenda was not too far from FAIR's. With 90 percent of legal immigrants entering through kinship preferences, our system of selection had only a slim connection to national needs, but was driven by the desires of recent immigrants to bring in related foreigners. In other words, it was based on nepotism. It was time, the Wyoming senator believed, to take up that part of the Hesburgh agenda for change. He also wished to place some curbs on refugee and asylum numbers, and to try again for a real ceiling on annual entries.

Kennedy, thinking ethnically and parochially as always, saw a new round of immigration policy legislating as a chance to expand the number of visas available to the Irish, who by now (like other Europeans) had few immediate family members in the U.S. to qualify them for migration. The irony was not noticed by reporters. Senator Kennedy, who had played such a prominent role in discrediting the older National Origins Quota system because it "discriminated" against certain nationalities and replacing it with the 1965 Act, now sought to reform the 1965 Act in 1990 because it was found now to discriminate against European nations, including the only one that concerned him—Ireland. A shift toward a greater emphasis on skills would benefit the Irish and other European nations without recent immigration flows to the U.S. Kennedy also had in mind making permanent the "visa lottery" invented in 1986 to enlarge the numbers coming from "underrepresented nations." He encouraged hope on our side when he agreed to support Simpson's call for a cap (of 590,000) on annual immigration.

In retrospect, Simpson should have stayed in his foxhole, as the legislative process quickly spun out of control of the leadership and the confining channel of the ideas sent forward by the Hesburgh Commission of a decade earlier. A growing economy sharpened the business appetite for abundant (cheaper) labor, and a widely circulated Hudson Institute study in 1987 (falsely) predicted a severe labor shortage ahead. The traditional voice favoring tight labor markets, organized labor, had weakened to the point where it was no match for the pressures from business. FAIR staff told the board in 1989 that the Expansionist coalition of business and big agriculture, free-market conservatives, ethnic and religious lobbies, immigration lawyers and liberal Democrats was still in place. Liberals in the House had stripped Ron Mazzoli of his immigration subcommittee leadership and conferred it upon a little known Bruce Morrison, who turned out to be an aggressive Expansionist.

In March, 1990, Morrison offered a bill essentially doubling the legal immigration numbers to 800,000. Efforts by a small band of restrictionist House members led by Lamar Smith of Texas to delete or modify these expansionist provisions were brushed aside. FAIR's staff had told the board at the end of 1989 that our organization's small lobbying team on Capitol Hill had the situation well in hand ("We were victorious! Congress adjourned before Thanksgiving without enacting any significant legislation," read one staff memo.). By the spring of 1990, new Executive Director Dan Stein and the staff realized that a major disaster was in the making.

"I'm exhausted, worried and anxious," Stein wrote FAIR supporters.

Not only was Morrison putting forward an expansion of legal immigration, IRCA itself was under attack. In the powerful Leadership Conference on Civil Rights, La Raza and Maldef demanded that the conference support repeal of *Employers Sanctions*, "our premier issue."

Dan Stein, hoping to break the legislative momentum with something dramatic, "borrowed" $125,000 from reserve funds to pay for a poll from the respected Roper organization. The poll, the first national sample on immigration in four years, conveyed news on public opinion that should have caught the attention of lawmakers.

Texas Congressman Lamar Smith cited the poll on the House floor: "The most recent national poll...found that 77 percent of all Americans [74 percent of Hispanics and 78 percent of blacks] believe that the U.S. should not increase current immigration levels," and 87 percent believe that the U.S. has a population problem."

"The American people don't support increased immigration," Smith said in the *Congressional Record*.

Nevertheless, public opinion polls, even public opinion, counted for little on the Hill. National politicians, it seemed, had adopted Tip O'Neill's view on this. Roper, and Congressman Smith, may have been right about public opinion, but to the average member of Congress there was "no constituency there." Public opinion delivered no money, or reliable votes—at least, public opinion on immigration didn't translate into real power, and was not to be feared. Expanding immigration wasn't only politically riskless, it was free, and the only governmental benefit that seemed to have no budgetary consequences. Smith, Simpson and the others who wanted to curb rather than expand immigration were repeatedly defeated on rules, committee and floor votes. The press showed no interest in the gap between public opinion and the direction of immigration policy, which was in any event far down the short list of policy issues preoccupying the media and public. In 1990, the focus was on the war in Iraq and a major civil rights bill. The presidency was not closely engaged.

* * *

1990: "We Were Alone"

"We were alone" on Capitol Hill," Dan lamented to his board. Almost.

The tiny organization, Population-Environment Balance, sent a lobbyist to voice complaints very similar to those of FAIR, and made FAIR look moderate by urging annual immigration totals of no more than 200,000 a year.

Later, Dan tried to emphasize for FAIR members and board a few "improvements" backed by FAIR and written into the 1990 law. These were skimpy even when exaggerated—the fact that IRCA was not repealed, that some enhanced border security measures were included, and a new national commission to study immigration was authorized. Along the way we had thought that Simpson's "cap" on immigration, written into the senate legislation, would be worth a lot in the inevitable legislative trading. Even if the 1990 law was too expansionist, the cap could be lowered in later years. We, and Simpson, had been conned. House liberals arranged that the cap was "pierceable" under certain circumstances, so there was no cap. Congress did not design benefit programs, budgets, or immigration laws with a firm cap, and probably never would.

Dan pointed to a few other small bright spots in the unfolding policy catastrophe of 1990. One was the emergence of Texas Republican Congressman Lamar Smith as a knowledgeable and forceful voice for reform in the direction of lower numbers: "Importing more labor instead of educating and training our own people," he said on the House floor, "Is not the answer." Smith, a conservative Republican, knew how to play on the liberal strings. He quoted John F. Kennedy, who wrote that "there is, of course, a legitimate argument for some limitation upon immigration. We no longer need settlers for virgin lands..." He pointed out that African-American academic Dr. Frank Morris told Congress that "many immigrants compete directly with blacks in the same labor markets..."

It might be considered a faintly promising sign that 165 congressmen voted for an amendment offered by Democrat John Bryant of Texas to kill the legislation altogether on the grounds that the U.S. had difficulty looking to the needs of its own population and didn't need 800,000 more immigrants a year.

The bright spots were few and small. The Immigration Act of 1990 was signed by President George Bush in late November. The law expanded the total number of visas from 500,000 to 700,000 (until 1995, when that targeted level was supposed to be reduced to 675,000), the expansion coming in the skills-based categories. Just one of the dubious new visa categories having nothing to do with the national interest was the new three-to-five year visa for "religious workers" pushed through by pressure from Catholic Bishops. By 2005, when a count was taken, 145,000 R-1 visas had allowed foreign priests and "religious workers" to spend their three to five years inside the U.S. A growing number came from Muslim countries. In 2005, an official with the Muslim Public Affairs Council estimated that half the mosques in Los Angeles had imams brought in on R-1 visas.

The law's "flexible" or "pierceable" totals were as always not ceilings, as they didn't include refugees, then amounting to more than 100,000 per year. When all features of the 1990 law were considered, analysts predicted that it would authorize a stunning 40 percent expansion in the number of legal immigrants that would be admitted annually. Two years after the law passed, the *Los Angeles Times* reported that the 1990 "Law Change Produces Big Hike in Legal Immigration," the 810,635 million people admitted in 1992 was the largest immigrant cohort in the second half of the twentieth century. Of these, 41 percent were estimated to have settled in California.

The law also included another amnesty, this time for 350,000 Salvadorans who came northward into the U.S. from the civil wars in Central America. It extended the life of the absurd "diversity lottery" which Kennedy had earlier slipped into the 1986 law to increase the number of Irish immigrants. Simpson's pilot program to develop a forgery-proof driver's license and to make it a national standard was dropped. The 1990 law, in the view of Cornell's Vernon Briggs, "is ill-conceived, deceptively designed, poorly timed," and based on a fabricated "myth of impending labor shortages." This time we had come away with nothing comparable to employer sanctions in 1986 to indicate that our offense had scored any points at all.

"Congress was clearly more liberal than the public," acknowledged Paul Yzaquirre, the head of an influential lobbying group with a racist name, La Raza, lavishly funded by the Ford Foundation.

"This is a lower ceiling than…we'd like to see," editorialized the *Wall Street Journal*, "but it'll do for now."

Chapter Thirteen:
California, 1992-1994: A Turn Against the Immigration Status Quo?

There has been a conspiracy of silence among liberals and conservatives on the subject of immigration. — Peter Skerry and Michael Hartman

In the immediate aftermath of the reforms of 1990, it seemed sadly obvious that historian David Reimers had been flatly wrong in predicting in the mid-1980s "a turn against immigration." He was, as it turned out, both wrong and right, depending on where one looked.

On what matters most, the number of foreigners coming to the U.S. to live here, there has been no "turn against immigration," from the 1965 reform law to the present time, across four decades and continuing. American policy, and the flow of foreigners through and around that policy, trace a steady expansion. Since the 1960s, the "turn" has been relentlessly *toward* more immigration, inaugurating an era of mass immigration which is now a major force in our national development.

Yet Reimers was right that something was taking place beneath the policy debates in Washington and the superficial and sentimental treatment of the issue in the national media. Change was evident at two levels, if one looked closely, or especially if one looked back with hindsight. In the contest of ideas and argument, the nineties saw a steady expansion of the cadre of critics of the immigration status quo, and a growing sense that they were winning the debate. At another, popular level, a grassroots activism began to organize in several states around the issue of illegal immigration, demonstrating the potential to alter not only the politics of immigration but the balance between the two national parties.

*　*　*

That Eternal Battle of Ideas

I have mentioned John Tanton's interest in "the war of ideas," which he saw as a multi-front engagement along a cluster of issues. He tried to pull these together as the agenda of *The Social Contract* and the annual Writers Workshops. He asked me in 1990 to make a written assessment of recent public discourse (and taboos) on those issues—immigration, population, American national identity and cohesion—and provided a small grant for research assistance. The taboo part turned out to be at least as important as what was being said on these topics.

I submitted my report dated the end of 1992, leading off with a comment by Peter Skerry and Michael Hartman made in a *The New Republic* article in June, 1991: "There has been a conspiracy of silence among liberals and conservatives on the subject of immigration." We knew this, but the importance of the observation was that it came in a liberal magazine from two respected academics (Skerry was a UCLA political scientist, Hartman at the Brookings Institution) who were outing the conspiracy. The problems associated with large scale immigration should be discussed, critics given their space and their views engaged, they argued. This was not happening.

The news for us here was that this complaint came from two establishment liberal scholars. They were right about the "conspiracy of silence," but that was only half of it. The rest of the conspiracy took the form of active instruments of taboo enforcement. The tools for silencing critical discussion of the immigration topic were familiar to us—motive assassination (restrictionists may talk of economic and other costs, but their real motives are xenophobic), and labels conveying association with historic Bads, from "racist" through "nativist" (never defined) to "divisive" and "mean-spirited." Each of us writing or talking on this issue had such stories to tell. I once wrote an essay on the 1965 Immigration Act, and called it: "Arguably the most nation-shaping measure of the Great Society," and the anonymous reader told my publisher not to

154

publish the essay since that sentence was "viciously racist." A more colorful episode was reported by western novelist Edward Abbey, who in the early 1980s was asked by the *New York Times* to contribute an essay on "Immigration and Liberal Taboos." This invitation was a sign of open-mindedness? Not as it turned out. Abbey reports, in his autobiographical *One Life At a Time Please* (1988), that the *Times* declined to print it. He was then rejected by *Harpers*, *The Atlantic*, *Rolling Stone*, *Newsweek*, and *Mother Jones*, who had not liked language such as: "How many of us, truthfully, would prefer to be submerged in the Caribbean-Latin version of civilization?" A minor regional weekly eventually published the piece.

The larger news in the early months of the 1990s was that something had changed for the better, at least for those of us long chafing under a taboo/motive assassination blanket. I found in my review of major magazines, journals, newspapers and books in the early 1990s what probably we all knew—that there was a growing condemnation of the stifling of frank and uninhibited discussion of a cluster of "sensitive" issues, beginning with race and extending through most forms of social difference, including being an immigrant. The condemners had discovered a splendid, attention-getting label for the weapons of the new "thought police"—Political Correctness, or PC.

The label was a new weapon for the counter-attack against taboos. "PC" was a phrase drenched in sarcasm and mockery, framed often in quotation marks. Richard Bernstein's "The Rising Hegemony of the Politically Correct" in *The New York Times* (Oct. 29, 1990) provided a map and glossary of the PC machine whose purpose was to intimidate the politically incorrect and control the agenda. *Time*, *Newsweek* and other major news organs took up the exposure of PC, finding it most aggressive on college campuses. The *Wall Street Journal* in December, 1990 editorialized that "Political correctness requires that students, faculty and administrators project 'right' opinions about women, sexism, race, and the numerous other categories of victimology." Campuses were exposed as hotbeds of verbal intimidation by leftists in books such as Dinesh D'Souza's *Illiberal Education: The Politics of Race and Sex on Campus* (1991). Other authors found the PC mindset well entrenched also in the news and entertainment media, foundations, religious and professional associations.

Now the thought and language police who freely wielded derisive labels had one around their own necks. This was "a brilliant propaganda victory" for the conservatives, some said (or complained). We restrictionists were not properly described as conservatives, but we certainly were taboo-stifled, and for us it was a relief to have the stiflers given an unpleasant name and reputation of their own. On May 4, 1991, President George Bush charged in a speech in Ann Arbor, Michigan, that PC "declares certain topics off-limits, certain expressions off-limits." Americans should be alarmed at "the growing tendency to use intimidation rather than reason in settling disputes." Amen. Perhaps the rising criticism of PC would lead in the 1990s to a more open immigration debate focused on issues rather than the debaters' alleged motives and notorious "nativist" ancestors

* * *

The Expansionist coalition also adopted a new justification for mass immigration. This was "diversity," a fuzzy new concept of uncertain lineage and now popping up everywhere. Prior to the elevation of the ideal of Diversity, Expansionists had appealed to the sentimentalist notion that the "meaning of America" would be lost if the country ceased taking in all or very many of the people of the world seeking refuge from poverty or some sort of local persecution. Diversity had a more fresh and modern sound.

This formerly innocuous word became a slogan in the precincts of the multicultural left in the 1970s. By the 1980s, it had migrated across the political spectrum and become a national "good." We needed it in our schools, our churches, our malls, and indeed across society. The way to get more of it was through mass immigration, as little of it from Europe as possible.

To fully understand what "Diversity" did and didn't mean, I needed three books published about ten years after I did my survey—Peter Wood's *Diversity: The Invention of a Concept* (2003), Peter Schuck's *Diversity in America* (2003), and Walter Michaels, *The Trouble With Diversity* (2006). All were lucid and skeptical. Schuck, a Yale law professor, was most interested in how the law should engage this new social goal, Wood in discovering what, if anything, it actually meant and warning that it meant trouble. In his book, I learned in 2003 what I only vaguely sensed in 1992—that Diversity was "big...everywhere," and at once vacuous as well as a radical challenge to the America we know. "We jeopardize liberty and equality by our friendship with this new principle," he wrote ten years after I reported that "diversity" and multiculturalism had become goals toward which mass immigration was helping to take America, and we would do well to give them the critical attention they were not getting.

* * *

As to national identity and cohesion, John had a long-standing interest in this, while I had a long-standing blind spot. As an historian coming of maturity roughly in the middle of this century, when America seemed to have successfully put far behind itself the divisions brought by regional secession, mass immigration, and even racial division enforced by Jim Crow, I found unappealing the once vital questions occupying earlier generations of historians such as, "What is the American character?," the "national identity," and how had the country held together in the face of sectionalism and other centrifugal forces? I was a historian trained in a top graduate school in the early 1960s, where I had been told that among historians the topic "The American Character," i.e., identity, was a very out-of-date subject that could harm your career. Once a central topic for historians and other students of American society, it was now (by the Sixties) boring and increasingly seen as parochial and flag-waving. What we young and rising historians should have been interested in was the non-white male forgotten or yet untold stories of American life—black people, women, other racial minorities, deviants, and cultural rebels. By the 1970s, most historians had concluded that whatever else the American character/identity had been, it had been and still was coercive—an oppressor of blacks, non-males, and others. Most historians shunned it as a research or teaching topic, or attacked the idea as a form of cultural domination.

Then as I reviewed the intellectual currents of the early 1990s, I realized that these old issues in American history had taken on a new urgency in the light of events overseas. Beginning in the late 1980s, events abroad cast a workable national identity and cohesion in a new light, as vitally important national assets easily lost. The mighty Soviet Union broke apart beginning in 1989, and secessionist movements destroyed what was once Yugoslavia, separatist impulses surged within Spain, Canada, Czechoslovakia, and elsewhere. This trend toward the dismantling of nations invariably had as its driver ethnic and cultural divisions that had become too intense for formerly functioning societies. In this light, the demographic transformation of the United States, driven by mass immigration, became a major story with a worrisome edge. What I found in my review of writings on this topic in the early 1990s was a sudden and unexpected rekindling of the sense that national identity and unity were again in play in the United States. *Time* magazine's April 9, 1990 cover story was "America's Changing Colors: What Will the U.S. Be Like When Whites Are No Longer the Majority?." This and other media stories on immigration-driven demographic and cultural change marked a new willingness to report in worried tones the changes that mass immigration was bringing. Even so, American journalism was not yet bold enough to ask if this was what the American people wanted immigration to be doing. As *Time's* writers began the story: "'The Browning of America' will alter everything in society, from politics and education to industry, values and culture." This demographic change "offers tremendous opportunity," but "also poses risks." What risks? Apparently, that the white natives might behave badly. "Racial and ethnic conflict remains an ugly fact of American life," the magazine concluded.

That was as far as this and most other such stories went. However, the theme of fragmenting American national identity and diminishing cohesiveness was becoming persistent, though not always with immigration linked to these changes: "Our great national achievement...a common citizenship and identity...is now threatened by a process of relentless, deliberate Balkanization," columnist Charles Krauthammer wrote in the *Washington Post* that year, saying nothing about immigration.

Another worrier about Balkanization, historian Arthur M. Schlesinger, Jr. brought out *The Disuniting of America*, a best-seller when published in 1991. Schlesinger knew that what he called disuniting had many causes and manifestations, and he was chiefly interested in the role of revisionist and ethnicity-centered history.

He briefly noted the scale and non-European character of recent immigration, and said: "No one wants to be a Know-Nothing. Yet uncontrolled immigration is an impossibility," and America "must confront…the criteria of control."

I saw Arthur at a professional meeting not long after, and asked, "Why he has not gone on to recommend immigration restriction to lower the numbers and give a better chance for the assimilative forces that he found in a weakened condition?

"Diane sternly warned me not to," he responded. "I would be viciously attacked."

Of course, I don't know (for sure) which Diane, and it doesn't matter. Arthur was a resolute man, yet he held back on the advice of a well-meaning, intimidated friend. The taboo against suggesting immigration as a cause of any sort of problem at all was even stronger, at least in New York City and in Arthur's larger world of liberal intellectuals, than I had realized.

* * *

Discovering in the public discussion of the 1990s a rising criticism of the stiflers who had been doing their best to stifle us, and a growing uneasiness with increasing cultural divisions and tensions, gave us beleaguered and battered immigration reformers some encouragement. It did not amount to a turn against mass immigration, but it was a promising change of climate, a small turn against the "Thought Police" who threw taboo blankets and invidious labels against those who wanted to make immigration a topic in which the arguments of policy critics had to be met with counter-arguments.

Equally encouraging, there was good news on the writing being done on the immigration issue itself. The ranks of immigration-status quo critics were growing, expanding and deepening the case for reform.

I will describe the emergence of four new voices, take brief note of others, and then recognize the intellectual debut of a think tank on immigration and a journal where mass legal and illegal immigration was in the 1990s regularly being connected to the other dots—national identity and cohesion, the many costs of population expansion, threats to national security, and community strains.

* * *

New Voices

From Australia came Katherine Betts' *Ideology and Immigration: Australia 1976-1987* (1988), a dazzling analysis of immigration politics and policymaking down under. The "growth lobby"(her term for what we sometimes called the Expansionists in the U.S.) in Australia had complete success in reversing a tight immigration regime that had been in place through the 1960s and into the mid-1970s, expanding immigration numbers in the midst of a severe recession and continuing that policy through the 1980s. Betts located a large part of the growth lobby's base in groups engaged in land development, housing, and manufacturing, who stood to gain from immigration-driven growth itself and the ample labor supply it guaranteed. The other vital component was Australia's elites, who took it as a "marker of intellectual status and identity" to be tolerant, cosmopolitan, committed to multiculturalism, and necessarily also "pro-immigrant" and thus pro-immigration. Betts described in some detail how Australian elites, with privileged access to communication media and influence over the terms of national discourse, stigmatized and stifled critics of the expansive immigration regime, who reflected the preferences of most Australians who paid the costs of an ever-crowded, environmentally strained, Asianized Australia. This seemed to American readers a very familiar story, with similar intimidation terminology used to smother rebellion by the racist, bigoted, xenophobic and nationalistic Australian masses.

George Borjas was a Cuban immigrant and an economist when I met him at UC Santa Barbara in the late 1960s, when we were both untenured assistant professors. I sensed then that he was incorrigibly rational on the immigration issue, and this time I guessed right. His first book, *Friends or Strangers* (1990), was a mixture of complacency and alarm at current immigration trends and impacts. He concluded that "immigrants have little impact on the earnings and employment opportunities of natives. Thus, Borjas concluded, the concern that has fueled much of the movement toward a more restrictionist immigration policy is…unjustified." But elsewhere he found substantial costs. The skill and educational levels of immigrants from the 1970s forward have been steadily deteriorating, and they were more likely to use public welfare programs than earlier immigrants. Thus the immigrant stream is changing, and not for the better, from the point of view of the nation's interest in a work force with substantial human capital. This finding called for policy reconsideration and revision, though Borjas had only general ideas about this. One year after his book was published, and apparently provoked by reviewers who interpreted his message as "no economic case against current immigration," Borjas wrote in a preface to the paperback edition that "there is no economic rationale to justify this huge increase in the size of the foreign-born population" expected in the 1990s. Borjas joined the Harvard Economics Department in the 1990s, and this Cuban immigrant's increasingly critical assessments of current immigration's economic impacts could not be dismissed as the ranting of some WASP bigot or a third rate economist.

* * *

Another major contribution to the critique of current immigration was written by an immigrant from Great Britain and economic columnist with *Forbes* magazine, Peter Brimelow. His essay, "Time to Rethink Immigration" appeared in the premier conservative magazine, *The National Review*, in June 1992.

Brimelow rebutted virtually every part of the conventional wisdom he found among conservatives on the immigration question, especially the wrongheaded economic conclusions of Julian Simon. His distinctive preoccupation was with the potential of massive non-European immigration for bringing about the cultural transformation of the American nation-state—"a sovereign structure that is the political expression of a specific ethno-cultural group." Those who think America is a nation built around "an idea"—that all men are created equal—forget or ignore the fundamental importance of "a common ethnicity" and the cultural values it brought. That combination was Anglo-Saxon Christian, and it gave the nation its distinctive nationhood, into which or at the margins of which other nationalities, ethnic groups and races made their contributions. Creating "the First Universal Nation" through mass immigration, as Ben Wattenberg urged and celebrated, was historically unprecedented, and amounted to a risky experiment to "deconstruct the American nation." It should have no conservative support. The American people should be asked if they wished to proceed with it.

Brimelow's article had a stunning impact. This multifaceted alarm bell on mass immigration had been carried in Bill Buckley's flagship conservative journal, suggesting an open break by some conservatives with the *Wall Street Journal's* open border line. In addition to opening a new front politically, the article, while it devoted much space to the economic side of the indictment of current policy, ignited a vigorous discussion of the cultural impacts, both in print and in interviews, where the telegenic and articulate Brimelow made a formidable figure.

* * *

Brimelow had broken through a hard taboo on critical or questioning discussion of immigrants' cultural inheritance. Former foreign service officer Lawrence Harrison's *Underdevelopment Is a State of Mind* (1988) displayed the same courage. Harrison argued that Latin America's economic and political backwardness was rooted in Hispanic culture, which was "anti-democratic, anti-social, anti-progress, anti-entrepreneurial, and, at least among the elite, anti-work." Bringing that culture into North America by unregulated immigration should be a public policy issue openly debated. Harrison's critique of Hispanic culture drew upon what was actually an old idea in Latin American studies (he cited the writings of Octavio Paz, Mario Vargas Llosa, Mariano Grondona, and Carlos Montaner) but in recent years it had not been given much attention.

Brimelow's article shook loose a vigorous, and to immigration reformers, a long overdue discussion. Unlike Harrison, who wrote five years earlier, Brimelow was not given the (mostly) silent treatment. Francis Fukuyama's "Immigrants and Family Values" in *Commentary* (May, 1993) argued that Brimelow was historically mistaken to link American nationality with race or ethnicity when it was rooted in "an idea." The two articles generated a flood of respondents. A few tried to invoke a taboo on the topic or call Fukuyama or Brimelow bad names, but most engaged in rational argument whether immigration on the current scale was overwhelming the assimilative capacities of a multiculturalist America where the elite classes at least were uneasy with the word Americanization.

Thus in the 1990s the problems of assimilation of divergent cultures were forcing their way to the surface in mainstream channels—even the taboo subject of whether Mexicans were at the head of the problem list. A month after the *Commentary* dispute began, the topic of cultural conflict received unprecedented exposure and centrality when Harvard's Samuel P. Huntington argued in "The Clash of Civilizations" (*Foreign Affairs*, Summer, 1993) that in the post Cold War era the fault lines of world conflict would run between civilizations or cultures. Rebuttals, rejoinders and clarifications poured into *Foreign Affairs'* editorial office, filled up two subsequent issues, and were combined in a book with Huntington's title in 1996. Cultural differences, which had earlier been almost uniformly welcomed as an enriching "diversification," were now discussed in elite circles as national security and global political issues with menacing potential. This was good news for those of us wanting cultural diversity to receive a balanced and wide-ranging critical appraisal.

* * *

The first years of the 1990s produced other writers who addressed immigration from a critical and reformist angle. If Brimelow awakened and encouraged soul-searching among conservatives, a California journalist with impeccable liberal credentials, Jack Miles, forced liberals to confront the costs black Americans in California and elsewhere were paying for mass immigration. Writing in the aftermath of the "Rodney King" riots in early May 1992 that tore apart portions of Los Angeles and exposed fierce ethnic-racial animosities, Miles offered a brilliant confession that California whites (including his own family) were turning, in home and shop, from black labor to brown, because "they trust Latinos. They fear or disdain blacks." "By an irony I find particularly cruel, unskilled Latino immigration may be doing to American blacks at the end of the twentieth century what the European immigration that brought my own ancestors here did to them at the end of the nineteenth century." Open borders, he now saw, was a formula for black displacement, and more LA riots. "FAIR [whose research assistance he acknowledged, along with help from Director George High at CIS] would admit 300,000 immigrants a year. How many would you admit? And if blacks get hurt, whose side are you on?"

Miles' article ("Blacks Versus Browns," *The Atlantic Monthly* (October, 1992) was one of the most powerful in the history of contemporary immigration discussion, and should have been particularly unsettling to the blacks and liberals lined up inside the open border coalition. Another liberal icon, former senator and flag-carrier for the opposition to the war in Vietnam, Eugene McCarthy, produced *The Colonization of the U.S.*, ranking undefended borders among the leading signs of American international enfeeblement. Liberal economic writer Robert B. Reich, soon to be President Clinton's Labor Secretary, brought out *Work of Nations* in 1991, arguing that immigration policy should be changed to aim only at bringing in high-skilled labor. David Rieff, author in 1991 of *Los Angeles: Capital of the Third World*, chose a subtitle conveying the basic story of urban pathologies brought to the largest city in the American state that received one-third of all legal and illegal immigrants. In an essay in the *Christian Science Monitor* entitled, "The End of the Migration Era," John Tanton noted that, with the human population growing by 80 million a year and expanding toward 10 billion, only a tiny fraction could hope to solve their problems by migrating. The rest "will have to bloom where they're planted," and if those who do leave include some of the most talented, "how will change ever come" at home? In my *Re-Thinking the Purposes of Immigration* (1991), I argued that U.S. immigration policy has no explicit national goals, responds chiefly to the desires of foreigners for a higher standard of living and employers for low-wage labor, and should have as its primary goal a demographic future chosen by America's elected representatives after extensive public discussion.

* * *

Mention of the growing ranks of individual writers on immigration impacts leads to the role of three new periodicals that helped bring their immigration and related work into view like quarterly artesian wells.

There were no such outlets in 1977, when I sat in my Hutchins Center office in Montecito searching for authors and expertise.

I have already mentioned the Petoskey-based journal that John Tanton published, *The Social Contract*, covering immigration and the issues connected to it. In that one journal, these were some of the offerings in the early 1990s: —journalist Georgie Anne Geyer wrote on the centrifugal forces eroding the concept of U.S. citizenship; Brimelow and Bouvier condensed their recent books into articles; German social scientists Viktor Foerster and Wolfgang Bosswick, frequent participants in the annual Writers Workshop, reported on European immigration politics and policies; *The New Republic* writer Robert Kuttner declared his support for a national ID card; several authors expressed reservations about the claims that NAFTA would reduce Mexican immigration; Georgie Anne explored the growing Islamic presence in Europe; Jack Martin of CIS wrote on the national security implications of porous borders; the increasingly prolific writer Roy Beck reported on refugee impacts on American communities and the immigration politics of national religious organizations; Ed Levy urged his fellow Jews to re-think their historic commitment to open American borders; and both James Robb and my brother Hugh Davis Graham (in his book *Collision Course* (2002) pointed out that affirmative action and immigration policies were on a collision course which must lead to fundamental policy adjustments on both issues. *The Social Contract* had become, at least for me, the liveliest (if uneven) and least PC journal that came into my mailbox.

In 1993 came the quarterly *People and Place*, published at Monash University in Australia, superbly edited by Katherine Betts and Bob Birrell. It focused on immigration issues in Australia with occasional attention to the U.S. and Europe.

CIS in 1989 began publishing a monthly periodical, *Scope*, that covered congressional and agency activities, and summarized its own reports on the results of IRCA and other topics, reviewing books, and noting immigration policy trends abroad. Deciding that the title *Scope* sounded "more like mouthwash than a policy journal," the new director of CIS, Mark Krikorian, changed the title to *Immigration Review* in the spring of 1994, and went to monthly "Backgrounders" and occasional reports in 1999.

The center also published books and monographs, and in this period the think tank's chief author was demographer Leon Bouvier, whose talent for clear exposition of what the demographic numbers meant gave his work considerable impact. In 1991, he produced *Fifty Million Californians*, a compact paperback informing citizens of that state that reasonable projections showed them multiplying from 31 million to 50 million in twenty years, almost all the growth immigration driven. A year later, Bouvier's book *Peaceful Invasions* projected population growth due to immigration for the entire U. S., along with the likely economic, environmental, and social impacts—most of them negative—and it made a case for policy change toward lower numbers..

In my report on the clamor of ideas about and around immigration in the 1990s, I claimed too much when saying that "the wind has radically shifted" toward our critical perspective. Still, the immigration topic seemed in unprecedented ferment at the level of ideas and public discourse. The voices critical of the status quo were multiplying. This was good news for those of us who for so long found it difficult to break through the suffocating blankets of taboo and myth.

Chapter Fourteen:
In the Washington Trenches

And if blacks get hurt, whose side are you on? — Jack Miles

A deeper bench of restrictionist analysts and writers, better institutional weapons—and still the inflow of immigrants in the 1990s was running higher than in the 1980s, which had been the decade with the largest immigration intake in American history. Estimates of the resident illegal population, and yearly replenishment, kept being revised upward. Mass immigration now had twenty-five years of momentum, and thicker chains of communication reaching back from affluent America to relatives in poverty-stricken countries.

FAIR by now had an annual budget of $2.5 million, permitting a Washington staff of about twenty-five, and one fieldworker in Los Angeles. We didn't know the budget of some of the organizations sending ethnic lobbyists to convince the Tip O'Neills on Capitol Hill that they had a real constituency, and only later learned that the Ford Foundation had given MALDEF startup funding in 1968 of $2.2 million. By 1995 they had provided $18.9 million to MALDEF and $12.9 million to La Raza. Louis March, in *Immigration and the End of Self-Government* (1994), filled four pages with the corporate sponsors of Maldef, from Nissan North America through Bechtel to United Airlines. By contrast, we were midgets in the league of issue lobbyist organizations, and had to catch attention with the merit and boldness of our analysis and ideas. Often asked, "Exactly what are you for?," FAIR began in 1994 to call for "a moratorium" on all immigration but immediate relatives. The idea of a moratorium had been proposed many times in the history of immigration politics, when there was a policy deadlock or confusion amid ongoing large scale immigration. Senator Robert Stump introduced a moratorium bill for which FAIR could claim some parentage.

FAIR's national image was only partly shaped by the tone and quality of its message. Much was a result of media habits of characterization. Initially labeled by an ignorant and deadline-pressed media as "rightist" or "conservative," by the 1990s the organization had been around more than a decade, and a few reporters improved their accuracy. "FAIR is at the forefront of the push to reduce immigration," the *Los Angeles Times* wrote on November 24, 1993. "The group's roots are in the environmental movement, and it is now an influential player." We were, they correctly (this time) said, "a tight corps of environmentalist and population control advocates—card carrying liberals all." Michael Kinsley of *The New Republic* agreed, "What little opposition there has been to immigration in recent years has come vaguely from the left…environmentalists [who] believe that immigrants contribute to overpopulation…and some blacks" worried about losing jobs to low-wage foreigners. That was close to accurate where the boards of directors of FAIR and CIS were concerned. Both boards were primarily liberals, with a rump of nationalist-conservatives. Slowly the media gave up on the liberal vs. conservative labeling game and sought other descriptive devices, most often "anti-immigrant group."

Contrast this with the media's handling of one of the open border groups with a name which translated into English as "the race," and that touted a motto: "*Por la raza, todo. Fuera de La Raza nada.*" (For the race, everything; outside the race, nothing.) No one complained about this in the media. There had been internal warnings about racism within the ranks of Latino politics by the sainted agricultural workers' union organizer Cesar Chavez. Chavez had this to say to his biographer Peter Mattheissen:

> *I hear more and more Mexicans talking about La Raza to build*
> *up their pride, you know. Some people don't look at it as racism,*
> *but when you say "la raza" you're saying an anti-gringo thing,*
> *and it won't stop there. Today it's anti-gringo, tomorrow it will be*
> *anti-Negro, and the day after it will be anti-Filipino…La Raza*
> *is a very dangerous concept. I speak very strongly against it among*
> *the Chicanos.*

La Raza, however, was the chosen label of a Latino group formed in 1968, and the media gave them a complete pass. FAIR, however, often was plastered by Expansionists with the term, always without evidence, as there was none. Cecilia Munoz of La Raza told the Los Angeles paper that "FAIR's appeal is blatantly racial." Then, lacking evidence, she came at the matter another way. They "may be race blind in their rhetoric, but the consequences of what they want hit people of color." It could get worse. Despite FAIR's moderate and fact-oriented rhetoric, in private, claimed freelance writer James Crawford, who had never been with us in private. The organization's "leaders have espoused a whole elaborate theory of race suicide." I felt cheated. I had sat through fifteen years of FAIR board and other meetings and my rascally colleagues never told me about this interesting theory.

* * *

Who Is Behind All This Restrictionism?

As for the real bumps, one came in 1993 with respect to FAIR's funding. Journalists dealing with new lobbying groups rightly want to go beyond (but not ignore entirely, which too often happened) the organization's published statements to know "Who is behind all this?" A look at the FAIR board of directors revealed an organization leaning a bit left of center, with strong environmentalist/populationist roots along with a business-conservative element. This was not the stuff of exciting journalism. Who gave the organization money? Could sinister rightist sources of funding be found? An occasional journalist pointed out that one of our steady funders was Cordelia May, a scion of the Mellon family. It wasn't clear what might be sinister about descending from this distinguished Pittsburgh lineage. Mrs. May herself was a charming, reticent sort of person, a bird-watcher and environmentalist. To protect birds and the environment, she was, I am tempted to add "of course," committed to human population stabilization, as was FAIR. When she died in 2005, the obituaries listed her chief beneficiaries as the Nature Conservancy of Hawaii and the National Tropical Botanical

Garden. Not very sinister. Her chief adviser in matters of finance and philanthropy through the 1980s and into the 1990s, Greg Curtis, was a highly intelligent forty-ish man who once circulated an essay lamenting the decline of liberalism among Writers Workshop regulars.

As a board member, I paid little attention to who gave us money, in the spirit of my former boss and friend Robert Maynard Hutchins, who had a sign on his desk at the University of Chicago announcing that "We Launder Dirty Money." Henry Ford had been a notorious anti-Semite, and when the Ford Foundation gave money to Latino lobbies, we did not denounce them for being anti-Semites by association. Our response was to see if we could get some Ford money ourselves. Once, only, we did. Senator Simpson and Dick Lamm lectured the head of the Foundation about partisan priorities, and Ford gave CIS about a quarter of a million dollars for a research project on agricultural labor in 1988.

Then in 1993 the media somehow learned that FAIR had received donations from a New York organization called The Pioneer Fund. It was news to me, for I had never been on the finance committee, and at general board meetings we didn't scour our donors' inner hearts for the purity of their motives. What was this Pioneer Fund? Dan Stein told the board of FAIR that it was a New York-based foundation established in the 1920s and run by an elderly lawyer, with a pattern of funding research into racial differences. An initial contribution to FAIR of $50,000 had been accepted in the usual way, with a note of thanks. Only the board's finance committee had it called to their attention. Then in 1993 the media rang with charges that Pioneer had a history of funding "eugenicist" research. So FAIR must be "eugenicist," whatever that meant.

Dan compiled a list of Pioneer's grant recipients going back to the 1930s, and in the record of funding in recent decades we found the names of many distinguished medical scientists from places like Johns Hopkins and Harvard, right up to the present. Among them I saw the name of a psychologist friend of mine at UCSB before he went to the University of Minnesota and became one of the nation's leading researchers on twin studies, Tom Bouchard. Tom, I knew, was rather far to the left in his social and political views. I assumed that he took Pioneer money in the same spirit as we at CIS took the Ford or any other money: We have zero interest in your "motives." Thanks for supporting this valuable work. Send more next year.

Put on the defensive by the "eugenicist" terminology, we pointed out that the Pioneer Fund made grants to many distinguished scientists at top institutions, and their grants amounted to only 5 percent of FAIR's funding since their contributions began.[3] The media coverage implied, to readers who didn't know us, a murky cloud of taint. I argued in board meetings that Pioneer funding came with too high a cost in public relations. Others prevailed with the view that the proponents of open borders shouldn't be allowed to dictate our funding options through the use of slander and innuendo. I still think I was right.

* * *

Despite rough patches, there seemed a slight and perhaps strengthening wind in our sails in the early 1990s. There was evidence of this apart from the buildup of writers on the restrictionist reform side.

To our discouragement but not surprise, the presidential election of 1992 followed form. The immigration question failed to be asked at any of the presidential debates. The national economy had slumped badly in 1991, and rising unemployment has always elevated the immigration issue. Two maverick voices in the campaigning for the White House let it be known that the daily violation of law at America's borders was one of their complaints against those now in charge in Washington. Writer and Republican Pat Buchanan was most outspoken on the problems associated with mass immigration, and especially the illegal component. He was, for me and others, a flawed messenger, despite his sound instincts on immigration. His main themes were those of trade

---

[3]Some years later, in a lengthy, measured and masterful web site commentary on a Southern Poverty Law Center smear beginning with a picture of John as "The Puppeteer," John wrote: "The Pioneer Fund was started in 1937 by individuals who still believed that "nature" (genetics) played a major role [in human outcomes]... To the displeasure of their opponents, they pursued this proposition by funding university-based studies of identical twins reared apart, now a standard genetic research technique. These showed that nature and nurture each played about a fifty per cent role. The debate continues. In the meantime, I'm comfortable being in the company of other Pioneer Fund grantees such as Johns Hopkins University, Cornell Medical School, Brandeis University, and University of California, Berkeley.

protectionism and opposition to abortion, matters on which FAIR resolutely took no position. Lacking a background of elective office and without funds, Buchanan was quickly marginalized, though he would prove to have admirable staying power as a commentator on public issues.

* * *

Ross Perot: The Indecisive Populist

Billionaire Texan Ross Perot more effectively tapped into a populist disgruntlement with the two major parties and America's global circumstances in 1992. He had created a national organization, United We Stand-America, to attack the free trade doctrine that in his view was leading to American de-industrialization. He denounced budget deficits and the arrogant political class that was spending its way to uninterrupted power and national bankruptcy. The approaching North American Free Trade Agreement enlarged his audience. United We Stand was not a political party, but its volunteers responded to Perot's February, 1992 television request and qualified him for presidential primaries in all fifty states. He won enough primary votes to elbow his way into the presidential debates. In his television interviews and campaign speeches, Perot made a few remarks critical of the loss of control over our southern borders. It was a minor and intermittent theme for this economic nationalist. He hadn't quite found a place for immigration restriction in his larger message. In the 1992 election, Perot received almost 20 percent of the popular vote, the second largest presidential vote in American third party history (Theodore Roosevelt polled 27 percent of the vote in 1912).

In immigration reform circles, we wondered if Ross Perot, whose presidential ambitions were expected to continue, might carry our issue into presidential politics for the first time. Some of us (but not all) welcomed this prospect, reasoning that it made little difference who injected the issue into national politics. One problem with Perot as an ally was that he was a strong critic of free trade, and we immigration reformers were divided on the trade issue. Some, most prominently John Tanton, held the free trade enthusiasm in considerable suspicion. Others among us did not want immigration reduction to be prominently associated with protectionism—a link that was already charged against immigration reform by some pundits. Our issue, some of us argued, was immigration, challenge enough to master. Let the pro-free traders and the anti-NAFTA forces fight about that complex issue in a different ballpark, as the issues of goods across borders and people across borders were not necessarily linked.

* * *

The president from 1993-97 was going to be Bill Clinton, whose views on immigration were unknown, if he had any. An early episode underscored our overall problem. In early January, Clinton nominated Zoe Baird as Attorney General. In the vetting process it was discovered that she and her husband had for the past two years employed two illegal immigrants from Peru, and failed to pay social security taxes on their payroll. White House Counsel, Secretary of State Warren Christopher (who gives an insider's account in *Chances of a Lifetime* (2001)), Clinton himself, and a panel of senators at her nomination hearing thought this a trivial matter to be ignored. This was the view of America's elite political class, but not of the American people, who immediately besieged senators' offices with angry correspondence, and Baird quickly withdrew.

We strained to find some promise of openness on our issue in the new Clinton administration, and Dan was initially encouraged by Attorney General Janet Reno's invitation to a personal session in her office. Generalities were all the agenda she had in mind, but Dan took the message to be that she was aware that border control was a part of her responsibility. Clinton had not been in office six months when he announced that "the fact is that our borders leak like a sieve. Those things cannot be permitted to continue in good conscience." A month later, he said, "We must not—and we will not—surrender our borders to those who wish to exploit our history of compassion and justice." Vice-President Al Gore led a task force to recommend reforms to "toughen" asylum provisions and examine illegal entry.

Also encouraging, we found what we thought was an immigration reformer ally in the senate, where democrat Harry Reid introduced legislation to limit immigration to 300,000 annually. He turned out to be quite fickle in his views on the issue. That our borders were under siege at many places was reinforced when on June 7, 1993 the freighter Golden Venture," after a 17,000 mile voyage from Thailand and around the Cape of Good Hope, beached at Fort Tilden, New York, with 296 Chinese illegal immigrants aboard. The Clinton administration was embarrassed by the public outcry. Federal prosecutors indicted the crew for smuggling, and half of the passengers were deported (many then successfully tried again to illegally enter the U.S.), and the rest were detained for several years and then pardoned by Clinton and allowed to disappear into the national population. The "Golden Venture" was no isolated incident. In the previous twelve months, more than a dozen ships had been detected dropping human cargo from China onto U.S. beaches or ports.

Dan Stein thought these and other developments grounds for writing to the board in October, 1993 that, "there has been a sea change in American public opinion." A few months earlier he reported that "California is heating up." Michael Kinsley, writing in *The New Republic* a few months earlier, had used the same language, "The politics of immigration may be heating up." The reformers had originally gathered from the environmental left, he conceded, but Kinsley, undoubtedly having read Brimelow in the *National Review*, wrote that "the re-emergence of anti-immigrant sentiment on the right." In retrospect, he was correct in sensing renewed passion on the issue, but looked in the wrong place for its epicenter. To see it first hand one would need to travel to the Left Coast.

That astute observer of America, Nathan Glazer, in a 1993 article in *Commentary*, anticipated the source of the rebellion to come. A huge social experiment was being conducted by policymakers in Washington who authorized large-scale immigration and augmented it with a growing level of illegal entry. The American people had not been asked.

"It seems we have insensibly reverted to mass immigration, without ever having made a decision to do so." Few Americans think our population too low, our industries short of labor. "But our politicians... end up looking as if we believe all this is true."

Chapter Fifteen:
California Growth Worries:
The Seeds of the Turn

We continue to have 1,500 new neighbors a day, a half million a year, monstrous misplaced freeways, park land scuffled and trampled like a pitcher's mound, a gray stink in the air. — Cry California

Knowledgeable people might say that the American public did not suddenly become unhappy with mass and substantially illegal immigration in the early 1990s. They had been against it since it started in the 1960s. It is true that public opinion polls reported steady majorities of Americans, without much difference among ethnoracial groups or sections of the country, opposing the expansion of immigration that was taking place inexorably despite the public's opinion. There were some minor fluctuations in the poll results, but the pattern was clear. The public since the 1960s has wanted less immigration than it gets, and its wants make no difference in policymaking.

Yet the polls tell more about opinion than about hard-to-measure intensity and emotion—which is why the Tip O'Neills who run our public policy machinery pay little attention to polls unless accompanied by some sort of political mobilization. What happened in the early 1990s was an intensification and deepening of public feeling against illegal and also million-plus legal immigration, and a resultant rise in citizen activism and activist organization. Finally, a substantial social movement had emerged, most visibly in California.

* * *

In retrospect, one can be twice unsurprised by this. California absorbed about 40 percent of the foreign immigration coming to the U.S., legal and illegal. Anyone could have predicted a backlash where the volume was highest. Beyond this, savvy Americans know where to look for new social trends, and it's not in South Dakota, Louisiana, or West Palm Beach. The future, we Americans tell ourselves with eyes rolled upward, seems always to originate in California and then move eastward inexorably.

This view of things makes the golden state, on the issue of immigration, too much the single originator. We at FAIR knew that there were citizens groups forming to urge immigration reform in Texas, New York, Illinois, Florida and elsewhere. In most cases they were spontaneous, in that FAIR had not mid-wived them, but hastened to establish contacts once these local groups surfaced. We also knew that a sort of upturn in the criticism of the immigration status quo was reflected in the late 1980s, in the formation of other Washington-based advocacy groups besides FAIR.

It Always Starts in California

A citizens' uprising there against incoming migrants in large numbers, much of it illegal, was not unprecedented. Californians in the past had been ambivalent about incoming migrants, and in times and places had become hostile to certain episodes in the history of in-migration. The Golden State had historically grown by the influx of migrants from the other American states, which was basically welcomed. This had not been so for Asian immigration when it began to grow from a trickle into a substantial flow in the 1870s and after. Asian immigration became a contentious issue for three decades until the Chinese Exclusion Act of 1882 and the "Gentlemen's Agreement" with Japan in 1906 essentially ended what might have become a significant and continuing migration from Asia. Thereafter, the state's business, professional, and educational establishment gloried in the growth that came both by native fertility rates and intra-U.S. immigration through the twentieth century.

Even so, there was a major exception in the form of fierce resistance to the caravans of thousands of "Okies" from the rural South and central plains states in the 1930s. Immigration-driven growth was welcomed again when prosperity returned after World War II, as it provided a pathway to mounting wealth for realtors, developers, the construction trades, and for business in general. When California edged ahead of New York as the nation's most populated state in 1963, a triumphant sign was hoisted over the Oakland Bay Bridge. Newspaper editorials hailed this achievement, but I recall hoisting an Irish ale that summer with my brother Hugh at the Buena Vista café in San Francisco to mourn the Golden State's historic mistake.

There remained, however, a contrapuntal theme through and after the booming 1950s. Resident Californians grumbled, some of them, about the pace of the state's growth during the 1950s, and they haven't stopped to this day. They cherished the remaining citrus groves and grassy hillsides, unclogged roads, state parks where one could get a reservation on a few days' notice. I know. They talked that way when I arrived in 1965, and I talked that way, too, from the first day I arrived.

* * *

California and We Migrants

I first visited California in the summer of 1954, after my freshman college year, a sort of pre-immigrant who was restless in the cultural confines of my native Tennessee. My uncle Wade Graham took me for a drive around parts of Orange County (south of Los Angeles) from his Garden Grove home and complained about subdivisions sprouting where once he had seen an expanse of lemon trees and roadside fruit and vegetable stands. He had nothing to gain from growth, and was against it—though his own migration there from Arkansas had been part of the growth.

I became one of those American migrants to California in 1965, pursuing academic career opportunities that led to one year in Palo Alto, then to Santa Barbara where a relatively new University of California campus (UCSB) was one of the state's many magnets of growth.

We recent migrants from other parts of America who had contributed to the state's rapid growth soon took sides on the lively growth issue, and I very early became an opponent of further growth. My family rented a house in a tract (that had once been a lemon orchard) in the Goleta suburb of Santa Barbara, where there were still hundreds of acres of lemon orchards, a clean and uncrowded beach, and no daily traffic tangles. Within months the local newspaper reported that a Milwaukee firm was relocating a work force of 600 to Goleta, and two local lemon orchards went under the bulldozers almost at once, to provide the housing. The Milwaukee company's migrants to Goleta arrived some time in the last months of 1966, and in a grocery checkout line I stood behind one of them who was talkative. Identifying herself as a Milwaukee transplant, she told the cashier that the newcomers from the Midwest were not feeling exactly welcomed by the community. I commented that, indeed, they were not welcome. Nothing personal against Milwaukeeans, or her. We just opposed further growth. The lady and the cashier were speechless, and she frumped off to her house where lemon trees once stood in green and yellow spotted rows.

For some reason, I didn't leave it at that, but wrote a letter to the editor of the local paper expressing my sentiments. When it was published, two reactions followed. The Chancellor of my campus, Vernon Cheadle, read my letter, and wrote me a scolding personal note from his home office on a Sunday. By what right did I, who had immigrated (he happened to know) only months before, advocate "pulling up the drawbridge" for immigrants to follow?

My wife begged me to climb into a foxhole (or, better, offer an apology), but I found the Chancellor's question interesting. If one concludes that population growth in one's homeland (however defined) has become excessive, who has the right/obligation to state this, and advocate some sort of growth control or cessation? Residents, seemed the answer. Only long-term residents like the Chancellor, who had lived in Santa Barbara for twenty-seven years? He seemed to think so. But why twenty-seven? Was not 2.7 years enough? Or 2.7 hours?

I wrote the Chancellor, posed this question, and argued that full citizenship came in something like 2.7 seconds, in my view, after the first breath of in-state air was drawn. I would continue to oppose more growth, thank you, and in other ways advocate what seemed best for my new homeland.

Fortunately, he took this exchange in good spirit. Others had read my letter, and I was asked to join a couple of local "growth control" groups—one working to revise citywide zoning to achieve a maximum urban population in Santa Barbara, and the other to mobilize local sentiment in order to demand an end to oil drilling permits in the channel for the dual benefits of environmental protection and curbing the oil industry's growth.

In both groups, there was a mix of third-generation Californians and recent immigrants like myself. The two causes seemed worthy, but I developed reservations early on. Most of my fellow growth-controllers assumed that the problems of growth could be brought to minimal and tolerable levels by some combination of land-use controls to combat sprawl, environmental regulations against the disturbance of fragile ecosystems, and above all, regional and statewide planning.

To me, this dodged the fundamental issue in the growth debate When, and how, to stop population expansion? Still, I was happy to be involved with groups who were critics of growth as usual.

* * *

California Tomorrow—Should We Have a Plan?

Just as I arrived in California in the mid-1960s the planning gospel as solution to the state's growth pains was given vigorous if sometimes longwinded expression by an influential organization, "California Tomorrow." It was established in 1960 by northern Californians Alfred Heller and Samuel Wood. In 1962, they published *California, Going, Going...* a vigorous rejection of the entrenched "growth is good" outlook. "How polluted can a bright land become, and still be bright?" they asked, condemning the loss of our land to "slurbs—sloppy, sleazy, slovenly, slipshod semi-cities." The organization published a magazine, *Cry California*, that took up in each issue one of the sub-topics of the larger question of the costs of growth—such as loss of agricultural land to sprawl, the pollution of Lake Tahoe, the harms from pesticides, and highway gridlock.

"We continue to have 1,500 new neighbors a day, a half million a year, monstrous misplaced freeways, park land scuffled and trampled like a pitcher's mound, and a gray stink in the air."

Always the remedies that were proposed were regional and state planning. The organization produced the *California Tomorrow Plan* in 1972, and in it identified four causes of the state's troubles. The third was "damaging distribution of population; there are too many of us, and we are living in the wrong places." Deep in this formidable and complex, and to many conservative readers shockingly "social engineering" document, came a vision of a future in which Californians planned for a population maximum of thirty million by 2000, and after that no more growth. This would be achieved by income tax deductions granted only for two children, abortion choice, and "setting up new, constitutional controls over in-migration," whatever that meant—perhaps charging immigrants $1,000 per head to cover their services.

This discussion of the population goals of California, and how to reach them, occupied no more than a page in a lengthy document that received modest attention. The book sold 20,000 copies amid much buzz for a short period, and was said to be influential inside the governorship of Jerry Brown. The message heard by the media was not population growth stabilization, in part because *Cry California* did not push it. The message foregrounded and heard was statewide planning.

Planning—the air of California in the 1970s and 1980s was full of talk of it. The growth-control through planning enthusiasms of the groups I worked with in Santa Barbara, and that I knew to be active throughout the state (and in other states and regions), seemed fatally flawed to me. We growth controllers were proposing to establish plans for "controlling growth," a topic under constant re-definition. Were we assuming that growth would then go on forever?

This was absurd. Endless growth, as Ed Abbey wrote, "is the ideology of the cancer cell." If growth must, obviously, come to an end sometime, then why not now, soon, sooner? Surely this was obvious, and the end of growth must be accepted and planned for. To me, the intellectual foundations of the Endless Growth notion were nonexistent. In the influential 1952 report of the National Commission on Materials

Shortages, *Resources for Freedom*, we find these words: "We share the belief of the American people in the principle of growth. Granting that we cannot find any absolute reason for this belief, we admit that to our western minds it seems preferable to any opposite, which to us implies stagnation and decay." Embarrassing.

California Tomorrow's planners had understood, if you read them carefully and to the end of their weighty publications, that we must meet the problems of growth not only with planning, but with growth-ending policies. Here they offered a few partially baked suggestions, but were spared the heavy lifting of growth-ending policymaking. For it suddenly seemed in the 1970s that the end of growth in America was coming through the free choice of individuals—the preferred American way. National as well as California fertility rates in the 1970s were dropping and would before the decade reach "below replacement" levels—2.1 live births per woman. There appeared no need to recommend policies to lower birth rates, stirring up the people who thought such policies a frightful error. With domestic increase ended (actual leveling off of population would take perhaps forty years, demographers thought, given "population momentum"), we would have only to discourage people from coming into the state (or nation). This was unexplored territory (except in Hawaii, as we shall see), but far less difficult than establishing policies to influence births--always a sensitive subject.

* * *

In the 1970s, planning/land-use reform groups such as the one I joined in Santa Barbara sprouted across the state. Population in our county in the 1970-1990 period grew by 70,000, producing traffic congestion, school crowding, suburban encroachment on agricultural lands, and pollution complaints—now central themes of local politics.

Why not just stop the growth, allowing us to get a handle on all these problems? "Whatever your cause, it's a lost cause without population control," somebody said or wrote about that time. One of my UCSB history department colleagues, historian of the ancient world Frank Frost, an opponent of further growth, ran for the county Board of Supervisors in 1972 on a "No Growth" platform. This was rare, if not unprecedented. Most critics of growth merely wanted to direct it away from sprawl into more compact forms. Frank, a Santa Barbara native from a distinguished local family, threw caution to the winds, arguing that when we become adults we stop growing and pursue stability, and it was time for Santa Barbara to make that natural transition. He was elected, to widespread astonishment.

Frank wasn't sure how to achieve the "no more growth" promise. Obviously one started by opposing growth-inducing proposals, such as the notion of building a spur canal eastward in order to import "state water" into the county from the pipeline running south to Los Angeles. Frank opposed it. Without state water, our local water supplies might serve as an absolute constraint upon building. This had much support, and resulted in a series of "temporary" building permit moratoria that sharply reduced new housing startups and other construction. The county rejected state water twice, before finally voting for it in 1991, long after Frank had left the political scene.

On Frank's first day in office, he announced another idea. He proposed that the county redirect the tax revenues derived from its "tourist bed tax." Instead of spending the money on advertisements of Santa Barbara's charms as a weekend getaway in the Los Angeles and San Diego markets, we should advertise the allures of Florida instead, reducing the tourist flow that consumed Santa Barbara's water supplies and freeway spaces. This went nowhere, and people began to realize they had elected a professor, i.e., a person with unusual thought patterns far ahead of (or hopelessly out of touch with) his time. I was greatly heartened, however. Frank was thinking in a "supply side" direction. So I tried to pursue the logic, and interest him in immigration restriction at the national level. This seemed to him like a faraway Washington issue, unsuitable for a mere county supervisor.

Frank moved back to the university full-time after his one term memorably spent delaying as many development proposals as possible. His successor was another growth controller, this time a moderate Republican lawyer. I served on a growth control committee for David Yager, and we tried to rearrange city and county zoning laws on the deck of the overloaded Titanic, enacting, where we could, mostly unconstitutional (the judges were saying) delays and moratoria on housing and industrial development. Local growth control saved some marshes from draining and infill, slowed the developers down, and offered forums for citizens to talk about the high price of housing, and whether the city should attempt to zone for a maximum population. Nevertheless, growth continued, and even on weekends the bulldozers grunted to uproot the lemon and avocado trees making fruit and absorbing carbon dioxide, in order to make room for the boxy suburban houses sprawling over the now treeless acres.

* * *

Growth Issues Move Up From Cities/Counties to the State Capital

In America, problems that are larger than local jurisdictions have a tendency to move upward to the next level. The new state of Hawaii experienced dismaying levels of population growth from mainland "immigrants" after statehood in 1959, and across the 1960s there grew a vast public worry about what growth was bringing to the islands, especially Oahu. Everyone saw the sprawling suburbanization up into the valleys, the high-rise hotels walling off Waikiki Beach, the snarl of traffic. Their island was being transformed physically. Its cultural distinctiveness was threatened, and it seemed that the Haole (Caucasian) invasion would soon produce a white majority—a prospect which even many Haoles thought undesirable. A widespread agitation prodded Governor George Ariyoshi to lead the state in an effort to plan for a different future. But how can one state limit or regulate immigration from other states? Hawaii had little legal room to maneuver, but experimented with measures to discourage if not prevent more immigration from the mainland, such as residency requirements before mainland immigrants could receive certain social services. This approach to immigration discouragement faced formidable constitutional challenges, and soon Hawaii decided to focus on state land use planning as a growth-coping tool. This launched an interesting experiment in controlling growth without controlling immigration. This venture is still ongoing if you visit (I lived on Oahu from 1958-1960, and have visited eight to ten times since) a traffic-jammed wall-to-wall Oahu and ask about the "growth problem," which they obviously have not solved. In the 1970s, even on the mainland where Hawaii's too-many migrants were originating, there was a certain sympathy among the public and even in the media, for the islanders' plight, and their effort to go to the root of the problem. In any other American state, discussing the "problem" of too many people, and in particular too many of the wrong ancestry, would have brought down a thunderstorm of "racist" denunciations. But this was Hawaii, and no one called Japanese-American Governor Ariyoshi any bad names for the cluster of concerns that made him the pioneer among American governors in attempting not just to "plan" to accommodate growth but find some way to end it outright.

* * *

In California, the population driver behind the growth broke through into state discourse early in the 1970s. In that year, the state Assembly, possibly influenced by California Tomorrow, created an advisory council on science and technology that convened a 1971 conference on California's future. Bob Moretti, Speaker of the Assembly, told the audience: "We can no longer accept the proposition that all growth is good." There must be "a balance" between resources and growth, he and the gathering agreed. This was a superficial start, but a start. In 1974, the voters of California elected thirty-four-year-old Jerry Brown as governor, and "Governor Moonbeam" proved to be a sixtyish figure with an openness to new ideas. He would not move into the huge governor's mansion that Reagan had built, or ride in the official chauffeured limousine. He gave top-level encouragement to governmental officials and Californians in general to ponder and facilitate the arrival of "an age of limits," to explore alternative energy sources and reduce our reliance on the automobile. Brown made state government in Sacramento, or at least the executive branch, an incubator of environmental and social novelties.

California Tomorrow had undergone several leadership changes, and a year before closing shop in 1983, had published *California 2000*, a last statement of the group's critique of growth. It called for statewide and regional planning, and if one looked hard enough, a stabilized state population. Jerry Brown's top staff had grown up with these ideas, so it was no surprise when two years earlier, at a luncheon in Washington, D.C., Jerry Brown's Secretary for Resources Huey Johnson told his audience that it was time for a population limitation policy in California. He suggested ending tax subsidies for larger families and support for abortion rights. Talking to reporters later, he added that the federal government "should tighten immigration rules."

Johnson wanted to begin a rational discussion, but he opened the way for a different outcome when he suggested that California should build less low-income housing lest it "draw poor people from Vermont." West coast newspapers briefly fanned these remarks into a controversy over whether Johnson was "a racist," and twenty-seven state senators wrote a letter to Governor Brown demanding that Johnson be fired for his population-limitation views. The Black Caucus would not meet with Johnson to hear his views directly, and Latino politicians denounced him in hostile tones. Several letters to the newspaper that most vigorously presented Johnson's remarks as a major scandal, the *Sacramento Bee*, agreed with Johnson and welcomed his courage. Governor Brown, who privately agreed with Johnson, ignored the flap, and it died away.

I remember thinking, at first, that the episode was encouraging. A top state official had raised the population growth issue, and had offered several policy remedies, including a brief reference to reduced immigration from both the Eastern U.S. and abroad. I probably should have been forewarned by how easily Johnson had been demonized by politicians and a mimicking media. His character and motives were made to be the issue instead of the consequences of runaway growth. A critique of the sources of growth, population increase, seemed suddenly to have become a subject you couldn't raise even if you tried. When you did, you became the issue, instead of it. You weren't only against jobs and progress, complaints the growth lobbies had long made without decisive effect, but also you now were against immigrants, which meant all Latinos, and for good measure, all "people of color."

Looking back, I now see this episode as a signal that the pro-growth lobbies had opened a new front against the "growth control" movement of which I was a part, and they had brought forward some new troops to man that front. The front was our idea of ending population growth itself, especially when we included as one tool a limit on foreign immigration. The new troops brought forward to defend the growth agenda were the ethnic politicians from minority groups who had formerly had almost no involvement in the heated discussions about growth and sprawl that reverberated within California. Johnson was assaulted and morally condemned in strong language by some of the indignant forces of the organized, self-appointed civil rights movement—the black and brown members of the California legislature. They claimed to detect racial bigotry, their professional *raison d'être*, even though Johnson had said nothing about race.

* * *

"No More People Than the Earth Can Take"

Not all growth critics carried their arguments as far as Huey Johnson had that day. We critics of growth in those days were a diverse lot. Most were moderates whose tool kit for growth controls was familiar across the country—zoning for more compact development; environmental regulation to prevent building in ecologically fragile or unique places; mass transit; and shifting more of the costs of development to developers. Then there were the radicals like Frank Frost and myself, tempted to use the phrase, "No Growth" to describe our ultimate goals. We were convinced that population stabilization itself was a pre-requisite for preservation of California's blessed natural endowments for the enjoyment of posterity.

We had no label, the term "populationists" not taking hold. There were a lot of us coming out of the Sixties, tutored by Ehrlich and the rough-edged western writer Ed Abbey. When the first Earth Day celebrations came in 1970, the population limitation theme was prominent. "What is the cause?," a student audience asked British writer C. P. Snow at an American campus in 1969. "Peace! Food! No more people than the earth can take!" he shouted, to tumultuous applause.

As we have seen, population stabilization had moved from environmentalist discourse and college campuses and had become a mainstream idea no later than 1972, with the appointment and report of the National Commission on Population Growth and the American

Future. Thousands of little "Growth Control" movements across the country were drawn together and legitimated when Democratic President Jimmy Carter convened a White House Conference on National Growth Policy in 1978. (I was a delegate, appointed by African-American Congressman Merv Dymally.) Growth management was so mainstream that it stretched from a left sector generated out of the 1960s to a conservative sector coming out of the Republican Party's concern over natural resources in a heritage running from Teddy Roosevelt to the modern Rockefellers. While population distribution was the core of the idea of a National Growth Policy, discussion of population size limitation was heard in a handful of panels and in the hallways. Limits on population size would have been a larger presence on the agenda, I believe, except that American fertility rates had undergone a steep decline across the 1970s. By the time of the 1978 conference, it appeared that population stabilization was happening without we growth controllers having to devise forms of intervention.

* * *

This receptivity to the population limitation issue was on an ebb tide even as we met in Washington in 1978, and Huey Johnson had learned a few years earlier when he made those remarks before an East Coast audience. He stated that there was a fierce taboo operating in California political circles when anyone made the immigration connection. One could see this as a sort of turning point in which the environmentalist/populationist discourse lost the little momentum it had gained and was thrown on the defensive. Prior to this, when I tactlessly in 1966 told the lady from Milwaukee that we did not welcome her in California, and the Chancellor told me that as a just-arrived immigrant I had no right to that opinion, he hadn't called me any ugly names, or linked me to racial bigotry. The immigrant I had unwelcomed in the grocery store was, after all, an American, and also Caucasian—as I was, and as the overwhelming majority of immigrants to California had been since the closing of the West Coast's door in the years between 1882 and 1906 to all but a small trickle of Asian immigration. Some black American immigrants moved to San Francisco and Los Angeles in the decades from World War I through the 1950s, but overwhelmingly the migrants to the Golden State were historically Caucasians with American roots—people like me and the lady from Milwaukee. We caused mostly suburbanizing sprawl, and a lot of Californians were unhappy about the scale and nature of it.

Native Californians who didn't welcome we westward-moving Americans in the 1930s and after had many reasons for their sentiments, but if you disagreed with their no-growth impulses, you couldn't dismiss them as racists. Their arguments or sentiments had to be disputed on the merits, not on murky alleged motives. We California growth opponents in the 1960s and after built our arguments out of many components— the environmental protection side of it appealing to liberals, the zoning controls on uses of property appealing to current property owners' self-interest, preservation of prime agricultural lands from development appealing to citizens devoted to agriculture as a business and way of life, and the idea of fewer or at least not more cars and trucks on our freeways appealing to everyone. Our motives were pretty obvious— preserving an environment for our descendants as clean and inspiring as when we entered it.

The new demographics of immigration to the U.S. and especially to California had changed the terms. For in the fifteen years after my grocery store expression of opposition by a Caucasian to more Caucasian immigration, the forces driving growth in the nation decisively changed—in California, radically. Congress had passed the Immigration Act of 1965, promising that the law would not substantially expand immigration numbers when it did just that. A new era of mass immigration to America, legal and illegal, had begun, and the Commission on Population Growth and the American Future told us that immigration now contributed 25 percent. A rising proportion of the nation's population growth, despite the decline of native fertility rates, marked no end to population growth. It now came from outside our borders. Immigration limitation would have to be brought into the picture as a policy lever, Huey Johnson and others began to see, and say.

* * *

This was especially true in California. The Golden State proved to be the strongest magnet in America. In addition to the Americans arriving from Tennessee, Milwaukee, or New York, who had been white and black Americans as late as the early 1960s, there was now a large and growing stream of foreigners. By the 1970s, one-fifth of all foreign immigrants to America were settling in California. By 1990, it was one-third. This meant a lot of new people, for the foreign migrant flow into the U.S. had at least tripled, jumping from 400,000 in the early Sixties to a million by the mid-Eighties, plus 300,000-500,000 illegals. According to the state's demographers, California got more than its share. The state's population doubled between 1960 and 1990, reaching 31 million, 8 million, or one-quarter of them, were foreign born. The state's total fertility rate (the average number of births per woman) had been 1.95 in 1982, below long-term replacement level. By 1988 it reached 2.33, driven by rising fertility rates among Asians and especially Hispanics, whose TFR reached 3.5. The California Department of Finance gathered this data, and concluded that "California soon will no longer have a majority population."

These vast changes were not limited to a numerical increase but also produced what one demographer (and CIS Board member) Leon Bouvier described as "shifting shares"—an innocuous and non-inflammatory way to describe rapid ethnoracial shifts in population numbers, and all that flows from that in the way of social advantage and disadvantage, as well as the cultural makeup of the population. In 1970, Anglos and non-Hispanic whites (Census Bureau categories into which people were forced to channel their self-assessment) constituted 77 percent of California's population, and Hispanics 12 percent. By the end of the century these percentages were 56 percent and 26 percent, and Bouvier forecasted that non-Hispanic whites would no longer be a majority in California by 2006. This happened in 1999. Forty percent of Californians did not speak English at home by the end of the century, and more than half the births in the state were to Hispanic mothers. Black Congressman Merv Dymally predicted that a majority of Californians would be "Third World people" by 2000, with the clear implication that this would be a fine thing—progress.

Probably not so fine, Bouvier argued in *Fifty Million Californians?*, published in 1991 by CIS. Under an optimistic "medium" projection assuming falling fertility rates and lower immigration, the state's population would reach 50 million by 2016. If current fertility and immigration rates continued unchanged, the 50 million would be reached by 2111, and 62 million by 2020. The result would be "overcrowded classrooms, clogged freeways, unemployment among the unskilled, cultural clashes, increasingly worse water shortages, environmental decay."

Through the 1970s and 1980s the explosive growth went on, as did the complaints of the growth critics that something must be done— better zoning, better planning, more roads, and more schools—the familiar litany. Efforts to get the "growth control" coalition to think about the brake called immigration restriction were always rebuffed, when not ignored. When rebuffed, the logic was usually muddled. I recall a fellow in Santa Barbara who was an activist and local chapter president for Zero Population Growth. My wife urged him to schedule a group discussion of foreign immigration, and while he agreed that we could not get zero population growth without immigration reduction, he insisted that "it was a diversionary issue for the group's membership at this time," and he would not allow it on the agenda until the "right time had come." But it never did, and he never told us what the right time would be. Mayor Pete Wilson of San Diego, who had made a reputation there for enlightened sponsorship of growth controls, came to Santa Barbara in 1982 while campaigning for the senate. In a cozy living room gathering I asked Pete (whom I had known at Yale and in the Marines) where immigration restriction fit into his strategy for preserving California's environment. He was visibly annoyed at the intrusion of an out-of-bounds idea. He barked something dismissive about "This is Washington's problem," still thinking like the mayor of San Diego.

Ironically, it was that same Pete Wilson who, as governor, became the first politician in statewide office to figure out that immigration was an issue chiefly decided upon in Washington, but that did not mean that state officials could have nothing to say about it. Congress had authorized the immigration and permitted the illegal traffic, and thus the growth, the problems, and costs that came with it. These were well-documented by the State Department of Finance. This was about a decade after he rebuffed my question in Santa Barbara. More on Pete Wilson's learning curve, just ahead.

* * *

So California grew, more orchards were cut down, the suburbs sprawled, the freeways choked to standstills, the air in the LA and even the Bay area basins turned brown with pollutants over the long summers after the spring winds eased. If you were a devoted user of the Sierras, or the beach parks and state forests and lakes, the trend over the faster-growth years arriving in the 1960s was toward crowding, filled campgrounds, and trampled public sites. When I first began hiking the high Sierras in 1966, we drank water directly from the streams, and only in the 1970s heard the term "giardia," an intestinal pest carried to the high lakes and streams in the feces of the mounting numbers of people using the mountains.

However, you don't need to hike high into the Sierras to see evidence of the underlying dynamic of sustained population growth in the U.S. from World War II to today. You have your cherished, once idyllic, now sprawl infected, bumper traffic places, and I have mine—the Harpeth Hills south of Nashville, up whose slopes boxy oversized houses climb like assaulting infantry; the San Francisco Bay area, where I saw in the late 1960s the first blanket of sickly brown smog on the Los Angeles model, and over four decades have seen the snarls of traffic, the Bay shrunk by wetland infill for development; the small-scale little Florida beach towns of Pompano Beach, Lantana, and Delray Beach, separated by green spaces with Miami and its high-risers far to the south, where my family visited every summer in the Fifties, swallowed up now in a continuous northward megalopolis to the east of a clogged Interstate 95. Isolated overgrown places? True, there was no real growth in the Dakotas, and cities in the "rustbelt" like Cleveland, Philadelphia and St. Louis lost population in the 1950s and 1960s. However, the U.S. population grew from 179 million in 1960 to 275 million in 2000, and the growth was almost everywhere—first in California, then the entire Sunbelt from Florida to Oregon, into the Rocky Mountain West, out from Boston and New York into the coasts and inner hills of Vermont and New Hampshire and Maine. The Rockefeller Commission told us in 1972 that 25 percent of that growth was coming from immigration. By 2000, 90 percent of it came from immigration and the nation added 32 million people in the Nineties alone. In California, 100 percent of their population growth came from foreign immigration, and the state added 12 million.

* * *

I left California in 1980 to take up a chaired professor position at the University of North Carolina, but returned to California two to three times a year for extended visits with my children. The superficiality and evasiveness of the discussion in the Golden State of the causes of growth and its related problems was a constant, with rare exceptions.

A crusty rancher and mayor of the town of Santa Maria in the north part of our country, George Hobbs, was quoted in 1989 as saying, "We have a Mexican problem in Santa Maria." He modified this to be "an illegal alien problem" and said it repeatedly, with accompanying illustrations of community pathologies. Hobbs was criticized in the town's newspaper with the usual language reserved for Caucasians who express anything remotely critical about minorities, but he held to his views, which were widely shared in the town, including among Mexican-Americans, who knew they weren't the target of his remarks. Hobbs was re-elected in 1990 with 62 percent of the vote, and again in 1992. In Santa Maria, Latinos are a substantial majority.

His gutsy, politically incorrect frankness was the one exception among public officials, to my knowledge, and thus stood out as the exception that proved the rule. California growth generated issues in the form of environmental damage, traffic congestion, water shortages, school crowding, crime, and strain on social services. These intruded everywhere in local political races and media reporting. But the state that was number one in receiving foreign immigrants was also number one in not talking in the main channels of public discussion about immigration as a contributing cause of any of this.

Chapter Sixteen:
A Turn Against Immigration:
The California Grassroots Rebellion

There are too many people coming into California. Immigration must stop. — Harold Gilliam

My wife, Delores, and I moved back to Santa Barbara in 1989 for a complex set of professional and personal reasons, expecting to find full-throttle growth still unshakably in place, and the immigration connection to growth-related problems a taboo subject. I was surprised to be increasingly wrong about the second. The full-throttle growth was still in place, as it had been as long as I could remember. However, a revolt against the immigration component of growth was taking shape in the southern part of the state, including Santa Barbara, and in the Bay area. I detected a deep and vocalized disgruntlement not present when I left in 1980 or in my frequent visits in the 1980s. It was encountered in discussions among friends, barbers, store clerks, folks at social gatherings, and even to some extent in the local newspaper, which frequently made the immigration connection to any number of social irritants. People seemed more agitated about burgeoning school populations with a lot of non-English speaking students, the appearance of Latino teen gangs in Goleta, neighborhoods in nearby Summerland and Carpinteria where zoning regulations against multi-family occupancy and goat-raising and slaughtering were routinely flouted by some of the Latino population. Friends from Los Angeles and San Diego reported the same sense of community stress from the population growth and its increasingly foreign and Third World sources.

My personal impressions about this change in the public atmosphere were in sharp contrast to another indicator—the news coverage of the region's dominant newspaper, the *Los Angeles Times*. When I returned to the state in the last year of the 1980s, the *Times* was more than usually full of stories depicting Los Angeles as a cauldron of urban problems. The Southland was stressed by crowded and unruly schools unable to hide collapsing educational performance, youth gangs spreading into the suburbs, rising crime rates, housing and water shortages, air and beach pollution. All of these were connected to growing human populations, which implied that they must be connected in some way to the vast surge of foreign immigration running through the Nineties. Of course, part of the smog, traffic, and depletion of water supplies and crowded campgrounds came from the lady from Milwaukee, from me, and from other earlier migrants. There were and had long been, in the words of California Tomorrow, too many of us already. A rising portion of such horde-pressures, and most of the mounting burdens on schools, hospital emergency rooms, gang formation and zoning defiance came from foreign, mostly Mexican immigrants. Yet the state's largest paper, and many other print and electronic news sources, never hinted at any connection between a rising portion of these growing pains and immigration or immigrants.

I remarked about this to a friend in southern California journalism, who offered me a conspiracy theory. The executives at the *Los Angeles Times* had assigned one of the paper's senior editors of Latino heritage, Frank del Olmo, as the "Immigration Exciser." According to this theory, which my friend hinted was more than that, Del Olmo enthusiastically served as the exciser. His job was to disallow and purge reports, allegations or even hints in news stories that whatever the social problem happened to be it didn't have any connection at all with immigrants. He was pictured as sitting at his desk with an oversized pair of scissors (a large Delete button was more likely), cleansing reporters' stories about community and regional pathologies of any immigration connection they might have carried when coming into the editors' cubicles.

Perhaps so. Del Olmo occasionally wrote Op-Eds on the editorial page about the many benefits of both legal and illegal immigration, and bitterly assailed "the bigots" who suggested otherwise. Whatever the mechanisms at work at the *Los Angeles Times*—and at the region's television news stations— there was, as far as I could see from observing these news media, no immigration problem in California (or anywhere else in America) as the 1990s arrived. I served a four-year term on the editorial board of the University of California Press, and the faculty and press had almost nothing to say about immigration in that most impacted state. My university friends generally flinched and changed the subject when I suggested that there was a research agenda going begging there. Minds, even research-oriented and inquisitive minds, along with discussions, snapped shut at any linkage of "immigrants" and "problems."

This was history at work. Immigrants had, back before our time (we had read about this in some book), been unfairly blamed for many alleged bad habits and behavior, which was scapegoating, preliminary to hatred and persecution. That door must never be opened again; not even a crack. At the first whiff of connecting an immigrant to some social problem, slam the door. I witnessed this in a memorable exchange with my friend (and one-time landlord) Wallace Stegner, that marvelous writer, gentleman and friend of the West. Over cocktails at his home in Los Altos we were having the usual genial, lively talk, and Wally was waxing eloquent in condemnation of smog and traffic on the Peninsula. Yet when I suggested that the intensifying traffic all around the Bay had some connection to large-scale immigration, Wally angrily denounced the very suggestion as a scapegoating attack upon the local Mexicans, and went off to the kitchen to calm down. I have seen this reflex many times. The mass media didn't really need a Frank Del Olmo to censor out any linkage of immigrants with school crowding, gang formation, population growth, or the like. Academics and journalists who do social research for a living have walled off an immense sector of society as too "sensitive," and thus professionally risky, for critical scrutiny.

* * *

Yet in the early 1990s the walls around this taboo zone seemed to be weakening, as more discussion of immigration-linked problems broke into the media, if not into discussion in the academy. *The New*

York Times ran a lengthy and probing "background" story on June 16, 1990 on the state's "Uncertain Future as Unskilled Hispanic Work Force Swells," and told of one vision of the future on the minds of many locals.

> *Over the next thirty years…the Hispanic population will swell…*
> *Failed by the schools and stuck in low-paying jobs, Hispanic*
> *youths will become frustrated and angry. Unable to find skilled*
> *labor, industry will flee and California's economy will crumble…*
> *most Latinos will live in squalid towns without paved roads…*
> *[while] retired whites…retreat into walled villages.*

The *Times* account ended on a more optimistic note, in which the state's political establishment finally spends the money to educate Latino youth, and this turns the tide. California emerges as "the paradigm of the 'happy fusion' of diverse cultural elements." This story was a rare exploration of both the severe hazards and the promising possibilities of the Golden State's immigration-driven future. It was not published in California, but brimmed with quotations from Californians who confessed that they had a new level of worries about immigration.

One of the rare scholarly books on immigration's impacts on the state was written and published in the East, the Washington, D.C. based Urban Institute's *The Fourth Wave: California's Newest Immigrants* (1985), by Thomas Muller and Thomas Espenshade. Using data from the 1970s, they concluded that Mexican immigrants "did not increase the aggregate level of unemployment among non-Hispanic California residents" yet "there is evidence of wage depression attributable to immigrants" and "the presence of Mexicans…reduced the average wages in manufacturing and some services," which confirms that "this issue is complicated." So was the question of whether immigrants in the 1970s cost more in services than they paid in taxes, though it appeared that on average Mexican immigrant households (again in the 1970s; the data on which *The Fourth Wave* was based was a full decade behind. They paid $1,425 in taxes compared to the $2,598 paid by other households, mostly because they sent more children to the public schools. The book noted the puzzling fact that one million natives left Los Angeles County over the decade for new homes elsewhere in California or in other states, a rate of outmigration far above other comparable American cities with robust economies. Why did they leave? The data didn't show the answers. Add to that the equally puzzling fact that there was "a virtual halt in net internal migration to southern California" and there may be some relationship to immigration there, for analysis some other day.

If there were any readers left awake after working through this dense and cautious monograph they hadn't been told of any causes for alarm or course correction. California's economy grew, and employers got the workers they needed (i.e., at the lowest wage), legally or illegally. To economists, this was a success story.

* * *

California's Populist Uprising

Then in the early 1990s the public temper in California abruptly changed—or, the changed temper was allowed to break through into mass media and politics.

A major precipitant was economic doldrums. California's economy slid into a steep recession in 1991, and the sunny optimism that had prevailed for so long gave way to worries about the future, both economic and demographic. "Bursting at the Seams" was the title of a story by *San Francisco Chronicle* environmental reporter Harold Gilliam: "The time has come to risk being politically incorrect...and speak the unspeakable. There are too many people coming into California. Immigration must stop." *Time* magazine ran a special issue on November 18, 1991 entitled "California: The Endangered Dream," a collage of pictures of sprawling, treeless housing tracts where there had once been rolling, oak-studded hills; of freeways gridlocked ten lanes wide; "eye-stinging smog, despoiled landscapes, polluted beaches, water shortages, unaffordable housing, crowded schools..." "The state is attracting far more people than it can cope with," *Time* concluded its special issue on growth-related problems. Unlike Gilliam and others, the magazine was not ready to speak the unspeakable, and to make the immigration connection. *Time* apparently had its own Frank del Olmo. Yet even he couldn't entirely purge the *Los Angeles Times* of the immigrant presence in stories on local problems. The rapid growth of the gang population made 1991 a record high year for gang homicides. Del Olmo was either taking a day off or could not prevent the paper's story on this from conceding that "the largest increases in gang homicides have occurred in predominantly Latino communities." Tuberculosis "is rising toward epidemic levels," the paper editorialized on another occasion, and noted that 27 percent of those with TB are foreign born.

By 1993 the Golden State was saying goodbye to more Americans moving out than were moving in—for the first time. The economic recession was the chief reason. What, if anything, did immigrants, legal or otherwise, have to do with this historic reversal of population flows within America? In a major story entitled "California in the Rear View Mirror," *Newsweek* in 1993 made a connection. "In 1992, 200,000 legal and at least 100,000 illegal immigrants settled in the state. Together with their American-born children…these new arrivals accounted for 85 to 90 percent of California's population growth last year. The resulting strain on government is enormous…the immigrant population costs state government $5 billion a year more than it pays in taxes." Better educated workers are leaving, poorly educated ones arrive, and the result is an erosion of the tax base, and a shift of taxation to businesses who then consider moves to Nevada, Oregon, or elsewhere. The state, *Time* concluded, had a strong allure for immigrants, especially from Mexico, but was losing its attraction to Americans to the east, and to some of its own citizens.

* * *

Finally, a Politician Breaks the Silence

The state's troubles in the early Nineties were a grim threat to the political career of first-term Governor Pete Wilson, who had ridden upward to the top office in Sacramento through tours as mayor of San Diego and U. S. Senator. At fifty-eight, he was known to harbor national political ambitions, but the state's economy had gone in the tank, and the California image had turned sour. Wilson had been in favor of unlimited access to Mexican labor for California's growers while a senator, and had the usual liberal outlook on immigration in general. I had learned at that dinner in Santa Barbara, already reported on, when he ruled illegal immigration an undiscussable topic. His view quickly changed during his first term as governor. Surely he read the 1991 *Los Angeles Times* poll that somehow got past del Olmo's scissors and asked a question phrased as "Do you think there are too many foreign immigrants in Los Angeles?" Six of ten Angelenos answered "Yes," and this proportion was essentially the same among Latinos and African-Americans as others.

Whatever these polled citizens based their views upon, the governor had access to alarming figures affecting the state's and thus his future. Tax revenues plummeted during the sharp recession in California, while expenditures on education and social programs surged ahead. Analysis by state officials showed that illegal immigrants were a net fiscal drain on the state treasury, and imposed high costs while paying lower than average taxes. In April 1991, the governor began to complain publicly about the costs of California's millions of illegals. In December, he flew to Washington to ask the federal government to either control the borders or send resources sufficient to compensate the state for this fiscal drain. He provided numbers: three of every ten school children was an illegal immigrant, costing the state $3.6 billion, and other social welfare costs, such as welfare, medical services and prisons, amounted to another $4.8 billion. Wilson's Department of Finance reported that "California's major tax receiver groups—students, welfare recipients, prisoners, and Medi-Cal eligibles—are growing more quickly than its taxpayer group," and "much of this growth" results "from immigration and a recent surge in the birth rate," which was also driven upward by immigration. Other public officials, including the mayor of San Diego and the governors of Florida and New York, began to make the same complaints and asked, or sued, for federal reimbursement. Surely Wilson noticed when a minor candidate for mayor of Los Angeles, Tom Houston, built his campaign (the election came in March 1993) almost entirely on the fiscal and social threats of illegal immigrants, and generated strong populist support and media attention (losing anyway).

Wilson's campaign to publicize the costs of illegal immigrants and shift the costs back to Washington may have helped to weaken the taboo on discussing the negative sides of illegal immigration, though the taboo was vigorous enough to bite him immediately. He was of course labeled by critics as a racist who was scapegoating innocent migrants, and was likened to Louisiana former Klansman David Duke, who had injected the immigration issue into his campaign for governor. Welcome to the unchanging netherworld of immigration policy discourse. No other elected official, certainly not one of Wilson's influence and visibility, had so vigorously stepped out as a critic of our nation's open borders and their costs.

Wilson, demanding federal reimbursement of certain governmental expenditures on illegals, called the intolerable situation in which the state found itself "a budget problem." He did not demand an end to the illegal invasion, saying only that "I'm persuaded that there is a limit to our ability to absorb immigrant populations." Journalist Richard Estrada called this "an historic pronouncement," and with some reason. Wilson's campaign was quite cautious, aimed not at curbing illegal immigration but at securing federal reimbursement of the social costs of immigration. This would not be enough for some Californians, many of them from his San Diego region where the U.S.-Mexican border daily released its northward flow of illegal people.

* * *

The Birth of Proposition 187

Barbara Coe of Huntington Beach, an Anaheim civilian employee of the police department and mother of three, took a friend to an Orange County social services office, and one or both of two things happened, in her account.

"Where am I?" she asked. "I walked into a monstrous room full of people, babies and little children, and I realized nobody was speaking English. What happened here?"

Her friend could not qualify for the requested service, she reported, but apparently the Hispanics in the room, many of whom she suspected of being illegal, moved through the system and received some form of welfare benefit. She allied herself with a sympathetic retired Border Patrol officer frustrated with noninforcement of immigration laws, and called a meeting in Costa Mesa where forty people showed up to hear a local Assemblyman welcome their activism. Coe formed the California Council for Immigration Reform, and the numbers and energy rose. Other groups were coming together at the same time in Orange County and San Diego, such as Glenn Spencer's American Patrol, and The Citizens' Voice in Monterrey Park.

I heard that citizen groups had formed in Orange County to combat illegal immigration, and knew of one in Marin. Then I received a call from "down south" asking if I would join other speakers in a "seminar" (it turned out to be quite large) organized by a group called "The Stamp Out Crime Council," based in San Diego. The action was there, not in Santa Barbara, so I accepted the invitation in order to educate myself about the front lines, and the people who were willing to hold meetings on this issue. One local made a special impression on me, Peter Nunez, a poised, affable and tough-minded law professor at a local university who had served in the Justice Department during the early Reagan years. His Hispanic identity was evident but never emphasized by him. I kept his phone number.

I have my notes from the talk I gave, in which I ended by endorsing a recent *Time* magazine statement: "The main problem underlying California's malaise is simple. The state is attracting far more people than it can cope with." The visit was indeed educational. My talk was of average quality by my standards, but the audience stood up to cheer, and one person shouted, "Run that man for president." A greater impression was made on me by the small mob outside, composed of Latinos with signs and angry gestures to match. There was ethnoracial hostility there, and it was outside the meeting, not inside. *La Prensa San Diego* ran a story on my talk the next day, announcing that "Eugenicist Keynote Speaker at Stamp Out Crime Seminar!"

"Dr. Graham, in his writings has made it clear that he is an Eugenicist [I had never written so much as one line on eugenics] who believes that America must purge itself of 'foreigners,' and his ideology 'sounds familiar' and 'was the basis for Hitler's policies of…creating a Super White Aryan Race.'" The conventional wisdom held that ignorant bigots (white) would come forward if immigration became a public issue. I was learning that ignorant brown bigots came forward, sure enough. The language on the outside of the San Diego meeting was saturated with ethnic hatred, yet I heard none of it inside.

After this experience and others, and as the only Californian on the Board of Directors of FAIR, I urged the board to move its next meeting to the West Coast, where something important seemed to be happening and the board ought to observe it. John Tanton was possibly, indeed very probably ahead of me.

"With the intense interest there is in Southern California," he wrote in a board memo I found in my files dated November 1991, "the time has come to play to our strengths by setting up a vigorous field operation there. I think it's time to go to the people…"

We convened in San Diego at the Del Coronado Hotel on Coronado Island, and invited as many local FAIR members as we could locate. When we held such meetings with members in Naples, Florida, where board member Sidney Swensrud wintered, our members had been overwhelmingly retired, white, affluent, and often at least as interested in talking about their golf game as the facts about immigration trends. They were happy to listen to FAIR staffers and board brief them on the Washington battlefront, but lived in gated communities, had no children in the local schools, and weren't angry.

In San Diego, we had not brought the battlefront from Washington. We had arrived at the battlefront. The core of those in attendance, FAIR members from the area, were mostly over fifty and white. This time the group was substantially augmented by local activists we had been able to reach through networks, and they had a different look and tone. There were many younger Californians, several blacks and a substantial representation of Latinos. All were angry and ready to tell us about the problem of runaway illegal immigration as they experienced it. Their stories were local—schools, like Belmont High in Los Angeles (I recall this example) overwhelmed by 2,000 illegal students, many non-English speaking, in a student body of 4,500; multiple families crowded into apartments or small homes, vacant lot "hiring halls" where young males clustered in large numbers, using trees and hedges for toilets. The tone was quite more serious than our earlier meetings with members in Florida or Texas. Nobody at that meeting talked about golf. Some didn't come as FAIR members, but as the organizers of activist groups in their own neighborhoods. Here I met the intense, diminutive, fearless, hard-edged Barbara Coe, whose Orange County-based organization CCIR put out an angry, patriot-oriented newsletter complaining of "invasion" and informed its readers of the reconquista rhetoric of Hispanic militants; Glenn Spencer, founder of the military-sounding American Patrol which was in fact another of these suburban and middle-aged networks; Black school teacher, Ezola Foster and her husband; outspoken Latino Jesse Laguna, with a flair for Op-Ed writing to local newspapers.

We from FAIR had two questions as in the early part of 1992 we visited this part of the American "grassroots" that was most energized. "What is happening out here?" was the first. As always, when we went to the grassroots, a question for ourselves was, Can we work with these people, or are they, especially the leadership, temperamentally or in other ways likely to produce more negatives for the reform movement than positives? The multi-racial composition of the group was encouraging, as was the relative youth, and the absence of crazies (so far as I could tell). We sensed the energy and the fermenting of a grassroots rebellion, and decided to open a California office in Sacramento, hoping to focus statewide reform energies on state and local politics.

As I recall, our meeting in San Diego came shortly before an event that notified the entire nation that California was encountering intense assimilation problems. This was the Los Angeles riots of April 29 to May 4, 1992. A jury in Sylmar, California cleared of charges of police brutality three (of four) LAPD officers seen on television beating a black fugitive, Rodney King, in 1991. For three days, violence and mayhem paralyzed parts of Los Angeles, leaving over fifty killed, 4,000 injured, and $1 billion in property damage.

What did this have to do with immigration? The violence for the most part did not take the form of black assaults upon white police personnel or white neighborhoods, but black-brown (and some Korean grocer) conflicts, with whites on the far suburban periphery. Televised riot scenes allowed the nation to see that Los Angeles, the American city most shaped by immigration (unless one nominated Miami), could quickly become a cauldron of racial and ethnic hostility. Some commentators, without excusing black rioters, pointed out that blacks and browns "were forced to compete for scarce economic and social goods," especially "jobs traditionally filled by black Americans," in the words of UCLA economist James Johnson. Confidence in California's assimilative capacities hit a low point. We Californians "must now watch Los Angeles become the Yugoslavia of U.S. cities, disestablishing itself into a murderous mosaic of warring parts," wrote state historian Kevin Starr after the riots.

* * *

That spring, FAIR opened a Sacramento office staffed by former INS Commissioner Alan Nelson, a Republican with a passion to establish control of the border and enforce IRCA, and Helen Graham, who had for years headed a tenacious growth-control group in Sacramento called Californians For Population Stabilization (CAPS). Nelson reported that politicians in the state capital were feeling the heat from what one California paper called "a fast-growing network of activist groups" across the state, helped by FAIR to "spread the message that illegal immigration costs taxpayers billions of dollars." Prior to this, in 1991-92, the only bills before the state legislature had to do with "immigrants' rights," but by 1994 there were twenty bills on curtailing the use of social services by illegal immigrants, most of them written with Nelson's help. The FAIR California office claimed to have nurtured immigration reform groups in Sherman Oaks, Marin County and San Francisco, with signs of activism in places like Petaluma, Redding, and San Jose.

* * *

California Voters Join in the Job of Controlling Illegal Immigration

By this time, the "Turn" had already commenced. We Washington-based FAIR people were intensely interested onlookers, trying to keep track of the growing list of California immigration reform groups, which reached about fifty. Then the locals acted. On Oct. 5, 1992, a group of activists and former immigration officials who had formed a network built around phone calls and e-mail, met in Costa Mesa. They included Barbara Coe, Ron Prince, an accountant from Tustin, political consultants Barbara and Robert Kiley of Huntington Beach, Al Nelson, former INS Western Director Hal Ezell, and others. Here, over an extended breakfast that lasted all day, they wrote a ballot proposition that required 600,000 signatures to become Proposition 187, dubbed SOS or Save Our State. They were undoubtedly encouraged in choosing this path of action by earlier successful state initiatives nurtured by John Tanton, establishing English as the official state language in California, Colorado, Florida and Arizona.

Prop. 187, declaring that "the People of California have suffered and are suffering economic hardships caused by the presence of illegal aliens in this state," was intended to set up a system to verify the immigration status of every person using public education, health care, and other public benefits. Trafficking in false documents was made a state felony, and persons "determined or reasonably suspected" by state social service and/or educational institutions of being in illegal status should be so notified and their names reported to the INS and the state Attorney General.

The network of activist reform groups then began a drive to gain the required signatures (600,000), and with little money, sought publicity wherever it could be found. Coe organized hundreds of supporters to drive to the border south of San Diego at night and illuminate the fences with their headlights. The California Secretary of State confirmed that more than the necessary signatures had been submitted in October 1993. The people were proposing to pass a law, since their elected representatives wouldn't.

I had my doubts about several aspects of 187, as did most of the FAIR board, while endorsing the general intent. It was one thing to strictly deny access to welfare, public housing and other benefits to people illegally in the country. A question could be raised about including certain health services where infectious disease epidemics might threaten. A more important concern was that Prop. 187 as drafted brought the public schools into the effort to control immigration, and teachers' and principals' complaints that they didn't want to be policemen would resonate with most voters.

"It's a real shame that the K-12 provisions are in the SOS initiative," Dan Stein wrote to his board.

There were also concerns about constitutionality, since the Supreme Court in a 1982 Texas case, *Plyler v. Doe,* had disallowed efforts in that state to deny public education to illegals. The situation in California involved far higher fiscal costs, and even lawyers opposed to 187 conceded that the court might be ready to overrule the Texas case.

These were design quibbles after the fact. Proposition 187 was now written, and, unlike legislation, was beyond modification. It would be voted on. Could it pass, given the array of forces? Its supporters had little money, and were merely citizens with no statewide name recognition and no institutional backing. The gathering opposition, by contrast, was a formidable and well-funded coalition—teachers' unions and educators generally, social service unions, the California Medical Association, the clergy, with the Catholic hierarchy in the forefront, most elected officials, most newspapers, and of course, the shrill voices of ethnic advocates who claimed persecution. The state's elites were solidly aligned behind the conviction that Prop. 187 was a terrible idea and the status quo—the easy availability of social services to illegal immigrants at taxpayers' expense—was just fine. The opposition was lavishly funded. The supporters were ordinary citizens, and their coalition, United We Stand America-California, claimed 200,000 members. Their leadership struggled to raise funds for the petition drive and media ads. FAIR was pressed to endorse the measure and to send financial help.

FAIR waffled a bit, unhappy at the prospect of aiming scarce resources at what looked like a losing battle. We then made the right choice (in my view), or some would say the only choice under the circumstances. We announced support for 187, rather later than the activists liked, and made a monetary contribution, rather less than they wanted.

I was asked to analyze the situation for a Santa Barbara group, and matched my endorsement of the goal with my reservations about the proposed remedies, most notably the involvement of schools in certifying immigration status.

"Then why are you for it?," asked a man from the back.

I paused. So he answered his own question.

"To send them a message?"

I nodded. Everybody in the room, it seemed, nodded vigorously. Send them a message.

* * *

What had happened in California had never happened anywhere in the U.S. during the three decades of mass immigration that had commenced in the 1960s. For the first time, the issue escaped the control of society's elites, and thrust itself from the grassroots upward into the mass media. Then it stormed into politics and radically altered policy—for a short, dramatic season.

Early polls showed 187 to be very popular, even with Hispanics. The *Los Angeles Times* polled Latinos and found 61 percent considered illegal immigration to be a major problem, and a columnist for the paper in September, 1994, suggested that Latino leaders critical of the measure "may be out of step with their communities." If so, they intended to whip their communities into line. A strident and well-funded campaign to demonize the leaders and goal of the proposition was launched by a coalition of all the educational, social service, religious and political leadership of the state. After weeks of ads emphasizing that the Proposition was "anti-Latino," when in fact it was intended to protect California's Latino (and all other) citizens from the costs of illegal and uncontrolled Third World labor flows, the Latino polls showed some erosion of support.

Then Governor Wilson changed the dynamics. Blamed for the economic slump the state was experiencing, the governor was trailing his attractive opponent, former Governor Pat Brown's daughter, Kathleen Brown, by twenty points in the polls. In April, 1994,

Wilson, who as senator had been a reliable supporter of guestworker programs for California agriculture, became the state's lead critic of illegal immigration by suing the federal government. They sought reimbursement of $2.3 billion for educational, welfare and prison costs due to illegal immigrants. His was not the only voice of complaint. Senator Diane Feinstein estimated that illegal workers were causing some part of the estimated 1.3 million unemployed Californians. The *San Francisco Chronicle* in March editorialized that "not since the 1920s has the debate been so inflamed and the pot for restrictionist legislation so ripe." In an extensive series on "The Immigration Backlash" in March and April, 1994, the paper found "the most intense public resentment in seventy years" directed against the immigration Expansionist coalition and politicians who voted with them. It was noted that other states such as Virginia, Iowa, and Nevada reflected California's mood.

During April, 1994, Wilson announced his endorsement of Prop. 187, calling it "the two-by-four we need" to get the federal government's attention. "People are unhappy about the impact on schools," Wilson frequently said, "and unhappy as taxpayers." One of his campaign ads depicted shadowy figures sprinting up the edges of a freeway running north from a border crossing, with the language, "They just keep coming." Wilson's comments through the campaign were a masterful blend of blaming politicians in Washington, D.C. for not defending California's borders, and a scrupulous refusal to make critical comments about the illegal immigrants themselves. He complained of fiscal costs in schools and social services, not of crime, community crowding, or failure to assimilate.

The opposition had nothing constructive to say about the issue of the fiscal costs of illegal immigration or how to enforce immigration law in a better way, but depicted the backers of 187 as racists and xenophobes.

"It's angry, it's ugly, and it's scary. The political atmosphere is charged with hate," said MALDEF's director of immigration programs.

As for Wilson's opponent, Kathleen Brown, she made an early error from which she never recovered. She drafted a speech in which illegal immigration was conceded to be a problem, but one for which Prop 187 was not the solution. Then at a planning session at her home she was intimidated by fierce complaints from Latino politicians, and inserted language saying illegal immigration was "wrongly seen as a cause" of California's problems. Her poll numbers fell sharply.

Voices of Hatred

I have in my files a number of the newsletters turned out by groups behind Prop. 187. The largest circulation probably belonged to Barbara Coe's CCIR newsletter, "9-1-1," distributed from Huntington Beach. It listed over twenty affiliated organizations, including Asian-Americans for Border Control, the Bay Area Coalition for Immigration Reform, and Stop Immigration Now! from Long Beach. She claimed 12,000 members for her CCIR, Americans who "are an ethnically diverse group representing members of every race, creed, color and religion," an "activist group" with a focus on media, peaceful demonstrations, and conferences. The newsletter provided a compilation of the immigration control activists' worries—"invasion," crime, social costs, and unresponsive local governments. They usually bent over backward to depict themselves as broadly inclusive in their memberships, not a solid white phalanx, and the "Letters to the Editor" section of southern California newspapers reflected this.

"I consider myself an American," wrote Hispanic Art Jacques to a southern California newspaper, "not a Mexican-American or any of those hyphenated names. Illegal immigrants are keeping a lot of these advocacy groups in a job."

"Latinos want a tighter border, too," wrote San Diegan Jesse Laguna in the *Los Angeles Times*.

Early polls confirmed this support for a tighter border among Hispanics, and this wasn't surprising, said writer Richard Estrada in the same paper. Farm worker union leader Cesar Chavez in the 1970s had called illegals from Mexico "a serious problem" for American agricultural workers of Hispanic descent, Estrada recalled. The current "self-proclaimed Latino leaders" from MALDEF and La Raza, he charged, ignored the economic interests of Latinos in order to build their own ethnic power base. Black voices were also heard in favor of 187.

"This isn't immigration," said James Coleman in an Op-Ed in the *Los Angeles Times,* identifying himself as an African-American. "This is an invasion, and you're paying for it."

The newsletters of the 187 groups were also a source of information on the public statements and tone of the Hispanic part of the anti-187 coalition. This was because newsletter editors on the 187 side ran short of material to galvanize their troops, and tended to repeat themselves. They soon found that they could gather and re-print what the Latino leadership was saying, by monitoring newsletters, pamphlets, media reports of public statements, and even attending meetings. In the case of a large meeting at UC Riverside, they taped the proceedings.

Much of this discourse must indeed have galvanized the 187 troops.

"We may not overcome, but we will overwhelm," Assemblyman Xavier Hermosillo was quoted as saying before the California Assembly in September,1992.

"We will take you over, house by house, and block by block." Prop. 187 "is the last gasp of White America," said the Honorable Art Torres, in what must have been his most widely quoted public statement (I have not tried to confirm these two statements, which have been widely quoted and never disavowed).

"Fuck you all, you are dead," came in a letter received at Barbara Coe's office and reprinted to the edification of her 12,000 members. "We're going to take your country whether you like it or not…187 continues the historic attempts at genocide against our people by the European colonizers. 187 is a declaration of WAR against the Mexican people in the militarily occupied northern half of our Mexican nation," were the opening lines of the lead article in the *Journal of Anti-Racist Activism* out of Burbank, in December, 1994.

A poster for a "*marcha*" in late 1992 commemorating "500 years of Raza Resistance" listed the location as San Ysidro Park in "San Diego, Califaztlan." *Voz Fronteriza,* published on the San Diego campus of the University of California, showed Governor Wilson's face framed in the cross-hairs of a rifle scope.

Welcome, you temporary Anglo occupiers of California, to the tone and style of Latin American politics, exported to el Norte in order to reclaim it.

* * *

A Case Study of 187 Politics in Santa Barbara

The immigration reform group in Santa Barbara that I became acquainted with was overwhelmingly Caucasian, with one Hispanic and a sprinkling of blacks. Most memorable of the latter was a large man named Stan who often expressed his resentment at being called a racist for advocating the rule of law in immigration matters. The leadership came primarily from Deborah Sutherland, an attractive, self-described "parent of a child that was in the elementary public school system who did an array of volunteer jobs within the school," as she wrote in an unpublished memoir. Debbie "became alarmingly aware of the negative impact that recent immigrant children were making on the learning process in the classroom"—crowding, high illiteracy among non-English speaking children even in the upper grades, and a certain amount of ethnic physical intimidation. When the local Catholic charities association petitioned the Santa Barbara City Council to officially oppose 187, without holding hearings or findings of fact, Sutherland, now joined by a local activist and later CAPS president, Diana Hull, formed a group to persuade the City Council to remain neutral. By this time Debbie had learned of FAIR and of me, and so I was invited to the meeting in which Sutherland's mostly school-mother gathering with signs urging "Take no position on 187," were shouted at with epithets of "bigots, racists, immigrant bashers and xenophobes." The shouters were young Latino males. The pro-187 placard carriers were mostly female, with a few middle-aged husbands among them. One dimension of 187 politics that wasn't much commented on was the far larger role of females on the 187 side.

Sutherland and Hull's Santa Barbara County Immigration Reform Coalition, which they described as representing "all age groups, incomes, races and political ideologies," was female led. They were buoyed by a rally at which former Senator Eugene McCarthy told them they were right and that he regretted his vote for the 1965 Immigration Act. They ran a newspaper ad urging the school board not to take the official position against 187 that had been demanded by Latino activists, and

211

they received threatening phone calls, remonstrated with the editorial board of the local newspaper because of biased coverage and non-coverage. They "made every effort to be non-inflammatory," in Debbie's words (found in her "Anatomy of a Grassroots Campaign for California's Prop. 187," a research paper for a class at UC Santa Barbara)." It was a time when Debbie Sutherland served dinners to her family at 10:00 p.m., after endless phone conversations and meetings.

I once told her, "You didn't miss the Sixties. This, now, is a social movement, and you're in it."

Looking back, Debbie Sutherland wrote of her observations during and after the battle. The opposition had charged the 187 proponents with arousing harmful emotions, but the inflammatory language, the "white supremacist" and "racist" labeling, was all on one side. A Republican, she readily put forward a "taxpayer vs. unions and special interest groups" explanation of the central dynamic of conflict. What should have been a debate about illegal immigration and how best to control it, she thought, became a war between "the individual taxpayer and large professional organizations...whose very jobs depend on the taxpayer." This accounted for the funding mismatch, with the California Teachers Association, the California Government Employment Association, and other groups drawing their payroll from services to immigrant populations contributing, along with ethnic lobbies and even the government of Mexico, to the anti-187 campaign.

* * *

Despite the polls, I expected the 187 campaign to be narrowly defeated on election day by the well-financed opposition representing the state's elite leadership and institutions in politics, education, social services, religion, and ethnic activism. But that side made a huge blunder, just as the election neared. In October, a massive anti-187 march of 65,000 (by police estimate; more, organizers said) people in Los Angeles was captured in color by all the state's newspapers and television media. Emotional, angry rhetoric accompanying the march must have offended some, but the coverage depicted something more powerful—a sea of colorful national flags from Mexico, Salvador, Guatemala and other Latin American countries predominating in and above the procession, and the American flag frequently carried upside down. Placards compared 187 to Hitler's racial laws; depicted Governor Wilson as a pig, and he was hung in effigy.

Signs read: "Go Back to Europe...Pilgrims Go Home...We Will Overwhelm You...We Were Here First!"

The Los Angeles march communicated nothing about 187, and everything about what mass immigration was bringing to California. Newspapers that month also carried the vigorous denunciation of 187 by a top Mexican government official, a blatant and much resented intervention in U.S. internal affairs.

* * *

Proposition 187 passed on November 8 by a margin of 59-41 percent.

"We done it!" read the headline on Barbara Coe's newsletter.

Underfunded, ordinary citizen David slew Goliath, or so it seemed. California Secretary of State campaign spending reports showed that $4 million was spent by those opposing the proposition, and $284,000 in support. These slippery figures do not include "in-kind contributions" of "free" media activities, where FAIR's paid ads went up against those of an impressive lineup of well-funded and mobilized educational, social welfare and ethnic organizations.

Then Goliath got back on his feet, and did David in. Lawsuits by MALDEF, Lulac, the ACLU and others were immediately filed, and a restraining order was issued on November 11 by a federal judge. At issue was a 5-4 1982 Supreme Court ruling in *Plyler v. Doe* that public education is guaranteed to all children in the U.S., legal or otherwise. Supporters of 187 were eager to test that ruling, believing that in 1982 Congress had not spoken emphatically on illegal immigration but did so in the IRCA law of 1986. The legal argument that Prop. 187 passed constitutional muster was made in a leisurely fashion by the state's unenthusiastic Republican Attorney General. An adverse decision came in 1997, and it was up to him to carry an appeal to the Supreme Court. This did not happen. Attorney General Daniel Lundgren unaccountably delayed, then Democrat Gray Davis was elected Governor in 1998, and the defense of the people's choice, 187, was dropped. There would be no Supreme Court reconsideration of the 1982 *Plyler v. Doe* decision. Proposition 187 had been voted into law, and then disqualified by two federal judges, without higher review. Elites seemed to have easily regained control after a populist outburst.

But was the immigration backlash cat now out of the bag, dashing unleashed onto the stage of American politics?

Chapter Seventeen:
Would the Rest of America Follow California?

Proposition 187 should be just the starting point. Immigration policy as a whole must be revised... The very identity of America is at stake. — Mortimer Zuckerman, Editor in Chief, *U. S. News and World Report*

Despite the blockage of 187, we restrictionists had good reason to believe by November, 1994, that the immigration issue had finally made a decisive turn our way, not only in California but across the country. In December 1994, FAIR held an awards dinner and post-SOS briefing session in Los Angeles for the key activists involved in the 187 effort. An emotional salute was given to Al Nelson and the other drafters of 187.

There was much evidence to support our sense of having seized the momentum. The media conveyed reports of citizens and politicians in other states, especially Florida and Texas, discussing the initiation of their own 187s.

The Editor-in-Chief of U. S. News and World Report, Mortimer Zuckerman, wrote at the end of 1994: "Californians have put immigration firmly on the national agenda." He meant *all* immigration. "Today, legal immigration is as much out of control as illegal...the difference is that it has not been politically correct to discuss legal immigration. Proposition 187 should be just the starting point. Immigration policy as a whole must be revised...The very identity of America is at stake."

These words were from an elite journalist in an elite journal of news and opinion. There was "grassroots anger" in places east of California—in Florida, Virginia, Iowa, and Nevada, reported the *San Francisco Chronicle*. The situation now is "very volatile," Senator Feinstein was quoted in the paper's "Immigration Backlash" series in March, 1994. We find "the most intense public resentment in seventy years" against the 'well mobilized immigration advocacy in Washington.'" The *Washington Post* after the 187 vote editorialized that "the failure of the federal government to control illegal immigration…has produced a backlash in the states" and these states "do have a genuine problem." The criticism from the states is "legitimate," and not "racism or xenophobia."

Prop. 187 "has profoundly altered the political environment in which we are working," Dan Stein told the FAIR board in early 1995. He and other staff could go on talk radio for five hours without receiving a single dissenting phone call. Dan agreed with Republican party head Haley Barbour in predicting that "immigration will be a major campaign issue for the 1996 presidential election."

* * *

Apart from the possibility of more California-style populist rebellions in other states, the immigration issue rode forward in the early 1990s on deep currents of public concern over the consequences of globalization. America's elites in and outside both political parties were wedded to internationalist values, were cosmopolitan and multicultural in outlook, attached to the expansion of free trade and the rapid and easy movement of people, ideas and projects across national borders. They pushed ahead in the early 1990s with NAFTA, despite deep-seated public worries over job loss and the erosion of the industrial base.

Beyond the news of industrial relocation abroad, and high unemployment and job insecurity among Americans (especially, in the early 1990s, in California), other events added to the public's worries. Foreigners crossing American borders gave us the World Trade Center bombing in 1992, the repeated stories of Chinese smuggling vessels entering American waters and ports, Haitian boat people, and Cuban raft people landing on Florida's beaches. In 1993, President Clinton nominated Zoe Baird as Attorney General, and her candidacy crashed upon the discovery that she employed illegal immigrants in her home. This elite female lawyer had forgotten that illegal immigrants were not just cheap help, but were illegally in the country, and that employing them was against the law. A daily occurrence in millions of American households had crushed a nationally-visible career.

* * *

Citing these developments, journalist Roberto Suro wrote in his *Watching America's Door* (1996), that "the U.S. reached a turning point (on immigration), beginning in 1993…" He noted, among the other signs of this, the handful of politicians with national ambitions who occasionally experimented with criticism of a broken immigration system as a winning topic, not necessarily a "third rail" to be scrupulously avoided.

Ross Perot muscled his way into national politics again in September 1996, forming the Reform Party out of remnants of the 1993 United We Stand America Party, and invited an open competition for the party's presidential nomination. The immigration dimension of his shifting message was minor and often invisible. USAP groups in California had been staunch supporters of Prop. 187, and to the extent that they flowed into the Reform Party, Perot's base could be expected to be strongly for restrictionist on immigration. Research was to confirm this. In *The State of the Parties*, (1999), edited by John Green and Daniel M. Shea, it was found that of the eleven top issues to Reform Party activists, control and reduction of immigration ranked second among their concerns, behind only reduction of the deficit.

It was not clear whether Ross Perot was aware of this, and if so, how he would handle this concern at the grassroots. We had ideas on this, but Ross had the reputation of being extremely secretive and all but impossible to reach. I was invited to participate in a "United We Stand America" (the official 187 support group) meeting in June, 1994, in Buena Park, California, and met Cordelia Spicer, Perot's "National Issues Coordinator." She expressed to me strong sympathy for "our position," and the hope that Ross would listen more carefully and sympathetically to Dick Lamm. I passed this on to Dick, who made unsuccessful efforts to meet with Ross to discuss immigration. This

217

seemed disappointing at the time, but in retrospect, it isit's difficult to imagine anyone influencing Ross Perot's thinking on anything. I had a go at it, and failed completely.

I am calling him Ross because I knew him as an older classmate at the Patty Hill School in Texarkana, Arkansas, from 1940 to 1943, where he was a buddy of my brother Fred, and his sister, Bette, traded frequent "sleepovers" with my older sister Jenny. When the FAIR board learned of this, they urged me to visit Ross and reinforce his negative leanings on the immigration situation. I wrote to him in the summer of 1997, and Spicer or someone on his staff told me he was enthusiastic about seeing me and catching up on family trajectories. I went to Dallas intending to urge him to expand his infrequent denunciations of our porous borders to include substantial immigration reform proposals in his overall program.

Before seeing Ross I was closeted with Russ Verney, his handler, who listened to my immigration reform views without comment. Then Ross would see me, in his offices taking up an entire floor in a conspicuous white tower on the rim of Dallas. Ross strode vigorously out to greet me, and we began what turned out to be half an hour visit. He consumed much time with gossip about our families, and insisted that I accompany him down the hall to his sister Bette's office to talk about my sister Jenny Margaret. Most of the talk was by Ross, and was superficial. Finally, I told him that I had come to urge him to give more concentrated attention to the larger immigration reform agenda, and I offered to connect him with wise counselors on how to do this, including a role for Dick Lamm. At that moment Verney appeared at the door, and announced that Ross had a television interview only minutes away. Was his intervention at this point an accident? I was cordially and quickly escorted out, with no invitation to be in contact later. I lamented to Richard Estrada later that day in his office at the *Dallas Morning Herald* that this professor had flunked in his effort to educate Ross on immigration politics. Richard would have none of my sense of missed opportunity.

He said, "One does not educate Ross Perot."

And no one but Ross Perot would be allowed to lead the Reform Party. Dick Lamm entered the contest for the party's 2000 presidential nomination, but Ross wouldn't permit a fair contest, and seized the nomination himself. In his campaign, he had virtually nothing to say about immigration. He also did not do nearly so well as in 1992, collecting only 8.4 percent of the 1996 vote. Ross Perot had failed his country.

My track record in persuading powerful political figures whom I knew personally to rethink their immigration position was now a dismal zero. I had a chance to educate Walter Mondale at a small dinner party at Sally Gamble Epstein's home in the early 1980s. Others were there, and Mondale always changed the subject. I couldn't get Pete Wilson to even discuss the issue at a Santa Barbara gathering later in the decade, and then Ross Perot had blathered his way past this issue when I raised it in Dallas. Not an impressive performance by me, over the years. I suppose that, as politicians, they all assumed that I "had no constituency."

* * *

But this gets a bit ahead of the story.

Some elected politicians at the national level seemed to read the winds of the early 1990s as we did. Public opinion polls registered rising criticism of the immigration status quo. A *Newsweek* poll in 1993 found that 60 percent of Americans wanted immigration reduced; a CNN/USA Today poll recorded 76 percent in favor of stopping immigration until the economy improves, and a Latino National Political Survey in late 1992 found seven out of ten thought that too many immigrants were entering the U.S. In 1993, Senator Harry Reid ((Democrat, Nevada) introduced the "Immigration Stabilization Act" drafted by FAIR—a comprehensive reform of legal immigration with "a real ceiling" of 300,000. FAIR's preferred legislation was an outright "moratorium" except for immediate family members of U.S. citizens, embodied in bills introduced in 1995 by Senator Shelby of Alabama and Republican Stump of Arizona Stump and his sixty-six co-sponsors of a moratorium proposed that it be lifted only when the president could report to Congress that illegal immigration had been reduced to 10,000 entries a year.

"If someone had told me twenty-four months ago that the things which have happened would have happened," Dan Stein wrote in August, 1993, "I would have said, impossible."

FAIR's proposals were now in the legislative game, with House and Senate sponsors who had sought the organization's advice. In that year, President Clinton admitted publicly that "our borders leak like a sieve," and this "cannot be permitted to continue in good conscience." Toward the end of the summer, Dan had his one-on-one meeting with Attorney General Janet Reno, who asked for "an ongoing dialogue with me." She was taking the lead position as the Clinton administration signaled that it would toughen its stance on illegal immigration. In 1994, Reno went to Los Angeles to unveil Operation Gatekeeper, an aggressive effort to seal the border in the San Diego sector, utilizing a system of high-tech barriers and a fourteen mile fence which became so successful that illegal traffic began to shift toward Arizona. Reno also bragged to the media about the administration's "unprecedented levels of federal aid" to help California and other border states with security.

After his meeting with Reno, Dan's spirits buoyed, and he wrote to the board in October, "There has been a sea change in American public opinion," and "eventually, the moratorium will be the answer."

This turned out to be too optimistic, but the beginnings of a significant shift could be detected even in elite opinion, here and there. Historian John Higham, author of the most influential critique of the earlier restrictionist movement, was quoted in the press as believing that it was time for moderate restrictions today to head off "an explosive negative reaction" later. Writing in the aftermath of Prop. 187, Hispanic journalist Roberto Suro noted "a new political landscape marked by torrents of citizen anger," and predicted decisive policy change toward limits on immigration.

Harvard sociologist and respected authority on ethnic matters in America, Nathan Glazer, wrote in a 1993 article in *Current* entitled "The Closing Door," "Clearly we are at the beginning of a major debate on immigration." The restrictionist case is gaining adherents, and "we are too prone to label them racists. An attachment to a country more like what it once was, a preference for a less populated country, are not ignoble." Indeed, the larger public "is now modestly restrictionist," though the policy elites ignore them, and repeatedly enlarge the legal flow and ignore the illegal. "It seems we have insensibly reverted to mass immigration, without ever having made a decision to do so."

At this moment of marked opinion shifts on the issue, former Congresswoman Barbara Jordan was chairing the early meetings of her Commission on Immigration Reform. Reform was in her commission's congressional charge, and could be felt as a growing sentiment from coast to coast. Reform still meant bringing illegal immigration under control and shifting legal immigration away from kinship selection and toward lower numbers.

* * *

Looking back, people like Dan Stein, Suro, and the congresspersons drafting restrictive legislation had reasons for their anticipation of a decisive turn in a restrictionist direction. Public sentiment by many measures had hardened against uncontrolled immigration. Again, those who welcomed this were giving too much weight to public opinion, and underestimating the Expansionists' control of congressional as well as White House politics.

A hint of the difficulties ahead came just weeks after Governor Wilson and Prop. 187 gained their victories. Two East Coast Republican figures, writer-pundit William Bennett and former Congressman Jack Kemp, visited California after the vote and gravely warned that Wilson's support for a measure to restrain illegal immigration threatened to "turn the [Republican] party away from its belief in opportunity, jobs, and growth, and turn the party inward to a protectionist, isolationist, and more xenophobic party." Whose idea was this, and who did they speak for?

In 1994, the Republican Party was split several ways on immigration, and the political convulsions in California had made a deep impression. Washington Editor of *The Social Contract*, Roy Beck, analyzed the immigration position of ten "national profile leaders" of the Republican Party in an article in *National Review* in July 1994. He started with the finding of a survey of the Republican National Committee in late 1993 that grassroots party activists polled 5 to 1 that immigration levels were too high. And the ten leaders? Two, Buchanan and Dole, agreed with that poll, but two others thought the grassroots activists were quite wrong, and six others dodged the question. Was resistance to illegal immigration a third rail, or a magic bullet? GOP National Chairman Haley Barbour declared in January, 1995 that illegal immigration would be a major issue in the 1996 elections, lending no support to Bennett and Kemp.

Wilson had just won a massive victory after trailing his opponent by as much as twenty-three percentage points. All conceded that his comeback was mostly because of his stance on illegal immigration. To turn this into a huge political mistake, as Bennett and Kemp proposed, seemed preposterous, as Wilson triumphantly began his second term as Governor of the nation's largest state. Yet the two eastern Republican figures had commenced the interpretive spin with a formidable ideological volley. Firmness on immigration law enforcement, they said, would put Republicans on a road away from free trade, internationalism, and growth, and toward protectionism, xenophobia, and the destruction of the Republican Party.

Who would answer this? Wilson, back East attending a Governor's Conference, jabbed back at Bennett and Kemp: "We really don't need any lectures from anyone outside of California," especially two easterners who seem confused about the difference between illegal immigrants, the target of 187, and legal immigrants, who have made "vast contributions" and themselves probably "voted for 187." Wilson clearly had a better grip on the rhetoric of immigration politics than any other Republican leader willing to address the issue. We in the restrictionist movement thought the scolding of Wilson by the two uninvited eastern Republicans an odd mission and easily rebuffed. He was a successful campaigner who had shown that control of illegal immigration was a winning issue, if done right, and had no necessary connection with all those negative, world-denying impulses the easterners invoked. Wilson had presidential ambitions, and would have the opportunity in Republican primaries leading up to the 1996 election to teach his party how to fold immigration reform into their general outlook, if he chose. Even those of us who were Democrats were enthusiastic about the clear meaning of the 187 Wilson experience in California, and unimpressed by the Bennett-Kemp attack.

We had substantial company in this view. After the 1994 elections, the Clinton White House regarded Wilson as a formidable potential opponent, and immediately sounded more concerned about porous borders. In January 1995, Doris Meissner, Commissioner of INS, announced that the administration was deeply concerned about the immigration pressures generated by the economic crisis in Mexico, and would soon decide upon some sort of "national computer identification system," either "a central registry" or "a national identity card." These formerly unacceptable words were coming from top administration officials. The winds from 187, augmented by the Jordan Commission, were being felt in the White House.

Chapter Eighteen:
Washington (and Local) Politicians Widen the Open Gate Again: 1996-2001

Admission and exclusion are at the core of communal independence. They suggest the deepest meaning of self-determination. Without them, there could not be communities of character, historically stable, ongoing associations of men and women with some special commitment to one another and some special sense of their common life. — Michael Walzer

Is the future decided no matter what the people want? Have the establishment and corporate money killed politics? — Pat Buchanan

In his recent detailed study of the politics of immigration in the U. S., *Dividing Lines: The Politics of Immigration Control in America* (2002), Daniel Tichenor accounts for the anomalous passage of the expansionist 1990 immigration law, despite public opinion running strongly the other way, by noting the "insulation of the policymaking process from restriction-minded publics." He was right about that, but saw much evidence that things seemed to be changing in the 1990s. Tichenor noted that immigration reformers after the 1990 setback had been energetically building their strength and numbers, and with what he viewed as impressive results. The revolt of the electorate in California reflected an unprecedented and mostly spontaneous mobilization of citizens into a social movement, and other grassroots groups spread across the nation, often spurred and encouraged by FAIR. Polls reflected the salience of the issue and a hardening public opinion, especially after the World Trade Center bombing in New York in 1992. Prior to the 1994 November elections, one poll showed 74 percent seeing mass immigration as a "critical threat to the vital interests of the U.S."

In those elections, the Republican Party gained control of both houses of Congress for the first time since 1952. This meant that Alan Simpson chaired the immigration subcommittee in the Senate and Lamar Smith in the House. House Speaker Newt Gingrich appointed a Task Force on Immigration chaired by California restrictionist Elton Gallegly. Senate Majority Leader Robert Dole denounced other lawmakers who were "not willing to protect our borders."

* * *

Reform Ferment in the World of Ideas

"The relatively young Center for Immigration Studies," Tichenor wrote, "generated a steady stream of scholarly reports and studies that supported a restrictionist policy agenda." Yet scholarly reports and studies documenting the costs and dysfunctions of current immigration did not gain the same attention as books with a strong point of view. One such was Roy Beck's *The Case Against Immigration* (1996), a book brought out by major publisher W. W. Norton and combining a revisionist history of immigration with all the costs noted along the way, especially those borne disproportionately by blacks and American workers.

"No book," said a reviewer for *Foreign Affairs*, "has made a better case for immigration reduction."

The book built a strong case for lower levels of legal immigration, but the distinctive feature was Beck's tone.

"I have a very personal stake in not wanting to provoke hostility or discrimination toward the foreign born who already are living among us...the number of immigrants—not their attributes [is what] causes many U.S. problems."

The reform case was made with equal force but from a very different angle of vision in Peter Brimelow's *Alien Nation* (1995). Here Brimelow stated again the argument in his 1992 *National Review* article on the costs of the immigration system and flows we had permitted, but broke through the taboo on letting worries about immigrant assimilation broaden into questions of cultural and racial difference.

"The American nation has always had a specific ethnic core," he wrote, "and that core has been white."

Current immigration flows were ending that, quickly, and without public discussion or consent. Beyond the lack of public consultation in this profound transformation of America, Brimelow wrote, multiethnic empires with no ethnic core do not work.

Many reviewers vigorously denounced this part of the book, including Mark Krikorian, writing in CIS's *Immigration Review* in 1995 that Brimelow sees American nationality "in excessively ethnic and racial terms." This is historically inaccurate, Mark argued, as the nation had always been ethno-racially diverse, as black Americans especially know, and skin color should not be re-injected into the immigration debate. Brimelow angrily objected that this misconstrued his argument. I wrote a "Second Opinion" for *Immigration Review* suggesting that Brimelow was right that "the American people should be asked what their preferences are in the matter." Nobody wrote in to denounce (or agree with) me, but a friend thought I had erred. Brimelow, she said, was wrong to want to re-start the conversation about whether the U.S. should accept large-scale non-European immigration, since one hundred years ago this had produced a nasty debate inflicting many open wounds. I responded that American society had moved far, far beyond the values and language of that earlier time, and our democracy ought not to let some of its elites transform the demographics and culture of the nation without open discussion. Eight years later, Victor Davis Hanson, writing for *National Review Online* in June, 2003, offered an observation I wish I had thought of myself.

"A multiracial society works. But a multicultural one...does not."

Brimelow's book at least had us talking about fundamentals such as what holds a multicultural nation-state together and how does such a society monitor and gauge the health of its assimilative processes?

* * *

The Jordan Commission

Then in late 1994 came the first of several installments of the report of the bipartisan Commission on Immigration Reform (CIR), established by the 1990 Immigration Act and chaired by former Congresswoman Barbara Jordan, a Texas African-American appointed to this post by President Clinton.

From the first, Jordan intellectually and personally dominated the deliberations of a commission initially split almost evenly between Expansionists and restrictionists. To our astonishment and pleasure, she proved to be a vigorous, even indignant opponent of illegal immigration as well as a critic of the current size and composition of the legal component.

"Those who come here illegally," she bluntly told a Congressional Committee in 1994, "and those who hire them, will destroy the credibility of our immigration policies. "Unlawful immigration...is unacceptable."

For immigration to continue to serve our national interest, it must be lawful.

"Those who should get in, get in. Those who should be kept out, are kept out. And those who should not be here will be required to leave. Limits must be enforceable and enforced."

As for legal immigration, it "has costs, as well as benefits" and "our current immigration system must undergo major reform..."

The Commission concluded that "immigrants should be chosen on the basis of the skills they contribute to the U.S. economy," and family-based admission categories should be reduced by the elimination of adult unmarried and married sons and daughters of U.S. citizens—a major source of "chain migration." Legal immigration totals should be curbed to cut back to 550,000 a year, with no preferences at all for unskilled labor.

Well aware that immigration reformers were often stigmatized, Jordan took the offensive at the start.

At the National Press Club in September, 1994, she said, "We disagree with those who would label efforts to control immigration as being inherently anti-immigrant. Rather, it is both a right and a responsibility of a democratic society to manage immigration so that it serves the national interest."

Little has been written about the CIR's internal dynamics, but it was clear even then that Jordan was not just Chair, but intellectual and moral leader. She sought a unanimous commission report despite the group's makeup of large egos and sharply divided views on immigration, and she essentially achieved it. CIR's recommendations were either unanimous, or reflected the predictable dissenting vote of the representative of the immigration lawyers whose livelihood was dependent upon the size of the immigration flow. The first report, issued in September, 1994, (before the Prop. 187 vote), looked at border control issues and recommended, along with stronger efforts at the border, a fraud resistant system for verifying authorization to work based upon a computer registry using Social Security numbers. The second report, in mid-1995, found the current immigration laws inattentive to the national interest, and recommended large cuts in chain family-based admissions, which would reduce legal admissions by one-third. Two final reports came in 1997 after Jordan's death, and dealt with refugee and management issues. The commission studied and rejected the idea of a guestworker program, which Jordan called "a grievous mistake."

A unanimous (except for the immigration lawyer member) national commission had placed recommendations for a substantial turn toward a more restricted regime of legal and illegal immigration on the nation's policy table on the eve of the 1996 elections. Enthusiastic about the commission's work, many of us regretted that CIR made no findings or recommendations on immigration's population and environment impacts, and published only a perfunctory and indecisive research paper on those topics. Their recommendation for a ceiling of 550,000 was not anchored in any national goal or commision-discovered interest, and seemed arbitrary and dismissible. It was both.

Jordan personally took the CIR's recommendations to President Clinton in June, 1995 and he quickly yielded to her persuasion and passion. He reversed the advice of top White House staff and issued a press release endorsing the commission's recommendations as "consistent with my own views." Similar endorsements came from the flagship liberal newspapers *The New York Times* and *The Washington Post.*

"A consensus had started to emerge among the Washington political establishment," journalist John J. Miller wrote in a 1998 assessment of "The Politics of Permanent Immigration," "to scale back on admissions, primarily for economic reasons but also because of cultural concerns, population worries, and environmentalism. Restrictionists appeared on the brink of enacting an array of policies that would have reversed America's history of generous admission levels..." We restrictionists had reached the high water mark, though we didn't realize it at the time, of the New Restrictionist reform movement in the twentieth century. There seemed abundant reason for Tichenor's history of these events to conclude that, in 1995-96, "immigration defenders poised themselves for a formidable restrictionist assault."

* * *

We knew, in a general way, that the Expansionists would mount their own formidable offense-defense. How formidable, we were about to learn. Big business and Big Agriculture had decades of experience in securing large annual infusions of cheap labor. The immigration lawyer bar was knowledgeable and well organized to promote the traffic in humans into the U. S. on which their livelihoods depended. The Ford Foundation and corporate funding had created imposing lobbying and public relations organizations for ethnic groups of all kinds. There was a substantial refugee industry enlisted in the effort to sustain large flows of people from abroad. American universities fielded in Washington a small but effective lobbying apparatus to press for easy access to large numbers of foreign graduate students in the sciences and technology. These elements of the Expansionist army were odd bedfellows, often disagreeing sharply on other policy issues. What united them was opposition to any form of restrictionism, and promotion of more immigration of whatever kind.

In an inspired phrase, journalist John Judis called this coalition "the Huddled Elites." Much of the credit for bringing them together for legislative strategy-making seems owed to two policy entrepreneurs— Dale F. ("Rick") Swartz, who founded the National Immigration Forum in 1982, and his successor (1990-) Frank Sharry, who arranged periodic meetings of a growing coalition of 250 national and local Expansionist groups. The Forum was a strange bag of otherwise unmixable elements— radical left activists from La Raza and the ACLU, union officials, Stephen Moore's Club for Growth and the U. S. Catholic Conference. Its meetings were firmly by invitation only. FAIR tried to send observers once or twice, and they were rebuffed. Perhaps this impressive coalition needed little coordination by Sharry or anyone else, as it built upon and mobilized decades of political contacts, lobbying ties, insider relations, money, and for the non-business elements of The Industry, the promise of continued employment in immigrant-importing industries and the moral intoxication of the Statue of Liberty's alleged symbolism.

They were unified by what they were against—the reforms moving into legislative form out of the subcommittees of Simpson and Smith, with free-lance bills from other Republicans intending to curb immigrant welfare eligibility, and even impose a moratorium (exempting spouses and children of U. S. citizens) on all immigration until 2000, a proposal of Senator Bob Stump of Arizona.

* * *

Warning: Congress is in Session

With these combatants mobilized around the expansion and against the contraction of immigration, congressional politicians, with vacillating and erratic input from the Clinton White House, began the legislative dance put in motion by the Jordan Commission's reform proposals. Lamar Smith in 1995 moved an ambitious bill that reformed legal immigration through the immigration subcommittee he chaired. The Immigration in the National Interest Act would reduce legal immigration to pre-1990 levels (535,000) under what appeared to be a real ceiling. Accepting one of the CIR's core reforms, Smith's bill curbed chain migration by eliminating two family-based preferences, while authorizing stronger border defenses. It called for fingerprinting all apprehended illegal immigrants, and expediting adjudication of asylum claims. Simpson's senate legislation began at similar points, adding stricter caps on refugee admissions.

Then, after sub-committee clearance, both came under fierce lobbying pressure from the Expansionist coalition and the Clinton White House, free to join the Expansionists now that Barbara Jordan was dead and could not criticize their role. With the Clinton administration's consent, the legislation was split, and the reforms of legal immigration were allowed to die—again. Both parties wanted to associate themselves with some sort of gesture toward controlling illegal immigration; both were quite happy with legal immigration as it was. The Illegal Immigration Reform and Immigrant Responsibility Act of 1996 passed, and was sent to Clinton and signed on September, 30, 1996.

The law was so complex that even FAIR's initial assessments were contradictory. However, it was soon obvious that the strengthening of policy toward illegals turned out to be minimal, and the important reforms of legal immigration that Smith and Simpson started with—most notably the cap on all legal immigration, and the abolition of the "chain migration" driver, the fifth preference for relatives outside the nuclear family, were in wastebaskets on Capitol Hill. Those Republicans and few Democrats who wanted to signal to the public that they were serious about containing illegal immigration claimed, without justification as it turned out, that crossing the border and then finding a way to stay in the U.S., even after being arrested, had been made harder by the 1996 law. The Border Patrol had received authorization for 5,000 new agents and the INS received 1,200 more (whether appropriations would follow was another question). Twelve million dollars was authorized to finish a fourteen-mile fence on the California-Mexico border. The deportation process was "expedited" in ways that immigration lawyers and judges could be counted on to interpret toward leniency and delays. Together with welfare reforms moving separately through Congress, the new law appeared to curb entitlements available to legal immigrants, but most of these provisions were dropped under White House pressure. Those remaining were soon repealed, under pressure from the Clinton administration and Hill Democrats. A proposal for a nationwide system to verify the immigration status of job applicants, arising out of the Jordan Commission, was dropped and replaced by three voluntary experimental programs at the state level, programs soon lost in the bureaucracy and leading to nothing.

One new tool in the 1996 law seemed very promising, and should not be forgotten despite its discouraging history to date. The "3/10 Bar" provision (sponsored by Republican Lamar Smith) would, for the first time, impose on illegal migrants a penalty more costly than a bus ride back to Tijuana. The provision barred re-entry into the U.S. for three years for those aliens with six to twelve months of unlawful presence, and ten years for those with more than a year. We catch you in the U.S. illegally, we deport you, and we penalize you—no more lawful entry into the U.S., and no path to citizenship, for three to ten years. I mention this provision of the 1996 law as a case study in the emasculation of Smith and Simpson's serious reform ideas going into the legislative meat grinder in 1995. Language added to the legislation in 1996 by Expansionist Senator Spencer Abraham dramatically narrowed its application. It was a task completed by subsequent INS administration—a story masterfully told in Jessica Vaughan's "Bar None," *CIS Backgrounder* (July, 2003). The new "3/10 Bar" in its first four years barred fewer than 12,000 previously illegal immigrants from coming into the U.S. This "sound idea" gave the 1996 law an initial reputation for "toughness" that it did not deserve.

So change was minimal, when the dust settled.

"The sad truth," truthfully said Dan Stein, "is that Congress failed to address any major problem."

Illegal immigration surged through the rest of the 1990s. The welfare reforms, especially, were of marginal importance in dealing with the problem of illegal immigration, and were in any event unenforced and soon repealed at the initiative of the Clinton administration.

* * *

We reformers had been bested again. Mass-scale legal immigration continued, and its composition was still determined on the legal side overwhelmingly by foreigners' family ties, with the growing illegal traffic bringing in low-skilled, low education workers, and often, their families. The entrenched elites had again rebuffed reforms that had appeared to have considerable momentum and backing.

Journalist John Heilemann, writing for *Wired* magazine, as the legislation moved to President Clinton's desk, described the astonishing reversal of the reform impulse.

"Congress was poised" in 1996, he wrote, "to pass the most severe anti-immigration legislation since the 1920s," pushed by "a powerful alliance" that had come together in a consensus based on the Jordan Commission recommendations.

"Restrictionists appeared on the brink of enacting an array of policies that would have reversed America's history of generous admission levels," John Miller wrote in 1998.

Then "six months later (Heilemann again) "the unstoppable alliance had been hacked to pieces by another, equally unlikely one," a corporate-dominated combination of high-tech business, libertarians, Christian conservatives, parts of the old left, supply-side Wall Streeters, and ethnic groups, the lot of them Judis' "huddled elites."

In Sharry's words, "the restrictionists wanted to impose…zero-immigration policies…but they failed. Not only did we keep them from getting everything they wanted…we kept them from getting almost anything. The deck was stacked in their favor," for the "backlash" against immigration "gathered such momentum in this country…restrictionists, both groups and politicians, effectively exploited the notion of economic insecurity…to really build a tremendous momentum." The "restrictionists really had the upper hand…but we outfoxed them. It was, I think, an astonishing victory," Sharry claimed.

"A stunning sea change," Miller wrote in *Reason* in 1998.

Well, perhaps not so astonishing. Sharry conceded that the coalition he helped pull together went up against only "two crazy restrictionist interest groups," FAIR and CIS, the latter a think tank with no lobbying capacity. No other organized opposition took the field. Even Barbara Jordan was not there to speak for her commission, as she had died of complications from cancer in 1995. Not much of a contest, if you look at the political muscle on both sides.

More Huddled Elites

It turned out that the "we" that Sharry referred to, the "huddled elites" working against any reduction of immigration flows, included not only the by now familiar ethnic lobbies and western growers and the Silicon Valley businesses worried about a labor shortage because of the surging late Nineties economy, but also some wealthy recent immigrants from Asia. Just months after Clinton signed the legislation from which virtually all of Simpson and Smith's reforms had been stripped, the *Boston Globe* reported that the administration's abrupt March shift away from support of the Jordan Commission's reform recommendations was the result of pressure from Asian-American campaign contributors, communicating with Clinton through Democratic National Committee Vice Chairman John Huang.

The prospect of more restrictive immigration "galvanized Asian-Americans like no other in recent times," *The New York Times* reported. Only 4 percent of the U.S. population, people of Asian descent made up 34.4 percent of the immigration flow in 1994, and "they want relatives to join them from overseas. They want their culture replenished with new arrivals." Nothing about the national interest here. These were recent immigrants whose thoughts, like all immigrants, were not first of the American national interest but of family and kin abroad; in other words, of further immigration.

Decades of post-1965 immigration had by the 1990s constructed inside the American fundraising and political lobbying universe another aggressive and politically savvy ethnic group to exert pressure for wide-opened gates. We were aware that Asian American groups lobbied actively on the 1996 legislation throughout the year, but we did not learn until 1997 that some of their money dangled before Clinton that spring had produced the sharp and fateful shift of his stance. I recalled that John Tanton in our first meeting in 1979 expressed a sense of urgency about restrictionist reform, as the passage of time increased the size and influence of recently-arrived ethnic and national groups. They created growing diasporas whose outlook was parochial and family-centered, with little conception of an overriding American national interest. The Sixties, and Ford Foundation and corporate funding, brought the Latino lobbying presence onto the political stage. By the mid-1990s, the multi-ethnic Asian American lobby had joined the anti-reform lineup. The reform hill was getting politically steeper as we worked.

* * *

As time went on, we discovered that our governmental policy challenge was not conveniently located in Washington, D.C. Other American governments were stepping into the arena, mostly to help make the apprehension and deportation of illegals more difficult. Local law enforcement agencies were closely involved in the handling of criminal aliens, but they generally had wide discretion in shaping their involvement in the civil side, i.e. illegal presence in the country. As early as the 1970s and gathering momentum in the 1980s, against the background of rising flows of illegals dislodged by the civil wars in Central America, religious organizations and ethnic activists launched the "sanctuary movement." This pressured major cities such as Berkeley, California, and then larger cities like St. Paul, San Diego, Los Angeles, Oakland, Seattle, Chicago and New York to declare themselves "cities of refuge" where local law enforcement officials and social service providers were ordered by mayors or city councils not to cooperate with the INS. In these hundreds of political battlegrounds across the country our reductionist troops only intermittently were engaged in a handful of them. We knew the results facilitated the illegal invasion. In the 1990s, we did not have the troops to effectively contest this local front of the battle.

* * *

Yet informed contemporary observers kept predicting that the restrictionists would soon mobilize again. *The Washington Post* editorialized after the 1996 election that immigration reform would inevitably press back upon the agenda and come to some sort of fruition "when the new Congress convenes in January," and well that it should, the paper (surprisingly) thought. Immigration levels are at historic and unjustified highs, the paper pointed out, and were driving U.S. population toward 400 million. A reporter for the *Wall Street Journal* detected "a new, harder attitude toward immigration."

Senator Diane Feinstein detected a "big mood shift" in 1996, "In California, it's my view that people want a slowdown."

Republican Howard Berman, a Judiciary Committee member who was one of those who voted to drop all tightening of legal immigration, "had no doubt" that the issue would be back just after the election.

What grounds were there for this expectation? Immigration reform, in the sense that we used it, was shut out of the 1992 presidential election entirely and made a marginal appearance in 1996. Pat Buchanan's candidacy was never formidable, but he was a persistent and often-quoted advocate of an immigration moratorium— "a timeout to assimilate those who have come here."

Pete Wilson, the only politician of national stature who had demonstrated the electoral potential of addressing the illegal immigration problem, entered the 1996 Republican presidential primaries. As it turned out, he could not carry the immigration-reform theme very far. His voice became raspy on the campaign trail and his vocal chords failed for several weeks in late summer, cutting short his candidacy and the possibility that an immensely successful, progressive Republican could fold immigration reform—if only the illegal part of it—into a winning package consistent with internationalism and harmonious

Still, the two eventual presidential candidates that year, when the issue came up, each tried to sound tougher on immigration than the other. Clinton boasted of increasing the border patrol to more than 4,500 agents, launching Operation Gatekeeper, and promised more deportations. Senator Robert Dole stressed his support of Prop. 187, and endorsed the new welfare bill that appeared to deny most forms of public assistance to legal immigrants. National politicians were not seriously engaged in this issue in the election year of 1996, but in recognition of the events in California were repeating their formerly successful litanies of "we strengthened the Border Patrol." Once again, immigration was kept out of the election, from the presidential level down through every congressional seat. We were in low spirits after the elections. Our issue had, again, made no appearance. The California "Turn" had been snuffed out.

Not every observer of American politics read the 1996 election results in this way. Some "informed" insiders argued that the populist revolt against out-of-control immigration that had surged into national politics in the early 1990s had only hit a momentary reversal in 1996. In this view, expressed by several responsible analysts of American politics, given the depth of these forces the resumption of a serious reform effort seemed assured. In the short run, this turned out to be quite wrong.

Chapter Nineteen:
The Flood of the Nineties Continues:
How Can This Be?

In no other realm of our national life are we so hampered and stultified by the dead hand of the past, as we are in this field of immigration. — Harry S Truman

The Numbers Coming In

The flow of immigrants through the 1990s continued to build momentum. Each year of that decade, 1.3 million (on average) immigrants settled in America. Adding births to immigrants, immigration accounted for 20-21 million new Americans, or two-thirds of the 33 million expansion of the national population over that decade, in California amounting to 99 percent of the state's growth. The U. S. foreign-born population expanded to 30 million, 11 percent of the total. One in five Americans was either born abroad or to parents born abroad. Census Bureau mid-range projections pointed to a U.S. population of 571 million by 2100, and slightly higher fertility levels would push that number to 1.2 billion. The Census Bureau had (under)estimated the illegal population at 6 million in the mid-Nineties (the INS guessed at 5 million), but after the 2000 census, CB admitted that the total was more like 11 million, and almost doubled the number the government statisticians had so recently estimated.

Occasionally these numbers received media attention, and sometimes these population dots were connected to familiar local problems—

overcrowded schools, traffic jams, pressure on public services, and crime. There were occasional stories about an ethno racial "power shift."

"White America: Ready to be a Minority?" was the headline of a series by journalist Jonathan Tilove that was carried nationally by the Newhouse News Service in 1998. "California and the End of White America" was the title of California businessman Ron Unz's 1999 article in *Commentary.*

"At some unknown date in the late 1980s...whites became a minority in California." He predicted "the coming of white nationalism... carrying the seeds of national dissolution." This prediction of some sort of white uprising could often be heard, but I am impressed with the point made most recently by Eric Kaufmann in his *The Rise and Fall of Anglo America* (2004), that there was remarkably little public notice taken at the century's end of the historic demographic transformation of America.

The annual incoming numbers themselves tell only part of the story. Immigration is not just an annual number of arrivals. It is a flow with constant internal communication from native land to destination, and develops (or loses, though we have not seen this since the 1920s) momentum, as early arrivals form bases and communicate back to kinship networks in the home country reporting a better way of life and pulling in friends and relatives to places with a growing ethnic beachhead. We need a momentum indicator for this, measuring not just annual arrivals but accumulated pressure from family and locational ties that sustain and increase future immigration. Our count of immigrants should not be merely the sum of who came in a given year, but also some calculation of who is likely to come in the channels already cut to the familiar niches already established. Nations anchoring their immigration selection system on kinship, and the U.S. leads that list, generate more momentum per foreign entry than those selected by other criteria. Immigration to the U.S. well deserves the label somebody gave it, "chain migration."

* * *

Post-Sixties immigration had initially clustered mainly in six states, but by the end of the century, the immigrant population was spreading to other parts of the country—Georgia, Iowa, Arkansas, Virginia, and North Carolina. In the Tar Heel state in the decade of the 1990s, the immigrant population increased 274 percent, the largest increase among all states and 22 percent of the state's growth. On moving back there in 1996, I found a vigorous discussion of the state's major problems—school crowding, air pollution, loss of timberland, wetlands and agricultural land, but only rarely a connection was made in the media between these problems and the influx of mostly unskilled workers and their dependents.

* * *

How Can This Be?

"How can this be?," was the well-aimed question asked in the late 1990s by Yale law professor Peter Schuck. This rising tide of foreigners, especially the illegal one-third, was unpopular with most Americans and was attracting growing critical attention. This seemed to Schuck (and to we reformers) to set the stage in a democratic country for immigration reduction. Yet the reformers were beaten again in 1996. Their well-deliberated proposals were squashed, while ineffective federal efforts to curb illegal immigration were paraded before the public as adequate to reduce that prominent part of the problem. How could it be that the restrictionist reformers pursuing a widely popular policy change were so easily defeated in Congress and the executive branch, as well as countless state and local settings?

An early and incomplete answer to this puzzle was offered by immigration analyst David North in a 1991 essay, "Why Democratic Governments Cannot Cope With Illegal Immigration." Like the United States, all fifteen nations of the European Union plus Australia and Canada were experiencing unprecedented levels of immigration—legal and illegal. North predicted larger flows of immigrants despite gathering public opposition, and he was right. In the first year of the twenty-first century, 350,000 people sought refugee status in the European Union, and the unsuccessful ones remained to swell the ranks of the illegal population—500,000 to 1.5 million estimated to reside in Germany, one million in the UK, and 300,000 in Italy. There were public complaints and a resurgence of nationalist political parties in Europe and Australia (not in Canada and the U.S.), but nothing effective was done to curb immigration in any of these countries.

Why? North offered a blunt answer:"Democracies...are unwilling to spend enough money...think hard enough, or be tough-minded enough to inflict pain (on otherwise law-abiding) disadvantaged persons."

The implication was that authoritarian governments, alone, were "tough-minded enough" to manage and restrict the movements of peoples. Not many people tried to immigrate to Cuba, North Korea, China, Syria, or Iran.

North's analysis, however, left too much out. It did not explore the question of why Western democracies behaved in this way, essentially voting benefits to people who were outside the polity and not voters, while at the same time permitted and even facilitated radical demographic and cultural change within societies that were quite comfortable with their older identities. Had he looked more closely at Europe, he would have found elements of the explanation in ruling elites locked into multiculturalist ideologies and contemptuous of the nationalistic impulses among the masses beneath them.

* * *

Context: Prosperity and Globalization

Historian John Higham taught his many readers to keep the economic context in view when studying immigration. The 1990s, as we have seen, saw more legal and illegal immigrants come to the U. S. than any decade in our history, though the decade started out with an economic slump that augured otherwise. The recession was more severe in California than in any other state or region—hence Prop. 187. However, recovery came quickly, and surged forward on the rails of internet-driven productivity gains into a bull stock market and an unprecedented run of prosperity. Immigration restriction, in our past, generally gained urgency when unemployment was high. Unemployment across the Nineties was at historic lows, and economic growth was strong. It was not a favorable economic climate for our restrictionist efforts, after the slump of the early Nineties.

The larger economic context is the advancing globalization of planetary economic life, which brought to America's middle and especially to the educated upper classes unprecedented consumer choice, rising affluence, and a bewitching cultural diversity to be consumed along with yachts and second homes. Globalization, to the leadership of both political parties and all business and professional elites, was perceived as much more than an isolated good thing. It was the indispensable engine of all modern progress—history's irresistible and universally enriching tidal wave. Goods and ideas should and did vault over all borders (increasingly a term of opprobrium), connecting and shrinking the globe. Why not labor also? Why shouldn't people, like ideas, money, and contracts, flow unimpeded across nations' artificial and troublesome borders? At the top of the corporate agenda was securing and replenishing the pool of lower-wage foreigners in order to bypass and discipline the domestic labor force while gaining brownie points for ethnic diversification.

There was, of course, an intense debate about all this across the Nineties, and a vigorous anti-globalization body of ideas was generated by environmentalists, labor organizations, and parts of the Left. One saw on television mobs breaking windows and disrupting the World Trade Organization (WTO) meetings in Seattle in 1999, and some form of street protest at every annual meeting of the WTO, the World Bank and the IMF. Seven days a week globalization had advanced. There were and are critics, even some economists from the "Chicago School" where free markets are most enshrined, who argue that goods and services should move freely, but labor is different. The marginality of such critics underlined the almost complete grip of the globalization creed upon the minds of the world's capitalists, economists and editorial writers. Unimpeded cross-border exchange of everything was the sure and only highway to world progress. This was the political and intellectual context in which our argument for closely regulating and limiting labor flows across borders ran against a fundamental tide of elite opinion, and could easily be portrayed as a rearguard action of outmoded prejudices and nostalgia, trying to "wall a country off" in an era in which "openness" was assumed to be the unerring engine of affluence.

At FAIR, we encountered these painful contextual realities early on, learning from the NAFTA debates that our issue was all tangled up with "free trade." Pro-NAFTA people claimed that free trade with Mexico would produce a booming economy there that was able to keep Mexicans at home. Anti-NAFTA advocates claimed it would mechanize Mexican agriculture and uproot millions of peasants who could only move north. Did we want to take a position on all this? A majority of us, including me, thought that FAIR ought to take no position on trade with Mexico or trade in general, as this was a complex swamp which threatened to engulf our energies and bring us new enemies that we did not need. John Tanton chafed at this, and frequently inserted materials critical of the religion of free trade into our Writers Workshop meetings, especially the writings of University of Wisconsin economist John Culbertson. Eventually we persuaded him that this complex issue was a diversion from our already intricate issue (or perhaps we just wore him down, without the persuasion). We immigration reformers were still sometimes called, or linked with, "protectionist" advocates who were also restrictionists—Pat Buchanan, as a leading example. My larger point is that in the 1990s any argument for limiting the free exchange of any of the elements of production beat against strong prevailing winds from the religion of Free Trade. In the 1990s, globalization was the faith of America's elites, and it provided a hostile intellectual and political context for we restrictionists, as well as those concerned with the well-being of American workers and the environment.

* * *

Such was our unpromising historical context, economic and intellectual, as we moved through the Nineties on our reformist mission. When you look at the order of battle on both sides of the issue in the 1980s and 1990s, you wonder why we restrictionists, or anyone else, expected immigration reformers to succeed in the great congressional battles of 1987, 1990, or 1996.

* * *

244

The Open Border Industry

One learns in the first week of political science 101 that a coalition of keenly interested and well-organized groups with money, livelihood and power on the line always prevails over the preferences of a broad but unorganized public. We immigration reformers participated in a case study of this fundamental dynamic of the American political system.

What was the size and composition of the Open Border Industry? I call it that because it is organized around delivery of a profitable product—foreigners moving to the U. S. Some would object that pecuniary gain is only one motive of this collection of immigration-expanders, and they would point to the leftist "global human rights" ideology that animates most of the religious and "human rights" groups. Indeed, Open Borderists are in some sense a part of a sort of social movement, a sector of the global "human rights" project. But most of The Industry is moved entirely or in part by money—cheap labor, or indentured labor, or immigrant clients, or jobs/careers as immigrant handlers or "ethnic shepherds" (California author Victor Davis Hanson's phrase). The cheap labor sectors are sometimes called "Big Business," but I prefer the term "employers," as it folds you and me into the ranks of those who like to import foreign labor rather than employ expensive and sassy Americans.

* * *

The big gorilla in lobbying for and luring more immigrants is an organized coalition of immigrant-addicted employers—agricultural growers, meat and poultry manufacturers, and the high-tech industries of our country's several Silicon Valleys. Doing little congressional lobbying but political allies in the cause of cheap foreign labor are restaurant and hotel owners, construction foremen, and you and I at gardener and nanny hiring time.

The constituent parts of the organized lobbying coalition did not all arrive at the trough of a governmentally-supplied cheap labor force at the same time. First came the southwestern growers, who used the labor shortages of World War II to win a Bracero Program supplying Mexican labor. After it ended in 1964, perishable crop growers were not only in the southwest but from Florida to Washington state, and they've won an expanding network of special agricultural worker visa programs. These had the effect, brilliantly described in Phil Martin et al, *The New Rural Poverty* (2004), of keeping perishable crop agriculture in America from following the course of other seasonal outdoor industries such as logging, shipping, and construction, where wages rose, fringe benefits spread, and mechanization eliminated much of the heavy lifting and other tedious and dangerous tasks. In these industries the concept and reality of what Martin and his co-authors call "a career in hired farm work" slowly emerged. This was not so in agriculture, where growers successfully pressured Congress to supply cheap and pliant foreign labor. With low wages came wretched or no housing, grueling work, dangerous work conditions, and an ever-replenishing rural poverty in America.

This entrenched agricultural guestworker lobby was joined in the last decades of the twentieth century by the large corporations increasingly dominating and radically restructuring the nation's beef, pork, and poultry slaughtering and processing industry at the end of the century a $170 billion sector. At mid-century, the meat processing industry had been much smaller, was centered in Midwestern cities, and its unionized workforce was one of the best paid with the lowest turnover in all American industry. In the 1980s and 1990s, meat processing rapidly shifted to rural areas in the Midwest and especially in the South, where huge feedlot operations supplied cows, hogs, and poultry to immense slaughtering and packing factories increasingly manned by Mexican immigrants, illegal along with legal. Wages have steadily declined from fifteen dollars an hour in 1979 to less than ten dollars at the end of the century, and that income was earned in bloody and dangerous disassembly lines.

"The past thirty years," wrote Donald Stull and M. J. Broadway in *Slaughterhouse Blues* (2004), "have witnessed a return to the jungle" described in Upton Sinclair's classic expose *The Jungle* (1906). Immigrant labor was an indispensable part of this transformation, and the large companies dominating today's meat processing industry have become active and influential lobbyists against workplace enforcement of immigration laws and for guestworker programs.

Another component of The Industry is made up of the 8,000 immigration lawyers profiting from the flow of bodies into the U. S. and organized in the thirty-five chapters of the American Immigration Lawyers Association.

Out in front and the most vociferous of all the several parts of The Industry are the now familiar ethnic lobbies, claiming to be still active parts of the civil rights movement and thus entitled to a moral arrogance that seems to come with victimhood in post-Sixties America. The most vigorous and numerous of these were the Latino groups that the Ford Foundation almost single-handedly either invented, or in the case of LULAC, converted from an earlier (and successful) assimilationist model into a narrow "civil rights" model focused only on ethnic advancement with no vocabulary for addressing national concerns.

"At the center of the movement was the Ford Foundation—the largest tax-exempt foundation in the world," reported William Hawkins and Erin Anderson in *The Open Borders Lobby and U. S. Security After 9/11* (2004). Ed Rubenstein, former Hudson Institute researcher, building on investigation of IRS 990 forms by Joseph Fallon, has added up the totals for Ford funding from 1968 to 2002. Ford spending on Latino activist groups began in 1968, when attorney Peter Tijerina, impatient with the middle-class social base and values, conciliatory tone, and conspicuous patriotism of LULAC (of which he was a member), and impressed with the NAACP's Legal Defense Fund, asked the Ford Foundation for a million dollars, which they doubled at the outset, beginning a run of financial support to the new Mexican American Legal Defense and Education Fund (MALDEF) that totaled $35 million by 2002. In 1968, Ford also adopted in 1968 the only "civil rights" organization in America with a racist name, the National Council of La Raza (routinely identified as La Raza), and by 2002 had provided the organization with $30 million 30$ million in funding. LULAC finally got the point, that the assimilationist, pro-American language and objectives that the organization had adopted in the 1920s were out of favor among the nation's liberal foundations.

LULAC abandoned its code that read in part:, "Respect your citizenship; honor your country, maintain its traditions in the minds of your children; incorporate yourself in the culture and civilization" (of the United States). In the early 1980s, a LULAC official could be heard declaring: "We cannot assimilate. We will not assimilate," and the new tone brought funding from Ford starting in 1981, when new President African American Franklin Thomas put out a white paper justifying a long-term strategy of opposition to all immigration laws on the basis of universal human rights.

We should not make too much of Ford money. While it was crucial at the outset and has for years expanded, lubricated and legitimized an ethnic lobby that quickly adopted its sponsor's open borders ideology, a glance at La Raza's and LULAC's corporate shakedowns tell us that Ford's yearly contribution is joined by big money from Bristol-Meyers Squib, General Electric, Coca-Cola, Bank of America, Burger King, and General Motors, just to browse a long list of corporate sponsors who can be counted on year by year. However, the big daddy has been the Ford Foundation, which by 2002 had supplied $67.5 million to the top three Latino organizations.

In the politics of immigration, the three big Latino organizations (measured by budgets; two of the three have no members), MALDEF, La Raza and LULAC, are routinely the most influential players the restrictionists faced, unless the issue was an ethnically narrowed dispute, such as a sudden pressure to admit Russian, Jewish, Haitian, or Cuban refugees. The size and political clout of diaspora lobbies in the United States continues to grow. The fastest-growing ethnic lobbies are Asian, as we learned in the Clinton years. There is even an Indian Caucus with 182 members in the House of Representatives (since 1994), with a counterpart in the senate with thirty-three members.

The refugee lobby component of The Industry transcends ethnic loyalties, and charges out like a ready cavalry whenever refugee issues come up, or can be brought up. The flow of refugees is large—in 2005, 70,000 refugees and another 70,000 asylum seekers and Cubans settled in the U.S. A flow of taxpayers' money comes with this, which has, of course, over the years built up a mini-industry of "non-governmental organizations (NGOs)" to argue for more refugees and thus contracts for themselves to settle them. We learned from journalist Don Barnett writing in *Chronicles* in August, 2005 that when the State Department's Bureau of Population, Refugees and Migration held an open meeting on the refugee budget for fiscal year 2004, no person or group representing the public appeared. More than twenty NGOs from religious, human rights groups, along with a cluster of immigration lawyers were told by the government where they could find refugee resettlement money from tobacco settlement funds, Department of Agriculture money for low-income farmers, or Department of Health and Human Services grants for services to "trafficking victims." The communities where these refugees would be settled were of course not present, or consulted. The largest NGO here is, always, the U. S. Catholic Conference of Bishops, which leads the other NGOs in lobbying for larger annual budgets for refugee resettlement. Welcome to the refugee sector of The Industry which can claim credit for the remarkable fact that the U.S. over the past three decades has resettled more refugees than all other developed nations combined.

If the right flank of The Industry is the big western growers, midwestern and southeastern meat and poultry factory owners, and Bill Gates and his friends from high-tech companies, the left flank of this odd-bedfellows alliance is a cluster of organizations working for immigration expansion as part of a "social justice" agenda. These include the ACLU's Ford-funded Immigration and Alien Rights Project, the Bay Area-based Immigrant Legal Resource Center , the amply funded Migration Policy Institute (MPI) which helped brainstorm the "grand bargain" between Mexico's Fox and President Bush which would result in "a North America with gradually disappearing border controls," the National Immigration Law Center that grew out of the Sanctuary movement and works to expand social services to both legal and illegal immigrants, and the Open Society Institute funded by George Soros to carry out various projects around the world. One of them was the Emma Lazarus Fund that used a $50 million endowment to fight "discrimination against immigrants" in the U.S.

This is the Moral High Ground part of The Industry—a mix of internationalism and ethno-nationalist lobbyists for more visas and refugee admissions from country X. The ugliest part of the immigrant-importing industry are the organized networks of human smugglers like the Mexican coyotes at the border, the criminal smuggling rings that take large fees to impound Chinese laborers in boxes aboard freighters headed for a U.S. port and years of indentured servitude to pay off the smuggling fee, and the human traffickers who bring 50,000 women and children per year (according to a 2000 CIA report, *International*

Trafficking in Women to the U.S.) to serve as slaves or indentured servants in the prostitution and child labor ranks of our nation. Writer Edward Abbey captured the tangled motives in a brilliant comment: "The conservatives love their cheap labor; the liberals love their cheap cause."

* * *

Is The Industry's lavish funding an adequate explanation for the coalition's success? Yale law professor Peter Shuck made the case, in an article in *Studies in American Political Development* (1992), that this left-leaning ideological component of The Industry brought to the immigration policy struggles a decisive advantage and edge in the contest of ideas. They brandished the "idea of diversity...the idea of universal human rights," the "rhetoric of egalitarian ideals," the "romantic...image of the U.S. as a haven," and "the conviction...that the U.S. was engaged in a high-stakes global competition" requiring it to scour the earth for brainy and "hard-working" people to move here and help us remain number one. These ideas and ideals, in his view, easily overmatched the reductionists' ideas, beginning with "the old idea of national sovereignty" which seemed "anachronistic, and perhaps moribund."

There is something to be said for this analysis. We reductionists built a devastating factual critique of the immigration status quo, with its costs to citizens so much larger than the benefits. In the realm of airy ideals, unanchored in anything but a mythologized history, those who crafted the Open Border rationale and appeal had staunch allies in every organized religious body in America, most social science and humanities university faculty and all top administrators, and so far as one can tell, most students, touching liberal hearts with personalized stories conveying, again in Schuck's words, "a remorselessly Panglossian view of immigration" which masked "the bitter distributional conflicts that lie just beneath the surface." Certainly in the Nineties, a heady time when the pursuit of unending economic and population growth through globalization seemed to work very well, we reductionists found it difficult to generate serious debate over our own vision of an America leading the world toward a different global model of a sustainable society demographically based upon an end to population growth.

* * *

In the 1930s, when it became clear that his beloved Marxism could not take over nations by mobilizing only the sheer numbers of the working class, the Italian theorist Antonio Gramsci, influentially urged a shift in tactics, from arousing the industrial workers for one spectacular revolution in the streets, to "a long march through the institutions" of middle class society by intellectuals of the left. In the U.S., the Open Borders coalition has done just that, taking control of the universities, the national bureaucracies of the churches, the news media, the entertainment media, the labor unions, and the corporate executive suites. What an Industry! Gramsci was a genius, as the Open Borders Industry had bested we restrictionists every time—so far.

There is an irony here that should bring pain to parts of that lobby. Gramsci had intended for the bourgeois allies of the silent working class to use their hard-won control over "the institutions" of civil society to bring the capitalists to heel and greatly reduce their power, if not eliminate their power and them. But the Open Borders Industy in America has been dominated by the Bill Gates's at the top, along with strawberry farmers in California and hog and poultry packers in Arkansas and North Carolina and Iowa at the base. The American Left, in a betrayal of American workers, supplied most of the educated elites of Expansionist ideology who in and after the Sixties made the "long march" toward control of the nation's leading cultural institutions. The big winners in this bizarre political alliance were the large American and multinational corporations. I never understood why we heard so little internal grumbling on the Left about their close alliance with international capital.

* * *

The Little Engine That Couldn't

As the century neared an end, we immigration reformers threw into the battle against this coalition FAIR's 75,000 members and one to two lobbyists with no PAC money to distribute; Roy Beck's five-person NumbersUSA office in Arlington; and two or three other Washington area groups (Population Environment Balance, Americans for Immigration Reform) too small to employ even one lobbyist.

We tried coalition-building, too—endlessly. As I related, FAIR had from the first tried to enlist the black civil rights organizations, knowing their members were paying a steep price in an era of mass immigration. Their leadership aligned unswervingly with their Latino civil rights allies, and thus with a large immigration influx that was not in the interest of African-Americans. We tried to partner with the larger environmental groups, and met the same frustration. The Izaak Walton League briefly endorsed immigration reform before retreating and The Wilderness Society was at one time briefly on record for reduction of immigration numbers. The flagship environmental organization, the Sierra Club, had for some time emphasized the importance of stabilizing populations, but their leadership firmly resisted internal pressures to endorse the only step that would have stabilized American numbers—immigration restriction. To have advocated less immigration, they concluded, would mean that the organizations might lose some foundation funding, and their boards and staff might be called bad names and placed in an intolerable social situation in the elite circles of Washington, New York, Berkeley, and wherever they operated. We made repeated efforts to change this, as we shall shortly see.

Thus our organizational strength, much larger than ten years earlier, was comparatively puny. We were an alliance of a handful of similar immigration reform groups—few, small, skimpily funded, our legitimacy constantly in question in the media and public forums. Our only source of political strength was the like-minded majority of Americans of all ethnic and racial groups, yet this public was poorly informed about incoming numbers, about who decided, what were the costs, and what were the remedies. Still, our potential numbers were imposing if poll data were consulted. One might think that at some level the evidence of public support for our general position would be, if not intimidating, then grounds for a certain respect and wariness from policymakers, media, and commentators on public issues. How many Americans answered "Yes" to the question, "Are there too many immigrants?" when Gallup asked it? Of those polled, 60 percent said Yes, which translates into 179 million Americans, if adults spoke also for their children. However you do the math, lowering the numbers of immigrants plainly was the preference of millions of citizens, a clear and undeviating majority over several decades. Expansionists never disputed this. What politician could long ignore it?

The answer was given early on by Tip O'Neill. The restrictionist millions were poorly informed and not focused on the issue. Their schools, prisons, and hospital emergency rooms in the border states could overflow, but most citizens seemed incapable of making the connection to a flow of low-education and low-income immigrants from impoverished Mexico and elsewhere. Those who did, and I hope I underestimate their number, were up to their necks in raising kids and living daily lives, and therefore only intermittently focused on the subject of immigration's concrete impacts and what to do about this tsunami from the parts of the world burdened with failed and failing societies. Many observers of this issue in American politics have predicted, often in fear and trembling, that the American public or some angry part of it was sure to break into open revolt against open borders, and severely restrict all immigration. This didn't happen in the 1980s or 1990s, apart from the easily contained rebellion in California. We reformers could only mobilize a small part of this latent restrictionist public.

In fairness, it was no easy thing for the public to make the immigration connection to incremental changes in daily life such as crowded schools and freeways, population pressure on ecosystems and resources, expanding fiscal costs of emergency rooms and prisons, the re-emergence of TB, formation of gangs in high schools and neighborhoods. These and other social ailments had more than one cause, but a major one, the immigration connection, was deliberately concealed. The news media were overwhelmingly liberal in outlook, traumatized and guilt-filled by the civil rights movement and attendant racial conflict. This meant that all "people of color" in America would receive sympathetic treatment by the enlightened elements of society, importantly including those who reported and commented on social trends and events. When a Vietnamese immigrant became high school valedictorian, or families who had recently immigrated from New Delhi revitalized the seedy motels in a bad part of town, room was made in the news for this sort of uplifting American success story. If Mexican high school aged males had high dropout rates from the schools and formed violent gangs in Modesto, or 70 percent of the births in an El Paso hospital were to Latinos who were unable to pay and probably illegal, the news media would write or air the story without connecting the social costs to immigrant status. Someone recently said that the eleventh commandment for journalists is that One Shalt Not Blame a Native American for Anything. This has been expanded to include all immigrants, legal or not.

I first called this the Frank Del Olmo effect, but learned that large metropolitan newspapers and broadcast news media all had mostly Anglo and Jewish editors and reporters; very few Latino editors. Del Olmo was able to do his censoring because the *Los Angeles Times* was editorially a liberal paper. The media in the early 1980s when we New Restrictionists worked to get their attention usually referred to FAIR and later CIS, as "an anti-immigrant group," or "anti-immigration group." We made very slow headway against this over the years by complaining to editors and reporters. John Tanton wrote more than one letter to newspaper and magazine editors like the one he sent to a Michigan paper near his home.

Don't keep referring to me as an "immigration foe," he wrote. "I am not opposed to immigration, anymore than someone going on a diet is opposed to food. Rather, the question as to both food and immigration is how much, what kinds, and how to abide by the rules decided upon."

It was only by the early years of the twenty-first century that both major papers on the coasts, *The New York Times* and the *Los Angeles Times*, switched to referring to FAIR as "a group advocating less immigration" rather than their customary "anti-immigrant group." Other major papers had a bit earlier eased their biased labeling, and referred to CIS as "a respected immigration think tank." The liberal bias of the media is well-described in Bernard Goldberg's *Bias* (2002), and in William McGowan's excellent book, *Coloring the Media* (2001), especially in a chapter devoted to nonreporting of the darker side of immigrant life in the U. S. such as the estimated 150,000 African girls subjected annually to female circumcision. This media bias amounted to a wind directly on the nose of our sailboat.

* * *

With this configuration of the opposing forces and their assets, and with the Democratic Party having shifted away from its earlier keen sensitivity to the interests of the American worker and now in fear of the displeasure of racial and ethnic lobbies, public policy outcomes on immigration were predictable. The unorganized/under-organized and inadequately informed are not "a constituency." So they lose, no matter which party is in nominal control of the machinery of policy. They are not under organized because of some failure of intelligence or will, but because it is very hard to organize people for sustained political action around something they don't perceive as a personal interest of a vital sort but as a citizens' interest they don't think about every day, or month. Historian Elliot Barkan wrote in 1998, with a hint of contempt, that "immigration reform had at that point 'disappeared' as a live enterprise because convictions on this by average people were 'not strongly held... only an inch deep.'"

This had been Roger Conner's conclusion ten years earlier, that our troops were broad but thin, like an inch-deep ocean. The Open Border industry was thickly organized, well-funded, going to work on the issue early every Monday morning, and keenly aware of their financial, ethnic, or professional stake in the large and growing traffic of foreigners into the United States. California journalist James Goldsborough, writing in *Foreign Affairs* in 2000, noted that the debate over immigration "has recently switched direction by about 175 degrees." Policy "today is driven by businesses that need more workers...Somehow, the process has gotten out of control."

* * *

Why Expansionist Politicians Never Paid the Ultimate Price

How was it that no politicians had ever lost their seat by voting against the public's known concern with runaway immigration? How *did* all those Tip O'Neills get away with ignoring our collapsing immigration system, year after year? Puzzling over this over these years slowly educated me, the historian of much earlier American politics, in the realities of modern political life. By the end of the 1990s, at least, and with the help of my brother and historian Hugh Davis Graham who had studied the Carter and Reagan eras, I began to understand a key development in recent American electoral politics—that the natural advantages of incumbents in the Congress (and in many state legislatures) somehow had reached the point in the 1990s (the trend had been visible earlier) that very few elected officials of either party were being defeated when they ran for re-election. The incumbent success rate reached 98 percent in 1998 and stayed there through the elections of 2004, a year when only seven incumbents lost their re-election bids. Of the winners in the congressional elections of 2004, 95 percent won by more than ten percentage points. Incumbents in both houses of Congress, especially in the House, were virtually unbeatable. The *Economist* magazine estimated in 2002 that only twenty House races were truly competitive; others put the number as high as fifty-seven. The incumbents usually won even in those. Some states had similar patterns in their legislatures. In California in the 2004 elections to state Assembly and Senate, 153 seats were open with an incumbent running, and none, zero, were lost to a challenger. This left elected politicians a lot of room for voting against public opinion and public interest. Incumbent politicians were virtually impossible to defeat no matter how they voted on anything, in the decade when we reformers hoped the public would defeat some of them on the basis of their voting on immigration issues. This incumbent advantage was a disheartening development for reformers trying to get the politicians' attention without using money, which was our situation. We never accepted the prospect that this electoral trend toward invulnerable incumbents could not ever, at least on our issue, be broken. Still, after twenty years of elections across the mass immigration era, the voters had taken only one scalp of a politician who made the mistake of appearing unconcerned about or even in favor of open borders. That was Kathleen Brown, who had led Pete Wilson by twenty points in the summer polls before he endorsed 187.

* * *

These changes in the American political system, along with embedded historical myths about immigration, plus the liberal bias of the media after the 1960s, seem to me to provide most of the explanation for how it came about that we and the majority of the American people lost three big legislative struggles between 1986 and 1996, and countless smaller media, court, and regulatory decisions along the way. During this difficult, discouraging period a few FAIR members (and some non-members) expressed their disappointment in letters or e-mail at the failure of reform, occasionally blaming the organization for using the wrong tactics and/or messages, and talking about the need for a new national organization that would lead us all to victory. I remain unconvinced that different basic strategy or formulation of the message by FAIR would have significantly altered the outcome through those years. Doubtless the organization's performance wasn't perfect, whatever that means. I wouldn't have taken the Pioneer money, but this had no impact on public opinion or mobilization. The other side had too many assets. It rode the tide of globalization, ran with the interest of business employers in cheap labor and of household employers in cheap gardeners, had more professional lobbyists and vastly more money to spend on politics, and deployed mythical tropes about immigration as the uncomplicated core of our national story that beguiled a sentimentalist public and stifled faint-hearted critics.

* * *

Georgie Anne Geyer asked in 1997: "Whatever happened to immigration reform?" Why was it not back on the national agenda, since the 1996 Act was so hollow and even harmful?

My reaction to that question was that in light of how we have been doing in Washington politics, did we want to get back on the national political agenda with the present configurations of power? We had learned that things could always get worse when you opened the congressional box and began the legislative dance. We were learning that "passing a law" is an effective way for ruling political elites to dissipate popular dissent and obscure the situation. "Reform" is declared, the actual results of a new and complicated statute are too complex to assess until time reveals (to those who followed the issue closely) its numbers-increasing result, while the rebellion against the immigration status quo was again contained and real reform energies depleted.

After the third legislative defeat, it did seem time to try other things far away from Congress, where there was in any event no eagerness to wrestle again with immigration. For one thing, our tiny pool of congressional leaders was just about dry. For Alan Simpson, after all, 1996 had been his third try, and he had seen enough. He was seventy years old in 2000, and retired from the senate. The loss was more than doubled when his appointed replacement as chairman of the immigration subcommittee in the senate was freshman Senator Spencer Abraham (Rep., Mich.) who would prove to be an energetic Open Border sponsor.

If part of the reason for the ebbing of immigration criticism after the flare-up in California was the weariness of the handful of congressional reformers, much owed to the national mood. It was the second half of the Nineties, and we knew that the times had cycled from the economic worries of the 1980s and the brief recession of 1990-91 into a boom era bringing tight labor markets, astonishing stock market gains, an internet-spurred surge of productivity, a real estate bubble on both coasts, and from all of this, widespread euphoria. The Nineties reminded this historian of that part of the 1890s after the economic depression of 1893-96 gave way to a boom time when everything good seemed possible, and the growing pains of industrialization were apparently left behind. Visiting British writer James Bryce wrote that Americans in the second half of the 1890s were "sailing a summer sea," ignoring problems building in their crowded cities. Our 1990s were like that—a bad time to ask the American political machinery to summon the will required to regain control of borders and workplaces.

Chapter Twenty:
Immigration Fatigue in the Rest of the West

After the Madrid bombings, it seemed more obvious than ever that Europe's elite was largely hopeless. — Bruce Bawer

It is five minutes to twelve, not just in the Netherlands but in the whole of Europe. — Pim Fortuyn

When David North wrote that democracies could not control immigration, he seemed to have in mind the entire West. If Japan were held apart as a unique part of the West where immigration problems did not exist because they weren't permitted, North called attention to a policy ineptitude common to the world's most advanced societies. When in the 1980s the U.S. found itself entangled in immigration policy dilemmas and the breakdown of control generated by migratory pressures on the southwestern border with Mexico and across the straits separating Cuba and Haiti from Florida, it might have given Americans a slight comfort, though no helpful solutions, to recognize that the rest of the west (minus Japan) was beset by similar pressures for which history seemed no guide.

Western Europe in modern times had a substantial, multi-century history of generating outward immigration pressures, not absorbing them. Fifty million Europeans relocated to what historian Albert Crosby has called the "neo-Europes" (North and South America and Australia) in the centuries between the Columbian voyages and the 1920s. This was an interval in which Europe completed its "demographic transition" from high to low fertility and from booming populations to a leveling off. Over that period, Europe was an immigration-sending, not an immigration- receiving, part of the world. Sending immigrants requires no real governmental capacity. Being on the receiving end is another matter, and it forces governments to try to learn how to regulate and control the human flows.

The immigration receiving role for Europe came unexpectedly after World War II, as most European nations, recovering from war and entering a period of unprecedented affluence after completing their demographic transition, began to experience inflows of people from the fast-growing undeveloped world, especially former European colonies. The Netherlands received 300,000 Indonesians, France absorbed thousands of Algerians, Tunisians and Moroccans, India and Jamaica sent large numbers to postwar Great Britain. These weren't exactly anticipated and seemed one-time additions readily managed. However, rapid economic recovery in Europe produced labor shortages in the Sixties, generating a considerable migration inside Europe of rural Italians, Portuguese, and Spaniards to their own central cities, and then to neighboring countries. Still eager for more cheap labor, industrialists pressured several European governments to contract for what seemed a good bargain (for the industrialists) at the time—guestworkers who would not be immigrants but would return home when no longer needed.

In the Sixties, France signed contract labor agreements with Algeria, Morocco and Tunisia, Germany with the latter two, Italy, Greece, Spain, and Turkey. Many of the guestworkers, and most of the Turks, turned out to be immigrants, after all, often bringing in their families. Foreign-born populations were augmented in virtually every European country by governmental hospitality to asylum seekers, whose reception seemed to ease Western guilt feelings about their colonial pasts. Another rationale for generous post-war immigration policies was the growing realization that European birth rates were falling to and below replacement levels, and a large flow of immigrants seemed to some people an obvious way to prevent that awful impending fate (welcomed only by the Greens), declining populations.

The result of European migration—sporadic flows of foreign guestworkers, millions of Algerians entering France during the Algerian War, and East Germans escaping into West Germany—was "forty million people in transit" within and into Europe through the 1960s and 1970s, as Tony Judt described this cross-border churning of peoples in his *Postwar: A History of Europe Since 1945* (2005). There was more to come, as outside Europe's borders, to the south and east, the world's supply of uprooted or economically desperate people was being increased by high birth rates and growing populations in the undeveloped world, plagued not only by poverty but by civil wars, overstressed environments, and failed states. Modern means of communication told of European affluence, and declining global transportation costs facilitated it.

A prediction of what was ahead came in 1974 from Houari Boumedienne, President of Algeria, speaking before the UN. "Some day millions will leave the world's poor Southern regions and surge into the Northern hemisphere seeking survival."

He was not alone in this vision. In 1973, French novelist Jean Raspail wrote *Camp of the Saints,* a sensational and highly controversial story of the voyage of a great flotilla of rusty steamships carrying millions of the poor from India to dump them upon the Mediterranean beaches of France.

He imagined them vividly:

"There they were! A million poor wretches, armed only with their weakness and their numbers, overwhelmed by misery, encumbered with starving brown and black children, ready to disembark on our soil, the vanguard of the multitudes pressing hard against part of the tired and overfed West." The boats disgorged their human cargo, the French army took up defensive positions—and commanders refused to order the troops to fire, as many soldiers deserted. The "million poor wretches" poured across France, into Switzerland, Germany, then all of Europe, and other such armadas loaded with the poor of the earth set out from Africa and Southern Asia.

"It is the end of the white world," one reviewer concluded.

The book was at first "badly received," Raspail conceded in an understatement, and the author, who presented the refusal to defend France as a societal suicide, was called a racist everywhere. A 1985 reprinting in France was again bitterly denounced by the elites for its unsympathetic portrait of the dark-skinned "refugees," though unlike the 1973 edition, this one sold briskly in and outside of France—a harbinger of shifting public opinion. Respected Yale political scientist

Paul Kennedy said that *The Camp of the Saints* will be to the twenty-first century what the book *1984* was to the twentieth—an opinion I share but apparently not the majority opinion among book reviewers. Raspail was unrepentant for writing a book so openly contemptuous of the governing elites who had failed to repel the "invaders."

"The West is empty," he wrote in an introduction to the 1985 edition. "The West has no soul left." Or ears to hear.

"We do have the ultimate weapon," said Mahathir Bin Mohamad, Prime Minister of Malaysia, said in a 1997 speech. "In a borderless world, we can go anywhere. We should migrate north in our millions, legally or illegally. Masses of Asians and Africans should inundate Europe and America."

* * *

The Europe-aimed "surging" from south to north that Boumedienne, Raspail, Mahathir and others predicted accelerated in the 1980s, at the same time when the U.S. was becoming preoccupied with its own northward-moving illegal Mexican and Central American workers. Almost all the asylum-seekers and illegals moving into Germany in the 1980s were Muslims from Afghanistan, Iran, Lebanon, and Bosnia-Herzegovina. Austria, Italy and Spain received a somewhat different but similarly growing flow of Muslim refugees or illegal immigrants. Italy, with many ports and Europe's longest coastline, estimated a tenfold increase of immigration across the 1980s, most from northern Africa and Asia, and most in illegal status. They were joined in the 1990s by boatloads of refugees generated by overpopulation, poverty, and civil unrest in nearby Albania. By the 1990s, the European Community had become the European Union, pushing the boundaries of "Europe" eastward and giving it common borders with countries of large or predominant Muslim populations—Macedonia, Albania, Belarus, and the Ukraine. Immigrants who successfully entered one EU country were able to travel to any of the others without passports. That, in itself, encouraged sustained large-scale immigration from parts of the former Soviet Union, North Africa and the Middle East into all corners of the EU.

* * *

In every European country there were, in varying degrees, mounting volumes of immigration-generated public complaint and even sporadic political mobilization. The rise of political parties expressing various combinations of nationalist sentiment, worries about the volume and composition of immigration, suspicion of globalization and the meddling of the EU bosses in Brussels began to re-shape the continental political landscape, country by country. Three such parties grew up in Germany in the 1960s and 1970s, but met with limited and local success, probably because Germany for good reasons was a country determined not to go again in a direction bearing any resemblance to the Hitlerian movement. In Austria, a charismatic lawyer named Jorg Haider took control of an insignificant rightist Freedom Party in 1986, and took its percentage of the vote from 5 percent to 27 percent with a message blending worries over large-scale immigration with taking the side of the "volk" in a culture war with the multiculturalists. One party banner attacked "*Uberfremdung*" or "over foreignization," another "Vienna Must Not Become Chicago." In France, the tiny FN (National Front) Party, founded in 1972, and never previously securing more than 1 percent of the national vote, surged toward 20 percent in municipal elections, and under the leadership of the openly xenophobic Jean Marie Le Pen. In Belgium, the Vlaams Blok ("Flemish Block") founded in 1978 was a very minor rightist-nationalist party whose parliamentary vote abruptly surged from 85,000 votes in 1985 to 405,000 in 1991, in response to a populist-nationalist message created mainly by Filip Dewinter, who insisted that immigrants were swamping his country, especially Antwerp, and no more "non-Europeans" should be admitted. The party's slogans, "Our own people first," "In Self-Defense," and "Big Clean-up," resembled the titles of two of Dewinter's books, *Our People First* and *Masters In Our House*.

In the United Kingdom, a 1968 speech by Conservative M.P. Enoch Powell predicted "rivers of blood" if commonwealth migration was not curbed and some immigrants expatriated briefly sparked for a time the growth of a new party, the National Front. This upstart party soon collapsed when rules governing Commonwealth migration were tightened in the early 1970s, and "Iron Lady" Margaret Thatcher, outspokenly in agreement with popular worries about the "swamping of

British culture" by immigration, began her leadership in 1978 through an eleven-year reign of a reinvigorated Tory Party.

* * *

Down Under

Australia was also part—along with Latin America, the U. S., and Canada— of Crosby's "Neo-Europes," prosperous countries in the temperate zone and therefore attractive destinations for Third World immigrants. The Down Under continent also experienced rising immigration levels, mostly from Asia, along with the public dissent and complaint that large-scale immigration everywhere generates, carrying the issue into Aussie politics.

I traveled there in late 1992 to attend a conference on immigration, and met many of the Australian reductionists. I found Australia unlike Europe (between 1985 and 2007 I visited Germany, the UK, Italy and Spain) in that the critique of current immigration levels had not yet been taken up by political parties. That critique came, as in the U. S., from a small but well-organized pair of "immigration reform" groups similar to America's FAIR and NumbersUSA, except that one (AESF) was mostly academics and professionals while the other (AAFI), was a more populist and confrontational group of "average" citizens. The Australian immigration reformers I met, people like academics/ writers Katherine Betts, Bob Birrell and Mark O'Connor of AESF, and Rod and Robyn Spencer of AAFI, did not seem to me "rightist" in any meaning of that term, but were talented, congenial and informed people, devoted environmentalists concerned about Australia's fragile ecology, patriots in the best sense. Like their U.S. compatriots, they were called racists and other vile terms. In a month there I found no racists, no haters (though I heard a Catholic priest tell of a cab ride in which the Muslim cabbie expressed an ardent desire to personally drive a knife into the heart of Salman Rushdie, a London-based Muslim author who had written a "blasphemous" book). One of the Aussie restrictionists, writer Dennis McCormack, was more than willing to open the issue of the assimilability of Asians and therefore the desirability of limiting their incoming numbers, a point of view explored controversially by the popular Australian historian Geoffrey Blainey in his *All For Australia* (1985). If Dennis represented the Australian hard right in immigration politics, folks from that side of their reform movement would be acceptable to date your daughter.

Thus in Australia in the early 1990s, large-scale and sustained immigration, most of it from Asia, had produced a small social movement, but not a political movement or party. That was in 1992, before newly elected member of the House of Representatives Pauline Hanson founded One Nation in 1997, after making a much-quoted speech lamenting that Australia was "in danger of being swamped by Asians."

Hanson, an attractive high school dropout and fish-and-chips shop owner, *was* One Nation, and she mounted an enthusiastic full-scale attack on government "affirmative action" subsidies and favoritism to aborigines, demanding also "an immediate halt to immigration until the unemployment problem is solved." Her party took 23 percent of the votes and eleven seats in a Queensland election in 1998. Then it collapsed from internal division and charges of misappropriated funds, and also because the Labor Party head, John Howard, began to sprinkle his speeches with promises of firmness on immigration, "stealing my message," Hanson said. One Nation dissolved in 2005. Hanson was "Australia's Hitler," said the mainstream press and other politicians, making France's Le Pen appear "broadminded." Some of my new Australian friends found her uneducated and not very bright (when asked if she was a xenophobe, Hanson said, "Please explain the term.") Others worked briefly for her party. Pauline Hanson now sells real estate, and appears occasionally on "reality TV," dancing and singing country and western music. For a brief, turbulent period she had brought together and expressed the populist resentments against both non-European immigrants and Australia's ruling elite classes, exploring the potential of the angry edge of populist politics.

* * *

The immigration flows into the core western nations of the European Union did not diminish in volume in the 1990s, with minor and temporary exceptions such as Belgium, where a rise in asylum-seekers to 27,000 in the early Nineties prompted a government curb returning the number to 14,000. Illegal immigration, increasingly organized by human traffickers, continued everywhere, despite sporadic governmental promises to curb it—500,000 to 1.5 million illegals estimated (nobody had confidence in the estimates) living in Germany, 300,000 to 500,000 in Italy, and 90,000 in little Belgium. Legal numbers also climbed. The UK statistics office reported that 500,000 non-EU immigrants entered Britain in the decade after 1994, and then admitted a 45 percent under-count and raised the number to 900,000. By the end of the Nineties, the entry into Germany of guestworkers, along with refugees, illegal aliens, and thousands of ethnic Germans from the states of the former USSR built a foreign-born population of 7.3 million by 2000, about 10 percent of the national total. France counted six million.

"There is a deep sense that we are full up, that we have no room, and that we are being exploited," said a migration expert in London in 2000, speaking of Europe as a whole.

* * *

My trips to Europe during those years, supplemented by reading, and annual discussions with the two German immigration researchers who showed up every year at the Writers Workshop, made me of three minds about the European encounter with large-scale legal and illegal immigration.

From one angle, European nations could be said to be handling this emotion-clouded immigration policy issue better than we did in the U. S., in that it periodically broke through into national politics, and was usually pushed there by third parties who were squelched in the American constitutional system. No U. S. presidential election from the Sixties forward, and very few local campaigns, had made room for the immigration question. The blanket of taboo could be found in every European nation, but it seemed far more suffocating of political speech and action in the U. S. (and Australian and Canadian) system.

Still, after the talk was talked in Europe, and after minority party immigration restriction politicians like Le Pen and Haider were heard, no European nation effectively controlled immigration from the Eighties forward. We and they came in the end to the same results—mass immigration ran on, with a large and ill-assimilated Islamic contingent.

* * *

Sustained immigration from east and south was clearly changing Europe in fundamental ways, carrying Europe no one knew where. The European Union seemed for a time to offer a vision of where Europe was headed, but in the early years of the twenty-first century, voters in France and the Netherlands rejected further expansion of the twenty-five member states, and it was understood that the prospect of admitting Muslim Turkey that brought into focus the religion culture-based conflicts I have touched upon here. Some Europeans, the best educated perhaps, thought the EU's evolution was a pathway to a post-nation state, post-nationalism world, and it was the only way to leave behind the horrors from the first half of the twentieth century. Certainly nationalism was on the defensive and not assertive. A German politician in 2000 said that the millions of foreigners in Germany must be made to adopt a German "*Leitkultur*" or guiding culture.

"The term is disgusting, and also menacing to immigrants," said a spokesman for Chancellor Gerhard Schroder.

"After Auschwitz there can be nothing specifically German," editorialized *Frankfurter Allgemeine*.

The Foreign Minister said: "This idea of '*Leitkultur*' today, in a post-national Europe, is completely crazy."

In 2001, teaching a graduate seminar composed of twenty-three young Europeans at the University of Bologna, the subject of their nationality somehow came up. I went around the room with the question of student nationality. The two Brits said they didn't think of themselves as British; the Hollander said the same; all the Italians somewhat hesitantly denied a sense of Italian identity; and the German girl vociferously rejected any idea of German-ness, for herself or any of her friends from Frankfurt. What are you, then? , I asked them. The group was hesitant.

Then someone said, "I guess we are Europeans."

Half nodded, but not enthusiastically. The other half were silent, and uncomfortable.

Chapter Twenty-One:
1996-2001 — A Stronger Reform Movement, But Still No Turn

The next time a politician gets spouting off about what this country needs, either hit him with a tubercular tomato or lay right back in your seat and go asleep. Because this country has got too big to need a damn thing. — Will Rogers

Now what should we do? As the legislative disasters of 1996 faded behind us, the situation became worse than when we started in 1978—a mostly self-selected legal immigration over a million each year, with illegal flows of at least 500,000 per year filtering into the growing resident illegal population with its insidious, hard-to-see spread of lawlessness. The overall immigrant population was growing six times faster than the native-born, and the immigrant poverty rate and welfare dependency was 50 percent higher than that of natives. *Now* what should we do?

At FAIR and CIS board meetings (I was the only person on both boards) everyone tried to be cheerful, but it was a discouraging time. On occasion, I tried dark humor. At virtually every meeting of the FAIR board, after we had reviewed the bleak legislative prospect, I would demand that Steve Swensrud, a successful Boston money manager, mobilize his considerable financial talents and maneuver America's overheated capitalism into a severe economic depression. I argued that as long as this euphoric boom psychology continued, fixing a broken immigration system (or anything else requiring hard choices) was off the Washington agenda. Steve shook his head, and with a weak smile, didn't dispute my point.

I tried my friends' patience further with another notion of mine, that what was needed to move our issue in the right direction was what I called "a beneficial disaster." The American political system often confronts festering public problems that our democracy will not face until some painful crisis forces action. Rational persuasion does not suffice. An example: the basic environmental law of modern times, the National Environmental Policy Act, was languishing in Congress with dim prospects in 1969 when Shell Oil drilling Platform 'A' blew out off the California coast at Santa Barbara on January 28. It dumped a foul-smelling flood of black tars on the white beaches. The public was horrified by television scenes of soiled beaches and oil-mired sea birds, and Congress quickly passed NEPA.

It was a Beneficial Disaster as one weighed the costs and benefits, and I proposed that such facilitating events should not be left to chance. An Office of Beneficial Disasters should be established in the West Wing (or the basement?) of the White House, to arrange for mild but timely disasters to focus attention and move blocked legislation forward. What we needed in the late 1990s, with mass immigration, legal and illegal, steaming ahead, was a Beneficial Disaster that would cast a quite negative bright light on our porous borders. Here my idea became fuzzy. An awful economic depression with double-digit unemployment might suffice, but the costs at some point could be said to outweigh the benefits. Perhaps a small catastrophe brought to us across our untended borders would do, something modest in cost but spectacular on television. I recalled an intriguing example. A leper came into Florida on one of the boats carrying the Mariel refugees in 1980, and caused a great consternation about what we were getting when President Carter flung open the door to the cargo of Havana's prisons. A few of us, in a light moment, charged that John Tanton or Roger had rented the leper and put him on the U.S. bound ship. It produced a sharp policy impact at little cost, however it happened.

The reaction to my cloudy idea was mixed, and I have not yet received the Nobel Prize for it. My idea needs work, but I believe I was onto something in exploring the educational and bottleneck-breaking potential of painful public events. I could not have known that the equivalent of an Office of Beneficial Disasters under the management of one Osama bin Laden was even then generating a plan for a disaster that in 2001 would re-focus Americans' attention on their broken immigration system. This office, however, was not located in the White House but in some cave in Afghanistan, and the plan was aimed at the World Trade Center in New York and the Pentagon.

This was, of course, not what I had in mind. The beneficial disasters I pondered would, like the Santa Barbara oil spill, just kill a few seagulls (which gave me some pain, yet was a price to be paid), not some 3,000 innocent people, in order to move the frozen gears of government. But even this ghastly disaster, designed by the wrong people for the worst motives, had some beneficial effects, as we shall see in a few pages.

This came in 2001. Much changed in immigration politics and the nature of immigration's human flows from 1996 to that pivotal attack from abroad.

* * *

The Clinton Administration's Pandering Politics

On the level of immigration politics and policy, we reductionist reformers and the public interest continued to lose in Clinton's second term, in smaller bites than in the debacle of 1996, but with a depressing regularity.

From our perspective, the high water mark of the Clinton presidency came when he met with Barbara Jordan in 1996, nodded respectfully during her strong presentation of her commission's reductionist recommendations, and then issued a press release that he agreed with the report. At about the same time a presidentially appointed Council on Sustainable Development issued a report, *Sustainable America* (1996). It noted that "continued population growth steadily makes more difficult the job of "moving toward sustainability."

The Council, in a section entitled, "Improving Immigration Strategies" stated:

Immigration amounts for one-third of total U. S. population growth [it was closer to three-quarters] and is a factor that must be addressed in the overall effort to stabilize population voluntarily.

271

Slippery. The linkage was noted and no recommendations for immigration policy change were made. We were glad to see even this language, knowing there must have been an intramural battle to get even that far. The report, linking sustainability to immigration reduction, drew no attention, certainly not from Clinton, who was, whenever he had a choice to make, now robustly headed in an Expansionist and on-sustainable direction.

In 1996, election year political considerations immediately took control of his administration's immigration stance. Asian campaign money, as the *Boston Globe* revealed, led Clinton to reverse his support for the vitally important repeal of the brothers and sisters' fifth preference (as recommended by the Jordan Commission), and it was dropped from the 1996 legislative agenda. It did not improve our mood when White House counsel Lanny Davis, asked about this policy shift, replied that it wasn't only Asian money that produced it but also pressure from the Roman Catholic Church and the Microsoft Corporation. Early in that election year, Vice President Gore pressured the INS to greatly accelerate its slow-moving "citizenship USA" program, with the goal of registering a million Hispanics so that they could, as expected, vote heavily for Clinton-Gore in November. In the rush, 180,000 applicants were pushed through without the usual background checks for criminal records.

Clinton did not stop thinking about immigration after he ordered that Gore-led acceleration of citizenship processing. He made a curious speech at Portland State University in 1998 in which he warned, as we restrictionists often had, that "a new wave of immigration larger than any in a century, far more diverse than any in our history, brings vast change, including "no majority race in California in five years," a point he made again in his 2000 State of the Union Address. "Unless we handle this well, immigration of this sweep and scope could threaten the bonds of our nation."

This seemed a good start. Then we discovered what he apparently meant by "handle this well," when the president, after praising immigrants as "the most restless, the most adventurous, the most innovative and industrious of people" (including American citizens?), condemned recent "policies and ballot propositions that exclude immigrants from our civic life." (It's wrong to exclude illegal immigrants from our civic life?) and called such measures "wrong, it's un-American." So "handle it well" did not mean prudently lower the numbers or make any adjustments of selection mechanisms. It meant raise no objections to any of this, including the illegal part.

These words were followed by administration-backed policy changes that expanded both legal and illegal immigration. In 1998, Attorney General Janet Reno directed the INS to terminate traditional worksite inspections for the presence of illegal aliens. Read that sentence again. In 2000, the INS quietly announced that it had ended all interior enforcement efforts to capture illegal aliens, leaving the Border Patrol the only American police force an illegal alien needed to get past in order to lead a peaceful life in the interior of the U.S. He would come into contact with law enforcement only if a felony were committed. Many did, and the INS deported 22,000 criminal aliens in 1997, and 8,600 in 1999. Presumably they came back across our porous border as soon as convenient. Repeated violations of our laws did not increase the penalty, meant only a painless plane or bus ride back to another starting point. Few Americans knew that law enforcement policy under Clinton's INS administrator Doris Meissner had become, without fanfare, *We give up on interior enforcement of our immigration laws.*

"Once inside the country," the *New York Times* reported in 1999, "illegal immigrants are largely left alone."

The executive branch had quietly all but abandoned immigration law enforcement.

Among us there were two explanations for the administration's collapse on law enforcement so soon after the president told Barbara Jordan that he "agreed" with her views. Some said it was lacking the political will to enforce the law and calculated—Doris Meissner said as much more than once—that the public really had little interest in such an effort. Others said that Gore's 1996 campaign exposed the presence of a more ambitious plan, to endlessly expand the number of lower-income people living in America in the expectation that the great majority would be reliable Democratic, pro-welfare state voters. If, however, one closely read the *Weekly Compilation of Presidential Documents*, one discovered, reading his June 13 remarks on meeting with his Advisory Board on Race, that Bill Clinton had a larger plan that guided his expansionist policies.

"We will soon be, in the next few decades, a multiracial society in which no racial group is a majority. And we are living in a world in which that gives us an enormous advantage in relating to other countries in the world since we have people from every country in the world here."

So the purpose of immigration policy was to end, as quickly as possible, the white majority, which was a serious handicap in dealing with the modern world. On to the First Universal Nation.

That is a rather large idea. It deserved wide and deep discussion. Or some might say, if you are convinced that it is correct and wise, you *can't* have wide and deep discussion, or the unenlightened public might repudiate and reverse such a radical policy.

* * *

There was Expansionist pressure on other fronts in the Nineties. A particularly indefensible guestworker program for skilled workers passed in 1990. The H1-B visa had grown from a program of last resort to one preferred by high-tech employers who were quick to claim that "qualified" Americans (i.e., those willing to accept lower than current going wages) could not be found. The original number of the visas, capped at 65,000, was doubled to 115,000 in 1998, while FAIR, the AFL-CIO, and a small organized band of American computer programmers protested. It seemed that every year there was a bipartisan congressional clamor to give in to employers and raise H1-B totals even higher. Congresspersons love to give away benefits that have no budgetary costs. In 2000, President Clinton reversed an earlier position. He asked for and received from Congress an increase of H1-B visas to 200,000. This meant 200,000 high-wage jobs in the U.S. would shift to imported foreigners, the wage lowered.

That was just one of many fronts where holes were constantly being punched in the broken fence of U.S. immigration law. FAIR claimed to have delayed some H1-B expansions, but in the end the critics of the H1-B program lost almost every contest.

Amnesties rolled through Congress virtually every year in the late 1990s—for Central Americans in 1997, Haitians in 1998, and Central Americans again in 1999. It was almost a feeding frenzy on the Hill in 1998-2000. Legislators were apparently convinced (for good reason) that they could reap the benefits of handing out permission to foreigners to live in America without paying any political costs. Senate Democrats in October, 2000, fell just short in an effort to suspend senate rules and vote on their "Latino and Immigrant Fairness Act," a massive amnesty to a variety of illegals from Central America and elsewhere. There had been no hearings on the bill. The political weakness of restrictionists was almost daily confirmed.

The executive branch ran with the same Expansionist current. The *New York Times* in March, 2000 quoted INS associate commissioner Robert Bach as conceding that illegal aliens who got past border guards were now left pretty much alone, the INS concentrating on deporting those coming to their attention because they were convicted of crimes.

* * *

Both parties seemed to smell Hispanic votes and corporate as well as ethnic lobbyist campaign contributions as the 2000 election neared. A potent coalition of conservatives and liberal politicians, Catholic bishops, Arab, Asian and Haitian ethnic handlers, and business groups came together in 2000 to press for a range of "pro-immigrant" policy changes, and launched an effort called "Fix 96," meaning repeal of those few aspects of the 1996 law designed to reduce illegal immigration and asylum abuse. These "Fix 96" backward steps included reinstating the notorious Section 245(i) program that allowed illegal aliens to stay in the country while they attempted to adjust their status—in effect, to successfully butt in line in front of others waiting abroad for visas.

To make things worse, potential allies with a mixed record on the issue increasingly veered away toward Expansionism. The Executive Council of the AFL-CIO, desperate to reverse the long-term decline in membership to 13.9 percent of the work force, voted in early 2000 to renounce its historic position on importing foreign labor, and called for an amnesty for all illegal aliens and repeal of employer sanctions—effectively recommending open borders.

* * *

The Sierra Club Stumbles Again

There was little we could do about a vote at the annual meeting of the AFL-CIO, but many of us were voting members of the Sierra Club and understood that unending population growth in America doomed the organization's mission of environmental protection. Indeed, members of that outlook were responsible for the Club's Population Committee and its urgings that the Club adopt an official position that immigration must be reduced if the American environment were to be preserved. This narrowly failed adoption by the Sierra Board in 1991, after which it (in 1996) adopted a "neutral" stance on immigration policy in an effort to stifle the issue permanently. It came to the front again in 1998 when members placed a resolution on the annual ballot placing the Club behind immigration reduction. The board denounced and undercut the referendum, offering the muddled argument that population "was an international issue," and the measure was defeated in a 1999 vote, 60-40 percent, with only 14 percent of members voting.

Gaylord Nelson, founder of Earth Day, wrote: "Until we address this growing influx of immigrants...our population will continue to grow indefinitely. . . . Never has an issue with such major consequences for this country been so ignored."

Legendary Sierra Club director David Brower, who was among those prominent members who had supported taking a position against what he called "overimmigration," indignantly resigned from the Club after the vote. Nevertheless, our side had lost again.

* * *

Our Case Gets Stronger

Still, looking back, a few sturdy optimists among us were right, even in the dismal , to insist that we were making considerable progress in some areas and better days might be ahead.

Intellectually, the weight of the facts and the accumulation of a multi-faceted critique of the immigration status quo began to convert respected academic social scientists and writers on policy issues. The National Research Council in 1997 published a study, *The New Americans*, and the first news reports told the public that the group's conclusion was the old, reassuring one. "Academy's Report Says Immigration Benefits the U.S.: A Major Economic Gain," was *The New York Times* headline. FAIR's press release read it differently, declaring that "NRC Report Confirms the Burdens of Immigration," and Mark Krikorian of *CIS* told reporters that the study found that "there are losers as well as winners" in the overall economic impact and that immigration brings a net fiscal burden to all states, amounting to $1,178 per family in California. The *Times'* headline version came under withering attack when two prominent economists whose work was central to the study, George Borjas and Richard Freeman, published in the *Times* an indignant Op-Ed rebuttal to the early news summaries, "Findings We Never Found." It soon became clear that the group's chairman in an early, rushed press release not vetted with the principal authors, and in subsequent congressional testimony, had spun the conclusions toward an endorsement of current immigration flows as benign because economically beneficial. Borjas and Freeman pointed out that the net gain to the economy was small, at most $10 billion, miniscule in a $1 trillion-plus economy. It was more than offset by the finding that current immigration imposed, and it was a substantial net fiscal burden (from $14-20 billion) on the states—thus on all taxpayers—for social services uncompensated by taxes, ranging from California's $1,178 to $235 per household in New Jersey. There were internal inequities not to be overlooked. "Immigration is not a free lunch," they wrote, and its impacts were unfairly distributed. Immigration produced winners and losers, the latter clustered among working class, poorly educated and minority Americans who had to compete with the newcomers.

Confirmation of these findings came again in the McCarthy/Vernez study of immigration's impacts on California, which was done by RAND in 1997. Large flows of poorly educated immigrants, they found, had imposed a great strain on public services, and pushed many native workers out of the state. Their recommendations lined up with the Jordan Commission: cut immigration to 500,000 annually, and shift selection criteria from family ties to the economic needs of the U.S. economy.

Another myth that was central to the unending call for more foreign labor was that there were "jobs Americans wouldn't do," and where foreign labor must be tapped. This was the age-old refrain of many employers, from the cotton plantation slaveholders of the Old South to the newest and wealthiest cluster of employers based in the Silicon Valley high-tech companies. No industry was more persistent in this demand for foreign labor or more successful in winning access to a subsidized labor force from Congress than the perishable crop growers of the southwest and south. The research on immigrant farm workers, however, had long been critical of the guestworker illegal alien solution to agriculture's labor needs. In the 1990s, the dean of those scholars, Philip L. Martin of UC Davis, began to publish in essays and congressional testimony versions of what would take book form as *Promise Unfulfilled: Unions, Immigrants, and the Farm Workers* (2003).

Expanding flows of illegal workers into the southwest and especially California had defeated the hopes of Cesar Chavez and his United Farm Workers (UFW) and other unions of winning higher wages and benefits. Martin found that the growers' argument that food prices would sharply rise without fresh infusions of Mexican labor collapsed on examination. Farm labor costs were less than half of one percent of the cost to households of fresh produce.

"If the influx of immigrant workers were slowed and farm wages rose," Martin argued, "the labor cost of one dollar's worth of fruits or vegetables would rise from five to six cents to seven to eight cents. The average American family's spending for fruits and vegetables would rise from $322 a year to $330. This would hardly be noticed, but other effects had the potential to bring the transformations Chavez had worked for. Growers would be spurred to mechanize, reducing the need for the arduous stoop labor that need not be a part of the American economy or the lives of Americans.

"If the U.S. closed the agricultural port of entry," Martin went on, "the result would be higher farm wages and more mechanization."

Since this wasn't U.S. policy, a flow of impoverished people came annually into the country, each new wave undermining the well-being of the one before it. "I conclude that, in the long run, there is nothing more expensive than cheap food."

Another respected economist sharpened his critique of the immigration status quo in the 1990s—Harvard's George Borjas who in 2000 published his influential *Heaven's Door*. "Our immigration policy has been spinning out of control for decades," he argued. The skills of immigrants relative to natives has been declining. "All native workers are worse off from immigration," net economic gains are small and accrue to the American wealthy, and the numbers are too high. In that year, George agreed to be the Richard Estrada Fellow at CIS, which meant doing some writing for us. (Richard died of a heart attack in 1999, a shock and loss to us all.) In 2002, I called on behalf of the CIS board and asked George to join us.

As I began my sales talk, he interrupted: "Otis, you don't have to persuade me. I'm concerned about my country."

He served a term on our board.

* * *

It might seem surprising that the words "our immigration policy has been spinning out of control for decades" were written in a Harvard office, the bluest zone of that blue state. The larger surprise came when this Cambridge, Massachusetts center of liberal-left thought and political correctness produced at the end of the century three other new immigration critics of the highest stature who formerly had little or nothing to say on the topic.

Respected sociologist Christopher Jencks, reviewing recent scholarly work on immigration at the end of 2000, concluded, to his evident surprise, that "the winners are the employers who get cheaper labor," and "the losers are unskilled American-born workers," with "an adverse effect on African-Americans...especially marked." Nathan Glazer concluded that "immigration not only contributes to growing inequality in general, but makes life more difficult for black workers in particular." The same focus on immigration's negative impact on blacks, the point we had so unsuccessfully urged upon the NAACP leadership in the early 1980s, came from another Harvard academic, Orlando Patterson. In 1996, he urged severe fines for employers of illegal aliens and a "halt" to the admission of unskilled immigrants.

In another building on the Harvard campus, the distinguished political scientist, Samuel P. Huntington, addressed immigration for the first time in his long career and minced no words: "Migration is the central issue of our time," and the "endless stream" into the U.S. was not assimilating as had "past waves of immigration," he wrote in *The American Enterprise* (December, 2000). "The Mexican problem" especially concerned him, as it was different from all historic immigration experience in four respects—it came across a shared 2,000 mile frontier joining a First and a Third World country; it contributed half of all U.S. immigration; a large portion of it is illegal; and it is concentrated in the southwest region. Assimilation cannot be assumed, since "the factors that made assimilation work in the past waves of immigration...are no longer present." Mexican immigration, "an endless stream, much of it illegal," amounts to "a major challenge to the cultural, and conceivably political integrity of the United States . . ."

While he did not work out of Cambridge, Massachusetts, , it sent shock waves throughout the Jewish establishment when Stephen Steinlight, Director of National Affairs at the American Jewish Committee, wrote an essay published by CIS in the summer of 2001 in which he reported "a deeply felt conversion experience" on immigration. Steinlight now urged American Jews to set aside all taboos and to discuss the remarkable demographic transformation that immigration was bringing to the U.S. and with it "the special problem of large-scale Muslim immigration." He urged a policy of lower immigration in general and a rethinking of all aspects of American policy, including "the open-ended entry of Muslim fundamentalists" with no means of keeping track of them.

The emergence of an articulate Jewish restrictionist voice was major news, but not entirely a surprise to me. In the spring, 1995, I received a phone call in Santa Barbara from Robert Pickus, head of the World Without War Council in Berkeley. He wanted to bring together a working group to make proposals to the INS on citizenship education for immigrants. To him, this meant listening to the views of the entire range of stakeholders, from Latino Open Border activists to restrictionist reformers from FAIR. I expressed doubt that the Latinos would come if we were there, and I had additional doubt that a civil dialogue could result. Latino activists, in sharp contrast to Latino citizens that I know, generally brought moral arrogance, harsh labels, and some race-based hatred, in my experience. Pickus brushed aside my concerns, and, being in favor of civil dialogue between these groups, I agreed to attend. At the meeting, Pickus, one of the most gifted discussion leaders I have ever witnessed, firmly refused to let the Latinos persist with their opening moralistic diatribe against we "xenophobes." He sternly insisted on civility in this meeting he had called and hosted, and the Latinos (I remember only two names, Martha Jimenez of MALDEF and Herb Castillo of some Bay Area group), were startled at having their diatribe against the racist xenophobes challenged. They made a polite apology and cooperated. We talked past each other for several hours, but at least in respectful tones. In private conversation, I found Pickus alarmed about mass immigration, especially the growing Muslim numbers.

"America is for Jews an aircraft carrier of refuge in a sea of deadly enemies. We must not lose our close relationship with those who own and steer that aircraft carrier."

If Pickus and Steinlight (not to forget that wise New Yorker Gene Katz, who in joining the CIS Board as early as 1986 had risked the displeasure of his Jewish friends and his wife, who was reluctant to welcome Gene's CIS colleagues in her home) were followed by other Jews in what Steinlight called his "conversion" to immigration reduction. It might contribute to a substantial realignment of forces, and would certainly be a major opening to the American left.

* * *

The end-of-century writers and intellectuals I have mentioned, taken together and added to the substantial pre-Nineties writing of scholars such as Vernon Briggs, Leon Bouvier, Phil Martin, Peter Skerry and Michael Teitlebaum, as well as journalist Georgie Anne Geyer, enlarged and strengthened the already vigorous and wide-ranging critique of current immigration patterns and policy. In the Eighties if one had asked, "Who are the reductionist voices identified strongly with liberal and/or black/Hispanic perspectives and identification?, there was a list of authors but it was a frustratingly short one: Vernon Briggs and Ray Marshall from the labor union camp on the left, Governor Dick Lamm whose focus was always on the environment and society we passed on to our children, Richard Estrada writing from a distinctly Mexican-American angle of vision, black sociologist Jackie Jackson and Dean Frank Morris.

* * *

New Liberal Critics of the Immigration Status Quo

The Nineties, fortunately, brought new voices from the left of center. Roberto Suro, writer for the *Washington Post* and author of two Twentieth Century Fund papers on immigration, offered a bold call for ending illegal immigration to protect American Hispanics from job, housing and other forms of competition with large illegal flows of Mexican and Central American labor.

In his *Strangers Among Us: How Latino Immigration is Transforming America* (1998), he wrote: "The wild card of illegal immigration "has to be taken out of play...Latinos have the most to gain by gradually but deliberately closing the doors...to illegal immigration."

Suro had a clear conception of how to end illegal entry.

"Ten years of consistent enforcement" based on entry-exit tracking and including serious and real "punishments" for illegal entry—such as a five- year ban, even for repeat offenders a lifetime ban, on entry into the U.S. for any purpose. "It can be done."

Suro had lined up with Cesar Chavez, most of LULAC's leadership from the 1920s through the 1950s, and Hispanic writers such as Richard Estrada in the 1980s, who had argued that Latinos already legally in the U.S. had the most to lose from annual streams of illegal and exploitable cheap labor.

Senior Editor of *Harpers* Michael Lind's *The Next American Nation* (1995) received wide attention in mid-decade. He argued that the multiculturalist-dominated era beginning in the 1960s was resulting in the fragmenting of the nation which he saw as a "project of the white Overclass" leading to what Lind called "Brazilianization"— a class division more dangerous than the ethnoracial "Balkanization" that worried some writers. Lind urged a return to what he called "liberal nationalism" in order to make fundamental changes in this social order, including strict reduction of the mass immigration which has been a chief tool of "the white Overclass" in their campaign to reduce wages and weaken unions. In an article in *Mother Jones* in 1998, Lind argued that "immigration reform is the best hope for a swift improvement in the wages and bargaining power of working Americans." In a 1995 *New York Times* Op-Ed, he stated that "the harmful effects of legal as well as illegal immigration on low income Americans are real." Lind was joined by another liberal writer, Ronald Steel, who wrote in *The New Republic* in 1997 that "large-scale admission of unskilled immigrants creates a cheap labor pool and renders unskilled Americans unemployable. The high social cost is hidden behind a smoke screen of sentimentality."

* * *

A critique of the immigration status quo also flourished in the latter 1990s within the conservative intellectual encampment, supplementing the earlier writings of Brimelow and Buchanan. William Buckley's *National Review*, flagship of conservative journals since the 1950s, gave increasing space to critics of the current immigration regime, adding to Brimelow's views the kindred arguments of John O'Sullivan, Paul Craig Roberts, and Mark Krikorian. At the end of 2000, the American Enterprise Institute, so long the home of Open Border thinkers such as Ben Wattenberg, signaled an abrupt change of heart. The editor of the Institute's magazine, *The American Enterprise*, acknowledging an intellectual debt to the Center for Immigration Studies, introduced a cluster of six articles on "Our Immigration Predicament" by saying "we are now importing problems," many of them "linked to sheer numbers overload." Four of the six essays strongly tilted toward alarm at the prospects for successful assimilation of the current immigration streams, especially Sam Huntington's bluntly titled piece, "Why Mexico is a Problem."

* * *

Intellectual Impoverishment Among Defenders of the Status Quo

On the Expansionist side during those end-of-century years, intellectual defenders of the mass immigration status quo thinned out, both in their numbers and the quality of their arguments. Julian Simon died in 1998 of a comment by Mark Twain that he had received an invitation to the funeral of so-and-so and had replied that, while he could not attend, he thoroughly approved of the occasion. While Simon's preposterous optimism about endless augmentation of American population growth and consumption would still be available in libraries, it would no longer be periodically updated and the author would not be available to be quoted in the media.

The sad intellectual condition of the Open Borders persuasion was painfully evident in two end-of-century books briefly reviewed and then forgotten. Stanford University educationist Sanford Ungar's, *Fresh Blood: The New American Immigrants* (1995), offered "a book of immigrant stories" to substantiate his closing argument that immigrants "renew, enrich" America with "concert pianists, rocket scientists," proving again that "there has never been any real basis for opposition to immigration but racism." A sentimental hymn to his grandparents, it ended in desperate name-calling. Equally sentimental and unengaged with the growing critical literature on immigration's impacts was Michael Barone's *The New Americans* (2001), another rambling set of immigrant stories said to reassure us that the successful assimilation of the Great Wave of a century earlier would somehow repeat itself again.

"We've been here before."

But of course, we had never been "here" before. Our assimilative capacities for the first time were working against a regnant multiculturalism and also for the first time with 60 percent of our immigration coming from one country sharing our southern border. Ben Wattenberg wrote a breathless book acclaiming America as *The First Universal Nation* (1991), perhaps the clearest statement of what America's elites were trying to do when they defended open borders. In Wattenberg's vision, immigrants from everywhere coming in an unending large volume not only solved all of our current labor shortage problems but something vastly more important. That diversifying flow allowed America to transform itself into "the first universal nation." "First" because no "nation" had ever been built out of such disparate materials, and "universal" because "we now come from everywhere, becoming one people."

This was indeed a bold and novel idea based on little more than multicultural enthusiasm. It should have generated more discussion— and heated discussion, as it wasn't clear who authorized such a grand experiment. Wattenberg and others in the 1990s added another new argument for mass immigration. It fended off the brand new and awful prospect of population decline,. restoring "growth" to dying societies as well as bringing, as immigration always does, the future Toscaninis, Navratilovas, Edward Tellers, I. M. Peis, Oppenheimers (Wattenberg's list), along with anonymous but essential nannies and busboys. Simon's therapeutical optimism lived on, but we were by this time better prepared to respond to such half-baked enthusiasms.

* * *

Mobilization at the Grassroots

One has to be impressed at the end of the century at our movement's considerable progress in creating an impressive body of critical policy analysis and the formulation of alternatives. However, change also requires political action, the mobilization of citizens until they gain policymakers' attention, and deploy muscular lobbies to match those of The Industry. For those of us who watched and participated in 187 in California, the rest of the 1990s gave the impression of a disappointing nationwide collapse of grassroots mobilization, even at the time when a reductionist-tilting body of policy analysis was building up so impressively.[4]

---

[4] Several people in the late 1990s were heard to complain that "restrictionist" did not have a good sound to it, and suggested "reductionist." I agreed, and will now use that term, though it is not much of an improvement. We still need a winning brand name for our project.

I cannot claim to have seen the small and multiplying signs that this too was changing. Only by looking back is it possible to see that there had been through the Nineties a growing political mobilization under the surface of things. John Tanton's, *The Social Contract* at some point began to list in every issue a selective, non-comprehensive list of groups large or organized enough to have web sites. Organizations sorted out into two layers, the Washington-based and the grassroots beyond the Beltway. From the issue of Summer, 1999, the Washington based organizations were FAIR (www.fairus.org), Roy Beck's NumbersUSA (www.numbersusa.com), Carrying Capacity Network (www.carryingcapacity.org), and Negative Population Growth (www.npg.org).

Outside the Beltway there was a substantial number of immigration reform groups (nobody seemed to know how many, but FAIR's website in 1999 listed thirty-one) with a state, regional or municipal focus. This was clearly a serious undercount, but this partial list included the persistent Prop. 187 California groups I was familiar with—Barbara Coe's California Coalition for Immigration Reform (www.ccir.net), Glen Spencer's Voices of Citizens Together (www.americanpatrol.com), recently moved to Arizona from Orange County, and Diana Hull's Californians for Population Stabilization (www.capsweb.org). Several states and many cities had one or more immigration reform groups not yet on *The Social Contract's* list. The most active of them (as far as I could tell) were in California (once home of about fifty groups), Arizona, New York, Colorado, Georgia, North Carolina, Florida, Tennessee, New York, Marin County, Austin, Texas, and Chicago. Fred Elbel's Colorado Alliance for Immigration Reform seemed to have the most complete list of links to other state groups (www.cairco.org). I suppose Dan Stein sat at the crossroads of more information on immigration reform efforts around the country than anyone else, since FAIR in the 1990s had moved away from its initial wariness about involvement with "chapters" or independent local groups, and had three regional field representatives working to encourage and guide local activities. Dan and those staff members came to each board meeting to report on developments in "the field," sharing information with the board. FAIR's newsletter in 1997 listed thirty-six grass roots immigration reform groups, from Mesa, Arizona through San Jose, California to

McLean, Virginia, and invited interested citizens to call FAIR's Field Operations Department for advice, ideas and encouragement. This list of organizations was dominated by the six or seven states receiving the most foreign immigration, but news stories were reporting the formation of reform groups in Arkansas, where FAIR played a supportive role, in Farmingville, New York, and in Siler City, North Carolina, where David Duke's KKK on one occasion unhelpfully organized a rally protesting "waves of immigration from Mexico," which reminded us that grassroots immigration politics were unpredictable.

* * *

We need another category for a third type of expression of rising public concern over immigration—a growing number of web sites providing opinion and analysis. In 2000, Peter Brimelow launched the New York-based VDare (www.vdare.com) with its lively stable of writers on immigration-related issues. UC Davis computer professor Norman Matloff offered his critical coverage of the H1-B program (www.heather. cs.ucdavis.edu.immigration), as did Rob Sanchez (www.ZaZona.com). Canadian restrictionist perspectives were found at www.canadafirst. net.. To mention only a few.

* * *

Connecting the Grassroots to Washington

Discouraged by the defeats in the 1990s in Congress, executive branch and courts, as well as in city councils and state legislatures, I approached the end of the century torn between two conflicting assessments of the health of our movement in the countryside, insofar as I could take its measure and pulse. On the optimistic side, one had to be impressed by the stubborn tenacity of many state and local citizens' groups, some of them entering their second decade. While some of the groups had dissolved, such as Debbie Sutherland's Santa Barbara organization or the Corpus Christi network held together by the multitalented Janet Harte who died in 2000, new ones kept springing up. There seemed more of them as time went on. Were they making an impact on local politics and politicians?

There was little systematic evidence on this, which left us a social movement story yet to be written. At first it seemed that attrition would match startups. Local groups found it hard to keep productively busy if all they could think of to do was to "write to your congressman." In the 1990s, and with its budget growing, FAIR developed a more coherent "grassroots" program, maintaining a small office in Los Angeles and two or three regional field agents. Their job was to travel to hot spots, cheer up the troops, and suggest local projects such as visits to editorial boards of newspapers and TV stations or lobby city councils on issues such as sanctuary resolutions or municipal establishment of official "hiring halls" that provided illegal labor. FAIR held its first national conference in D.C. for over 200 local activists in 1996, and found it an energizing occasion to encourage the grassroots soldiers, give them a sense of a national effort, and go down to the Hill on Friday afternoon to lobby congressional staff.

This "rally in D.C. in the spring" occasion was repeated several times by FAIR in the 1990s, and from these "IRAW" (Immigration Reform Awareness Week) gatherings, supplemented by visits to local groups, we FAIR board members learned something very heartening about what was not happening to the movement—intrusion of people representing what Theodore Roosevelt called "the lunatic fringe" often attracted to protest movements. We didn't quite know what sort of lunatics might show up, but since the issue was immigration, the worry was (and had been from the beginning) that our movement might attract, despite our moderate tone and complete absence of any language that could be construed as a racial agenda, white or otherwise, a handful of people who disliked certain ethnic or racial groups or had a white nationalist agenda (whatever that might be). The good news was, this was not happening.

* * *

White Nationalism? What Was It, and Where Was It?

As an historian of the United States, I knew something about the long history of an institution that was once a sizeable force but was now a scattered rabble—the Ku Klux Klan. Farther out on the Right, there had been surprisingly few American Nazis in the 1930s, but David Bennett's impressive survey, *The Party of Fear: From Nativist Movements to the New Right in American History* (1988), described (and explained) the virtual disappearance of what he called "antialien extremists of the Right." By the 1980s Bennett calculated that there were less than 500 American Nazis--one-third of them "nuts," one-third people who liked to wear military uniforms, and one-third FBI infiltrators. The KKK by the mid-1980s had perhaps 12,000 members scattered around in rivalrous groups. A violent shadowy group called (sometimes) The Order, was shattered by FBI raids in the mid-1980s, but occasionally the media would discover violent neo-Nazi cells such as the Aryan Nation, White American Resistance, Posse Comitatus, Creativity, and the shifting political cult gathered around the erratic Lyndon La Rouche. There was "no real movement" arising out of the "stunted" remnants on the contemporary neo-Nazi right, Bennett concluded, and no prospect of one. Rising immigration levels produced a reform movement of which FAIR was the primary organizational voice, and Bennett saw in the arguments of FAIR and the broader immigration reform movement "no return to the nativist traditions of the past."

When a journalist during the Prop. 187 episode in California called immigration historian John Higham and asked: "What do you make of the nativists?" Higham responded, "I don't know any nativists."

I knew nothing about contemporary white nationalism. The media at the end of the century gave the sketchy impression that the tiny "white power" movement was in disarray and fragmented, its leaders harassed or imprisoned by the FBI. Whatever the size of the far right political fringe of American life, we were gratified at FAIR to find that these people didn't join up as members or write letters espousing white supremacy, and did not come to the meetings we hosted. Our field representatives reported no contact with Nazi types in the local groups with which they had contact. The grassroots engagement of FAIR over the years was on rare occasions punctuated by prickly and angry individuals in grassroots leadership positions, wanting our endorsement of a harder line, noisier protests, and more money for and fewer restraints on their projects from FAIR—that rich and complacent Washington outfit that had lost every Washington battle and didn't seem to understand that the illegals in the Farmington, Connecticut hiring hall were defecating in the shrubbery and flooding the local school system with their children.

But white nationalism? Whether this meant advocacy of "white supremacy" as in the Old South, or white separatism, or some other formulation, I (and others in our movement with a keen interest in detecting and expelling it) have not found it in our movement. There were a few black and Latino immigration reform activists in virtually every immigration reform group that I visited over the years, which was good evidence of the absence of any racial emotion. I met a member from a Chicago suburb who made it clear more than once that she didn't like Mexicans, who had too many children, etc. A room full of Mexicans seeking to go on welfare in her home place of Orange County made Barbara Coe upset, as we remember. Perhaps Coe would have been equally upset to find a roomful of Swedish immigrants all speaking only Swedish and going on welfare upon arrival. The lady from Chicago seemed to express a barnyard variety of ethnic (she might say cultural) dislike, which I encountered so infrequently in meeting immigration reform activists that only this one example comes readily to mind.

This is a far, far cry from white nationalism, as I learned from Carole Swain's book of interviews with those she identified in the 1990s as prominent White Nationalists (see Carole Swain and Russell Nieli, eds., *White Pride, White Protest: Contemporary Voices of White Nationalism*, 2002) and her *The New White Nationalism in America* (2002). Some of the white nationalists interviewed by Swain and her colleagues aligned themselves with immigration restriction as they spoke of what needed to be changed in America, but they had no program on that front, preferring practicing militia tactics in the mountain states or (a different set of people) taking on the role of intellectual/writer challenging multiculturalism. Swain, like many others writing on this topic, worried that white nationalism might spread, and recommended that the U. S. substantially reduce immigration levels in order to interdict one of the movement's energy supplies. The entire history of debate over modern mass immigration has been punctuated by predictions of a vast nasty arousal of white bigots, and reality has (so far) disappointed the hate-industry entrepreneurs like the managers of the

Southern Poverty Law Center who—we know from a meticulous expose by reporter Ken Silverstein in the November, 2000 *Harper's*— make their living by finding or simply labeling "hate groups" around which to organize oppositional fundraising.

* * *

Looking back, it seems to me that four writers occasionally attending the Writers' Workshop probably qualified as some sort of white nationalist intellectual—Larry Auster (see www.amnation.com) who stopped coming to the workshops in the 1980s; Peter Brimelow (see his e-journal <u>www. Vdare.com</u>); Jared Taylor (see his print journal, *American Renaissance*, on the web at <u>www.amren.com</u>); and Sam Francis (who died in 2005). Scott McConnell, editor of *The American Conservative* and board member at CIS wrote a short obituary salute to Sam Francis in March, 2005, and denied that Sam had been a white nationalist. When challenged on this by Taylor, Scott offered what seems to me a useful clarification. If white nationalism means white supremacy, and the hope of a return to the sustained legal and social subordination of all the other inferior races by "whites," Scott reckoned that Sam (and I would add Peter Brimelow, Jared Taylor and Larry Auster) did not fit the bill. The people who do fit the bill drive pickup trucks with mounted rifles in the West Virginia or Idaho mountains, I suppose, and I have not met them.

If, on the other hand, Scott went on, white nationalism meant "wholehearted opposition to the more flamboyantly anti-white aspects of liberal multiculturalism...the regime of discriminatory racial quotas, an assault on the American remembrance of white historical figures, the propagation of guilt among American whites for the purported crimes of their ancestors, the manipulation of hate crime statistics," and mass immigration policy "designed, implicitly or explicitly, to bring about an ethnic upheaval in American society," he thought Sam Francis did fit the bill. I would add Taylor and Auster, and point out that if the first cluster of attitudes is white nationalism, the second is quite something else with no agreed upon label. In a thoughtful and erudite history of *The Rise and Fall of Anglo America* (2004), Eric Kaufmann argues that FAIR and (as far as he can tell) the rest of the organized immigration reform movement (and also the movement to promote English) are "civic nationalists" moved by cultural, environmental and economic concerns but have no ethnoracial agenda, despite the insults thrown at them by their enemies. Writers like

Auster, Brimelow, Sam Francis and Chilton Williamson, by contrast, Kaufmann sees as "ethnic nationalists" who outspokenly prefer that America continue to have an Anglo-European majority. He is certainly right about the FAIR and CIS boards. People like Roger Connor, Liz Paddock, Sherry Barnes, Dick Lamm, Vernon Briggs, Roy Beck, Frank Morris, and many others (myself included), were determined that our leadership ranks not be hospitable to or infiltrated by the "ethnic nationalists," white, black or brown. We were always uneasy with the word "white," and saw no need for it, and didn't agree with the people who did.

A few immigration reformers of this persuasion felt that John should not have invited to the Writers Workshop intellectuals like Auster, Frances and Taylor who thought an Anglo-European ethnic majority essential to the American future, and who thought and could be expected from time to time to say that. After all, since the idea of a black interest group and a Hispanic and several Asian interest groups promoting the interest of their ethnic clan was accepted as entirely legitimate, why not a white interest group, especially as whites slipped into minority status?

FAIR stayed a thousand miles from this sentiment. As for the Writers Workshop, I sympathized with the concern about possible public relations problems posed by the attendance at this annual meeting of people whose list of concerns and themes included the conviction that the Caucasian element in America deserved some sort of defense rather than a straight diet of condemnation and the shrinkage of its influence. Yet I recoiled from disinviting intelligent and productive writers who sometimes used (as I didn't) the word "white" in speaking of what they believed to be legitimate interests. John Tanton made up the invitation list for the Writers Workshop, and he always sided with the big tent, as long as people were rational, collegial, and intellectually serious. Auster, Brimelow, Francis and Taylor always were—as was another occasional participant in the Writers Workshop, Australia's Denis McCormack, an articulate, smiling fellow whose chief interest was the implications of a loss of a white majority in his country. That struck me as a legitimate question.

Chapter Twenty-Two:
Their Big Industry and Our Little Movement

We lack entirely a working term for citizens defending their community interest when immigrants, wittingly or unwittingly, put them at risk. — Chilton Williamson, Jr.

Without question, our social movement was still outgunned by the Industry arrayed against us. A large majority of Americans wanted less immigration, but few would give up their personal time to go to group meetings where they might be asked to volunteer time and effort toward immigration policy change not only in Washington but right here in Costa Mesa, Denver, Herndon, Raleigh, Boulder, Seattle, Atlanta, and Tampa. We were a social movement by Prop. 187 days and after, but a small one, anchored not among the young college generation but among an older cohort. We had no self-interested industry behind us, groups or institutions with a financial or ethnoracial or religious stake in smaller and more selective immigration.

Our opponents were such an Industry, and this mélange of agribusiness, employers small and large, immigration lawyers, and university diversifiers could draw upon a sort of social movement of its own, the Hispanic and to a lesser degree Asian ethnic "civil rights" groups organized on campuses, in communities, even in state capitals where public funding was increasingly available. When it came time for conventional lobbying, or the sort of lobbying expressed in the street, or event, or governmental office picketing, or demonstrations, we were almost always outnumbered and always outspent. In 1997 the racially-titled organization La Raza had a budget of $13 million;

MALDEF and LULAC added another $4.5 million to the Latino part of the Open Border Lobby. If one can judge by results, in the 1990s we immigration reformers' letters, phone calls, and city council appearances seemed most frequently to be on the losing end of local struggles over sanctuary policy, or whether local police should cooperate with the INS, or whether illegals should get drivers licenses or free or in-state college tuition.

So I pondered evidence to support two contradictory assessments.

One, that grassroots mobilization of immigration reform groups as the 1990s closed was very important work taking place all over the country and attracting decent, patriotic people and some admirable local leadership with very few irascible cranks. FAIR had been right, and possibly too slow, to shed its caution, and in the 1990s, engage and encourage these grassroots groups.

Second, that two decades of such grassroots activism, assisted and supplemented by the Washington-based lobbying groups, had lost every major national policy battle and many local ones.

Half full, or half empty? This ambivalent assessment was in my *fin de siècle* mood, tilted to the pessimistic side, and reflecting the discouraging 1990s without (of course) the more optimistic perspective of the post-9/11 future. The reductionist social movement aimed at immigration reform was in the 1990s quietly gathering the size, simmering indignation and energy for a larger role in turning around the discourse on immigration and creating a climate open to policy change. In the 1990s, I did not appreciate the dimensions and potential of this relatively unreported mobilization at the grassroots, and I didn't even know that the D.C.-centered national groups had begun to meet together regularly in 1999 as a coalition informally dubbed "the Exchange" for its' information sharing first purpose.

Nor did I realize the degree to which a few politicians were sensing the shift in the public mood and outlook. Late one night in 1999 on CSPAN, I saw a lone Republican congressman addressing an empty House. He was a late-forty-ish dark-haired fellow (of Italian heritage) named Tom Tancredo, complaining about the broken immigration system of the United States. A former high school teacher and president of a Colorado-based institute devoted to term limits and reducing government spending, he had just been elected to a congressional seat in Colorado after a campaign in which he expressed alarm over illegal immigration. There he was on CSPAN almost nightly, it seemed, talking alone to an empty House about the urgent need for immigration reform—primarily, illegal entry and long-term residence in the U. S. At first I took this as sad, this lone nightly complainer with no audience. But events would soon enough cast a different light on the late vigils of Congressman Tancredo.

* * *

Our Movement Inside the Beltway

How healthy and promising was the movement institutionalized inside the beltway, as the century ended?

My perspective on this was of course skewed by where I sat—on the FAIR board until 2002, and on the CIS board from the institution's founding in 1986.

When John planted FAIR in Washington in 1979, two pre-existing and tiny D.C.-based population limitation organizations quickly sensed that immigration reform had the potential to become a more visible problem than their original focus on America's population size, and shifted their emphasis. Population-Environment Balance, established in the mid-1970s, had created a parallel organization, Carrying Capacity Network (CCN). Both operated out of the same address on P Street in Washington and had the same leadership—essentially a man named David Durham (I never learned his background) and Vanderbilt University Anthropologist Virginia Abernethy. A newsletter was virtually their only activity, and their impact on immigration policy discussion was, as far as one could see, negligible. Abernethy played a useful role elsewhere, as the fearless editor of her own journal, *Population and Environment*, which published well-researched articles on the environment-population-immigration connection.

Negative Population Growth (NPG) was founded in 1972 out of frustration with ZPG's unwillingness to focus on U.S. population reduction. Led for many years by Don Mann, a congenial person of good judgment, NPG ran ads in national media on population size, and produced white papers and occasional books of good quality by respected authors such as Leon Bouvier and Lindsey Grant. There was a third "national" immigration reduction organization located in a remote Virginia town, the tiny American Immigration Control Foundation (AICF), a publishing house run by John Vincent. They put out small, price-subsidized paperback books by conservative authors concerned about the ongoing immigration-driven cultural decline and impending breakup of the United States.

None of them—Balance/ CCN, NPG or AICF—developed any substantial staff expertise in the complex subject of immigration law and policy, available for high-level testimony or media appearances in Washington's policy game. They did no lobbying, and could provide no informed spokesmen at a convenient phone number five days a week for news inputs or Congressionalcongressional deliberations and conferences. Their occasional short statements, papers and books were intended to inform their membership and hopefully the larger public.

How to measure their influence? There is some evidence that this "inform and arouse the public" mission had some impact, primarily on Americans already inclined to share these concerns. AIC specialized in publishing short polemical books, brief and inexpensively produced, such as Larry Auster's *The Path to National Suicide* (1990) and Sam Francis, *America Extinguished* (2002). Such books are not much reviewed or discussed in the mainstream media, but it would be hasty and probably wrong to conclude that they were a waste of time. Tom Paine's *Common Sense* (1776) was such a short polemic, and for a certain busy audience at a time of public confusion, short polemics have a place that is sometimes (not in Paine's case) difficult to assess. When Proposition 187 in California told us that many Americans were awakening to the immigration issue for the first time, John Tanton and Wayne Lutton quickly wrote a 190-page paperback, *The Immigration Invasion* (1994) which had a large circulation and must have had much educational value. Of the three organizations just mentioned, NPG's authors (Disclosure: I became one in 2005, publishing with NPG a piece on the Immigration Act of 1965) were the better credentialed and their point of view more focused.

Writing pamphlets and white papers is not, finally, what moves the gears in Washington. The mass media and congressional staff rarely called on these organizations for expert testimony or cited them for expertise on complex immigration issues. Balance/CCN lived on revenues from their small memberships nourished by a newsletter, which was virtually their only activity; well, public activity. Durham and Abernethy, with a light work load in the office, spent much behind-the-scenes energy criticizing FAIR in the hope of winning a larger share of a common donors' contributions. Though inconsequential within the policy discussion, these groups made the largest contribution they could to public education on immigration issues, and deserve credit not only for this task but also for doing no harm to the public image of immigration reduction, striking a moderate tone on this emotional subject. They reinforced the reductionist instincts of their few members with newsletters and occasional publications documenting the cost side of America's immigration status quo. There was plenty of work here for all of us, and for an even fuller orchestra.

* * *

At FAIR, despite the setbacks in Congress in 1996 and after this at state and local levels, Dan's Director's Annual Reports to the board in 1996 and after were invariably upbeat. Part of this was predictable and perennial. Paid staff of lobbying organizations, even when the organization had a tough year, always tell the directors that the group's brilliant performance has prevented worst defeats and launched very promising counterattacks. This is to be expected, and may be a modest part of the truth. We directors, to some extent, discounted somewhat the more optimistic reports from staff. On reviewing them, however, I see that Dan built a convincing case for progress in at least one sense. FAIR was growing stronger as an organization and becoming somewhat better armed. Membership had reached 70,000 at the front of the decade, and the budget reached three million. Our income came from a diverse and reliable donor pool counting 211 people or institutions giving $500 or more.

Larger size had not, of course, translated into success at changing policy. In the 1990s, there were precious few legislative achievements in the reform direction to report. Yet the FAIR staff understood the immigration issue thoroughly by now, no small achievement, and were skilled and connected enough to discover the parts of the government where policy weakening or erosion was taking place or proposed. This allowed FAIR to reach out to a national constituency and attempt to mobilize and focus the protests of members and activists to prevent the situation from getting worse, which was the trend of the times. We played defense, it seemed, every week. At least we were there to defend, without which things might well have been worse. Our executive director, Dan Stein, was a lawyer, and a skilled and experienced participant in congressional hearings and in appearances on national media. He was frequently called upon.

In the 1980s, when FAIR staff discovered a legislative or administrative plot to enlarge refugee numbers, grant a new amnesty or enlarge the H-1B visa numbers, the only resort had been to urge our modest sized membership to "write your congressman." We had learned that this was not far distant from futile. A few letters could be coaxed from busy citizens, but legislators ignored them.

By the mid-1990s, however, it seemed that more citizens out there were aroused by the immigration mess, and there were new ways to reach, inform, and spur them on. New technologies, especially the internet and fax machines, energized activist ranks and facilitated quick mobilization and response.

Yet something larger was under way in American mass media. The liberal tilt of the leading television news channels came under a fierce counterattack in the latter half of the Nineties. Media entrepreneur Rupert Murdoch launched FOX news channel in 1996, to offer what FOX executives called "a haven" for viewers unhappy with the uniformly liberal leanings of the four major television news organizations This meant "conservative" perspectives—on crime, sympathy for the victim; on the environment, skepticism about government regulation; on terrorism, a flag-waving aggressiveness; and on illegal immigration, outrage at the collapse of border protection. FOX's ratings climbed steeply, especially after 9/11, and by 2001 FOX reached more homes than CNN. In 2004, FOX had 51 percent of the prime time cable news audience, and was clearly drawing viewers from the centrist ranks of the older networks.

FAIR and CIS staff were called with increasing frequency by FOX's Bill O'Reilly news show for advice, data and speaking appearances.

* * *

The same expansion of public agitation and information about immigration issues came from the growing audiences for talk radio. Several FAIR board members were present at a Writers Workshop in 1998 (I think it was) when a radio talk show host from the Boston area told the assembled immigration critics in the most convincing and passionate tones that public anger over illegal immigration was fast growing out there, in case we didn't know it, and we ought to seek out talk radio hosts since their listeners/callers were predictably incensed by illegal immigration and were our "natural audience." He surely had in mind the hosts who had most aggressively and persistently focused audience attention and anger upon the multiple social costs of our porous borders and fast-growing resident illegal population— George Putnam, whose "Talk Back" program had long been popular on KRLA out of Los Angeles, Terry Anderson on KRLA and the John and Ken Show on KFI 640 radio, both beamed from Los Angeles, Roger Hedgecock on KOGO San Diego, and many others. Few of us knew how to reach, so as to encourage and inform, the growing talk radio audience discussing mass immigration, but I later learned that Don Mann at NPG in 2000 hired CIS's retired director David Simcox to "make himself available" to talk radio hosts on the immigration issue. David told me "how much more cordial radio talk show audiences were" than when he began making radio appearances in the 1980s. Then, you were constantly fending off charges of racism. In 2000 and after, "my callers rarely raised those issues, but rather one hears a note of real desperation and boundless anger." Requests for his participation "skyrocketed," and "99 percent" of the talk show hosts proved "friendly and encouraging."

This friendly and encouraging tilt toward immigration-regime critics could not be observed in the print media, but was growing on talk radio and in the Fox and CNN sectors of television. The tilt continued in the twenty-first century, with the conversion of CNN's news anchor, Lou

Dobbs, to a sort of crusade to expose the problems associated with a porous border. But we are getting ahead of the story.

* * *

How much of this growing public concern had come from our educational efforts and how much from the relentless growth and geographical dispersal of both legal and especially illegal immigration was impossible to know. Never mind. Losing every Washington battle, we felt an urgent need to do a better job of animating and engaging the grassroots. Dan's idea of the ideal DC-grassroots relationship emerged somewhat slowly. By the end of the 187 battle, he sketched for the board a plan to establish, under FAIR's general umbrella, a "national network" for both defense and offense, nourished by annual meetings of activists in Washington. FAIR seemed to me to have finally gained a clear view of how to engage the unpredictable, far flung, impatient, sometimes volatile grassroots, and a structure to guide, encourage and offer expertise to the independent impulses out there in the countryside. This was Dan's creation and had taken some time to construct. Those of us who were impatient along the way had forgotten that aroused citizens do not present a simple management problem taught in the MBA schools.

* * *

Thus FAIR, entering its third decade in 1999, was a mixture of a success story in institutional innovation, and if judged against its goals, more loser than winner. The organization was well managed, had low staff turnover, and among a staff of about thirty, remarkable devotion to the cause. The board was smallish and very congenial, spanned the political spectrum, did their homework, and had no deep divisions. Some of us had little gift for fundraising or administration, but that was the (or, a) strong point of John and Sidney, and later Sidney's son, Steve Swensrud, and his niece, Nancy Anthony, whose strong managerial skills and Sidney's "cut to the heart of the matter" instincts were matched by those of Sherry Barnes. With indispensable public appearances by Governor Lamm, the philanthropic contacts and savvy of Janet Harte, Don Collins, Sally Epstein, San Francisco lawyer Max

Thelen, and the addition to the board of New York philanthropist and homeless activist Henry Buhl, FAIR's fundraising produced reliable and rising annual income and a budget of three million by mid-decade.

Some people who heard of the legendary institution-creating role of Dr. John Tanton of Petoskey, Michigan have asked me over the years if John was a dominating figure. No and yes. He said less than most of us most of the time, tolerated long stretches of difficult or poorly focused discussion, and let other members' agendas come forward. John was actually quiet parsimonious with words and tolerant of our occasional long-windedness. But his was a decisive presence. When we had wrangled to weariness over complex and difficult decisions, John would sense when it was time to move ahead. He would summarize the options and suggest a way to proceed. This was almost always decisive, and indeed, a relief.

The staff that Roger and Dan had collected gave FAIR many points of contact with the public. If you were a news reporter drafting a story with an immigration angle or focus, a Hill staffer planning congressional hearings, a foreign embassy who wanted a briefing on American immigration law and issues, or an activist from the West Coast in need of information on the intricacies of immigration policy or how to get press coverage for an appearance before city council to protest a sanctuary resolution, you called FAIR or consulted their steadily improving web site. Sometimes FAIR offered a simpler service. Every day the mail seemed to bring at least one hand written letter of thanks for "being out there, working on this problem." "I thought I was all alone in my worry for the future of my country" was the language of frequent reports from the field on the most intangible work FAIR staff were doing.

* * *

The emergence of CIS was not entirely welcomed by Dan, who like Roger before him, had always pressed to expand a FAIR research/ writing/publication program in the hope that the organization could be a "full service" institution. I tried with limited success to clarify the different and complementary missions of a lobbying group and a think tank. It was fine for FAIR to put educational materials for activists and to produce occasional white papers on policy issues, which it did with increasing effectiveness after adding Jack Martin to the staff. However, a lobbying group like the National Rifle Association, the National Association of Manufacturers, or FAIR, had limited credibility with the media and policymakers as a credible research institution.

I would call FAIR's record in the 1990s of anticipating and warning about the terrorist vulnerabilities inherent in our nation's sieve-like borders a commendable B. It didn't predict an airliner attack on the Towers in New York, but Dan spoke on the national security vulnerabilities of a country that had lost control of its borders before military and national security audiences, FAIR produced some useful short papers on terrorism and internal security, and peppered its newsletter with warnings that our open borders were also a national security issue. No one seemed to be listening, as Clinton aide Dick Morris learned (as he reports in his book *Off With Their Heads*) when in 1995 he received a cold response from the president when he urged Clinton to push for national drivers' license standards and database so the government could find and deport terrorists. Clinton was unresponsive, White House staff was hostile, and Morris' urgings were ignored.

* * *

FAIR inevitably endured criticism. Expansionists hoping to discredit the organization threw bad labels at it in an unending effort to get FAIR associated in the public mind with ugly far-right impulses. Typical, if unusually high-profile, was a 1997 *Wall Street Journal* Op-Ed, "The Intellectual Roots of Nativism," by journalist Tucker Carlson. Without documentation beyond a brief and uneasy phone interview with Dan Stein, he opined that FAIR's "ideology" was to be found not in any of its published materials but hidden deep in the writings on various non-immigration topics of former board member Garrett Hardin and a nineteenth century British author John Tanton liked to quote, Parson Thomas Malthus (1766-1834). FAIR, Carlson reported ominously, received donations from the sinister Pioneer Fund. Dan Stein, he recalled, once uttered a criticism of some immigrants for "competitive breeding." Add it all up, said Carlson, and Stein and FAIR represented not a "reasonable" critique, but nativism—not defined, but clearly sinister, like the Pioneer Fund.

Carlson's technique was the standard guilt-by-association lynching in print, Joe McCarthy style. Dan claimed that this attention given to us in the *Wall Street Journal* proved that FAIR was effectively slowing the Expansionist project, and there was much truth in that. As further proof, the Anti-Defamation League decided that FAIR was a sufficiently prominent policy player that it needed to be undermined, and piled on in 2000. "Is FAIR Unfair?" was a pamphlet offering a rambling repetition of criticisms of FAIR by various parts of the Expansionist coalition, but no original research. The tract ended with a summary of what FAIR's open border enemies had said about the organization, and on the basis of this sort of evidence came to its conclusion—"FAIR's activities in support of immigration control have been characterized by some political observers as promoting nativism and xenophobia." These criticisms by "some political observers" must be true, since the organization took money from the Pioneer Fund.

FAIR held a twentieth anniversary dinner in 1999. Several of us, discussing such attacks, noted that the organization's critics had not changed the basic style of their assaults across that entire period— innuendo, guilt by association, "critics have charged" FAIR as "nativist"/ racist/xenophobic. These were the stocks in trade of McCarthyism, and of an opposition that did not want to do the hard work of arguing that immigration reformers were wrong on the facts.

Was this tactic of questioning hidden motives instead of arguing the facts an effective strategy against the growing immigration reform movement? The goal had been to push FAIR to the extremist margins and then off the page of public discussion. Goal unachieved. FAIR as early as 1982 had run ads in the *Washington Post* and *The New York Times* in which the organization and its message were endorsed by the likes of President Gerald Ford, Rabbi Marc Tanenbaum, retired General Maxwell D. Taylor, actor Edward Asner, former Rep. Barbara Jordan, Claire Booth Luce, Senator Eugene McCarthy, and George Frost Kennan. The organization had been asked to testify before Congress hundreds of times over these twenty years, and appeared countless times on national news networks, such as *60 Minutes*, and *Good Morning America*. Called "xenophobes" and other negative labels, our performance in shaping a consistent message that was fact-based and explicitly affirmed non-discrimination had over time earned us an expanding access to mainstream leaders and debate channels. This was quite an achievement.

Had we made errors? I still regret the decision to take Pioneer Fund money, not because the money was tainted by the fund's unknown motives, but because accepting the contribution would be cited, and perhaps by some accepted, as proof of some deep inner motive invisible in our Statement of Purpose that read, "FAIR believes America can and must have an immigration policy that is non-discriminatory and is designed to serve the social, economic, and environmental needs of our country." Apart from Pioneer money, perhaps Dan should not have trusted the professionalism of Tucker Carlson, forgetting that everything would be taken out of context by a combative journalist writing for the Open Border editorial page of the _Wall Street Journal_ to whom he should not have granted an interview in the first place, or if so, a brief and bland one. Wisdom after the fact.

* * *

Our board chair during these years, Sherry Barnes, was an executive at Prudential Life, and at her urging FAIR went through an intensive scrutiny of an outside consultant to determine if "our message" needed rethinking and revision. After months of meetings with the consulting firm, Dan concluded that "we achieved a great deal in refining and developing our message." The consultant told us that a large majority of the public were alarmed when they learned from us (or someone else) the pace and scale of U.S. population growth and immigration's role in it, and we should continue to let "the population numbers speak for themselves" while "keeping it simple." This should be our main theme, they recommended, because the public was overwhelmingly against a larger population. Beyond this, the public lacks a "permissive structure" to speak out strongly in criticism of mass immigration, and "lacks the basic language to discuss cultural concerns," unless they are attached to English language maintenance. A recommended shift was to "match our opposition point for point on the motive of compassion and caring for the downtrodden," by which FAIR would clearly mean Americans burdened by mass immigration.

I had given lukewarm support to the idea of an outside consultant on "our message," and found the exercise healthy, though hardly leading to some sort of public relations breakthrough.

* * *

FAIR was also subject to occasional attacks from within the camp of those wanting immigration reduced and reformed. Frustrated activists in the countryside wrote angry letters to Dan, the board or each other, denouncing FAIR for not "fixing the immigration problem" and sometimes threatening to start up a new national organization that would turn the national ship around—a suggestion made by Chicago activist Joe Daleiden in 1999, calling for a National Grassroots Alliance, his name for a new "coordinating" national body. Nothing came of it. Good luck, I thought, in finding another John Tanton. Virginia Abernethy at Balance/CNN contacted many reform activists and donors in the mid-1990s, and in bitter tones, charged that FAIR had not supported the moratorium strongly enough. On the idea of a moratorium, you were damned if you did and damned if you didn't. Writer Ramesh Ponnuru in *National Review* (2001) charged that the restrictionists' "first tactical mistake was to insist on a moratorium on immigration."

* * *

It was John who seemed always to situate our effort in history. He published an essay in 1994, "End of the Migration Epoch," foreseeing a time not far off when the developed world would realize that it couldn't absorb the 80 million people a year born in poverty and ecological devastation in the undeveloped world and enticed by television and cheap transportation to give up on their countries and migrate. "The forces working worldwide to secure borders and decrease immigration will prevail," he predicted, possibly by the end of the century, bringing an end to the "Migration Epoch." How will we know when we have won? In 1995 he imagined that some president a few years ahead, recognizing that the planetary numbers could not be accommodated in the available space, would say in a State of the Union Address: "The era of mass immigration is over." For the gloomy among us in our vastly outgunned effort to return to America's small immigration traditions so that the nation could get off the path of population growth and environmental degradation, John predicted that we were in fact lined up with history. And the change was coming soon. I couldn't put out of my head another prediction I had heard somewhere: "Mass immigration to the U.S. will end when you can't drink the water there," someone had said, possibly Garrett, who added, "We are closer to that than you think."

* * *

CIS Expands Output and Influence

The Center for Immigration Studies was a different institution on a different track. Our first director, former Foreign Service Officer David Simcox, brought many talents to a job no one had ever done before (to my knowledge)—establish and manage a research institution to study immigration from the point of view of its impact on the national interest rather than the story of the immigrants themselves. We knew the evidence well enough to anticipated that our findings would make us more often critics than celebrators of America's post-60s immigration regime, and this would make some news. David was a fine writer and editor, knew the international scene, had experience with the visa process, spoke Spanish, and had a tension-breaking Kentucky wit.

From one angle of vision, the center could not fail to succeed. No other institution tried to fill the huge niche of critical policy analysis from the perspective of the nation rather than the immigrants. Mass immigration to the U. S. had been underway since the 1960s, making multiple and large social impacts, some positive, but many negative. The negative impacts were ignored or denied by the reigning political correctness in the universities, research centers, foundations, and media. The few research centers focusing on immigration turned out surveys of immigrants' numbers, origins, assimilation, hardships inflicted by our xenophobic society, contributions of entrepreneurship and of course "cultural diversity," of which the U. S. was suddenly in dire need.

CIS thus began its work in a world with no institutional competitors for the study of that part of the impacts of immigration on America and Americans where there were substantial costs and much harmful policy. That niche as policy critic was a vast one. If we did impeccable scholarly work and offered intelligent, constructive interpretation our work would gain attention and have weight that the limited research efforts of activist lobbying groups like FAIR and NumbersUSA could never hope to achieve.

* * *

This open field was the first part of the optimistic prospect before the new center. Add to that the quality of the CIS board, which over the years brought together immigration scholars such as Vernon Briggs, Malcolm Lovell and George Borjas, scholar of Mexican politics George Grayson, three African Americans along with one Latina and one Latino, all who had written on the topic. Lawyer Bill Chip, writer and editor Scott McConnell, and Carole Ianonne brought a cluster of valuable skills in policy advocacy, writing, and NGO management. The board from the beginning held political views from a bit right of center to a bit left, and if we had been the only people to vote in the 2000 election, Gore would have won, but not by much. We published an annual report, and one from the 1990s which I found in my files listed the foundations supporting us, ranging from Carthage on one political persuasion to Hewlett from another, along with the German Marshall Fund and the Luce Foundation. It was also a plus that our first two directors were grown men with Foreign Service skills and seasoning, underpaid but enthusiastic about institution building in this cause. They established a habit and culture of professionalism and serious purpose. Our mission statement described CIS as "an independent, non-profit organization...the nation's only think tank devoted exclusively to research and policy analysis of the economic, social, demographic and environmental impact of immigration on the United States." All the other think tanks on immigration studied immigrants, and advocated more of them.

As against these assets, CIS still had the skimpiest of budgets in the early and mid-Nineties, and apart from Liz Paddock and Roger Conner, our board (and our first two directors, both former government employees who had never needed to know where the money came from) was not skilled in raising money. CIS received a substantial grant from the Ford Foundation in 1989 after Alan Simpson and Dick Lamm scolded Ford's President Franklin Thomas for the institution's grotesquely one-sided pattern of grants in the immigration field. The Ford grant gave CIS a boost in reputation, but a two-year grant to study the impact of IRCA on perishable crop agriculture gave us expertise on a story nobody was much interested in. Our first publication, a CIS Paper entitled "Illegal Immigration and the Colonization of the American Labor Market," (1986), was authored by respected University of California (Davis) economist Phillip Martin, a boost for us if not for Phil, who complained when it didn't get much notice.

Nothing we did seemed to get a great deal of notice at first, including a volume of essays, *U. S. Immigration in the 1980s: Reappraisal and Reform* (1988). We were delighted that the Sierra Club agreed to publish a study we had funded with grants from the Compton and Weeden foundations, Leon Bouvier and Lindsey Grant's *How Many Americans? Population, immigration and the Environment* (1994). It was easily our most noted and important publication to date, but the relationship with the Sierra Club never developed. Our periodical, *Scope*, contained high quality little essays on immigration trends and issues, and some people in Washington and around the country thanked us for these brief reportorial pieces. Still, that sort of policy reporting and short research pieces let no single finding or author stand out. This was not the way to build marketable experts needed by the media, Hill hearings, and conferences. David Simcox was a combination of director, publications editor, chief fundraiser, and for a time our only real in-house immigration expert, publishing several papers on the problems (which had a low profile in those days) of secure identification. His first staff member apart from clerical staff was writer Richard Estrada, a man of great intellectual depth who had completed all course work toward a PhD in history at the University of Chicago. He confessed that an incomplete doctoral dissertation sat on his desk at home.

In 1992, David decided to move back home to Louisville, while accepting a place on our board. His successor, George High, was another former Foreign Service officer (they had pensions, and could work for less, so we exploited them)—intelligent, reliable, of sound judgment in editorial and personnel matters, with no personal bent toward research or writing and the modest level of entrepreneurial flair to be expected of a career Foreign Service bureaucrat. By mid-decade CIS had a solid reputation for our small output, and had occupied a niche and started to fill it with high-quality analysis not drawing a great deal of attention.

Then in 1995 we hired Mark Krikorian as director, a former employee of FAIR (who had left in a struggle over leadership when Roger Conner retired). Mark knew the subject, had a Master's Degree in international relations, and some background in journalism. And an Armenian heritage which, we later learned, made him instinctively pro-legal immigrants in a way that became one of his many assets. Scope had become *Immigration Review*, but Mark recognized that even a top quality quarterly periodical assessing important immigration policy issues would not make the policy or public opinion impact we hoped for. He shifted to stand-alone *Backgrounders* and *CIS_Papers*, research reports of substance making the author an expert ready for Washington policy discussion. Some were written by "Senior Fellows" of the center, some by staff in the office, such as former Foreign Service officer Jessica Vaughan whose knowledge of the visa process led to impressive written output as well as congressional testimony. Then Mark added our first Ph.D. staffer, public policy analyst Steve Camarota, who proved to have everything one could want in a director of research—clarity of expression, capacity for high-level analysis of more than one subject at a time, and an instinct for applying demographic and economic data to policy questions. It was another plus that Steve liked to be interviewed on TV and to tell congressional panels what they needed to know and ought to do.

The output at CIS in the second half of the 1990s began to gain a remarkable prominence and impact, considering that the center had a staff of about six, a budget of half a million, and was only ten years old. In 1998, CIS published an attention-getting report explaining how the settlement patterns of immigrants caused six states to lose seats after the 2000 census. Leon Bouvier continued to produce influential papers on the impact of immigration on individual states. Steve Camarota began to publish an annual summary or "snapshot of America's foreign-born population," which reporters could and did turn into news stories on how the annual arrival of a million or more legal and uncounted illegal immigrants had pushed the total number of immigrants to 10.4 percent of the national population by 2000, their poverty rate 50 percent higher than that of natives, and their use of welfare programs 30 to 50 percent higher. By the end of the decade, CIS research papers were coming out almost monthly. Demonstrating remarkable courage, Steve analyzed the Mexican component of incoming immigration, *Immigration From Mexico: Assessing the Impact on the United States* (2001), with highlights from the Executive Summary such as: "Almost two-thirds of adult Mexican immigrants have not completed high school...less-educated natives face significant job competition from Mexican immigrants... There is no evidence to indicate that the U.S. has a shortage of unskilled workers...Welfare use among Mexican immigrant households remains much higher than that of natives...Mexican immigrants have a significant negative effect on public coffers...allowing more unskilled workers from Mexico would not be in the best interest of the United States..." In another Center Paper responding to occasional questions as to what sort of immigration policy the center was in favor of, Dick Lamm and Alan Simpson edited a series of short essays in *Blueprints for an Ideal Legal Immigration Policy* (2001).

Center publications, at first available only in print, were freely downloadable at the CIS website after 1999. At every board meeting, Mark could report more media attention to the Center's work, more quoting of our staff in print media and radio and appearances on TV, more congressional testimony, and more hits at the web site. He launched two e-mail information services, "CISNEWS," a daily list of full-text news items, and "This Week in Immigration," a weekly roundup of links to immigration news, new publications and upcoming events. Both listservs presented news and information from all angles of vision, and by the end of the century had 2,000 subscribers, and 5,000 by 2005.

Mark was also augmenting CIS's impact by gathering a substantial roster of writers, one or two of them each year designated as Center Fellows, available for public appearances. The mail and e-mail from policymakers, immigration specialists, and interested citizens was overwhelmingly positive. In public statements Mark began to say that the Center was pro-immigrant if they are legal, while in favor of reduced numbers of them. He had found a tone of moderation joined with a quick marshalling of facts and a sharp sense of humor sometimes at the expense of the ill-considered rhetoric of the Expansionists. People who had given up on the American work force and promoted multiculturalism without limit, along with essentially open borders represented a new school of thought, Mark would say. They represented "Post-Americanism," an advanced state of consciousness that had outgrown old-fashioned notions of national patriotism.

While Steve and others wrote Center papers, Mark began to find his own literary voice in short essays for *National Review* and *National Review Online*. More foundations began to bet on the Center, the most welcome being a large, multi-year grant in 1999 from the respected Hewlett Foundation in California. The media rarely labeled CIS any longer as "anti-immigrant" or "conservative," substituting phrases like "a group advocating reduced immigration." Dan Stein graciously e-mailed his thanks and congratulations when a Center publication made an unusually strong impact, and FAIR chairman Sherry Barnes wrote to me more than once in the late 1990s with praise for the Center's "unique contribution."

* * *

Thus the immigration reform movement faced a paradoxical end of century prospect. It was gaining strength, even as immigration politics and policy ratcheted the numbers higher each year, and the illegal influx mounted. At the end of the century, two new nationally focused and Washington-based reform organizations sprang up to fill niches that no one (but their inventors) had even imagined to be there.

* * *

Roy Beck

I do not remember the first time I met Roy Beck. He was a journalist who had covered business news in Cincinnati and a religion beat for a national syndicate of newspapers based in Dallas, taught Sunday School, and led groups of teenagers on Habitat for Humanity summer camps. Deeply influenced by the environmentalist fervor of the 1960s while at the University of Missouri School of Journalism, Roy became a prize-winning environmental reporter. But his mind was too active and oriented toward fundamental causes to remain stuck in battles over water pollution or the extinction threat facing small frogs. He soon perceived that the environmental protection cause was lost without population stabilization, and then saw that this was prevented by the mass immigration regime launched in 1965. Moving to Washington as a correspondent for a chain of Michigan newspapers, he covered the congressional hearings on the 1990 Immigration Act and was dismayed by the absence of resistance to the law's large increase in immigration. He called Roger Conner who introduced him to John Tanton who made Roy the Washington Correspondent to The Social Contract, allowing him to begin to study and write about immigration. He made a major national splash with his piece on the impact on a small Wisconsin town of a sudden deposit of refugees from southeast Asia, "The Ordeal of Immigration in Wausau," in *The Atlantic Monthly* (April, 1994).

Then came *The Case Against Immigration* (1996), a book I have earlier described, which Jack Miles in a review in *The Atlantic Monthly* called "a powerful—indeed, nearly overwhelming—case against the status quo."

When it came to "the numbers," Roy emerged as a kind of lecture hall equivalent of that talented demographer, Leon Bouvier (who was a writer, not a speaker). Roy created and toured the country with an illustrated lecture on global and American population growth, using large charts and jars of colored gum balls to convey to demographically illiterate audiences that even doubling America's immigrant intake would absorb only about 3 percent of the world's annual population *increase*. I have watched Roy's "gum ball" lecture and video several times, and the crowd is invariably stunned by this graphic and colorful depiction of global population increase in our time, the balls, representing population growth, overflowing out of the large glass containers and spilling out noisily onto the table and floor.

Roy founded NumbersUSA with offices in Arlington, Virginia, and put up a web site to reach and educate whoever he could. The site was distinctively Roy Beck. The emphasis was upon "the numbers" and, mostly, their environmental and community impacts. If one clicks on the button labeled "No to immigrant bashing," you get a serious lecture, "Nothing about this web site should be construed as advocating hostile actions or feelings toward immigrant Americans." Roy had an edge to his words, however, when describing the long history of our elected officials who tolerated illegal immigration and foisted on the American people a demographic future they did not choose—indeed, the opposite of the one they *did* choose, which was population stabilization.

Roy soon saw another niche not adequately filled. In 2001, he hired Rosemary Jenks, a former CIS staffer who had just graduated magna cum laude from Harvard Law School, and rented a red brick house on Capitol Hill, just a few blocks from the congressional offices. They had a bright idea, and it worked almost overnight. Rosemary—tall, attractive, smart, young, and equipped with an immigration lawyer's knowledge of the topic— established close contacts with Hill staffers (who often came to Roy and Rosemary's offices for drinks and snacks after long work days). If the Expansionists were plotting a surprise enlargement of the numbers of H-1B workers or refugee admissions, Rosemary soon knew it, and Roy's staff put out the word to his growing list of activists via e-mail and the website, offering to pay for a FAX message to any activist's congressman or senator. Roy suggested some facts to use, but the activists wrote part or all of their own messages. As a journalist, Roy knew the importance of the labels the media chose to use, and mounted a successful campaign to have his activists write letters or faxes of complaint when they called reformers "anti-immigrant."

Now *this* was lobbying, a Hill lobby housed on the Hill in a red brick three-story house, backed by a constituency—real voters, motivated and irritated, who put piles of differently worded messages of protest on the desk of a legislator about to enlarge the numbers again in some traditionally un-noticed way. Could NumbersUSA be dismissed as a hate group? Not if you go to the web site and get lectured against "hostile actions or feelings" toward immigrants. Not if you meet Roy

Beck, with that quizzical smile, that never raised voice, and that perfect pitch for arousing resentment only against our elected officials.

* * *

Project USA

Upstairs in the top room in Roy's office-house you could, some time in 2001 and after, find his renter, Craig Nelsen, inventor of another new way to put public pressure on Expansionist legislators. After college he spent two years in China teaching English. Stunned by seeing the multifaceted burden of so many people and realizing that the U.S. was on a rapid growth path itself, Nelsen became, in his words, "a former open borders advocate whose eyes were opened to the severe problems associated with overpopulation." He returned to the U.S. and became established in Astoria, New York, apparently by himself and with no financial backing (he owned a small Manhattan restaurant with his brother), ProjectUSA. The organization's sole activity commenced in 1999. It rented public spaces to put up billboards around New York City, carrying simple and factual short messages about immigration. "Tired of sitting in traffic? Every day, Congress lets in another 6,000 immigrants. Every day." Another read: "More than 80 percent of the American people say they want reduced levels of immigration. Anyone listening?" Visible from the Brooklyn Bridge was the billboard: "Immigration is doubling US population in my lifetime," next to a picture of a young American.

I would have advised Nelsen that this flimsy stuff would catch no one's attention, and was a waste of time. I would have been quite wrong, at least about the attention it would get. The armies of political correctness are strong in New York, and apparently had little to do that summer. The New York liberal multiculturalist establishment brought out all the squelch guns. A New York state legislator in Albany railed against this "type of racism and bigotry," and one pronounced the billboard message, "Immigration is doubling U.S. population in my lifetime" a "loathsome message." Another spoke of "the putrid stench of the kind of racism that Craig Nelson [sic] embraces." Nelsen's billboards were splattered with graffiti and slogans like "stop racism." Newspaper articles associated ProjectUSA with "hate groups," including that well-known hater, John Tanton, who was said to be one of Nelsen's funders, along with the Pioneer Fund, whose mention is a reliable indicator that the "anti-hate" industry was again inventing and injecting hate where it wasn't, in order to raise money for their machinery. The New York City Council voted 43-2 to condemn the billboards, and the New York Port Authority which owned the land under Nelsen's Brooklyn Bridge sign demanded that it be removed. It was. Speech suppressed.

Nelsen, a trim and youthful-looking man, made an ironic mistake on the way to this media event. While a New York small restaurant owner, he was charged with and admitted to hiring illegal aliens without checking their records or paying required social security and other taxes, and responded by blaming the government for a chaotic system. Poor career move, but unlike Zoe Baird or (later) Linda Chavez, he hadn't been nominated for any post he now had to withdraw from. He also turned out to be fearless, the tone and totalitarian coloration of the attacks on his billboards seeming to spur him on. Or perhaps it was the supportive response he got from around the New York area and the country. Apparently some money flowed in, and he rigged up a "Truthmobile" as a sort of traveling billboard, taking his signs to the Midwest and South. His website drew readers and allies who liked his message: "We believe a modern immigration policy will be one that places more importance on the long-term consequences of current policy on our grandchildren, and less importance on the mythologized nation of our grandparents.... We believe that the United States is a country, not a market, and we believe a country should do its own work...We believe that it's possible to advocate a moderate immigration policy without being anti-immigrant in the same way it's possible to be on a budget without being anti-money." Small donations from around the country kept Project USA going.

* * *

Thus our movement, at the end of the century, was finally developing, here and there, the attributes of the effective artillery fire that I was

315

taught in the Marines. The shells were launched from close to the front lines by privates and sergeants, given guidance and direction from the spotters and command posts with a central view. But our salvos were merely harassing fire, at this stage. The sponsors and managers of the Open Border abandoned no positions, and were still on the offensive.

Chapter Twenty-Three:
New Century, New Open Border President:
The Worst of Times, 2000-2001

Prime Minister Winston Churchill, when asked by a reporter in 1942, "Why are we fighting?" responded: "If we stop, you will find out."

We reductionists had never faced a more unpromising policy climate than when the elections of 2000 arrived. The presidential campaigning, as usual, was almost entirely unmarked by any discussion of immigration. Journalist Robert Samuelson correctly called immigration "the great forgotten issue of the 2000 presidential campaign." Both major party candidates pandered to Latinos with occasional Spanish phrases, Republican candidate Texas Governor George W. Bush somewhat less awkwardly.

The dying little Reform Party's Platform endorsed the reductions recommended by the Jordan Commission, but its candidate (Pat Buchanan), marginal to start with, was plagued with ill health and failed to qualify for the presidential debates. The Democratic Platform, that unread phalanx of words, acknowledged a need to control the borders, frowned at the H1-B program, and rejected guestworker programs. But even these firm-sounding words were not heard from the Democratic Presidential nominee, Al Gore, who probably agreed with Bill Clinton, who in his June, 1997 remarks to reporters gave a rare articulation of the liberals' view of the purpose of the immigration policies they presided over:

We will soon be, in the next few decades, a multiracial society in which no racial group is a majority. And we are living in a world in which that gives us an enormous advantage in relating to other countries in the world since we have people from every country in the world here... We'll be in a unique position to show people... they don't have to give in to those darker impulses...

Immigration was already doing this to, or for, America, so for Clinton/Gore the status quo was fine. It was fine for another reason important to Clinton and the party's 2000 nominee—immigration, they were convinced, was pouring Democratic voters into the country. It was not enough that they came. They must be registered to vote, an act of government well understood by the urban bosses and machines of the nineteenth century, where the motto was "vote the Irish early and often." First the new immigrants of the 1990s had to receive citizenship from the INS, and for the 1996 election Clinton assigned to Gore the key role in forcing the INS to expedite its "Citizenship USA" program, which was slowed by the necessity to fingerprint all applicants and eliminate those who the FBI found to have criminal records, as well as administering a test for English and civics. The INS was hesitant to follow White House orders to politicize its work, along the way rushing the process and inevitably giving citizenship to some convicted felons. INS head Doris Meissner finally gave in White House political pressure in 1996, and the agency cut all necessary corners in order to qualify one million aliens as citizens and voters in time for the 1996 election. The Gore campaign repeated this rushed naturalization again in 2000, a story told, among other places, in David Schippers' *Sellout: The Inside Story of President Clinton's Impeachment* (2000).

No wonder, then, that the Democratic nominee in 2000 did not raise the immigration issue as a problem. Mass immigration, most of it from Latin America and Asia, was in the view of party leadership transforming the U.S. into something better than it had been—the first multicultural society available to lead the world. Pursuing that policy also promised to expand a liberal Democratic political majority. Win-win.

The Democratic Party displayed no internal opposition to the Clinton-Gore approach to immigration. By the 1990s, organized labor had made its strange, almost inexplicable long march away from its historic support for strong employer sanctions. Labor now for the first time in its long history wanted exactly what the bosses wanted—a free flow of Third World labor—most of it unskilled, some of it computer savvy, all of it cheaper than Americans. The Executive Council of the AFL-CIO in 2000 actually called for the repeal of IRCA, which they had supported in the 1980s. Long forgotten was the core commitment of organized labor as expressed by Secretary of Labor, Ray Marshall in the 1970s: "I have worked all my life for a labor shortage."

With Gene McCarthy and Dick Lamm out of office, and Barbara Jordan gone, elderly Senator Byrd of West Virginia was the single voice from the ranks of America's nationally elected officials on the Democratic Party side who sometimes spoke out for a closely regulated immigration policy. The Democratic Party had become what it had never been historically—a mass immigration party, legal or otherwise.

* * *

The other party in 2000 was actually a tent harboring some reductionist reformers—but apparently not many were willing to step forward on the issue. Alan Simpson had retired from the senate. A handful of GOP House members, most prominently Texan Lamar Smith, Congressman Tom Tancredo from Colorado, and Elton Gallegly from California had for years openly resisted the expansionist project. Tancredo founded an Immigration Reform Caucus inside the party, and at first rallied only fifteen members. This probably understated the strength of reductionist sentiment inside the GOP, for the party's 2000 platform denounced "lax enforcement of our borders" and endorsed the core Jordan Commission recommendations. The Open Borders wing of the party was able to write into the platform contradictory commitments, such as a demand for larger H-1B and H-2A guestworker programs for high-technology and agriculture. At the state level some Republican political entrepreneurs calculated that Open Borders was a formula for a winning politics. Tom Vilsack, GOP Governor of Iowa, asked the federal government in the summer of 2000, to designate Iowa "an immigration enterprise zone" exempt from all immigration laws. Republicans in California and elsewhere were tutored by easterners Jack

Kemp and William Bennett that Pete Wilson's support for Prop. 187 "proved" that any proposal to reduce immigration swung millions of Latinos toward the Democrats. Yet a Zogby poll in early 2000 showed Hispanic respondents quite divided, a slim plurality favoring a cutback on immigration. The chief finding was that Hispanics do not align in predictable ways around the immigration issue at all.

Wary on the immigration issue during the 2000 campaigning, the managers of the GOP presidential campaign kept it out of the speeches and policy proposals of Governor George W. Bush, except for an occasional comment indicating that their presidential candidate had a philosophical aversion to borders and affection for "hard-working" Mexicans. He told a newspaper editorial board in January, 2000, in response to a question, that there was "a xenophobic, dark side of American politics" that liked to "pick on the downtrodden." We should "do a better job of enforcing our border" but "we ought to increase legal immigration for our country's advantage." Well-aimed questions from activist Craig Nelsen at an informal Q&A session in New Hampshire, however, exposed Bush as remarkably ignorant of immigration policy and mistaken on the few things he did know. What was his position on Chain Migration? He hadn't heard the term before. When it was explained, Bush admitted ignorance as to whether the law permitted the immigration of "cousins and in-laws," about which he in any event took no position. He knew nothing about immigration's impact on U.S. population growth, which he thought to be at an all-time low.

* * *

When Gore and Bush were nominated, the political situation seemed to me hopeless on the immigration issue, and I couldn't disagree when the *Christian Science Monitor* titled a 2001 story, "On Immigrants, a Great Softening…Anti-immigrant political fervor of the 1990s may have largely disappeared." I nonetheless took a strong interest in the election, as I was full of guarded optimism when it came to the possibility of electing Al Gore, a long-time friend of our family and a man well qualified to be president—except for his acquiescence in mass immigration, of course.

John Tanton, immune as always to pessimism or defeatism, wrote another "Quo Vadis?" memo to us in 1999, beginning with: 'It seems clear that we're losing ground in the immigration reform battle." He listed as causes the "bullish economy," the confused linkage in the public mind of immigrants with our civil rights movement, and the abdication of the environmental and labor movements. To break out of these constraints using our core advantage, public opposition to mass immigration, it seemed time to "descend into the cauldron of electoral politics." John did not mean that FAIR would do this, of course. The organization was prohibited from political work due to 501(©) (3) tax status. He was considering running as a Reform Party candidate against Michigan Senator Spencer Abraham in 2000, in part as an example to other individuals in our camp.

Abraham, who somehow inherited Alan Simpson's chairmanship of the Immigration Subcommittee, had quickly become a major advocate of a range of measures to increase immigration even further, especially from his ancestral Middle East. Yet he showed weakness in early polls. Abraham's Democratic opponent, Debbie Stabenow, would not touch the immigration issue, and her voting record was no better on the matter than Abraham's. Nevertheless, she was not chairman of the Senate Immigration Committee and thereby in a position to be an active dismantler of remaining limits. If Abraham's immigration voting record were given visibility by John's candidacy, and Stabenow either shut up about the issue or tilted our way, national attention might be gained when he lost his seat because of his Expansionist record.

In the end, John decided not to run, to the relief of most of his friends, who knew the financial and physical burdens of such a race. A handful of immigration reform groups formed a coalition that ran TV and radio "issue ads" intended to educate Michigan voters on what Spencer Abraham had said and done about immigration. His opponent said little about immigration, but on election day, she took Abraham's seat.

It seemed to me that the result justified a little internal celebration. An Expansionist politician had made the mistake of being out of touch with his voting base on an issue where he had a substantial voting record—immigration. Prior to a gathering of reformers in early 2001, I found in a party costume store in a seedy section of downtown

Washington a male wig with black hair resembling Abraham's. I walked to the front of the large meeting and, in what I hoped was a triumphant fashion, presented it to Dan Stein, who held it aloft. The applause was thunderous, out of appreciation for the Michigan voters' punishment of an Expansionist with political death. I would have preferred to give the wig/scalp to both John and Dan, but Dan was chairing the meeting and John would not come forward to claim any personal credit for this unusual event, though he was a Michigan voter. He was probably right. FAIR was in the education business, not the political campaign business. Still, it was a cherished and rare moment for our side.

* * *

We glumly expected newly elected President Bush to move to promote some sort of amnesty/guestworker program package, as the media was full of talk about how his chief political strategist Karl Rove had embraced the dubious but widely accepted theory that the key to the Hispanic vote for Republicans was to further open the borders. This strategy would only work if it gained many Hispanic voters and did not at the same time offend Republican voters who thought immigration in need of reduction, not expansion. All indications were that Rove and others had convinced Bush that this was a political winner. The empirical base for this strategy seems to have been the hard times experienced by the California Republican Party and officeholders after the second term of Governor Pete Wilson.

Evidence for the emergence of this Bush White House Hispandering Strategy (an unknown somebody coined this useful word at about this time) came in the adoption by the president and then other administration officials and elected Republicans of a new language. The entire immigration system "is broken" and there was an urgent need for "immigration reform," soon to become "comprehensive immigration reform," something Bush had said nothing about in his election campaign. This was irritating news, and not just because the new president and his repeaters were trying to steal a phrase we had used as early as a CIS lead article, "Comprehensive Immigration Reform," in *Immigration Review* (Spring, 1994). We could insist on our own meaning of "comprehensive reform," but the public would be (further)

322

confused, and a president had several big pulpits he could mount each day in full view of the media, while we had to be grateful for published letters to newspaper editorial pages, occasional (mis?)quotations by reporters, our organizational newsletters going to the faithful, and our writings aimed at the same audiences.

We soon learned that Bush had some powerful allies who were lined up to support (and were probably the original architects of) this new campaign to further expand immigration, as if the status quo of 500,000 illegals and a million legal immigrants a year were not enough. "A powerful alliance of labor and business groups, immigrants rights organizations and the Republican political strategists has gathered to lobby for immigration liberalization," The *Washington Post* reported in August 2001. At a Washington meeting, "representatives from the U.S. Conference of Catholic Bishops have met with State and Justice Department officials," joined by leaders of the immigration bar. LULAC activists met with Vice-President Cheney. A well-funded "Coalition for a Sensible Immigration Policy" had begun running radio, TV and print ads. Rallies were held in several large cities. "This is probably one of the most friendly environments for positive immigration reform that I have seen," said an official of the chief pro-immigration business group, the Essential Worker Immigration Coalition.

"Positive reform." They were now raising the banner of "immigration reform," redefining it to stand for widening, not narrowing and making more selective, the intake of foreigners, legal and illegal. The early months of 2001 were in many ways our darkest moment. "The situation we face at present," Dan wrote to the FAIR board on August 7, "is as dire as any we have ever confronted." Since the Democrats had formed a special task force on immigration and seemed to have decided to go along with the Bush plan in the hope of at least sharing if not stealing ownership, "both parties are moving toward endorsing an amnesty program" and some sort of guestworker component open to foreigners not already in the U.S. And "all of this is taking place against a backdrop of other adverse proposals at the state" level, Dan went on, such as in-state tuition and drivers licenses for illegal aliens.

Six months after his inauguration, President Bush responded to Mexican President Vicente Fox's overtures for some sort of grand bargain between the two countries. Their emerging proposals—described in July,

2001 as ideas the White House was "considering," were breathtaking and historically unprecedented. They would legalize all Mexican illegal immigrants in the U.S., signaling to the world that our laws against illegal entry had been set aside—for Mexicans. They would also ask Congress to approve a new, permanent guestworker program supplying cheap labor from Mexico for employers in every economic sector in America, a program open to all nations. The media gave much less attention to another radical idea, extending to Mexico the sort of "totalization" agreements on Social Security that the U.S. had with twenty nations, mostly in Europe. With those countries, legal residents who split their careers between two nations and paid (depending on where they were stationed) into two systems could get a proportional retirement benefit. But the agreement with Mexico proposed by Fox-Bush extended American Social Security benefits to illegal aliens in the U.S., without requiring that they previously become citizens.

The audacity of the Fox-Bush proposals had no precedent, especially as the details were left vague. A president of a foreign country joined with our own chief executive to recommend dismantling the immigration restrictions constructed over more than a century of U.S. history. The United States, as the world population grew from 7 toward 9-10 billion people, would declare open borders for workers and then their families, but Mexicans first.

Fox visited the U.S. in early September to address a joint session of Congress with his proposal to set aside immigration law for this one country to our south, allowing free movement of people (presumably only Mexicans) and goods across the U.S. – Mexican border. His speech was an unprecedented but meekly tolerated intrusion into American domestic policymaking. He demanded action by the end of the year and barnstormed in several U.S. cities. Democratic leaders made no objections to the Fox-Bush plan. Polls showed strong public opposition to Mexico's meddling in U.S. internal politics and to the thrust of presidential proposals, but American policymakers had never paid much attention to polls on immigration issues, and held to that tradition. The deal seemed done. As the summer ended, the media generally predicted that the two presidents were on their way to an astonishing historic agreement under which Mexicans (but not Guatemalans, Dominicans, Nicaraguans?) would be allowed to come northward for work and eventual citizenship. Without impediment. But Bush would not stop with dismantling the border with Mexico. He was thinking of an unlimited guestworker program allowing American employers to hire any foreigner for jobs deemed (by the employer) as unwanted by American workers (i.e., at sub-standard wages and conditions). The guestworkers would be eligible for citizenship at the end of a six-year term.

This, I submit, is the most radical and ill-conceived proposal ever made by any president in the history of American immigration policy. Everything was to be swept away--the entire 150-year effort to regulate the immigration of foreigners into the U.S.

The second big news was the restrained, scattered, and puny resistance from American policymakers and public figures. Mark Krikorian wrote in *National Review Online* in early September that administration efforts to call an amnesty "normalization" or "earned adjustment" should not obscure the reality of what was being proposed—a "prospective amnesty" under which illegals would receive green cards in a few years, compared to the "retrospective amnesty" of 1986. But an amnesty is an amnesty, and none of them in the past had solved the problem at hand.

Congressman Tancredo said: "This is a kick in the teeth to the thousands of individuals across the world who are legally attempting to enter the U.S. Instead, the U.S. is saying, "Why wait? Sneak on in.""

Senate Minority Leader Trent Lott correctly understood the import of the Fox-Bush proposal, and expressed caution: "A mass amnesty is probably not the way to go."

House Democratic Minority Leader Richard Gephardt commended Bush for his promising ideas. In late summer, 2001, we reductionists seemed only months away from the decisive defeat and repudiation of our entire historic effort, from the 1880s to 2001, to limit, and regulate immigration to our country.

The Brookings Institution in 2000 published a study that found immigration policy the second most incompetent policy performance of modern American governance. In the summer of 2001, immigration policy was ready to move into first place.

* * *

In January, 2000, the great Bull Market of the 1990s peaked, and collapsed. The Dow lost 1,926 points by March. The Nasdaq crested on March 10 and then a bear market settled in, wringing out the huge gains of the 1990s. By 2003 what Federal Reserve Chairman Alan Greenspan had called the "irrational exuberance" of the 1990s was a painful memory. The Dow settled in at 38 percent of its 2000 high, the Nasdaq at 78 percent. The Wall Street bubble was over, though the housing bubble ran on.

At a FAIR board meeting I thanked Steve Swensrud for his work in bringing the bull market, finally, to an end. He smiled and made no comment, though I later learned he was selling his yacht. I had enjoyed a brief visit on that yacht in financially more exuberant days, but the stock market implosion that separated man from boat did not immediately bring sanity to the national discussion of the immigration binge we had been on. The financial euphoria of the 1990s and deficit-based growth had lubricated the immigration binge (among other errors and excesses) for so long that it had a formidable momentum.

In narrowly elected President George Bush, the Expansionist project now had a powerful sponsor of proposals to open the Mexican border to unlimited low-wage workers. It seemed certain that the ending of the financial bubble had come too late, our strengthened reform efforts had been too small. As the summer of 2001 inched toward fall, we immigration reformers faced the grim prospect that an intolerable mass immigration status quo, one-third of it illegal, might soon become worse, and through the open processes of American democracy.

PART V:
THE HINGE OF HISTORY:
ACROSS OPEN BORDERS,
AMERICA'S ENEMIES ENTER
AND ATTACK

Chapter Twenty-Four:
Terrorist Attacks of September 11, 2001:
Had The Turning Point for Immigration
Policy Come?

Our vulnerability to these abominations is not merely a failure of intelligence but also of border control. — Mark Krikorian

The costs of America's porous borders were stunningly piled even higher on the morning of September 11, 2001. While Mexican President Fox traveled northward to Washington on his mission to open America's southern border to his surplus population, Islamist terrorists commandeered jetliners and struck the World Trade Center in New York and the Pentagon, killing nearly 3,000 persons.

The Fox-Bush deal, at least for the moment, slipped into limbo.

"We were moving slowly but surely to do these things (amnesty for all illegals, a new guestworker program)," said Daniella Henry of the Haitian-American Community Council, "and all of a sudden everything was crushed…"

The day's events changed many things in America. Surely one of these would be the immigration policy debate. How could there not be broad agreement that the terrorist attacks harshly illuminated a range of key defects that had not formerly been acknowledged by our nation's managers? Our porous borders and governmental abandonment of virtually all interior immigration controls allowed terrorists to move at will into, around, and out of the country, legally or illegally, as they prepared for their deadly work.

* * *

<u>Getting Some Benefit From the Disaster?</u>

Just as I remembered being on the steps of Low Library at Columbia on November 22, 1963, when I heard students shouting that John F. Kennedy had been assassinated, so I recall that I was in a faculty meeting at UNC-Wilmington on September 11, 2001, when a colleague burst in with the news of two airliners striking the World Trade Center in New York and the Pentagon. America was in a new kind of war.

It was only later in the day that I began to sort out the implications for immigration policy. We critics of the immigration status quo had warned of this, and we had been right. Our borders were shockingly porous, and one result was that America's enemies were easily crossing them. Surely this would lead to a radical change in the politics of immigration. Reformers of America's wide-open system would gain the upper hand, and defenders of current policies would be put on the defensive. Of course, much would depend on how clearly and forcefully we reformers brought forward the lessons and defined appropriate remedies for the newly energized national security concerns. Americans had been killed on our soil, not by foreigners in some sort of Pearl Harbor attack from across the seas, but by foreigners we had let into the country and then onto our airliners. Our critique of the immigration status quo now had a bloody and shocking resonance. Feeble immigration controls, the act of letting foreigners in for a variety of purposes and then losing track of them, had just become a national security issue of the highest importance. Our opportunity was to aim our research and arguments at the flaws in immigration policy and practice exposed by 9/11, and formulate remedies. Apart from keeping terrorists out of the country and keeping track of foreigners (any of whom might be a terrorist) in the country, could we also advance our larger goals of a smaller immigration flow tailored to America's national needs?

Mark Krikorian and Steve Camarota at CIS, who had not previously written much about national security issues associated with immigration, seized the day, and quickly shifted their research agenda to focus on topics related to the new national security realities. By May, 2002, Steve

330

produced an immigration history of the forty-eight terrorists convicted of (or admitting to) acts of terrorism against the U.S. since 1993 (*The Open Door: How Militant Islamic Terrorists Entered and Remained in the U.S., 1993-2001*, Center Paper 21). He found that they had readily exploited every possible means of entry into the country.

"They came as students, tourists, and business visitors," he found, and seventeen had worked the system to enter and stay legally, despite their terrorist associations, becoming lawful permanent residents and even citizens of the nation they hated.

Twelve were illegal aliens when they boarded the planes for the attacks, and twenty-one had been undetected in illegal status at some point in the last ten years. They had no reason to fear our law or our government as they went about their lengthy preparations inside the country. Steve concluded:

> *Because every part of our immigration system has been exploited by terrorists, we cannot reform just one area, but must address the problems that exist throughout. The solution is not to single out Middle Easterners for exclusion or selective enforcement. Instead, we need to more carefully check the backgrounds of all visa applicants, better police the borders, strictly enforce the law within the country, and, most important, reduce the level of immigration to give the INS the breathing space it needs to implement fundamental reforms.*

Camarota's report was a stunning indictment of the government's performance as the enforcer of immigration law, the first of a cascade of writing (a good amount of it by CIS authors) exposing the frightening vulnerability of a nation entering a new struggle with global Islamist terrorism, led by a government that would or could not bring immigration under control. Mark Krikorian had placed immigration reform at the center of the War on Terrorism agenda within a month of the attacks.

"Our vulnerability to these abominations is not merely a failure of intelligence but also of border control."

Incredibly, there was early resistance to this linkage.

"We're not talking about immigration," announced James Ziglar, head of the INS,: "we're talking about evil."

He was fired before the year was out, as the administration realized that the existing immigration apparatus was part of the problem. Many would not acknowledge this, and openly denied it. Cecelia Munoz of La Raza offered the idiotic observation of the year when she stated that "there's no relationship between immigration and terrorism."

The Director of the American Immigration Lawyers Association, Jeanne Butterfield, former Director of the Palestine Solidarity Committee, told reporters, "I don't think the events of last week [9/11] can be attributed to the failure of our immigration laws."

These were the voices of the radical, irresponsible Expansionists, for whom open borders always came first and American national interests were not even conceivably a separate and over-riding subject. In the new era marked by 9/11, many of them, in denial about what had actually happened to the context in which immigration was situated, became virtual collaborators with the terrorist enemy, who also wanted open American borders. Some Expansionists were wiser.

Linda Chavez quickly recognized the changed circumstances, and in a column in the *Wall Street Journal* six weeks after the attacks, conceded that "U.S. immigration policy was in need of a major fix before 9/11, but the issue has taken on a new urgency."

She endorsed "keeping better track of those who come here, better screening of visa applicants, tightening up student and refugee visa programs—indeed, "For the time being, it might be better simply to hold off admitting any refugees…from nations known to pose a terrorist threat."

Chavez sensed what some Expansionists did not, the strong reductionist public sentiment and emotions on the immigration implications of the 9/11 attacks, as well as the national security case against what formerly she and other Expansionists had liked, the porous borders of yesterday. A Zogby poll, the first after 9/11 asking citizens whether the government was doing enough to control the border, found 76 percent answering No." Congressman Tancredo's House Immigration Reform Caucus jumped to fifty members, and Roy Beck's chief lobbyist, Rosemary Jenks, predicted in early 2002 that "serious immigration reforms' would be part of the recommendations of the 9/11 commission then at work. The *U.S. News and World Report* conceded that after 9/11, "nativist sentiment has come to be viewed not so much as old-era paranoia as new-era prudence." What a welcome change it was when it was not one of we reformers, but an editorial writer for a respected national magazine (*National Review*), who wrote that we needed "tighter policies, and tighter enforcement of them. Most important, lower levels of immigration overall, to shrink the haystacks in which needles must be sought. We have long known that high immigration and slack enforcement were economically null and culturally disruptive. Will we be serious now that we know they are deadly?" That was now the question in this radically altered climate.

* * *

My last year on the FAIR board was 2002. I decided that twenty-four years was much too long for any board member of any organization, and FAIR should fill my seat with new talent. Both the FAIR and CIS boards recognized that we had an unprecedented opportunity to ride the 9/11 wave of national urgency toward needed changes. Immigration's linkage to national security, a topic that both organizations (and many other groups and individuals) had attempted with little success to elevate in the public mind, was now an urgent national concern. A broken system must be fixed so that it did not permit foreign terrorists so easily to enter, overstay, and attack us from inside. We welcomed this new and logjam-breaking attention to illegal entry, illegal overstay, and visa screening, long on our agenda. We were determined to align our project with a new wave of public concern, steering where possible toward our larger goals—a great shrinkage of the illegal flow and domestic presence, a smaller legal component chosen less for family ties and more for labor market considerations.

So the opportunity now was to turn the attacks of 9/11 into a disaster with some offsetting benefits. What parts of our broken immigration system deserved the most attention, in light of 9/11? Exactly what had gone wrong? Where were the vulnerabilities? It was time for investigative journalism, and for think tanks that could match journalism for speed and policy relevance while bringing to the topic a convincing factual integrity and analytical rigor.

* * *

CIS had taken the lead in linking a failed immigration policy system to the deaths of Americans in New York and Washington, and in framing remedies. Every 9/11-linked publication by the Center received wide media attention, and CIS had no institutional rivals in developing the immigration policy lessons from the experience with homeland terrorist attacks. A Nexis search in October, 2001 found CIS the most frequently cited reform-minded organization in immigration-related print news stories. I remembered a line from the British poet A. E. Housman: "We were ready when trouble came."

Others, fortunately, were also exploring the immigration-policy/terrorism connection. With the publication of *Invasion* on the first anniversary of 9/11, Michelle Malkin, the daughter of two Asian immigrants, became a powerful new voice critical of the immigration status quo. "Sick and tired of watching our government allow illegal line-jumpers, killers, and America haters to flood our gates," she nominated herself as "the new face of the immigration debate." Her attention in *Invasion* was focused on the incompetent immigration policy bureaucracy and the open border industry that, both before and, inexcusably, after the 9/11 attacks, lobbied for ever-larger holes in the "Swiss cheese" that was the American immigration apparatus.

Problems began with the visa issuance machinery abroad, in nations required (over twenty are not) to present them upon entering the U. S. Malkin found visa issuance officers under pressure from the tourism industry and U.S. diplomatic officials to offer "efficient" (i.e., quick and superficial) processing of the burgeoning numbers of foreigners heading for the U.S. under one of a rapidly growing array of visas for travelers, students, religious ministers, technical workers, and people from "under-represented countries" (as with the Diversity Lottery). This accelerated and perfunctory visa granting process permitted most of the 9/11 terrorists to come to the U.S., along with over three million overstayers—some of them, we now know, with known terrorist backgrounds. Malkin drew upon the resourceful investigative reporting by Joel Mowbray published in *National Review* a year after 9/11. Submitting the visa records of the nineteen 9/11 terrorists to six experts in visa procedures, Mowbray concluded from their comments that, "If the U. S. State Department had followed the law, at least fifteen of the nineteen [terrorists] should have been denied visas for obvious discrepancies such as providing as a U.S. address "California" or "hotel," or, in one case, simply "No." There were other irregularities and discrepancies, all traceable to the visa officers in the U. S. Embassy in Saudi Arabia.

Indignant at this lax and fraud-prone process, Malkin became even more incensed as she moved from the issue of getting in the U.S. to staying there illegally. The foreigner tracking system required by Congress in the 1996 Immigration Act had been stalled by a coalition of trucking companies and immigration lawyers. In 2000, Clinton persuaded Congress to abandon it. So nobody knew how many overstayers there were or where they might be. They had butted in line ahead of others abroad, and despite illegal status, immigration lawyers stood ready to explore for them the multiple avenues for moving from illegal to legal status while in the country. Asylum claims and marriage to a U.S. citizen were among the most reliable.

"It ain't over until the alien wins," she concluded.

She described the rare decision of immigration courts to "deport" illegal aliens convicted of aggravated felonies—after which the INS fell back upon a sort of honor system, releasing the alien into the general population, with a letter (a "run letter," in the trade) going to their last address asking them to voluntarily leave the country or turn themselves in at an appointed date. Ziglar of the INS admitted that the agency didn't know the whereabouts of 324,000 fugitive deportees. An INS fingerprint database ordered in 1994 was incomplete, and had never been linked to the FBI database. The government's "serial incompetence" was her main theme. At the end, Malkin compiled an imposing list of necessary reforms: ban temporary visitor visa programs from all countries with al Qaeda strongholds, end the investor, H1-b and Visa Waiver programs, replace "catch and release" at the border with detention and deportation, militarize the borders until control is restored, and "pull up the Welcome Mat" for illegal aliens in the country, and "no more amnesty programs, period."

We invited Malkin to speak at one of CIS's Friday night board dinners, where she made it emphatically clear that *Invasion* was a report not only on the "Swiss cheese" system prior to 9/11, but her research extended into the summer of 2002 and recorded almost no change after the attacks. This attractive, articulate, and fearless young journalist might better have called herself "a new face" rather than "the new face of the immigration debate," as there was no one new face (fortunately). If she meant that her Asian background made her a unique voice among restrictionists, she hadn't yet met Yeh Ling Ling, a California-based immigrant of Chinese heritage who had for several years been an active speaker and Op-Ed writer (www.diversityalliance.org) on the need for better immigration regulation. Never mind. Malkin's book had vaulted her into the ranks of nationally syndicated columnists, and this new face quickly became an unrelenting and prolific critic of the immigration system which had made 9/11 possible, past and present.

* * *

In the months after 9/11 a scatteration of immigration policy reform ideas came from writers, politicians and others unwilling to wait for the findings of a national commission on 9/11 that was beginning work on a report that would arrive in 2004. Reporters and editorial writers pressed Mark Krikorian at CIS for a well-considered list of the most important immigration policy changes required by national security priorities. A CIS Backgrounder by Krikorian and Camarota (*Immigration and Terrorism*) in November, just two months after the 9/11 attacks, recommended reform in four areas: 1) Improved visa application processing and thorough screening overseas, by State Department overseas officers reminded that they worked for the American people, not for the convenience of foreigners; 2) take a major step toward controlling the border by creating a computerized, entry-exit tracking system with biometric identifiers; 3) take a major step toward interior enforcement by, at long last, creating the national computerized system allowing employers to screen and submit data on new hires, along with a tracking system for the one million foreign students and one million special work visa holders (a program that ought to be shrunk); 4) "Give the INS the breathing room it needs" by reducing overall immigration to around 300,000 ("Less immigration means better enforcement"). "Cuts across the board," Krikorian argued in a paper ("Safety in [Lower] Numbers") published just after the anniversary of 9/11.

Fortunately, such a policy change would serve other important national interests as well. It has been clear for some time that current immigration policy is an anachronism, on balance doing harm to the economy, the public fisc, national cohesion, and environmental quality.

This was now mainstream advice. That fall a study by the Chicago Council on Foreign Relations found that most Americans supported reductions in legal immigration, and 70 percent thought ending illegal immigration an important goal.

"Tighter policies, and tighter enforcement of them," editorialized the *National Review*. "Most important, lower levels of immigration overall, to shrink the haystacks in which needles must be sought...We have long known that high immigration and slack enforcement were economically and culturally disruptive. Will we be serious now that we know they are deadly?"

FAIR came out with its own overall wish list at about the same time, recommending a secure national ID for all citizens and legal resident aliens, while anchoring state drivers' licenses in a biometric identifier. Instead of fierce opposition or silence, this proposal, long derided as an Orwellian intrusion into American privacy by a dreaded "National ID card," was entertained and even supported in unlikely places. Liberal Harvard law professor and celebrated television pundit Alan Dershowitz said in his *Why Terrorism Works* (2002) that he now supported national identity cards (as well as the deportation of all illegal aliens), because things had changed.

* * *

National security-driven government reorganization was inevitable, and was launched immediately after 9/11, though it was not necessarily also immigration reform. On November, 25, 2001, President Bush signed the Homeland Security Act, and submitted a reorganization plan affecting intelligence, security and immigration functions of the government. A year was consumed in wrangling with Congress and interest groups about details, and on May 14, 2002, he signed the Enhanced Border Security and Visa Entry Reform Act of 2002. Each of these major laws, along with the October, 2001 USA Patriot Act, made changes in immigration policy, at least on paper. An early academic survey of these measures, published in the *American Political Science Review* in late 2003, termed them all "restrictionist." We reductionists were not so sure, as the letter of the law is a dense undergrowth of contradiction and loopholes, while subsequent policy decisions are not always tightly tethered to statutory language. Our task, after participating in the legislative process, was to put a spotlight on the actual results on the ground, and object when they were not in the national interest.

As a place to start, it seemed good news that the incompetent cop guarding borders and interior, the INS—given a grade of D for 2002 in the annual *Government Executives Federal Performance Report* would be dismantled. The troubled life of the INS was ended, its functions divided and housed inside a large new cabinet Department of Homeland Security (DHS). The border enforcement roles went into a new U. S. Customs and Border Protection (CBP), the interior enforcement into U. S. Immigration and Customs Enforcement (ICE), and the service functions to the U. S. Citizenship and Immigration Services (USCIS).

What did this mean, beyond box shuffling? Each of the major reform laws of 2001-2002 made complex structural and substantive changes to immigration policy on the way to national security rearrangements. Was American immigration policy and practice being radically re-shaped toward a less porous border, smaller numbers, and tighter controls on terrorists? Or were the apparently sweeping rearrangements only cosmetic, leaving our borders and interior as vulnerable as ever, the numbers of illegals and legals just as high and unmanageable?

* * *

In a March, 2002 *National Review* article, "Immigration Policy Six Months Later," Mark Krikorian pointed out that key measures were being talked about with much urgency, such as computerized entry/exit tracking, a foreign student tracking system, and federal standards for state driver's licenses, had been passed in 1996 and were subsequently watered down or repealed. So in a sense Congress after 9/11 had been discussing whether to finally make good on earlier promises. Other than that, he wrote, "relatively minor administrative measures" had been taken, "mere baby steps." In fact, a large step backward was actually being proposed, without hearings or a recorded vote. House Republican leaders and the White House almost slipped through an extension of Section 245i of the basic Immigration and Naturalization Act which would allow illegal aliens who pay a fee and have sponsors to remain in the country and apply for permanent residency, while continuing to work. This was an amnesty for those who broke our law and butted in at the front of the line, as well as providing adrenaline for more potential illegal immigrants abroad when they heard about it. Congress would have done this six months after 9/11, if Senator Robert Byrd had not noticed and blocked it.

FAIR offered at the end of 2002 an assessment of 9/11-related immigration reforms, and awarded a grade of "D" to post-attack immigration changes. There had been some progress in visa issuance, interior enforcement, sharing of information between law enforcement agencies, and domestic document security, but most of it was "spotty and haphazard." The Government Accounting Office report at that same time found the State Department's system for issuing nonimmigrant visas still lax and underfunded and in need of "immediate and dramatic changes."

This was discouraging news one year after our devastating immigrant-brought attacks in New York and Washington. Dan wrote in his end-of-year *Immigration Report* that the Homeland Security Act of 2002, capstone of twelve months of legislating security-aimed changes, was "a major victory for immigration reform." Well, gratifying, but it was too late to call it a major victory. The despised INS (not the Border Patrol, a hard-working agency) had long been a miserable bureaucratic failure, its nadir reached under Doris Meissner in the Clinton years. Wait and see what sort of agency replaces it. Still, the fact that the politicians and policy elites were now continuously talking (and the public was hearing) about the necessity for significant changes in the ways we processed foreigners into and out of our country was for us an exhilarating transformation of the policy climate and a great broadening of the agenda of items conceded to need corrective attention. Before the planes hit the towers in New York, the agenda had been proposals for a massive guestworker program, free entry for all Mexicans, and amnesty for ten million people who had broken U.S. law—essentially, a dismantling of the entire century and a quarter of efforts to regulate immigration. These notions had retreated offstage in 2002 and 2003, replaced by concerns about border security and tracking foreigners as they came into and left the U.S. The agenda was again what it had been for Barbara Jordan—how to see to it that those who are invited in, come in with a welcome, and those not selected, stay home and wait. I had to agree with Dan that there had never been such a hopeful climate for our efforts.

* * *

Formulating The Post-9/11 Reform Agenda

Eight of the forty-eight foreigners convicted of terrorist acts since the first Trade Center attack in 1993 had held student visas. This visa program had been launched after World War II to educate bright students from abroad who would then return to provide leadership to their developing countries. It had grown (65,000 student visas were issued in 1971, 325,000 by 2000) into an industry providing thousands of universities, colleges, and trade schools with students who sometimes paid high out-of-state tuition and were increasingly sought after as graduate students in engineering and science programs. They would work longer hours (and on Sundays) than the American students whose numbers in these fields was in decline in any event. This had become a quite large flow of foreigners—583,000 were studying at 3,500 accredited U. S. colleges and universities in the 2001-2002 academic year, along with uncounted others in trade schools like the Florida flight school that trained some of the young Saudis who guided the planes into buildings in New York and Washington.

This American program must have seemed a providential opportunity for young Islamic extremists who needed easy entry and overstay opportunities into the country. Now that we knew how many of the 9/11 terrorists had used this program to swim into, around and out of the country for purposes not intended by American policymakers, it drew critical attention for the first time. The student visa program was "riddled with corruption," George Borjas wrote in a 2002 study, and "ineptly run." The visas were issued when any one of 73,000 American schools (some of them colleges, most of them trade schools in subjects like acupuncture, cosmetics, or golf) sent the applicant an I-20 form confirming admission. There was much fraud and bribery at the admissions end in the U.S. and also abroad, where phony letters of recommendation and other aids were available for a price. In the U.S., there was no system of tracking students to their specified academic destinations, determining if they registered, or if they left the country when finished. The program had developed many problems long before 9/11. Most students didn't return to work in their home countries but found ways to stay in the U.S. (and take well-paying jobs wanted by Americans). Nobody tracked these students, and their employers if they stayed after graduate studies. They ran no risk of penalties. Efforts in 1996 to collect basic information about foreign students were easily squashed by university and college officials, who sternly insisted that they were not "policemen."

A federal panel a year before 9/11 had recommended that colleges be compelled to account for the arrival, campus presence and departure of overseas enrollees and be prepared to report on their location and status to immigration authorities. This was ignored, there being no apparent problem. After the terrorist attacks the foreign student visa program came at once under scrutiny, and California Senator Diane Feinstein proposed a six-month moratorium on the entire program. This called out the lobbying power of the foreign student industry based in the universities, and her proposal sank from sight. A tracking system for foreign students was ordered, but did not require schools to periodically verify the students' whereabouts. Other questions had not been faced, Borjas pointed out, such as, "Should foreign students belonging to particular national-origin groups be barred from entering particular types of educational programs?" American taxpayers subsidized each foreign student, he found, and advanced students in science and engineering posed security issues—acquiring U.S.-based knowledge, and carrying it back to Iraq, Syria or Iran—even if none were or would become terrorists.

The effort to raise fundamental questions about the program went nowhere. In 2003-2005, the numbers of student visas went down—about 3 percent, accompanied by loud complaints from university officials and faculty—an important component of The Industry. Minimal entry-exit tracking was hampered by computer system flaws. Three years after 9/11 there had been almost no reform in the student visa program. It is very hard to bring discipline to, let alone shrink, a flow of bright young foreigners into trade schools thirsty for fees and into universities whose faculty and administrators believed and preached that American youngsters were no longer motivated so do these jobs. "They [Americans] are in a decades-long flight from science and engineering," an engineering faculty member once told me on campus, "and even when they enroll in graduate studies they will not attend the labs on Sunday afternoons. The Asians will, so we recruit in China, Taiwan, and India," and we're glad to have students from Egypt, Pakistan, Saudi Arabia, and Iran.

* * *

Identification: Who Were the Terrorists, and How Did They Get In?

The nineteen plane hijackers of September, 2001 had, with no apparent difficulty, collected sixty-six American drivers licenses as they prepared for their mission. They had acquired, that is, a national ID card, and with that could obtain credit cards, enroll in schools, open bank accounts, and board airplanes. Another weak link in immigration control that we restrictionists had pointed out for two decades at last escaped the obscurity of the pages of our reports and newsletters and went to the front of the national security/War on Terror agenda. Again, a disaster did what rational persuasion and argument could not.

The best-known immigration reformer, after retirement from the senate and relocation to Harvard, was still Alan Simpson. Two months after 9/11 he testified before a House committee, and told them the dismaying story of the government's failure to listen to those who saw trouble ahead. Improving the security of identity and work authorization documents, Simpson recalled, "has been under review by policymakers since at least the late 1970s." The Hesburgh Commission had recommended use of the Social Security card for national work authorization. IRCA in 1986 had been stripped, at the eleventh hour, of such provisions (sponsored by Simpson). In 1990, a provision to add biometric identifiers to state drivers' licenses was killed with language likening them to the "tattoos" used in "Nazi Germany." The Jordan Commission urged a computerized registry allowing employers to check workers' legal status, and the 1996 Immigration Act launched a pilot program of this sort. Outcry against "a National ID Card" repeatedly blocked any action. Thank you, we can imagine the terrorists saying, as in early September, 2001 they benefited from this paralysis.

Simpson's story of repeated efforts to narrow the holes through which the 9/11 terrorists easily walked should have shamed those who over the years had blocked reforms—but Simpson was too much an insider to settle up accounts in this blunt way. He just told the story of the futility of his reformist efforts, and concluded that, while we don't need a new "national document," we urgently need congressionally mandated standards for state drivers' licenses, national standardization of birth certificate documentation, and use of the Social Security/INS combined database in all states.

Simpson spoke at the end of 2001. A year later, the General Accounting Office (GAO) sent agents with counterfeit driver's licenses into the U.S. via sea ports and border crossings. In twenty-five attempts to enter, they were not challenged once on their documentation. Porous borders, same old story.

* * *

Sociologist Amitai Etzioni was a member of a the Subcommittee on Reliable Information, a national task force on national security, and in his work found driver's licenses in the fifty states "useless...as a means of identification." Less than half the states, as of 2002, checked Social Security numbers offered by applicants, or required proof that applicants were legally in the country. There was no common practice regarding the "breeder documents" used to determine identity. Some states claimed to be tightening up documentary requirements for the driver's license; some plainly were not. With unreliable identification documents issued by the fifty states, anti-terrorist new programs like the No Fly List and Terrorist Watch were undermined. Mandated national standards were obviously required, Etzioni wrote, or the fraud-vulnerable old system would endure. In a forum on identity fraud, CIS author Mari Dinerstein's call for "mandated national standards for driver's licenses" was vigorously seconded by an ally from an unlikely place, the Heritage Foundation. Licenses with an electronically readable biometric identifier, a fingerprint and the ability to verify users' identity via an electronic database was "absolutely essential," said Heritage Senior Fellow Robert Rector. "We have to move forward with this type of system...I think it's inevitable."

When legislation aimed to achieve this was introduced by Senator Richard Durbin in early fall,2002, it was stubbornly resisted. Complaints about this archaic, decentralized and fraud-prone system, and proposals for federal standards met similar objections. The states' motor vehicle departments did not welcome federal intrusion into their historic autonomy, and want another unfunded mandate. The ACLU and Phyllis Schlafly's Eagle Forum (which would soon alter their position and become our allies) railed against "a National ID card," and Republican legislators wrote this sentence into the law establishing the Department of Homeland Security: "Nothing in this act shall be construed to authorize the development of a national identification system or card."

The sentence had no practical effect, but the sentiments behind it prevented progress on national identification through 2002 and 2003. Indeed, living illegally in America with fraudulent documents had been made easier beginning in 1996, when the Internal Revenue Service (IRS) began issuing Individual Taxpayer Identification Numbers (ITIN) to foreigners, many of them presumably illegal, who did not have Social Security numbers. By 2002, 5.5 million of these had been issued, and immigrant advocacy organizations urged illegals to use the ITIN to open bank accounts and, in some states, obtain driver's licenses.

During these months of discussion about the national driver's license vulnerability it turned out that two governments, not one, had initiated programs to make it easier for any foreigner illegally in the U. S., terrorist or not, to remain there and acquire the documentation necessary to function in a modern society. The Mexican government in 2002 began distributing to Mexicans in the U. S. a new, "high-tech" version of an identity card sometimes issued by Mexican consulates abroad. The new card, the matricula consular, spread rapidly, as some 200 U. S. municipal police departments, as well as many banks and agencies of city and state governments, accepted it as official identification. "It's part of a creeping amnesty," Mark Krikorian commented, representing "a growing institutionalization of their status." Guatemala, Brazil, Poland, Nicaragua and Haiti announced interest in providing such a card to their nationals in the U.S., but an FBI official in congressional testimony in June 2003, said the agency had concluded that the Matricula Consular "is easy to forge" and "is not a reliable form of identification." A witness from the Department of Homeland Security said his agency shared these concerns, but made no recommendation.

* * *

Special Treatment for Middle Eastern Nationals?

The 9/11 attacks by Muslims from a cluster of Middle Eastern nations (mostly Saudi Arabia) raised difficult issues about the limits of the U. S. commitment to uniform treatment for all nationalities applying for some immigrant benefit. After 9/11, should the U.S. treat travelers and immigrants from Islamic countries just like the Irish and the Brazilians? Should we treat young Arab-looking males like elderly pale-skinned grandmothers? The American public seemed to have quickly decided that it was time to discriminate, not just in internal security measures but in the initial decision as to who could come to America, temporarily or permanently. A Chicago Council on Foreign Relations poll in 2002 found that 79 percent of the public agreed that the U. S. should simply bar all immigration from Muslim countries. "No more ragheads," I heard a newspaper reader on a Washington, D.C. street announce to no one in particular.

The government took a few small steps in that direction. The INS decided just after the attacks to fingerprint, photograph and track all visitors from Iran, Iraq, Sudan, and Libya and all males aged sixteen to forty-five from several other Muslim countries. In late 2002, it launched a special registration program for visitors from twenty-five Arab and Muslim countries. Some 82,000 came forward to be interviewed, 13,000 were found to be here illegally, and were ordered to be deported. A voluntary "Arab exodus," in the words of one reporter for *The New York Times*, took place in Brooklyn, and presumably in other Middle Eastern ghettoes, where "families are packing up." Before 9/11, 120,000 Pakistanis lived in Brooklyn. Some were deported as illegally present, but many—15,000, the Pakistani Embassy estimated—had "self-deported," either back to Pakistan, or to Canada.

They were reacting to an apparent decision to "profile" legal immigrants, tracking some nationalities more closely than others. Yet there was extended confusion about such "profiling." The Bush administration in early 2003 announced new guidelines on "profiling" in law enforcement, and the standards of scrutiny for visa applicants would include suspicion that a terrorist motive or history might be involved, but would not include "racial or ethnic stereotypes." Whatever that meant. Mark Krikorian in 2002 wrote that "expanding ideological exclusion to prevent the admission of Muslim radicals would be an important contribution to homeland security," but recoiled from grounding it in nationality. "If we were constructing a long-term, Muslim-specific immigration policy," this would be "contrary to American principles and politically unsustainable." His alternative to ideological or national origin "profiling" in nonimmigrant visa granting and in routine security measures was a sharp reduction in the numbers of immigrants from certain "Muslim" countries.

Not much was known about America's Muslim population. Steve Camarota, in his timely CIS Backgrounder, *Immigrants from the Middle East: A Profile of the Foreign-born Population from Pakistan to Morocco* (2002), supplied informative statistics and argument. What was the real size of the Muslim population in the U.S.? Middle Easterners, defined as people from Pakistan, Bangladesh, Afghanistan, Turkey, the Levant, the Arabian Peninsula and Arab North Africa, were one of the fastest growing immigrant groups in America. Their total size within the U.S. had increased by sevenfold since 1970, to between 1.5 and 3 million, of which 150,000 were illegal. Their large numbers in the recent immigration flows to America meant that State Department visa issuers abroad are overwhelmed and do perfunctory screening, and large ethnic enclaves in the U.S. allow extremists to operate with no hindrance. More important, cultural adaptation—assimilation—is especially difficult for Middle Eastern Muslims.

"Some conservatives have suggested doing away altogether with immigration from the region," at least for a time, Camarota wrote.

He may have been thinking of Michelle Malkin, who had said: "Why don't we just start with all of the countries that are already on the State Department's list of designated state sponsors of terror, and freeze visa issuance to those countries?" Not one Member of Congress has proposed such a thing, Camarota noted, and "Congress would never single out one region of the world for exclusion from green cards." This is "politically inconceivable, in our equality-obsessed society, that we would return to the days prior to 1965…"

Still, other useful steps could be taken to shrink the Muslim flows to levels that would permit adequate initial screening and expose the new Muslim Americans to assimilative forces. Ending the Visa Lottery would reduce Middle Eastern immigration. We could scrutinize visa applications from the region more carefully. The single step of reducing overall immigration promised the most benefits.

There was not much follow-up discussion of these early ideas about the advisability of ethnic or ideological filters, or deliberate shrinkage of Middle Eastern immigration. The public discussion of Muslim-specific profiling in visa granting and airport searches, on the other hand, stumbled along indecisively, accompanied by howls of protest from Muslim organizations in the U.S. who had little to say about how they might aid their adopted country in this fight against Muslim terrorism.

* * *

Assessments of Progress, 2002-2003

The attacks of 9/11, we reformers thought, would surely spur far-reaching and beneficial change in how we checked the backgrounds and intentions of *all* those entering the U.S., kept track of their departure/overstay, and enforced the law against illegal entry at borders and "choke-points" such as work sites and transportation hubs in the interior. "The momentum is with us," a FAIR field coordinator assured me in early 2002. Certainly it seemed indisputable that the national security imperative now aligned itself with changes in these areas that our arguments had never been able to initiate. We expected to direct some of that urgency toward the other components of real immigration reform.

Apart from a tightening of controls over foreign students, however, real immigration reform deriving from national security concerns made remarkably slow headway in 2002-2003. The program to monitor nonimmigrant student entry and exit, the new Student and Exchange Visitor Information System (SEVIS) was said to be fully operational on August 1, 2003; it was not. More than one million foreign students entered the U.S. in 2002, a seven percent decline from the year before, and university faculty and administrators complained persistently and demanded more foreigners.

The entry-exit tracking system for all foreign visitors, US-VISIT, was formally inaugurated in January, 2004, and faced an awesome eventual task of tracking the 190 million temporary visitors to the U.S. annually. When officially launched, US-VISIT fell far short of the vision of an entry-exit tracking system for all foreign travel to and from the U.S. It registered arrivals but not yet departures, so was initially of no use on the problem of overstays. It was operational only at major air and seaports, and did not apply to the twenty-seven Visa-Waiver countries, or to any traveler entering from Canada or Mexico—88 percent of the total. The system's effectiveness was hard to assess at this early stage, but the gaps were immense. Middle Eastern-born terrorists living in Canada, immigration officials acknowledged to reporter Paul Sperry in 2004, could still enter the U.S. at an airport with no visa or background check. A phony birth certificate could get them across the border with Mexico and a forged passport would ease them into America from one of the Visa Waiver countries. Homeland Security Secretary Ridge often claimed that America was "far safer" than prior to 9/11, and hadn't again been attacked. DHS claimed that it caught thirty wanted criminals with the startup system in its first three weeks.

As for interior enforcement, Mark Krikorian in a _National Review_ essay in early 2004 pointed out that while the construction of the new visa-issuance and entry-exit tracking systems enjoyed a broad consensus among governmental officials and politicians, interior enforcement was politically contested by influential corporate employers at both national and local levels, and little progress had been made. The problem of fraudulent procurement of driver's licenses was if anything getting worse, with the proliferation and persistence of state-level political campaigns to grant licenses to illegals. "Sanctuary" policies were still widespread, the term broadly referring not just to the church-harboring of aliens of the 1980s but official municipal policies prohibiting city employees, including the police, from reporting immigration violations to federal authorities. Employer sanctions were rarely enforced. During the next year, 2002, the INS fined thirteen, that is _thirteen_ employers within the U.S. for hiring illegals, and across America they arrested the grand total of 451 workers on site.

Across the range of interior enforcement programs, Krikorian found "ambivalence," and "a general sense among many political leaders that enforcing the immigration law is futile, and in any case would displease important constituencies." These constituencies included the Mexican government in one much-publicized case, when in August 2003 Border Patrol agents arrested five illegal aliens near the Mexican Consulate in San Diego, and loud protests by the Mexican Consulate and local Latino activists prompted patrol officials to order agents to make no interior arrests, only border stops. It is worth adding that such a sense of futility and "mission shrink" among those involved in immigration law enforcement owed much to the fact that no chief executive of the U.S. since the emergence of the illegal alien issue in the 1970s had ever communicated down through the law enforcement bureaucracies and political classes a firm determination to make illegal entry and residence costly and rare. INS Commissioner Doris Meissner once commented to the press that the problem of illegal aliens was almost impossible to solve because the American people were forever "ambivalent" about it. Well, she was certainly right about the political elites, such as herself.

* * *

After 9/11: Where Were We?

We were caught in cross currents. The fundamental change was that the national security imperative put wind in the sails of our immigration reduction and reform boat. The terrorists within had accelerated our own movement's mobilization. More people had been awakened to the realities and costs of a broken immigration system.

Yet a year after 9/11 we were impressed, sadly, by the small progress in tightening the immigration net. There were grounds for saying of the U.S. what Prime Minister Tony Blair said of the UK, that two years after 9/11 it seemed that much of the world "turned over and went back to sleep again."

What astonished us, however, was the defiant resurgence, after only a few months of relative silence, of the Expansionist, Open Border coalition and movement. Within a year of 9/11 they were back on the offensive. The president never officially withdrew his endorsement of a broad amnesty and open-to-all-comers guestworker program. Certain Hill legislators were bolder than the White House. GOP Representatives Flake and Kolbe of Arizona submitted a bill in the summer of 2003 to create a new, unlimited "guest worker" program for every foreign worker who could find a U.S. employer, and a massive amnesty for illegals now in the country. Texas GOP Senator John Coryn crafted similar legislation, as did GOP Senator John McCain of Arizona and Democratic Senator Ted Kennedy. Democratic Senator Joseph Lieberman of Connecticut endorsed a limited amnesty, and Democratic Congressman Richard Gephart, like Lieberman, a presidential aspirant for the 2004 race, told a La Raza conference that he would sponsor a major amnesty for all illegals. The cheers of the La Raza activists were not matched by any attacks from Gephart's (or Lieberman's) rivals. In the Democratic Party, it seemed, amnesty had no critics, and was becoming the Democrats' only idea when the "problem" of illegal aliens was raised.

* * *

Outside of Washington, there continued to be an unending campaign at state and local governmental levels to move illegals piecemeal into a sort of semi-legal, authorized status. Beginning in 2002, state legislators in California and other states pressed for in-state tuition at public universities and driver's licenses for those not lawfully in the country. In many cities there was aggressive political pressure to sustain, and where possible, extend "sanctuary" measures to prevent local police from any form of cooperation with federal immigration authorities. The Expansionist army could mobilize platoons, if not battalions, in every state and many cities.

* * *

On the other hand.

Our own reductionist army was also expanding and going on the offensive. New groups were constantly being formed—in Vermont, North Carolina, Georgia, Tennessee, and Utah. The Colorado Alliance for Immigration Reform held a press conference outside the offices of the Denver Mayor protesting his sanctuary policies. Vermonters for Reduced Immigration lobbied their Department of Natural Resources for a population policy. The New York-based cluster "of 9/11 Families" who had lost relatives in the attack began to take an interest in immigration reform and exert their formidable influence.

In parallel, the national, D.C.-based reform organizations were more deeply and skillfully engaged in Hill lobbying than ever. Rosemary Jenks and Jim Edwards of NumbersUSA were frequently asked to brief congressional staff, and the two basically wrote the CLEAR ("Clear Law Enforcement for Criminal Alien Removal") Act legislation submitted by Georgia Republican Charles Norwood to require the federal government to pick up every illegal alien apprehended by local authorities and pay local police for their detainment expenses. FAIR reported similar gains in local activism, and that more doors were opening to its lobbyists on Capitol Hill.

* * *

Thus the post-9/11 political climate was not better for us, or worse, but both. The public was rightly fearful of foreigners inside the country with murderous intentions, and journalists, politicians and national security bureaucrats responded with a short season of critical re-examination of immigration policy and a flourishing of tightening up ideas and projects. There was much evidence that the wind was blowing our way.

Yet in this weather there were two prevailing winds. The Open Border Industry, after a very brief (if any) pause after 9/11, had become increasingly aggressive, and launched offensives on local and national fronts.

* * *

Mass Immigration Rolls On

The immigrant flow in the 1990s had been unprecedented in size. The INS in 2000 raised their estimate of illegal entry, and concluded that 700,000 a year had entered during the 1990s. But this was an average, and the numbers rose as the decade ended—817,000 in 1998 and 1 million in 1999. Some returned home, some found ways to legalize their status, and the agency now acknowledged that the illegal population inside the U. S. was growing by 500,000 a year. That suggested an illegal population of 8-9 million by 2002, far larger than the government had ever acknowledged. Predictably, it was spreading to new parts of the country. In the 1990s, North Carolina's illegal population was estimated to have increased 692 percent, Colorado's 364 percent, and Georgia's 570 percent.

After 9/1, the flow of illegal immigrants abated briefly, and then surged again. In late 2002, the Border Patrol reported that the brief slowdown of illegal entry pressures at the Mexican border had ended, and apprehensions were back where they had been before the attacks. "We're running about even with last year," a Border Patrol official in south Texas said a year after 9/11, "maybe slightly higher." The

352

overwhelming majority were Mexicans bent on work and income, not on terrorist acts. However, it was not only Mexicans who crossed that border illegally. In 2002, 28,048 OTMS (other than Mexicans) were detained, and the next year, 55,890. These included nationals from Afghanistan, Bulgaria, Russia, China, Egypt, Iran, and Iraq, who had figured out that entry across America's southern border avoided airport contacts with authorities that for some reason they wished to avoid.

* * *

A Turn? Autumn 2003

I describe a stalemate, yet my notes for the autumn of that year contain signs of an accelerating momentum on our side. At the October, 2003 meeting in Washington of the Writers Workshop, we learned from lawyers giving pro bono services in RICO-based lawsuits against employers that there were encouraging signs that companies employing illegal aliens might under that statute be assessed damages sufficient to attract lawyers to such suits for compensation. We heard a powerfully moving presentation from Peter Gadiel, father of a young man killed in the WTC bombing. Gadiel's parental anger at a government that tolerated inside its borders the men who killed his son had gained him coverage on Bill O'Reilly's TV show as well as Lou Dobbs. We saw first hand the power of legitimate emotions in an immigration debate that from the 1970s had been a place where any sign of emotion was held against the restrictionists. We saw the same parental outrage and resolve when Bonnie and Bob Eggle, parents of Kris Eggle, narrated a documentary of the life and death of their son, a ranger in a national park on the Arizona border who had been killed by illegal aliens. We heard another new voice, LA talk show host Terry Anderson, a large, supercharged, indignant African-American new recruit in the struggle against illegal aliens in California. We heard Congressman Tancredo again, and I was impressed by his progress in finding his voice on this difficult issue. We heard the thoughts of Steven Steinlight, former official with the American Jewish Committee and in 2002-2003 a CIS

Senior Fellow, describe his conversion from unthinking Expansionist to deep alarm over the impacts of mass immigration upon the future of American and world Jewry. Steinlight and FAIR West Coast office head Ira Mehlman reported the remarkably positive responses they were getting in synagogues and before other Jewish audiences they visited in their recent tour of major U.S. cities.

That weekend Mark and Steve told me that the staff of news show host Lou Dobbs (CNN) had been calling weekly with questions about illegal immigration, and when I returned home I found Dobbs had become a vocal and often impassioned nightly critic of open borders. In an October article in *U.S. News and World Report* Dobbs sounded like the CIS staff and board, warning that "our rapidly growing population," driven by "unchecked immigration," was straining healthcare and educational systems, and burdening our land, food production, water supplies and air quality. His nightly newscasts raised the visibility of the debate over illegal immigration and the open southern border. Mark, Steve, and several CIS authors became frequent talking heads. Between October 1 and late December, CIS staff appeared on CNN a remarkable twenty-four times.

Roy Beck and Rosemary Jenks were also frequent visitors to both the Dobbs and O'Reilly news shows. Bill O'Reilly's Fox Newscast, launched in the fall of 1996, had surged to the top of the major news shows. That gave frequent prime time coverage for a critical view of immigration trends. O'Reilly, in the fall of 2003, covered the Mexican Matricula Consular, the importation of Mexican labor into Wal-Mart stores and Midwestern pork and poultry industries, and the cost of incarcerating illegal aliens in American prisons.

What a change. The mass media, when we started, had always been a part of the problem for us, avoiding discussion of the costs unchecked immigration brought, or sentimentalizing the topic with stories of Vietnamese kids who were valedictorians of their high school graduating class or of a hard-working Mexican family who started a successful bakery in Phoenix. It was a sea change in late 2003 to be invited to a different relationship in which we helped steer the media toward the heart of the larger story of a broken system, legal and illegal. The staffs of CIS, FAIR, and NumbersUSA helped educate the staff of the Dobbs, O'Reilly, McNeill and Lehrer and other news programs, earned their trust for accuracy, and appeared as expert commentators while responding during the day to increasing calls for interviews on talk radio.

* * *

<u>Big News in the Form of No Reform</u>

The year 2003 ended with no amnesty passed, and no guestworker program. I was surprised at our ability to fight off the formidable Expansionist coalition's radical proposals. However, when I encountered Roy Beck and FAIR's Rick Oltman that fall, they were not surprised, and told me why. NumbersUSA had become a lobbying force to be reckoned with, sending 750,000 faxes in 2002 and exceeding that in 2003. Roy told me in late 2003 that his list of activists had more than doubled over that summer, and that public anger at open borders was running at a fever pitch. Roy felt the public pulse that year in a way that I could not.

So did Rick Oltman, FAIR's western field representative. He sensed the same surge of public sentiment on illegal (and mass legal) immigration among groups he visited in the west, where there were now immigration reform groups in places like Idaho, Utah, and Arizona, not just in the major cities of California. At the 2003 FAIR-sponsored annual IRAW gathering in Washington, the activists from across the country made their usual visits to congressional offices. But this time instead of cool response or even "rudeness" in some offices, there was a warmer reception. "Politicians listened this year," Oltman reported, and attributed the difference not just to the terrorist attacks, but to the politicians' awareness that the issue of out-of-control immigration had surged to the top of the worry list of their constituents back home.

Chapter Twenty-Five:
2004—America's Political Elite Pushes Their Plans to Surrender

The challenge for national security in an age of terrorism is to prevent the very few people who may pose overwhelming risks from entering or remaining in the U.S. undetected. — The 9/11 Commission Report

When Presidents Bush and Fox in early September, 2001, agreed that the U.S. should grant amnesty to Mexican illegals resident in Bush's country, there was no opposition in either house of Congress. Then came the Al Qaeda suicide bombers, and the U. S. President, in the words of *Congressional Quarterly Weekly* in early January 2004, for two and a half years "had been largely silent on the issue." On January 7, 2004, an election year which would decide, among other things, whether George Bush remained in the White House for four more years, the president proposed an initiative to allow illegals currently in the country to obtain work visas for three years, renewable for an unspecified period if they could show that they had jobs and their employers certified that no Americans would take the work. "The system is not working," he conceded, since there are many illegals living in "fear and insecurity. Our laws should allow willing workers to enter our country and fill jobs that Americans are not filling." The remedy was "a new temporary worker program" to include both the 10-11 million illegals who had a job and "those in foreign countries" who received "a job offer." Their legal status would last three years, and perhaps be renewable, but in the end (six years?) all these "temporary workers" would "return permanently to their home country." By the way, "I oppose amnesty." If we do this, not only will we fill jobs Americans will not fill, but "Our homeland will be more secure when we can better account for those who enter our country, instead of the current situation in which millions of people are unknown to the law."

The president's short statement, delivered to a friendly audience of cabinet members and representatives of Hispanic groups, left all details skimpy and was an intellectual mess. He took no questions, and the press referred to the event as "a ceremony." The President of the U. S. had (again) proposed an amnesty for illegals and a broad and apparently permanent guestworker program reaching across the entire economy, based on the explicit assumption that America had a permanent need for millions of foreign workers and that employers would be the judge of how many, and at what wages and conditions.

At one level, I was not surprised—none of us were, in our camp. These ideas had been in the air for years, and when the history of this is written we will undoubtedly find many people claiming that they hatched and nurtured the Bush(Fox) proposals. That President Bush early in an election year would cobble them together again could have been predicted. The masterminds in the White House and their Expansionist allies had actually concluded that it was time to mount a major counter-offensive. A de facto abandonment of immigration regulation in favor of an employer-driven system of open borders, they were gambling, was at least a vote-getter in the campaigns ahead, whether or not it could be pushed through the legislative process. If they were right and it *was* a vote-getter, after the 2004 and succeeding elections it would be hard to stop in Congress.

Either the Bush camp had miscalculated, or we had. On my hopeful days, I reminded myself that anyone who had looked at the Latino poll results over the years and understood the dynamics at work knew that Americans of Hispanic heritage had views on illegal immigration reasonably close to those of other Americans, and that immigration policy was not high on their list of issues nor one on which their individual votes (there was no "Latino vote," only a diverse ethnic mosaic) hinged. Rove-Bush had also made the risky gamble that the

Open Borders tone of his immigration proposal would not alienate any part of his base.

On some days I felt that Bush had just made an egregious political miscalculation, not just because I have some Republican friends whose views on lawbreaking and a permanent flood of foreign workers I am familiar with. Like anyone paying reasonable attention to immigration politics, I knew that Tom Tancredo's Immigration Reform Caucus was steadily growing and that Tancredo spoke for a large and expanding national Republican following. My instinct about the reaction of ordinary Republicans was strongly confirmed within days of Bush's proposal. I was in Santa Barbara through much of January, and as it happened, local immigration activist Gwat Batcherje persuaded me to give a luncheon address before the S. B. County Republican women. I talked about the immigration issue in general, and initially said nothing about Bush, not wanting to start a fight with folks I knew to be partisans of their president and who had paid for my lunch. Then I was asked my opinion of the president's recent, early January proposal. I called it the worst piece of proposed public policy I had ever heard of in my lifetime or studied in history. I expected a few boos, but mild boos, and possibly many nods. Instead, the entire audience at tables in the Montecito Country Club came to their feet in thunderous applause at my comment.

George Bush had, I now sensed from contact with real Republicans, made a substantial political mistake—unless I had somehow encountered an out-of-step group of Santa Barbara GOP malcontents. I later learned that David Frum, a Bush speechwriter inside the White House during some part of 2002-2003 was on a book tour touting his new *An End to Evil* on January 7 when the president's proposal hit the news. Frum met with audiences and appeared on talk radio, and "every show you did, every question" was an angry complaint about Bush's proposal. Frum called the White House and told them "there's a problem up here in Americaland; the Americans are unhappy about this," but it was too late. "Hideous errors" of this sort were sometimes made, he conceded, when White House working groups brought only a few interested parties together and made policy that alienates the "upper working-class American" who is the "voting bulwark of the party."

The initial reaction as conveyed by the mass media suggested that the Bush plan pleased his big business supporters and had considerable support in editorials from prominent newspapers ("the president, who yesterday announced a proposal to reform this country's "broken" immigration laws, deserves applause," was the stance of the "liberal" *Washington Post*). A vice president of the Chamber of Commerce said that "we (employers) are extremely pleased," and Senate Majority Leader Bill Frist promised "most serious consideration and attention to this proposal."

Elsewhere the plan stirred up a swarm of doubts and fault-finding of various sorts. To Vermont Democratic Governor Howard Dean, then the front-runner for his party's presidential nomination, the plan did not go far enough in the direction of re-defining illegals as legal. It would do "nothing to place hardworking [illegal] immigrants on the path to citizenship" and "would create a permanent underclass of service workers with second-class status." *The New Republic* editorialized in the same direction, that the plan did not put illegals on a sure path to citizenship without a return home. Why not ignore Bush's inadequate plan and solve the entire problem of illegals by passing the AgJobs Act and Dream Act that were stalled in Congress? Several politicians and leaders of Latino lobbies, perhaps to Bush's surprise, agreed with Dean, wanting illegal immigrants to be treated more leniently even than Bush proposed. "It's not amnesty, that's for sure," and many illegals wouldn't sign up for a three or six- year tour that led to a return to and waiting period in Mexico, said a United Farm Worker official.

Yet there seemed more conviction and combativeness among those who found the amnesty-guestworker plan entirely too lenient and bad policy to begin with. John J. Sweeney, head of the AFL-CIO, objected to the creation of a "permanent underclass of workers" who will constitute "a second tier." The *Los Angeles Times* sent reporters to interview three dozen Border Patrol agents, including the president of their union, and found all of them of the view that "Bush's proposal is...a grab for Latino votes" and "an insult" to their profession, causing them to wonder "why they get up in the morning, and why they go to work." Immigration scholars seemed unanimously critical. "I think it's a terrible mistake," George Borjas was quoted, "and it's doing nothing to prevent the problem from recurring again in our future." Phil Martin and David North warned of widespread fraud in all guestworker programs, especially one aimed at perhaps eleven million resident illegal aliens and un-numbered foreign applicants. Bush's program, especially, "put(s) employers in charge," pointed out Professor David Abraham of the University of Miami.

These were some fragments of opinion and observation in the early media-reported reaction of interested parties and experts to the president's January proposal. The only coherent and sustained critique of the Bush plan in those weeks after its January debut came from CIS.

* * *

The Center was uniquely ready to analyze and expose the many flaws and confusions in the Bush initiative. Phil Martin had written a Center study in April, 2000, on the sorry history of guestworker programs in the U.S. going back to the Bracero Program, and had another CIS Backgrounder scheduled for publication in January, 2004, describing how guestworker programs plus illegal immigration had ruined the hopes of Cesar Chavez and the United Farm Workers. Mark had developed expertise on the topic, publishing a study of agricultural guestworker programs in June, 2001. Informed that the president would make some sort of amnesty-guestworker proposal in early January 2004, Mark, with another Backgrounder ready for February ("Flawed Assumptions Underlying Guestworker Programs"), quickly wrote a cover story for *National Review*'s January 26 issue, "Against Amnesty: Mark Krikorian on a Policy Disaster." His shorter version, "Jobs Americans Won't Do: Voodoo Economics from the White House," appeared in *National Review Online* the day of Bush's immigration "ceremony." Just minutes after the president's talk, Rush Limbaugh was reading whole chunks of Mark's essay on his radio program. Message: This is an amnesty, despite Bush's denials. It will be impossible to administer without fraud, will invite further illegal immigration which will be "guaranteed" to contain Middle Eastern enemies of the U.S., and will build pressure for other amnesties. Control illegal immigration first, and "after eight or ten years of proven, ongoing border control and interior enforcement, with a properly functioning and motivated immigration bureaucracy and a steadily declining illegal-alien population," perhaps we will discuss the issue of amnesty, at which time we will see that the illegal population has shrunk through attrition to insignificant levels.

Mark's "Not Amnesty but Attrition" article in *National Review* (March 22, 2004) introduced a new idea which he called "a third way" between mass roundups and "the surrender of our sovereignty." It was "attrition," "squeezing the illegal population through consistent, across-the-board law enforcement to bring about an annual reduction… rather than the annual increases we have seen for more than a decade. Over a few years, the number of illegal aliens would drop significantly, shrinking the problem from a crisis to a manageable nuisance." Like any brilliantly original-sounding formulation, this one owed something to earlier work. Former CIS Director David Simcox had argued in a 2002 NPG *Forum Paper* "Amnesty: Overpopulation by Fiat," that tighter enforcement and a small increase in individual deportations "could reduce the unreplenished illegal population by as much as 4.0 million over a decade." These attrition concepts could not be described as "draconian, inhumane roundups" in the language used by Open Borderists to describe any alternative to amnesty. Illegals would deport themselves after finding daily life in unlawful status in the U.S. too full of jeopardy, and return home to get in the legal line and otherwise make the best of life in the country where their Creator had initially placed them.

As for the guestworker idea, in "Jobs Americans Won't Do" Mark drew upon earlier studies such as Phil Martin and Michael Teitelbaum's superb "The Mirage of Mexican Guest Workers" published in *Foreign Affairs* (November-December, 2001), as well as Vernon Briggs' CIS *Backgrounder* scheduled for March publication ("Guestworker Programs: Lessons From the Past and Warnings for the Future"). Mark reported that all U.S. experience with guestworker programs had been negative in the long run. Guestworkers don't go home, as the president promised this time they really would, and such programs inhibit agricultural innovation, depress wages, and amount to a public subsidy to employers. The White House should have consulted the reports of the Hesburgh and Jordan commissions, both of which had rejected any sort of guestworker program.

This was a remarkable intellectual performance for any Center, especially a very small one. How was CIS ready with well-considered analysis and recommendations on exactly the topics the president decided to put front and center? I am prepared to believe that some mole in the White House phoned Mark at CIS in 2003 and warned him of the upcoming Bush proposal, giving him time to prepare a January counterblast. Or not. We (Mark first) knew it was coming, and that the media would immediately need some critical and informed response in order to frame their stories. Sure enough, the media reaction to the Center's early analysis was intense. In the week following Bush's proposal, Mark appeared twice on Fox News and also on "The News Hour With Jim Lehrer," while Steve Camarota carried the analysis to CNN and CBS. The "amnesty word," along with troubling questions, was now attached to the Bush plan, though the president had said at the end of his remarks, "I oppose amnesty" and the White House kept insisting that his proposal to require illegals to take several steps as well as pay a fee should be called "earned legalization."

* * *

"The Amnesty Word"

The amnesty word, and the guestworker idea, had driven a wedge in Republican ranks. At a major, three-day national meeting of Republicans in late February, "immigration proved to be the hottest issue," a *Washington Times* reporter found, and "many in the audience booed and hissed Manhattan Institute analyst Tamar Jacoby's defense of the guest worker proposal" and "sided heavily" with the views of Pat Buchanan and Phyllis Schlafly. Very soon some prominent elected Republicans began to back away from the president's idea. Congressman Tancredo's immediate opposition, and that of his fifty member Immigration Reform Caucus, was assumed. But a more prominent House figure, Majority Leader Tom DeLay (Republican, Texas), told the press he had "heartfelt reservations about allowing illegal immigrants into a U.S. guestworker program that seemed to reward illegal behavior." Rep.

Elton Gallegly (Republican, California), a member of the immigration subcommittee, said it "amounts to the forgiveness of a criminal act." Un-named "House Republican officials" told the *Washington Post* that the plan would have a low priority.

Behind this unenthusiasm was a remarkable outpouring of public complaint. Talk show hosts fielded clouds of angry calls. Negative mail was said to have washed into the White House and Hill offices, running 400 to one (some said 1,000 to one) against the proposal. Some of this backlash mail was engineered by NumbersUSA and FAIR, but surely more of it was spontaneous (as a testimony to these organization's growing public relations skills, politicians often couldn't tell). In the Santa Barbara luncheon with Republicans, I had been asked "What should we do?," and I suggested that they contact their GOP local politicians and party leaders and tell them that the immigration plan sapped all enthusiasm for turning out to vote in November. It seemed that Republicans in California and across the country had figured this out for themselves, and sent negative mail to their political leadership and threatened a fall-off in contributions. "This [immigration] is the number one issue that comes back from voters no matter what we talk about," a GOP consultant in California's March elections told a reporter in late February. "It's a very powerful issue."

A CNN-USA Today poll toward the end of January found that 55 percent of Americans opposed Bush's proposal, while 42 percent favored it. George Bush had not produced a breakthrough in the lengthy, stalemated war over immigration policy.

Yet the plan was "out there," in general concept if not in legislative form, and there was a brief, energetic, if intellectually muddled campaign to explain and sell it. Cato's Dan Griswold in a May/June *Cato Policy Report* said we had to eliminate the "underground" pool of labor because it "drags down working conditions and wages on the lower rungs of the economic ladder," but thought better of that line of argument and tried to correct himself. "They don't drive down wages or cause unemployment." Not much was heard from him thereafter. Margaret Spellings conceded in a Cato panel in late January that the guestworkers were expected to bring in their families, which would be a big problem for those who, like the president, expected these workers to eventually return home. Spellings soon went back to her other White House duties.

A more skilled polemicist, Tamar Jacoby, came forward from the Manhattan Institute where she had just established a marginal immigration expertise serving as editor of the 2004 anthology of essays on assimilation, *Reinventing the Melting Pot*. In congressional testimony and in essays and media appearances, Jacoby honed the core arguments for the Bush initiative. Our "immigration system is broken…Enforcement isn't going to fix it, because we tried that…the border is uncontrollable" and "the flow is inevitable…" The Bush plan "isn't perfect, but it's a bold step in the right direction." It merely needs a clearer "track to citizenship."

This nicely caught the Bush proposal's logic, the logic of surrender to the demands of foreigners and some American employers, retroactively. Eleven million illegals would be brought into a legal relationship inside the country for six years, after which they would be expected to return home (leaving any America-born children behind?) and submit themselves to the legal immigration process they had already faced down. Was it contempt for the public intelligence, or merely a muddled mind, that brought the president to claim that this massive bureaucratic signup of foreigners, eleven million now here and who knew how many millions of others from overseas, would actually allow the government to "keep track of people in the program and better enforce our immigration laws?" Vice President Dick Cheney told reporters shortly after the president made his proposal, that "from the standpoint of homeland security and securing the nation's borders," the legalization of illegals (at least they were no longer using the term "undocumented") was a great plus, since, as it is now, "we have millions of illegal, undocumented workers in our midst. We don't know how long they stay. We don't know what they do while they're here. We don't know when they leave."

This was a new side of Dick Cheney, worried about "securing the nation's borders." How did amnesty fit into this? In his view a key benefit from the proposal to sign up all the illegals and making them legal was to "better enforce our immigration laws." It made no sense. Bush himself had not expressed a single clear idea about enforcement, which would be an even larger problem dealing with the enlarged flood of illegals after the word went out that we intend to forgive the eleven million already illegally here. Even Jacoby, the enthusiast who welcomed Bush's "critical step forward," conceded that "the most glaring gap has to do with enforcement," which of course the president was making ever more difficult with his frequent talk of amnesty. Her one sentence on enforcement was as close as she or any Bush supporters would come to referring to the problem of the millions of illegals who would rush north when they heard about this latest forgiveness of their predecessors.

I did run across one explanation of Bush's brief claim and Cheney's implication that legalizing all illegals would make border defense in the future a whole lot easier. Writer Peter Laufer, in *Wetback Nation: The Case for Opening the Mexican-American Border* (2004), a book published just after the Bush announcement, welcomed the plan on the grounds that, with Mexican workers now able to come north legally, "the Border Patrol will know that the people trying to break into the country—the ones in the tunnels, those running across the desert and jumping the fences—are the real villains...drug traffickers and the terrorists" who the Border Patrol can then easily capture. Presumably the legitimate, legal immigrant workers hired abroad, sight unseen, by U.S. employers, would ride in on planes or buses, armed with a paper designating them as guestworkers under contract to an American boss. From Bush through Cheney, Griswold, Spellings, Jacoby and Laufer, the White Flag Reformers and their allies insisted always on their superior "realism," and ignored the enforcement problem that an amnesty only intensified for the next round. They came across as either tired, new to the subject, contemptuous of their audience, or all three.

* * *

With the president's election-year immigration proposal short on details and with no legislative embodiment or sponsor, as well as quickly and widely unpopular among some Republicans, the year 2004 certainly granted us the Chinese wish that we live in interesting times. Anxiously interesting times, for those of us with the reductionist perspective. We soon found what we expected, that the Democrats would not be outdone in the new race to explicitly dismantle immigration regulation and redirect our immigration policy bureaucracy toward recruiting foreigners wanted by U.S. employers and granting citizenship to those who had come by breaking the old rules. In May, Senator Edward Kennedy and Representatives Robert Menendez and Luis Gutierrez introduced a bill under the cover-all-bases acronym SOLVE (Safe, Orderly, Legal Visas and Enforcement Act). Denouncing Bush's plan as too restrictive, the Democrats demonstrated that more disastrous immigration policy ideas could be hatched on the Hill than in the White House. Their bill established a guestworker program with no numerical cap, the workers after two years eligible to apply for citizenship. Their amnesty made the Bush proposal look positively stingy—all aliens in the country for five years get citizenship, as do their family members abroad.

By early summer, 2004, dozens of bills we abhorred were in various places on the clogged congressional conveyor belt. Most gave legal status to millions of foreigners already in the country illegally, and/or inaugurate new guestworker programs run for the benefit of employers who disliked the expectations of American workers. The most dangerous bill seemed to be the AgJOBS monstrosity of Congressman Chris Cannon and Senator Larry Craig, which by mid-2003 had sixty-one co-sponsors in the senate. A few legislators, like Tom Tancredo, proposed to impose new limits and tighten enforcement to enhance national security, but these had small numbers of sponsors and got little serious attention.

A growing part of the policy confusion and volatility of 2004 derived from competitive labeling. Both sides, all sides, were pushing "immigration reform." Could Americans, on this complex and emotional topic, look carefully behind the "reform" brands? The options under the reform banner were radically different, and the future of the country was at stake—which was not so with other important policy measures, such as taxation, agricultural subsidies, or whether to terminate Amtrak.

* * *

Dodging the Bullet

Yet in 2004, again, the Expansionists did not achieve their version of national immigration "reform," to my relief and surprise. Neither did we. The year stretched out as a dangerous, volatile stalemate, as the issue built toward some unforeseeable political breakthrough.

At the city and state levels, ethnic lobbyists were pressing for new laws offering drivers licenses and other identification documents, in-state college tuition, and publicly funded and managed hiring halls for illegals. Such activities generated a fierce and widespread series of grassroots battles over these issues running throughout and beyond 2004. "States large and small in every corner of the country are wrestling with the issue of driver's licenses and identification for immigrants and illegals," the *Christian Science Monitor* in mid-summer quoted a National Immigration Law Center staffer who tracked political currents. "The debate has become high profile." On this sprawling field of conflict, we won some and lost some, but our troops were beginning to show up under effective leadership in most local contests over immigration law enforcement and illegal alien policy.

Looking back at 2004, the main story, to me, was the strengthening of the real immigration reform movement. At both the local and the national levels our side got stronger as the year went on—more recruits and converts and grassroots organizations, more effective arguments and arguers, the opening of new fronts. It could have been a very bad year, and it wasn't.

Was the momentum truly shifting our way? A cautious case could be made for this, but the basic stalemate, if it seemed now to be preventing Bad Immigration Reform, also prevented Good Immigration Reform. We were blocking things, but our reforms were also bottled up.

I cornered Roy Beck in a hotel bar as 2004 turned into summer. "If it seems to you that our nation is hanging precariously in the balance right now," he had written to his NumbersUSA mailing list on January, 30, 2004, "I don't blame you. Every few days, another major national leader proposes some kind of mass amnesty and guestworker program. But don't despair. Incredible outpourings of citizen outrage seem to have created a firewall against all those incendiary proposals." Over a drink in June, 2005, he told me that, two years earlier, NumbersUSA had 3,000 reliable and active faxers who would respond when Roy or his lobbying staff signaled that something major needed to be resisted, or endorsed. At the end of 2003, that number was 12,000. In the months after Bush's early 2004 proposal on immigration, the list soared to 55,000. It would reach 115,000 in mid-2005. Roy reported a surge in visits to his web site, now receiving more hits than the web site of, for example, the National Rifle Association or the American Civil Liberties Union. "We have burst through to a whole new level of citizen mobilization and Capitol Hill influence."

* * *

In July came publication of the The *9/11 : Final Report of the National Commission on Terrorist Attacks Upon the U. S.* (2004). In this unusually readable document, published in paperback by W. W. Norton and selling more than a million copies, national security and immigration policy were firmly joined, and the assignment of immigration policy was large and vital:

> *More than 500 million people annually cross U.S. borders...*
> *another 500,000 or more enter illegally... The challenge for*
> *national security in an age of terrorism is to prevent the very*
> *few people who may pose overwhelming risks from entering or*
> *remaining in the U.S. undetected. In the decade before September*
> *11, 2001, border security . . . was not seen as a national security*
> *matter... The immigration system as a whole was widely viewed*
> *as increasingly dysfunctional and badly in need of reform. In*
> *national security circles, however, only smuggling weapons of mass*
> *destruction carried weight...Had the immigration system set a*
> *higher bar for determining whether individuals are who and*
> *what they claim to be . . . it could potentially have excluded...*
> *several hijackers who did not appear to meet the terms for*
> *admitting short-term visitors.*

This must change, the report insisted. We must in the future make it impossible or surpassingly difficult for the ninety-four terrorists operating in the U.S. from the early 1990s to 2004 that were studied by the 9/11 Commission staff task force on terrorist travel to commit immigration fraud (as fifty-nine of them had done with impunity) or obtain immigration benefits to facilitate life in the U. S. (as forty-seven had been able to do). The Commission recommended a comprehensive border security system, and appraised the steps thus far taken in that direction. The report rang with language we reformers had used for decades. "There is a growing role for state and local law enforcement agencies." "The federal government should set standards for the issuance of birth certificates and sources of identification, such as drivers licenses." There should be "a biometric entry-exit screening system," "an integrated watch list." "All people, American or otherwise" should carry biometric passports.

The 9/11 Commission Report said nothing about immigration levels or selection procedures, but it vastly magnified the warnings we had been raising about the national security risks of porous borders, and created a climate in which policymakers who weakened or abandoned immigration law enforcement were aware that they ran against a strong tide of public opinion and sentiment generated by the meltdown of the twin towers in New York. The report ignited again the fading public discussion of the 9/11 attacks and their lessons, and that meant, among other things, the appearance of national television of lobbying organizations composed of the families of those killed in the attacks of that day. We saw again the controlled but intense anger of Peter Gadiel of "9/11 Families for a Secure America," who had lost a son in the attack and went on the FAIR Board as I left.

* * *

The changed climate also was shaped by mounting evidence of the social costs and dysfunctions of the mass immigration era. The numbers alone were unprecedented, and the few measures of restriction taken after 9/11, such as the minor shrinkage of the number of foreign student visas so complained about by universities, did not much change the annual totals. Looking back to the 1990s, on average, 1.1 million legal immigrants came to the U. S. each year. A sharp spike upward came in 1999 and 2000, with 1.5 million new Americans and their subsequent children. The events of 9/11 probably accounted for a slight reduction in 2002-2003 back to the earlier, unprecedentedly high 1.1 million annually on which the century had ended. In 2004, the upward trend re-asserted itself, with 1.2 million legal new Americans, who would have children to augment the national population. The foreign-born percentage of the population in 2003 was estimated by the Census Bureau as 33.5 million, up from the year before, reaching 12 percent of the whole. Latin America was the source of 53 percent of the foreign-born cohort.

Nine million illegals resided in the U. S. in 2003, by an estimate made by Steven Camarota of CIS, "probably 10 million or more" by the end of 2004 (10.3 million, by the *Congressional Research Service* estimate). More than half of these were Mexicans. The economic slowdown that began in 2000 seemed to have no effect on the flows, legal or illegal. What did seem to influence the numbers of illegal entries over the southern border, especially, in the view of Border Patrol officials, was the lure of Bush's amnesty proposal. The number of apprehensions on the Tijuana-San Diego sector of the border from the ocean to the mountains had fallen from 531,689 in 1993 to 111,515 in 2003, as it was now fortified with a steel and concrete fence (two in some places) running eastward some forty-four miles. These physical barriers, combined with improved Border Patrol technology and numbers, had shifted the growing human pressures eastward to Arizona, New Mexico and Texas, where coyotes led their paying customers into a more dangerous crossing through a harsh desert environment

* * *

Time magazine recognized that a nation-changing drama was unfolding in this new sector of the border, and assigned reporters Donald Barlett and James Steele to write a special report that became the cover story, "America's Border: Even After 9/11, It's Outrageously Easy to Sneak In," for the September 20 issue. They began at little Bisbee, Arizona, five miles north of the border, and described a steady stream of illegals pouring northward. Most were Mexican, but the BP detained in this sector 55,000 OTMs in 2003, tripling to 155,000 in 2005 (of perhaps 190,000 OTMs who came over this part of the southwest border undetected)—other Latin Americans, but also people from Afghanistan, Bulgaria, Egypt, Iran, and Iraq. Of the 155,000 OTMs arrested in 2005, lack of detention space and the cost of overseas deportation meant that 70 percent were given the "catch and release" process, which meant a brief detention with a "run letter" requesting their court appearance at a later date.

For Arizonans living near the border the impact was more immediate and outrageous. "The masses of incoming illegals lay waste to the landscape," the article reported. "They discard backpacks, empty Gatorade and water bottles and soiled clothes. They turn the land into a vast latrine." When arrested, or injured, the illegal's medical needs were unloaded on Arizona medical facilities with no federal reimbursement, pushing hospitals like Copper Queen in Bisbee and the medical facilities at the Tohono O'odham Nation reservation toward bankruptcy. The reporters' story was suffused with outrage at the situation they found, but the anger was directed at faraway corporate employers like those at Tyson Foods, and at congressional politicians who acquiesce in the almost total breakdown of both interior and border enforcement.

* * *

The Piling Up of Illegal Immigration Bads

What the *Time* reporters described for a national audience in a politically quite incorrect tone of anger was a breakdown of social order at the border, a part of America that few saw. Less attention was given to the rising level of immigrant-connected criminal behavior across the interior. The Department of Homeland Security's inadequate and not fully integrated databases revealed that 80,000 of the 400,000 illegals ordered deported had criminal records, and the government had no idea where they were inside America. They had been given Run Letters, and had run. The *Time* story's account of illegal immigrant crime in the interior was sketchy, crime being a formidably elusive topic for journalists and other investigators. They did tell the story of Jesus Franco Flores alias Victor Manuel Batres-Martinez, who first entered the U.S. from Mexico in 1986. Convicted of felonies and imprisoned once, he had been deported three times for various crimes. He re-entered the U.S. each time, and late in the summer of 2002 raped two nuns in Klamath Falls, Oregon, and then strangled one of them with her rosary.

We immigration reformers had been insisting for years that part of the social cost of contemporary immigration was an unusually high crime rate among illegal aliens—drunken driving, robbery, rape and murder. Discussion of this dimension of the issue had long been suppressed by charges of "immigrant bashing," and the media, not wanting to risk that sort of label, had long avoided or sanitized social problems that seemed somehow connected to immigrants. The Frank Del Olmo scissors had been active in most media editorial offices. There were a handful of exceptions. Perhaps the most prominent mainstream media critic of the mass immigration status quo over the past decade had been *U.S. News and World Report*'s Editor-in-Chief Mortimer Zuckerman, an outspoken reductionist. Toward the end of 2004 he wrote: "There has been an utter failure to deal with the tidal wave of foreigners to America's shores and borders...placing a strain on our social resources, creating huge security risks, and, ultimately, challenging the very identity of our nation." The only major newspaper in the country editorializing for firmer regulation, and encouraging its reporters to give balanced coverage, appeared to be *The Washington Times* (some would add the *Christian Science Monitor*). To us, the *Time* front page story in September 2004, appeared to mark an important conversion of at least part of the liberal mainstream mass media to our argument that the cost side of our nation's collapsed border filters and interior enforcement was and is a major story that must be researched and told, along with the stories of Vietnamese valedictorians in Dallas and successful Korean merchants in New York.

One example of media attention to the problematic side of large-scale illegal immigration was Latin American gang expansion inside the U. S., an old story that had not been much of a story until 2004. Manhattan Institute writer Heather Mac Donald pulled together police estimates that exposed the dimensions of the problem. The California Department of Justice estimated in 1995 that 60 percent of the 20,000 members of the southern California-based Eighteenth Street gang were illegal. Soon they were not the largest gang complex fed into the U.S. from Mexico and Central America. The Central American street gang Mara Salvatrucha—or MS-13—had been migrating from its base in Guatemala to U.S. cities since at least the early 1990s, chiefly to L.A., without much notice being taken. In 2004, the media gave increasing coverage to urban law enforcement officials' concern over gangs in general and in particular to MS-13, whose numbers were by one estimate between 70,000-1,000,000 in the U.S., with 5,000 in Washington D.C. alone. ICE officials believed a majority were illegal. In many cities, most importantly in gang-infested Los Angeles and New York, the local police were banned, under "sanctuary policies," from reporting immigration violations to federal authorities.

These large numbers for international criminal organizations migrating into and flourishing with the U. S. were an ominous trend. Black, Hispanic and to a lesser extent Asian gangs were sprinkled across and down through American history. In my own home town there had been Hispanic gangs in Goleta schools just north of Santa Barbara in the 1980s, and some conflict with black gangs in Santa Barbara High occasionally made it into the local news, though the local newspaper had a Del Olmo-type editor or editorial dictate, and ethnicity and race were usually left out of the stories. The numbers nationally had surged in the two decades after, coinciding with the flood of Hispanic immigration. The street gangs' livelihood was stolen cars and other goods, stolen documents, and the drug trade. The recruiting grounds were often in nearby high schools, where gang members with names like SOK (Still Out Killing) and HTO (Hispanics Taking Over) learned the ropes. California high schools in heavily ghettoized neighborhoods reported mounting trouble with gangs, but in 2004 the newspaper in my neighboring city, Raleigh, North Carolina explained that the graffiti tag, "X13," claimed that territory for Sur Trece, a Hispanic gang with California roots. In California and elsewhere, school gangs had some involvement with out-of-school crime, but most of their violent energy went into inter-gang, inter-racial maulings and killings. Their members were saturated with an underclass culture hostile to authority and placing no value on education, especially for women. The result for many was gang affiliation, crime, dropping out of school, and fathering illegitimate offspring. George Bush frequently said that "family values don't stop at the Rio Grande," a muddled remark taken to mean that

Spanish-speaking people arriving in the U.S. had strong family values. Whatever that meant, the young Mexican and Central American males, at least, either brought some not-so-family values with them or picked them up quickly in the wicked cities of North America.

* * *

There seemed two major reasons for the upward spike in the media attention directed to the costly and darker side of contemporary immigration in 2003-2004. The general public was without question more aroused than at any earlier time, and this could be seen in virtually every state and in all regions. The grassroots anger seen in California in the early 1990s was now nationwide. The electronic and print news media slowly realized that immigration was a high-up-the-pole and rising issue. However reluctantly and warily, reporters and editors made room for immigration-related troubles in their coverage.

Of course, on talk radio the critical attention to America's broken borders came earlier than in conventional news channels and with considerably more passion. I had my own exposure to talk radio during a book "tour" in 2003 to promote my new book, *Unguarded Gates: A History of America's Immigration Crisis*. It offers a sharply revisionist view of American immigration policy history, arguing, among other things, that our national eras of small-scale immigration have been better for the country than the "great waves," one of which we were now caught up in. To promote the book, the publisher arranged over thirty interviews on talk radio medium, from stations in California and Texas to New York. In all the conversations with callers, only one was hostile to what he understood to be my point of view on this issue. All of the hosts were sympathetic. Several radio hosts, most notably Terry Anderson, John and Ken, and Doug McIntyre, all broadcasting from California, impressed me as entrepreneurs who took up the critique of immigration not only because it magically expanded their listener base, but also out of personal outrage at the growing illegal presence. Terry Anderson was uniquely impressive in person.

* * *

Arizona Brushfires

One could have guessed that if the embers of the Prop. 187 brushfire in California drifted east to start another flare-up of resistance to illegal immigration it would be in Arizona. The success of border reinforcement in the San Diego sector had pushed the human flood eastward, and in the fiscal year from October, 2003 to October, 2004, 600,000 people, mostly Mexicans, were apprehended along the Arizona border, a four-fold increase in one decade. With these swelling numbers came the intrusions I have earlier described—drug trafficking along with the human, petty but also occasionally deadly crime, crowded safe houses, trashed landscapes, and hundreds of immigrant deaths. "The signs of strain are everywhere—emergency rooms closing, overcrowded schools, families living in garages, homes converted to hiding places and gangland-style crime," reported the *New York Times* (October, 16, 2004) in a biased story that opened with several criticisms of Arizona critics of illegal immigration, and only at the end got to the "signs of strain" that animated the critics.

Resentments in Arizona boiled over, and Prop. 200, like 187, was a local invention to deal with a federal government failure. It was put together in late 2003 by an organization called Protect Arizona Now, headed by a Quaker Sunday school teacher named Kathy McKee. It had two aims—to prevent illegals from receiving welfare or other public benefits, and to require proof of citizenship when registering to vote.

As in California, the entire state establishment rose up in opposition and indignation—the Democratic Governor, popular Republican Senator John McCain, the state's three Catholic Bishops, virtually all the business, journalistic, religious and educational leadership. Their arguments were not too different from those against 187—there is no voter fraud in Arizona, to enforce the provisions against public benefits would require a huge bureaucracy and much expense, a witch hunt will follow, and you people are racists. McKee responded succinctly: "This is about protecting the voting process and prohibiting welfare fraud. Nothing more, nothing less." Proponents were outspent by a wide margin. With FAIR's legal help, they survived several early court challenges bankrolled by Ford Foundation money. The pro-200 ads stressed the $1.3 billion a year spent by the state in services to illegals.

Again as in California, polls steadily showed strong public support for the initiative. Also again, the local proponents raised less money than they hoped, and faced lavishly funded opposition. Efforts to gain signatures to put the initiative on the ballot faltered, and FAIR in Washington heard appeals for financial help. FAIR western field director Rick Oltman visited Arizona frequently, and he and long-time FAIR activist in Arizona, Bob Park both found McKee administratively incompetent, irritable, over-supplied with ego and a desire to be paid a large salary. She embodied the problems that sometimes came with local leadership in this movement. Dan Stein soon shared these impressions, but he and the FAIR board judged that Prop. 200 already had such national visibility that its defeat would be a big setback. FAIR committed to financial and legal advice, and found strong and moderate local leadership to work with in Rusty Childress, a Phoenix businessman who had helped launch Protect Arizona Now, and Republican National Committee member Randy Pullen who chaired the Yes on Proposition 200 Committee and gave it an impressive spokesperson. Citizen volunteers were mobilized, the necessary signatures were certified, and a persuasive public information campaign was mounted.

Given McKee's shortcomings, there was no way to avoid a nasty split in the pro-200 ranks. It had little effect on the outcome but made life harder for everyone. Vanderbilt professor Virginia Abernethy, the dominant force within the two small DC-based virtual organizations, CNN and Balance, whose marginality I have described, had since the 1990s been intensifying her attacks on the successful parts of the reductionist national organizations, FAIR and NumbersUSA, calling them "Reform Lite" organizations. As the Prop. 200 campaign heated up, she moved to Arizona, allied herself with the equally erratic McKee, and also declared herself an "ethnic separatist" and a member of the Council of Conservative Citizens, thereby giving unfriendly media an opening for distortion. Abernethy had evolved into a bomb-thrower in organizational wars she often fomented, and, it was my impression from several conversations, that she was not a happy person. Graf, Childress and Rick Oltman of FAIR got the required signatures, and managed the campaign. On election day in November, the Arizona Taxpayers and Citizens Protection Act was adopted by a margin of 56 percent to 44 percent. Exit polls indicated that 47 percent of Hispanics voted for it, and 72 percent of Arizonans with incomes less than $15,000. "This is a movement that is going to gain momentum," Graf predicted, and there were news reports of activists in other states eager to adopt the Arizona model.

* * *

In late July, California activist and writer Joe Guzzardi wrote that, "with Congress safely adjourned until Labor Day (phew!), now is a fine time to evaluate how the immigration reform movement is doing on Capitol Hill...The news is quite good. We've hung tough and stood off furious attacks." A near doubling of the number of H-2B visas took legislative form, but never came up for a vote. AgJOBS, with its sixty-three senate co-sponsors, met the same outcome, apparently because Senate Majority leader Bill Frist heard "bottle this thing up" advice not only from some of the sixty-three senators who had been hearing from constituents but also from the White House. "Five amnesties were passed by Congress in the 1990s," Roy Beck recalled, "but since 2000, not a peep of an amnesty has been able to get through." An "incredible victory" for our "rag tag army of loosely organized, modestly funded national and local organizations," sending e-mails and faxes, showing up and raising their voices at meetings with their elected politicians, at rallies and city council sessions.

* * *

Another Presidential Election Without Immigration

Now it was time for the national conventions, and the presidential race. The good news of 2004 was that a second nationally visible state plebiscite on illegal immigration (the first was, of course, Prop. 187 in 1994) had produced another successful populist uprising rejecting the analysis and advice of America's Open-Border-minded Overclass. The disappointing side was that the presidential race, again, left immigration reform off the agenda. This left Arizona's vote on Prop. 200 the largest arena in political year 2004 in which American voters were presented with a sharply defined choice between Open Border politicians and programs and reformers of our "reduce the numbers and enforce the law" perspective.

* * *

We reformers always hoped to be involved in a presidential race in which immigration policy was a large factor, but we had learned that the politicians and their advisors kept a firewall up to screen out this issue. In 2004, the Republican Party platform committee heard from some party leaders who wanted a strong border control statement along with the usual language expressing Statue of Liberty sentimentality. But the White House seemed to have written the platform, which endorsed the president's "plan" with his own words about "matching willing foreign workers with willing U.S. employers." The Democratic Party's counterpart began with the sentence: "We will extend the promise of citizenship for those still struggling for freedom," and was more lopsided than the GOP platform toward sentimentality and welcoming more immigrants. President Bush never brought up immigration before non-Latino audiences, but addressed a gathering at the seventy-fifth anniversary of LULAC and reminded them that he "proposed reforms that would match willing foreign workers with willing American employers" and "grant legal status" to workers now here illegally. (Applause) was inserted after this part of the press release put out by the White House. Neither Bush nor Democratic nominee Senator John Kerry mentioned immigration in their acceptance speeches heard by a national audience, though Kerry went before a conference of La Raza and said that he would, within one hundred days of taking office, propose "a path to equal citizenship" for all illegal aliens, i.e. amnesty, and would endorse and sign AgJOBS guestworker program and the DREAM Act giving young illegals preferential college tuition as well as a path to citizenship.

The issue was briefly but conspicuously forced on the candidates on one major occasion when they faced the American people, not an audience of ethnic lobbyists.

In the third presidential debate on television, moderator Bob Schieffer of CBS asked, "Let's go to a new question, Mr. President. I got more e-mail this week on this question than any other question, and it's about immigration. I'm told that at least 8,000 people cross our borders illegally every day. Some people believe this is a security issue. How do you see it, and what do we need to do about it?"

Bush agreed that he saw it "as a security issue . . as a serious problem." And said he favored a "temporary worker card" and "I don't believe we ought to have amnesty."

Kerry said, "I will...toughen up our borders," and "we need a guestworker program" and "earned legalization."

That was Bush-speak, and I remember listening intently to that exchange, still after all these years astonished when I heard a liberal Democrat say "we need a guestworker program" and by "we" he meant we employers, not we American workers. Some liberal.

* * *

The 2004 election was the fourth in a row in which the success rate of incumbent congressmen did not fall below 98 percent. If virtually every seat was safe, how could we immigration reformers hope that mounting evidence that public opinion was hostile to illegal and mass immigration would push Open Border politicians or those on the fence (all of them in safe seats) toward more reasonable positions?

Yet this election contained signs that the times might be changing. Congressman David Dreier of California was a powerful and respected politician who had been overwhelmingly re-elected in every race following his first win in 1980, and he had never faced a serious challenge. He also had an Open Border voting record. Two southern California radio talk show hosts, John and Ken, whose show on KFI-AM, Los Angeles, was popular with conservatives, rigged up a Hit List of Congressmen with the worst (Open Border) records on immigration. One of them was Dreier. They hammered him (and the others) relentlessly in the summer and fall in what they called their "Fire Dreier Campaign." Dreier outspent his opponent by $900,000 to $31,000 and won re-election, but received just under 54 percent of the vote. This was the narrowest margin in his twenty-five-year career. Dreier did not wait for the end of the race to respond to what he was hearing. He moved toward restriction in October, introducing legislation to toughen penalties against employers of illegal aliens and anchor law enforcement in a counterfeit-resistant Social Security card. Sometimes, democracy works.

Slowly. Too slowly? Arizona Congressman Dana Rohrabacher, a recent convert to tighter border controls, told Lou Dobbs in the autumn of 2004 that he did not think the American political system was responding adequately to the "influx of millions, out of control influx of millions of illegals," and "I predict that within a year or two, there will be a third party that will emerge and it will sweep out the existing parties."

* * *

The 9/11 Commission Reports

The waning days of 2004 still contained one last spasm of high-profile immigration politics, and this time we lost—at first, and then at the end of the year, won— a rare experience.

The 9/11 Commission recommended national rules to standardize state documentation for driver's licenses, and a few other immigration reform measures to our liking, such as limiting asylum claims. These passed the House under the leadership of the Chairman of the House Judiciary Committee, Republican Jim Sensenbrenner, and were folded into the ongoing Homeland Security bill. The senate dropped them in December, and a stubborn Sensenbrenner rallied House conference members to insist that the immigration control measures would be guaranteed a hearing in the new Congress in January. They were, and the Real ID Act passed the House in February, 2005. This was a step in a heartening direction on identification documentation.

* * *

In his December e-mail newsletter, Craig Nelsen of ProjectUSA said that 2004 had been "a wonderful year" for our immigration reform effort. That was not my own experience. It had been nerve-wracking, from my place on the sidelines. But Craig worked out of Roy Beck's brick house on Capitol Hill, and Roy and his staff had their institutional finger on the pulse both at the grassroots and in the congressional corridors. It must have been for Roy and the FAIR staff, for Craig and all the real immigration reformers across the country, those red, white and blue reformers and not the White Flag reformers, was a year like no other, in which you could watch and feel the American people finally awaken.

* * *

President Bush at a year-end news conference on December 20 reiterated his commitment to a new guest worker program as a permanent part of America's labor and immigration policies. *The New York Times*, a liberal paper from which one once could have counted upon protective feelings about American labor when capital begged for permanent access to cheaper foreign workers, in a lead editorial commended a president who "understands this issue on a personal level" and is trying to deal with the large problem of "jobs Americans won't do." They did not add, "at the prices offered." Vicente Fox could have written the *Times* editorial. For 2005 and the foreseeable future, we reformers faced another year in which the president wanted the current mass immigration vastly expanded and illegal immigration re-classified as forgiven; another year in which almost all Democrats complained that his proposals didn't open the border enough; and a year in which the media, business, religious, educational, and other elites would be in favor of either or both.

In that context, some might say that calling 2004 "a wonderful year" had some justification. The Expansionist reform agenda had aroused an unprecedented stiff resistance, and had been bottled up. No colossal amnesty had been extended to 10-11 million illegals and their overseas relatives, inducing more millions to decide to illegally enter America; and there had been no permanent program to bring foreign labor to work where employers claim that Americans do not accept the conditions of employment.

Still, I thought "wonderful" the wrong, too enthusiastic word. Yes, we restrictionist reformers had gained strength, and staved off disastrous border openings. However, the costly status quo of mass legal and illegal immigration remained, and plans to make it worse had impressive backing. Our own proposed immigration reforms, some of them taking legislative form on the outer ring of the national legislative conveyor belt, had also not been enacted or even voted on, but remained thoroughly bottled up—except for Congressman Sensebrenner's still-alive and front-burner plans for driver's license standardization, expedited deportation, and tougher asylum rules.

* * *

"Democracy," Senator John McCain was quoted as saying in the early months of George Bush's second term, "isn't very good at addressing incremental problems." If he meant the policy system could not respond to serious problems if they came upon us slowly, on this, at least, we agreed. My pessimism about reining in immigration, a pessimism which was now over thirty years old (and probably becoming quite a drag for my friends), was rooted in part in my studies of the modern U.S. political and policymaking system. In addition to a sustained mishandling of immigration pressures, our political system had in the last decades of the twentieth century and the first years of the twenty-first avoided or made worse a cluster of "incremental problems"—including the growing entitlement/social security/medical care fiscal cancer, the global build-up and national proliferation of nuclear weapons and delivery systems, the time bomb of climate change/global warming, and the approach of Peak Oil production followed by horrendous energy costs. Who could have confidence in the prospect of reforming immigration as we meant to do it, in light of this policy record?

In this frame of mind, and even though the events of 2004 had not turned out as badly as I had feared, I complained to Roy Beck that the year should not be categorized as "a wonderful year." Roy, one of the world's cheeriest (and shrewdest) people, begged to differ. "Otis, they are listening to us now, the mainstream politicians who had so long ignored or scorned us." Look at David Dreier, he suggested. The influential congressman was re-elected in November by the narrowest margin of his impressive twenty-four year congressional career because two California radio talk show hosts (Jon and Ken) had repeatedly denounced and encouraged call-in ire directed at Dreier's immigration voting record. The very next month, in December, he submitted legislation in the House to tighten up the deportation process. "Democracy, eventually works," Roy said, or something to that effect. He knew more about the machinery of contemporary American politics of immigration than I did, especially on this issue. I retreated to the concession that 2004 had been in some important respects and on balance an encouraging if not "wonderful" year—compared to all those I could remember, with the possible exception of 1994 in California. Bring on tomorrow.

Chapter Twenty-Six:
Ninth Inning, Score Tied?

Illegal immigration is a severe and growing threat. — Michael Chertoff, Secretary for Homeland Security

At a news conference on December 20, 2004, President Bush, just re-elected, asserted again that the American economy "needed" more foreign workers, and made it clear that one of his objectives in 2005 would again be the passage of a guestworker program and a pathway to citizenship for all illegal aliens and their relatives. And a secure border, of course, which was also a good idea and ought to be tried someday soon. Behind all aspects of this proposal was an unspoken assumption: You can trust me to properly administer this mammoth inspection and certification of more than 11 million foreigners and their overseas families without admitting a single terrorist, despite the difficulties the federal government is currently having in reconstructing Iraq and Afghanistan, reining in the fiscal and trade deficits, managing Social Security and medical insurance crises, and keeping New Orleans above water.

* * *

It was tempting to accept media guesses that this persistent White House pressure to open the borders to all who wished to come, had its roots in Karl Rove's calculations, dating back at least to 2000-2001, of what an expansion of Latino Republican voters could do for the party's future (and George Bush's place in history). Doubtless this was and is

Rove's (and others') reasoning, and that George Bush is persuaded by it.

Close watchers of the Bush presidency knew that the sustained campaign for "comprehensive immigration reform" that takes the form of opening the nation to a limitless supply of foreign labor had deeper roots than simplistic Roveian electoral calculations. For those who received their news only from television, Lou Dobbs, in a June 9 CNN news broadcast, reported on the recent recommendations to Congress of a Council on Foreign Relations Task Force on North America (*Building a North American Community*) that the U.S. join Mexico and Canada in establishing a common border for a new regional entity presenting common policies on immigration, trade and security. This was a vision that had been germinating for years, and which led to and underpinned President Vicente Fox's agreements with President Bush in 2001. Dobbs was more alert than the other major news commentators, but still he was at least three months behind the story. In March, 2005, Bush convened a special summit of heads of state of the three nations at Waco, Texas, and they signed a joint report establishing a new "Security and Prosperity Partnership" (SPP) of North America. It was now out in the open that three nations' economic and political elites had set ministerial working groups to work—doing what? It was all very secret, including the names of the bureaucrats in the Department of Commerce who were working on SPP. They were drafting a framework for a North American version of the European Union, planned to take form by 2010, charged (among others) Jerome Corsi, a Havard PhD and independent scholar who had written on national security matters, and whose articles on SPP ran in *Whistleblower* magazine (www.wnd.com), in Phyllis Schlafly's Eagle Forum (www.eagleforum.org) and elsewhere. One element of this union, Corsi claimed, would entail re-negotiating U.S. borders, and moving them southward to the edges of Mexico and northward to the edges of Canada, in addition to setting the rules of entry in consultation with our new partners. Corsi seemed right that the idea of some sort of North American Union had impressive multinational sponsors and had been germinating for years, and that the CFR report, written by Robert Pastor, a writer long advocating the economic and political integration of the hemisphere, had been going the rounds of Washington foreign policy circles. Had George Bush ordered the

Commerce Department bureaucrats to draw up such a plan, with deadlines? I had a call that summer from a booking agent for college lecture tours who claimed that she could book me at every Ivy League university and guarantee large left-leaning and sympathetic audiences if I could lecture on "the findings of Jerome Corsi." The issue then sank out of Dobbs' sight, and into the blogs, where it festered . The White House in 2008 posted a website (www.spp.gov) describing the "trilateral initiative" as only a "dialogue" carried on by ten working groups. In a list of "Myths vs. Facts" the site denied that SPP would "modify our sovereignty . . . or change the American system of government."

* * *

Just a few days before his second inauguration in January, 2005, Bush renewed his immigration proposals. He justified the amnesty offer to illegal aliens (which he insisted wasn't amnesty) by saying, in part: "We see millions of hard-working men and women condemned to fear and insecurity in a massive, undocumented economy." I will spare readers the rest, but concur with the editors of the conservative magazine, *The American Enterprise* that "never before has a prominent U.S. politician, let alone a president, rationalized illegal immigration that baldly. Bush's remarks placed illegal aliens on the same level with legal immigrants as seekers of opportunity." Again, Bush made the foggy argument that "a program that enables people to come into our country in a legal way...will help make it easier for us to secure our borders." The logic of this oft-repeated idea seemed to be: If foreigners who want to live in the U.S. gain admission after they find an employer sponsor within one or more guestworker programs, then the 500,000 or million or more who now enter illegally would be legal immigrants, and the problem of illegal entry would be nonexistent or very small. Illegality ends when everyone is declared legal. Homeland Security head Michael Chertoff tried to give Bush's idea a clearer re-statement, saying that the president's proposal "would make it possible for the government to channel foreign nationals into a legal regulated and temporary way to do work and then go home again." No analysis of costs, administrative challenges, or fraud potential was ever offered in support of this fuzzy notion, and there was no claim that history held a single example of a successful guestworker program or an amnesty that didn't make matters worse. The White House neither submitted nor endorsed specific legislation. That was left to congressional entrepreneurs.

Others, most of them Republicans, had different ideas for how to fix a broken system. Within days of Bush's statement, House Judiciary Committee Chairman Sensenbrenner re-introduced his 2004 border-tightening legislation, which blocked illegal immigrants from obtaining driver's licenses, and it contained no guestworkers or amnesty. He declared that his committee would entertain no other proposals until his own passed. Restrictive measures had jumped ahead of the president's agenda, at least in the House. The media reported other resistance to the Bush proposal among Republicans, responding to immigration's high profile in public opinion. A conservative web site echoed a sentiment frequently heard: "Soon after the dust settled from the 2004 elections, the most divisive issue to dominate the political landscape...became U.S. immigration policy."

Well, I guess this is what we wanted, a higher place on the agenda for immigration reform. But we wanted *our* version, not theirs.

* * *

The Minutemen of Arizona—and Elsewhere

Operation Gatekeeper, which put more agents and physical barriers along the line in the Tijuana-San Diego sector, proved that border defense can have real deterrent effects, as the growing human traffic then shifted from California eastward, much of it to Arizona, especially the Tucson sector. The entire border zone, north and south of it, increasingly resembled a sort of war zone, with Mexican coyotes, drug traffickers and even Mexican Federales exchanging fire with Border Patrol officers and some ranchers outraged by a flow of illegals leaving a trail of clothing, trash, excrement, and some dead bodies. When there wasn't death there was always garbage. A local Arizona activist told WorldNetDaily.com in 2001:

> *The foot traffic is so heavy that the backcountry has the ambience of a garbage dump and smells like an outdoor privy. In places, the land is littered…deep with bottles, cans, soiled disposable diapers, sanitary napkins, panties, clothes, backpacks, human feces, used toilet paper, pharmacy bottles and syringes.*

Porous southwestern borders produced complex results in states far north of the border. Mexicans and others who went north to cut the grass in Denver or wash dishes in restaurants in Chicago could be and were seen by some as useful workers. Yet the news media revealed that some unknown percentage of them, when not working, might be driving drunk without a license or auto insurance, forming urban gangs, or committing felonies and crowding the courts and jails. Mixed in with them as they crossed the southwestern border were rising levels of OTMs—39,000 arrested in the fiscal year 2003, 64,000 in 2004, and 85,000 in 2005. CIA Director Porter Goss told the Senate Intelligence Committee in 2004 that "several al-Qaeda leaders believe operatives can pay their way into the country through Mexico." Whatever that meant. An Arizona journalist reported in the *Wall Street Journal Online* that local ranchers reported finding Muslim prayer rugs and Arabic dictionaries along the trails the illegals had worn in the brush.

If any of this upset a citizen, she could always write her congressman. We at FAIR had recommended that for over twenty years. But the public mood had changed after 9/11, and had become more short-tempered and activist. A new response was the mobilization of what sympathizers called citizen border patrols and what critics called vigilantism, a word defined in Merriam-Webster as a combination of "a volunteer committee organized to suppress and punish crime summarily" with "a self-appointed doer of justice." Volunteer patrols had a long history along the U.S. border, and emerged in California in the 1990s, the most prominent being Glenn Spencer's Valley Citizens Together/American Patrol, a group called Light Up the Border in San Diego, and U.S. Citizen Patrol formed in 1996. By 2001, a CRS study found that "Arizona produces the largest amount of unauthorized migration and the largest numbers of civilian border patrol organizations," with much activity of this sort also in Texas.

These civilian border patrol groups were small, scattered, and at first little noticed. Chris Simcox, a California school teacher much upset by 9/11, took a long hiking vacation along the Arizona-Mexican border and was shocked by the flood of at least 300 illegal migrants he encountered. He toured the border for three months, and then moved from Los Angeles to Tombstone, Arizona. He bought a small local paper, and on one of his travels into the border area, he met U. S. Park Ranger Kris Eggle, serving at Arizona's Organ Pipe Cactus National Monument. Eggle told Simcox startling stories of park rangers too busy defending their territory against organized and heavily armed drug runners out of Mexico to do what rangers in other National Parks expect as their main mission—interpretation to tourists. Shortly after, Simcox learned that Eggle had been killed on August 9, 2002, while pursuing a drug cartel hit squad. "Our border is a war zone," Simcox concluded, and in late 2002 established the Homeland (then Minutemen) Civil Defense Corps, with a fuzzy idea of what it might do. There were conflicting accounts of the history, but friends in California tell me that the Simcox beginning took on extra energy and focus when Jim Gilchrist joined up. Gilchrist, an ex-Marine and Vietnam veteran who was a retired CPA living in Orange County (California) decided to get "a few volunteers" to "observe and report illegal immigrants." He then linked up with another ex-Marine from his Vietnam unit, James Chase, who was outraged when an illegal alien shot and killed a police officer in Oceanside, California. Chase drove Gilchrist to Arizona, where the action was most intense and where they met with Simcox and hatched the Minutemen Project. They invited volunteers from all parts of America to spend the month of April 2005, helping the Border Patrol detect and apprehend illegals.

There was a substantial, newsworthy response from volunteers, and eventually 800-900 citizens (by the organizers' count; open border advocacy groups such as *La Tierra Es De Todos*, "The World is For Everyone," claimed the turnout was a quarter of that). "Macheted in the press" as dangerous vigilantes—the word President Bush used to describe them—the Minutemen, when followed around and interviewed by reporters from the east, turned out to be "hard to place politically and seemed pretty moderate" and late middle aged, in the words of a writer from the *Weekly Standard*. Simcox and Gilchrist, now calling themselves co-founders of the project, were keenly aware of the catastrophic effect if the national media found that they had recruited "an unsavory element." (Chase had returned to California to form the California Border Watch in July, eventually said to be the largest and most continuously active of all such "Minutemen" groups). They advised against carrying weapons (except for self-defense, having received several death threats), fashioned a strategy in which Minutemen would not confront illegals but would detect and track them for federal and local law enforcement officials, and even demanded that one volunteer not wear a Confederate cap. "We don't blame the people coming across," Simcox said. The month passed without any Minuteman shooting anyone, or being charged with an offense, although it was said that local law enforcement authorities were not all that happy to have them there. Interviews with desert-weary volunteers from Illinois, Vermont and Washington State revealed how deep the frustration ran, and it was national. The major news networks covered the Arizona Minutemen almost nightly, bringing to Americans who had never visited the border the disturbing images of young men (and women) running northward in twilight and dawn, breaking into America.

And "it worked, more or less," in the words of Arizona writer, Leo Banks, writing for the *Wall Street Journal Online*, The number of illegals coming across the sector they guarded fell—perhaps merely pushed east and west to more thinly manned sectors. Still, part of the border had been made less porous. A pair of congressional staffers sent by the Congressional Immigration Reform Caucus reported in May that the 900 volunteers in one month had demonstrated that with "realistic manpower increases illegal immigration on America's southern border would be dramatically reduced."

The largest effect of the Minutemen's April campaign was political. California Governor Arnold Schwarzenegger said to the press: "I think they have done a terrific job…It's a shame the private citizen has to go in there and secure our borders." Gilchrist and Simcox, displaying a growing sophistication at PR, went on national television, declared a small victory, and invited volunteers to come back to all four border states for duty in October. Then they went their separate ways, Gilchrist running for Congress and heading the Minuteman Project, and Simcox forming the Minutemen Civil Defense Corps, raising funds for mostly Republican congressional candidates. "We have really become a political movement," he said in 2005, claiming thirty-four chapters in thirty states, including borderless North Carolina, Tennessee, Maryland and Florida. Time would tell. The Northeast Central Florida chapter admitted finding few ways to address illegal immigration in their part of the state, but the California Minutemen under James Chase and the San Diego Minutemen under Jeff Schwilk energetically protested at Day Labor Center sites. They showed up at city council meetings to urge an end to sanctuary policies, and established web sites full of news and motivational hate mail received from Latino ethnic activists—"You are a fucking gringos you stinks, this is our territory, you stole us" received by www.minutemanproject.com from "Guillermo" and "you're a Nazi-racist bastard" from "Luis."

It was "a redneck revolt," Banks and others said, but one that wasn't marked by "nativism" or hostility to immigrants. The Minutemen brought together by Gilchrist and Simcox that April in Arizona, rank and file, continued to display a remarkably smart PR. "We are not anti-immigrant" as described in the press, a female volunteer was quoted. "We are anti-illegal-immigrant." The immigration reform movement had struggled from the beginning under the albatross from history, labeled and delegitimized by words like "nativists" and "anti-immigrant." The Minutemen in their initial campaign, despite extremely close scrutiny, came through as patriots who hated nobody, though they confessed anger at their own congressional representatives—and, despite being mostly Republicans, their president. They did their border stint, vilified in racist language by angry Latino open-borderites and left behind the impression that some American patriots of middle age had left home to defend their country.

This public perception at the end of April was the first defeat for the Stigmatization Department of the Open Border machine. Our side had looked good in carrying out their uprising, a media impression not granted to the California Prop. 187 rebels. The populist border revolt in Arizona had put in place, at least for the moment, a disciplined, attractive, patriotic image and evaded an ugly one.

* * *

The news media was shifting toward a recognition that something large was happening in America, and perhaps more facts and analysis were called for, and less avoidance or ridicule. The immigration numbers, even before analysis, at one level told their own story. Estimates of the illegal population resident in the U.S. continued to rise. The Census Bureau in 2005 estimated 8.7 million, the Urban Institute 9.3 million, CIS 10 million, *Time* magazine 15 million, and the investment banking and securities firm Bear Stearns made a news splash late in the year with its own estimate of 20 million. In a 2005 report for CIS ("Immigrants at Mid-Decade: A Snapshot of America's Foreign-Born Population in 2005," Steve Camarota distilled from recent Census Bureau data the news that 8 million immigrants had settled in the U.S. since January 2000, nearly half of them illegally. The 35.2 million immigrants in the country was the highest number ever recorded. Looking beneath the population totals, he found that 31 percent of adult immigrants had not completed high school, three-and-a-half times the native rate. Their poverty rate was 18.4 percent, which was 57 percent higher than that for natives.

We were surprised at CIS to see from a Lexus-Nexis search how widely these cold figures were spread upon the national media. Then we were surprised again when another CIS report on immigrant birth rates, which I thought sure to be ignored, gained wide attention from newspapers and TV stations in the cities and states of the southwest.

"Nearly one in three babies born in Yuma County in 2002 came from illegal immigrant mothers," the *Yuma Sun* condensed the findings of this CIS study.

"Central Valley foreign-born mothers are delivering a record number of children," declared the *Fresno Bee*, and births in California to immigrant mothers had jumped from 15 percent in 1970 to 46 percent in 2002.

The *Napa News* noted that their county ranked thirteenth nationwide for percentage of babies born to illegal aliens, and pried loose from the California Hospital Association the estimate that California's hospitals spent $500 million a year on illegals.

Cold figures? A La Raza spokesman called the numbers "inflammatory," and he was right, though "shocking" would be a better word for it. A Fox News series on illegal alien effects on health care and educational systems quoted an official of the State Association of Hospitals saying, "California's public health system is on the brink of collapse" and the central problem was uncompensated care to illegals.

The $500 million was a guess, and because so many states did not have anything like accurate current information on the fiscal costs of illegals, FAIR in 2004 published estimates for all fifty states. This was useful for activists and some researchers, but the media and politicians paid more attention to official estimates, and these began to emerge, often based on data from the Pew Hispanic Center since most states did not keep statistics on immigration status or ethnicity. Arizona officials had shown no interest in the subject until 2004, when—prodded by Congressman J. D. Hayworth— they estimated the costs of illegals in that state was $1.6 billion a year, or $700 per Arizonan. A study by a University of Florida economist David Denslow found a net annual cost of $1,800 per immigrant family, and thought "that would be close to the national figure" for other states.

An instructive example of this flurry of state accounting on the fiscal impacts of illegal immigrants came from Minnesota, where a report to Governor Tim Pawlenty, *The Impact of Illegal Immigration on Minnesota* (2005), estimated the costs of the state's 80-85,000 illegal (not "undocumented," another sign of a shift in opinion) immigrants in the areas of K-12 public education, public assistance health care, and incarceration to be $180 million. This left out a lot of costs, such as hospital care, and no estimate of taxes paid was offered. The governor was accused by Latino activists of "scapegoating for political reasons." The police chiefs, in a closed meeting, apparently told him the report saw only the tip of the iceberg. The issue gained high visibility across the state, while the governor did not say what he recommended be done about this fiscal drain. High up there along the Canadian border, a rumble had occurred over the gap between what Spanish-speaking illegals were costing in services and contributing in taxes.

* * *

A motif in the story of the immigration reform movement was the emergence from time to time of a new voice, usually a researcher/

writer with a special skill at illuminating yet another dysfunctional dimension of an immigration system out of control. Economist George Borjas, unassailable as an anti-immigrant bigot because of his Cuban immigrant background and Harvard credentials, lit up the nineties with articles and books building an increasingly strong indictment of an immigration stream whose losers were lower-tier American workers. Michelle Malkin, invulnerable to charges of "anti-immigrant" due to her Asian features and Filipino immigrant parents, was articulate and fearless in media appearances following her 2002 book *Invasion* that drove home just after 9/11 the vital importance to the terrorists of our "Swiss cheese" borders and interior controls. My brother, Vanderbilt historian Hugh Davis Graham, described in *Collision Course* (2002) the "unlikely and unanticipated convergence of affirmative action" with immigration policy. Black Americans who had gained affirmative action in the latter 1960s found these preferential policies, originally intended for the ancestors of slaves, granted also (read the book to understand this indefensible turn in civil rights policy) to Latin American, Asian and other immigrants, intensifying the competition for jobs, "displacing black, low-wage workers and "unsettling the liberal coalition." But it was not unsettling enough that black political leadership would raise questions about either mass immigration or immigrants' inclusion in the racial preferences blacks thought they had won for themselves. Hugh Graham did not think that the acquiescence of the African-American political establishment with mass immigration from Latin America and Asia could survive this "collision" over affirmative action policy preferences.

In 2003, seventh-generation California rancher and scholar of ancient Greece, Victor Davis Hanson published *Mexifornia* (2003), a memoir describing how the post-1960s surge of illegal immigration from Mexico brought mounting community tensions and was transforming the California where his family had lived with Mexican American neighbors for five generations. "Wherever you live, if you want your dirty work done cheaply by someone else, you will welcome illegal aliens, as we did,…slowly walking the path that leads to Mexisota, Utexico, Mexizona or even Mexichusetts—a place that is not quite Mexico and not quite America either."

My nomination for that new voice in 2005 would be Madeleine Cosman, who made her debut writing on immigration in an out-of-the-way place, an article in the Spring, 2005 issue of a medical journal, "Illegal Aliens and American Medicine," *Journal of American Physicians and Surgeons*. How I came across this I cannot recall, though it may have been pointed out to me by one of my wide-reading new friends on the board of Californians for Population Stabilization (CAPS), which I had joined in 2004. I in turn commended Cosman's article to several people, and all agreed that she had entered a highly important but almost unexplored terrain. Cosman, identified in the article tersely as a medical lawyer (whatever that is) and PhD who had taught at CUNY, turned out after a Google search to be a professor emeritus from CUNY, a prolific writer and lecturer on medicine-law connections. She left New York for San Diego in the 1990s, and the reality of California plunged her into research on her new topic, which she brought to the October Writers Workshop in the form of a slide show delivered in a vibrant, rousing performance ("I get standing ovations whenever I lecture on this.")

Bush's illegal but "hard-working laborers" who only "pursue the American dream" are presented in Cosman's heavily footnoted article as having a major and almost unreported public health impact. "Illegal aliens cross America's borders medically unexamined. We don't know what they carry in their bodies." And once here, their "free medical care...has degraded and closed some of America's finest emergency medical facilities...eighty-four California hospitals are closing." She described in detail the 1985 federal law (Emergency Medical Treatment and Active Labor Act, or EMTALA) requiring every hospital's emergency department to treat the uninsured and absorb the costs (another unfounded federal mandate). She then laid out the expense of "anchor babies" (the U.S., unlike most countries, grants citizenship to babies born here to foreigners) who immediately qualify for public aid including the network of translators and advocacy organizations helping illegals qualify for that aid. Next, the rising incidence of Third World diseases such as TB in new drug-resistant forms, chagas disease, leprosy, dengue fever, Hepatitis A, B and C, and polio among illegal alien populations. Cosman concluded with "tough medicine" recommendations: Close America's borders, deport illegal aliens, rescind the grant of citizenship to children of illegal immigrants, punish those who aid and abett illegal aliens, and grant no new amnesties. "It's either surrender or fight."

Her grim catalog of immigration-borne diseases and health care costs had a large impact on the audience for whom none of this was exactly a surprise. Her presentation came at a time of considerable contemporary media speculation about the coming of a worldwide Asian Flu pandemic, transmitted by travelers and wildlife on airliners and boats moving from country to country.[5]

* * *

Other costs of illegal immigration did not attract their Borjas, Malkin, Hanson, or Cosman to dig deeply into neglected topics and illuminate reality. The news media, however, kept several stories before the public, even if the analysis was superficial and the attention fleeting. ICE agents in the spring and summer carried off a twenty-seven state sweep of more than eighty violent street gangs including MS-13. They arrested more than 1,000 gang members;, more than 90 percent of them illegal aliens. "Street gangs in America have grown and expanded their influence to an alarming level," said Homeland Security Secretary Michael Chertoff, "marked by increased violence and criminal activity. Illegal immigration is a "severe and growing threat." My own state of North Carolina, the Raleigh newspaper reported in August, led the nation with seventy-seven arrests. There were black gangs in most North Carolina cities, but the gangsters seized during this sweep in the capital itself, Raleigh, were all from either Mexico, El Salvador, or Honduras.

Homeland Security head Michael Chertoff in 2005 was emerging as much tougher-talking on immigration and border issues than his predecessor, Tom Ridge, who had repeatedly stated that immigration regulation was not a part of his assignment. This improvement in leadership outlook was either our random good luck or a sign that some public officials were hearing the rising pitch of public frustration at border issues. News reports of Latino gangs added a darker side

---

[5] We were not to hear again from Madeleine Cosman, who died in March, 2006.

to the sentimentalist Open Border/Bush depiction of all illegals as "hardworking" and entrepreneurial, taking jobs Americans won't do.

* * *

Immigrant Indigestion in Europe

One cost not put on our national ledgers by illegal aliens in those years of policy stalemate was more terrorism to add to 9/11. The U.S. was not attacked again at home, though the government implied that several violent attacks had been narrowly averted. Our national media, however, occasionally carried news of other nations' immigration-generated social problems that might easily have been our own. A stream of reports from Europe told of the growth of unassimilated, disgruntled immigrant Muslim communities whose second and even third generation youth were drawn to radical Islam. By the arrival of the twenty-first century, Europe had acquired interior colonies of 22 million foreign nationals, a legacy of empire and also of guestworker programs whose "return to home country" components did not work. European immigration policies had allowed the build-up of what Brookings Senior Fellow Robert Leiken called "the equivalent of a Saudi Arabia in the heart of Europe." Eurabia.

Troubles followed from it. The most spectacular event of 2004 was the ghastly November murder on a street in Amsterdam of popular Dutch filmmaker, Theo Van Gogh, who was shot off his bicycle, beheaded and left with the knife in his chest by Mohammed Bouyeri, child of Moroccan immigrants and linked to jihadists in Holland who had links to other militants in Spain, Italy and elsewhere. The tolerant Dutch were profoundly shocked, and the brutal murder intensified a spirited internal reconsideration of their three-decade record of liberal immigration and asylum policies, resulting in a minor tightening of identification documents and some feeble steps toward curbing the influx of immigrants.

Neighboring countries recognized that the dangerous divisions within Dutch society were not confined to the Netherlands. "Holland is everywhere," commented a German expert on internal dissidence, referring to what writer Paul Belien writing in *The American Conservative* called "pockets of Eurabia" in and around every major European city—neighborhoods filled with mostly young, underemployed and hostile North African immigrants and well-known to Europeans as high-crime "No Go" zones for citizens and tourists. In 2005, the Netherlands voted against expansion of the EU, a surprise turn that owed much to the Van Gogh murder.

Then on July 7 jihadists claimed credit for four bomb blasts in downtown London, killing 56 and injuring 700. It was time for immigration and assimilation reconsideration among the Brits, heretofore proud of their multicultural achievements. "Coming to Britain is not a right," Prime Minister Blair sternly said for the first time, "and staying here carries with it a duty…to share and support the values that sustain the British way of life." In August came disturbing TV images from a different part of Europe's immigrant-pressed perimeter. Hundreds of would-be immigrants from sub-Saharan Africa could be seen on American television news shows climbing nightly onto and sometimes over the barbed wire fences between Morocco and the Spanish enclaves of Ceuta and Melilla, pieces of Europe on the African coast from which immigrants could move to any EU country.

Then on October 27 in the town of Clichy-sour-Bois, a "banlieu" or immigrant-filled and public-housing dominated suburb ten miles northeast of Paris, two boys who were being chased or thought themselves chased by police jumped the fence into an electrical facility and were electrocuted. The town exploded into violence, rock throwing and car burning. The violence spread to other French cities over the next several days, and was clearly out of police control. The French government's timorous response may have encouraged this outbreak to extend itself and others to be more likely. At the peak of the riots it was estimated that 1,000 cars were wrecked and burned each night, along with public buildings, buses and even ambulances. The riots seemed to have no organized Muslim leadership or political purpose, but the neighborhoods where the outbreaks were rooted were all filled with a North African Muslim population recently immigrated to France. European officials began to talk for the first time, though in vague terms, of extruding and possibly excluding "Islamist" (meaning "radical

Islam") immigrants. The Defense Minister invited British Islamists, even those born in Britain, to leave: "Go to another country. Get out." Even those unprecedented statements did not amount to calls for changes in which ideology or countries of origin might become factors in immigrant admissions.

* * *

What did these European ordeals mean for the U.S.? Quick to sense that the American public might interpret these riots (and the London and earlier Madrid bombings and the murder of Theo Van Gogh) as warning signs to the U.S. not to continue to go down the European road to large scale immigrant and especially Muslim immigrant intake, the *Wall Street Journal*, Chief Defender of the era of unlimited immigration, counterattacked with a lead editorial in November. Those who said the riots were a consequence of Europe's liberal immigration policies were "flat out wrong," the paper opined. The U.S. should pride itself that it has no "Muslim Problem" such as recent events exposed in Europe. Muslim foreign-born living in America constituted only 2 percent (6 million) of the population (when the Netherlands had 6.2 percent, Germany 3.7 percent, and the UK 2.7 percent by official statistics, known to be on the low side). More important, Muslim immigrants were generally upwardly mobile in the U.S., the paper claimed, and intermarried at close to the national average for Americans marrying outside their religion, and were not crowded into isolated ghettoes like those surrounding Paris and other European cities. American assimilative influences were robustly doing their integrative work, the editorial concluded, even for a group whose culture was vastly different from America's European heritage. What we saw in France "was not a Muslim problem or an immigration problem. It's an underclass problem." France needs to make its government-stifled economy more like the Americans—providing job growth to end the *banlieue* crisis.

The *Wall Street Journal*'s editorial opinion always came out in the same place (less government, or none) no matter what subject matter it started with, but its editors' fear that the French riots might spur demands for stricter controls on Muslim immigration to America was not immediately borne out. Still, the violence in France and London was splashed across all American media, and one did not have to be an American Jew or ardent friend of Israel to harbor doubts about sustained high-volume Muslim immigration. A few isolated questioners were heard. A British immigrant, Tony Blankley, editorial page editor for the *Washington Times*, published *The West's Last Chance* in October, warning that "An existential threat…hangs over our nation and civilization," the threat of "radical Islam." Europe's populations are aging and soon will shrink; the continent is being repopulated by Muslims. To prevent this suicide, the West should declare war on radical Islam, Blankley argued, give the president wartime powers, secure our borders, and stand ready to engage radical Islam in many Afghanistan's and Iraqis. He made no recommendations for legal immigration changes, and the book was not much discussed in the U.S.

In France, however, the riots opened a vigorous if inconclusive public debate. *"Le Pen l'avait dit!"* was the new slogan of Jean-Marie Le Pen's National Front, and there was at least briefly reflected in French media channels a grudging acknowledgment that the immigration-warnings of perhaps not only Le Pen but also Jean Raspail's *Camp of the Saints* and Oriana Fallaci's best-selling (in France) *La Rabbia e L'Orgoglio* (published in English in 2002 as *The Rage and the Pride*) had been dismissed too quickly.

* * *

State and Local Battles in the U. S.

Arizona for a few months was the nation's hot zone for local immigration politics in 2004 and 2005, with Proposition 200 delivering another message on what the public thought and felt about illegal immigration, and the Minutemen patrolling the border for three weeks in early 2005. The border volunteer idea had become a sort of movement by early summer. The Associated Press counted "at least forty anti-immigration groups [that] have popped up nationally" (note the terminology; they should have been designated as anti-illegal immigration groups), 18 of them Minuteman Project "chapters." Some were in border states, which gave them something to do along the international boundary or in relationship to it. Some, like the group in Tennessee, planned a rally in Memphis but had a long-term activity problem. By the end of the year, enthusiasm for volunteer border patrolling seemed to have waned, except in California, where such volunteers were encouraged by Governor Schwarzenegger, though they hardly needed it. By Labor Day, a campaign began to put an initiative on the June, 2006 ballot to create the first state border police in the nation. California businessman Mark Chapin Johnson wrote in July for the *Wall Street Journal* opinion page: "I sense that another sea change may come about [like Prop. 187]…I can sense a deep and intensely growing concern and fear that illegal immigrants are completely overwhelming our state infrastructure."

* * *

The Suburban Combat Zone

A newly emerging zone of conflict over illegals was suburbia, where across the country the growing economy and hot housing market of the 1990s stoked demand for workers—the more inexpensive, pliable and exploitable the better, in construction, gardening, and a range of daily hires. Day laborer sites for such workers first appeared spontaneously, sometimes near Home Depot and other building supply stores, sometimes in convenience store parking lots. The workers were Mexican or Central American natives, unskilled, male, and—nobody denied this—overwhelmingly illegal. Soon local governments, pressed by Latino lobbyist organizations, began to sponsor and thus legitimize these sites and the transactions taking place there. Behind this day laborer site proliferation was the National Day Laborer Organizing Network started in 1999 (apparently with Ford Foundation money) and held a national assembly in 2005 where it sold T-shirts that read, "No Human Being is Illegal."

There was no reliable count of these centers, the informal or the sponsored. A *Wall Street Journal* article in July counted eighty sponsored day laborer centers in the U. S. by the summer of 2005, which seemed quite low, as the reporter estimated one hundred formal and informal markets for job seekers in Los Angeles County alone. When I lived in Santa Barbara in the 1990s the day labor site (informal, i.e., without city or other sponsorship) was at the corner of Carrillo and Santa Barbara Streets near the harbor. The sponsored centers were part of a larger effort, pushed by Latino lobbyists and the Catholic Church, to institutionalize and essentially legalize illegal workers. The city council of Longmont, Colorado voted to hire a full-time "immigrant integration coordinator" to help Mexican immigrants, legal or illegal, to "mesh more fully into society." Some officials went so far as to urge that an illegal alien be hired for the post. Municipalities moving in these directions often had backing and funding from private foundations (the Longmont "integration coordinator" was one of ten in the state funded by the Colorado Trust) or corporations. The city of Houston, Texas used a federal grant to establish a day labor center, and the Bank of America contributed $50,000. Some police departments, such as in Duluth, Georgia, or cities like New Haven, Connecticut, issued identification cards to lend legitimacy to these illegal workers. A growing number of large corporations also expanded the space in which illegals were treated like everybody else—that is, merged into society. Blue Cross of California and Georgia accepted Mexican and Guatemalan IDs. Cincinnati-based Fifth Third Bancorp, America's thirteenth largest bank, began accepting the *matricula* in 2002, and Sprint telecom in 2004.

These pro-illegal immigrant municipal policies attracted only scattered criticism until 2004-2005, when the visibility of gathering points for daily labor market transactions involving illegals quickly sparked a brushfire of local protests across the country with the same complaints—the laborers were illegal, swarmed around shoppers in their cars, asked for work, urinated in public and defecated behind stores, raised the levels of crime, and if you did not understand this the first time, were illegally in the country and community.

Unsurprisingly, California ignited first, with protests not only by the substantial number of Prop. 187-era groups but more importantly from new ones aroused in 2004-2005 by the visible day laborer phenomenon. A group called Save Our State was founded in 2004 by a twenty-nine-year-old stock trader and graduate of USC named Joseph Turner. He was turned into an activist on immigration by the Jon and Ken talk radio campaign that mobilized the radio audience against Rep. David Dreier's immigration voting record. Turner-led SOS members picketed Home Depot stores in Redondo Beach and elsewhere to protest day worker congregations outside the stores, and Turner became a local celebrity.

The backlash of opposition to day laborer sites, especially local government-sponsored and funded ones, quickly spread nationwide, and gave focus to a growing public uneasiness and anger with the immigration status quo. Citizens in communities in New York (little Farmville broke into national news), Connecticut (reporters gave Danbury a moment of fame), Virginia (a 7-Eleven parking lot in little Herndon, near Dulles airport became familiar to D.C. residents), Colorado (Longmont received its first national media exposure), Arkansas, Texas, New Hampshire, Nevada, Colorado, and other states picketed Home Depot stores and other sites where illegal alien day labor sites had emerged. They complained to local officials that the crowds of laborers (150 showed up every weekday morning in Herndon) were illegally present, urinated in public, brought with them rising levels of nuisance crimes such as public drunkenness and trespassing as well as some drug trafficking, expanded the untaxed underground economy, and brought into the community dependents who strained the budgets of schools and hospitals and introduced new strains of tuberculosis. And were illegal—a point which ought to speak for itself, *res ipsit loquitur*, somehow seemed to need reiteration.

In all of this there was a shift in momentum. Municipal elected officials who had formerly responded to illegal immigrant support groups heard the noise from a resentful public, and responded by reversing themselves and withdrawing support for taxpayer financed day laborer sites and outreach personnel to assist any immigrant to gain access to social welfare programs. This tactical retreat from pro-illegal alien policy was not enough for other local politicians, who switched over to efforts to deal with the underlying problem. In Idaho, Canyon County (west of Boise) Commissioner Robert Vasquez broke with the Latino party line and proposed to sue local businesses under federal anti-racketeering laws if they hired undocumented workers, and sent a bill to the Mexican government for the $2 million he estimated that illegals cost his county. Called a racist and a traitor to his heritage, Vasquez did not flinch: "There is nothing racial about this. The only color involved is green—for money." The Mayor of Fresno, California proposed a two-year moratorium on all immigration. All across the country, said Las Vegas resident Mark Edwards, Marine combat veteran, radio talk show host, and founder of one of the town's illegal immigration protest groups, Wake Up America, there is a grassroots movement such as one could see in Las Vegas, where hundreds of local residents were said to meet monthly in several groups formed to discuss the problems that came with the estimated 150,000 illegal aliens in Clark County. Edwards organized a national convention of local groups to give the movement focus and leadership.

States Make Immigration Policy, Too

The Open Border social movement that had been working for at least three decades to eliminate the very concept of illegal entry into the U.S. had never confined itself to lobbying in Washington. It applied steady pressure all the way down the chain of federalism through states and to municipalities. Their staple demands on state governments were to keep the issuance of driver's licenses free of any real test of citizenship, grant-free or in-state tuition to illegals, and accept the Mexican ID. By contrast, our social movement was for decades so puny that we exerted only scattered pressure on local governments, and at the state level (to my knowledge) only once in a sustained way, when FAIR hired former INS Commissioner Alan Nelson to open an office in Sacramento in 1992-94.

By 2004-2005, our fast-growing social movement had gained the size and energy required to discover and object to the concessions won from state governments by the Open Border lobby, and to take the battle over illegal immigration to the state level. In my own state, North Carolina, with the fastest-growing illegal population among the fifty states, the issue took a sharp turn in 2005. For more than a decade prior, the Open Border lobbies had been active and mostly unopposed in the capital city of Raleigh, and had helped shape a fraud-vulnerable driver's license issuance process anchored in acceptance for identification purposes of a Taxpayer Identification Number issued by the IRS to any immigrant without a Social Security number. North Carolina had the reputation on the East Coast as the easiest state in which illegals could get a license. Then in early 2005 the Open Border lobby made another bold move, persuading sympathetic legislators to introduce legislation, which quickly had thirty-one co-sponsors and the backing of the *Raleigh News and Observer* and former Governor Jim Hunt, to offer illegal immigrants in-state tuition at the state's public universities and community colleges (North Carolina estimates that 300,000 illegal aliens are residents of the state).

Then they discovered that 2005 was different. Somebody informed New York talk show host Rush Limbaugh of the proposed legislation, and his passionate critical coverage awakened local talk show radio programs and provoked a storm of e-mails and calls to state legislators—a "torrent of anger" in the words of a local reporter. One Raleigh talk radio host reported 600 calls against the proposal and three in favor. An existing immigration reform group, Ron Woodard's N.C. Listen, experienced a membership growth from fifty to 200, and, joined by a new group, Americans for Legal Immigration led by William Gheen, pressured legislators in Raleigh, who in substantial numbers did their arithmetic and backed away from the bill. Within days it was withdrawn by the leadership. Open Borders = 0, Restriction of immigration = 1. In November, five Republican members of Congress from North Carolina aimed their critical fire at the state's lax driver's license procedures, and threatened to cut off $890 million in federal highway aid if the state did not stiffen its requirements. Prior to 2005, none of them had said much on the immigration issue. Politicians were shifting positions.

* * *

Our Social Movement: Still Flying Without a Left Wing

The media was biased and sloppy in its labeling, but it was not entirely wrong to identify our social movement, even as it expanded and added new constituencies in 2004-2005, as "conservative" or "from the right." I knew this to be false and misleading as to the political leanings of the boards of directors and staff of the principle organizations—FAIR, CIS, and NumbersUSA. There were more liberals than conservatives at both board and staff levels, and more votes for Clinton, Gore and Kerry than for the Bushes. But there was some truth in this labeling. Our grassroots activists, based on my visits with local groups and my reading of our incoming mail and e-mail at FAIR (CIS was not a membership organization, and I have had no access to Roy Beck's organizational mail) remained in 2005 as they had mainly been since the beginning, predominantly Republicans.

We reformers who had been or still were Democrats of course saw this as a limitation, and even our Republican allies agreed. I have told of our repeated efforts to make common cause with left-of-center constituencies who were clearly harmed by current immigration—African Americans, Hispanics, and organized labor. The results were dismal, since we could not effectively reach and reason with the rank-and-file of these organizations but were forced to deal with their college-educated multiculturalist politically correct staff. We never gave up on this effort to broaden our base, and because almost all of us were "Greens" to one degree or another, our most persistent efforts were directed toward the environmental groups. New York family foundation head Alan Weeden spread his grants among a selected group of environmentalist organizations until they had come to count on it, and then threatened a cut-off if immigration reform in order to limit population growth were not added to their message and program. I have urged Alan to write the history of that endeavor, getting from that wise veteran a weary smile for my efforts to have his efforts better known.

Another Sierra Club Battle Lost

Environmentalists who understood the immigration connection to their cause mounted three major and countless minor efforts to align the flagship environmentalist organization, The Sierra Club, with our effort to steer the U. S. toward population stabilization as a precondition for sustained ecological protection. The club seemed a good choice among the large environmental groups, not only because of its visibility and the fact that it was governed by directors elected by the membership, but also because for several years there had been a strong internal movement within the ranks and elected leadership to commit the club to a view that linked environment to population limitation to immigration restriction. California activist Judy Kunofsky, chair of the Club's Population Committee, seemed to have pulled this off in 1989, when the Club adopted the statement, "The club would always make the connection between immigration, population increase and the environmental consequences thereof." This advance was erased in the 1990s under intense pressure from a leftist coalition including the "environmental justice" groups allied with the National Immigration Forum in Washington, the Political Ecology Group operating out of San Francisco ("race-baiting hooligans of the Left," Earth First co-founder Dave Foreman called them), leftist Club staffers and foundation staff, and from "one Hispanic member of Congress from Southern California" who said he wouldn't support the Club on air pollution legislation if they continued to take an official "anti-immigrant" position. Judy and her like-minded Club policy reformers were soon outnumbered, and I have described the policy reversal of 1996 when the Club declared that it "will take no position on immigration levels or on policies governing immigration into the U. S," and the failed effort to reverse this by a referendum of the members in 1999.

The position of legendary Club Director David Brower, was clear: "Overpopulation is a very serious problem, and over-immigration is a big part of it. We must address both." Sierra Club dissidents came back in considerable force in 2002, 2004, and 2005—this time organizing to put up board candidates explicitly supporting the immigration reductionist position. In 2002, UCLA astronomer Ben Zuckerman ("the number one environmental problem—and it's not even close—is overpopulation"), who with others like Alan Kuper had formed Sierrans for U. S. Population Stabilization (SUSPS) in 1998, was elected to the Sierra board (along with two allies) with the largest total among the five candidates. Zuckerman, a formidable opponent of Sierra's ostrich policy on immigration and U.S. overpopulation and two allies (Ben called them "immigration realists") were inside the tent.

A showdown came in 2004, when an impressive slate of Sierra Club members with national reputations ran for the board, with the potential to tip the board toward change. Three were national figures—former Colorado Governor Dick Lamm, African-American educator Frank Morris, and Cornell entomologist-biologist David Pimentel. Their effort was endorsed by an impressive list of environmentalists, including David Brower, Lester Brown, Dave Foreman, Gaylord Nelson, Stewart Udall, and Edward O. Wilson. But the interior lines belonged to Club staff, aggressively led by Executive Director Carl Pope, who "pulled out all the stops and the race card," in the words of Georgetown University demographer-historian Frederick Meyerson. Handicapped by a thin and unconvincing argument against taking a position on the need for immigration reduction (such a position "would be damaging to the club and its alliances around the country," said President Larry Fahn), Pope gave several media interviews laced with the words "racist," "xenophobia," "Nazi" and "it's hate, " a "virus," to characterize "the forces behind" the "takeover by outside forces" which included white supremacists and elements of the Animal Rights movement. When Club members and others complained that the hateful Nazi outside forces were three of the most respected members of the Club—Lamm, Morris, and Pimentel—Pope said he had not called the three racists, just pointed out that racists were "behind them." So they were doing racists' work, a distinction without much difference. "This is classic McCarthyism," objected Sea Shepherd Society head Paul Watson.

The media printed without comment, and more than once, all of Pope's slurs, and chose headlines such as "the greening of hate" to lead off stories on the Lamm/Morris/Pimentel challenge. Club headquarters sent out mass mailings repeating this language, and the 23 percent of the members who voted rejected the insurgents and elected the board-endorsed candidates by a large margin. In early 2005 came another ballot question and more board candidates pledging to reverse Club policy on immigration, and "The Good Guys" lost again.

All this futile struggling produced at least one revelation. The vehemence and character assassination McCarthy-style that Carl Pope injected into these three episodes seemed so extreme that Dick Lamm and Frank Morris questioned whether an anonymous big donor might be calling the shots, and demanded that Pope reveal the names of those who recently and anonymously gave $102 million to the Sierra Club Foundation. Did Dick and Frank know something no one else (but Carl Pope) did? Apparently so. Pope refused to disclose the names of donors wishing to remain anonymous. But this is America, and out the story came. Reporter Kenneth Weiss of the *Los Angeles Times*, in a 2005 general interview (having nothing to do with the Sierra Club) with wealthy southern California philanthropist David Gelbaum, quoted Gelbaum as admitting that strings were indeed attached to at least some of his sizeable gifts. "I did tell Carl Pope in 1994 or 1995 that if they [Sierra Club] ever came out as anti-immigration, they would never get a dollar from me." At stake, it turned out, was more than a dollar. Gelbaum's donations in 2000-2001 exceeded $100 million. This one donor was effectively dictating—without making a plausible argument before anyone—how other Club donors and members' money would be used, while Pope covered this up for years and denied that any anonymous donor made Club policy. But Gelbaum certainly did.

* * *

The sordid behavior of Sierra Club leadership and the cowardice and denial of staff and voting members were doubly disturbing to immigration reformers, especially those who were also Greens. White guilt, leftist ideology and political correctness had again prevented a flagship environmental organization from facing the population dimension of the assault upon nature, and thus from making progress on the core mission. The nation's deeply flawed immigration policies were spared from a formidable new critic. As we talked about the outcome, some said we should give up on the Sierra Club but not give up on the project of alliance with the environmentalists. Why not work to ally with the Audubon Society, which gave local chapters considerable autonomy and in whose ranks FAIR had found many immigration reformers? What about the Izaak Walton League, which seemed worried about the population element in the mix? But the same basic ideological and PC forces were at work within the national headquarters of all major environmental organizations. We could make no breakthrough.

After three decades, our social movement still flew with a stunted left wing. Several liberal intellectuals and public figures associated with the liberal project in America had spoken out over the years for lower levels of immigration and an end to illegal immigration—*The New Republic*'s TRB and Senator Paul Douglas as early as the 1950s, Gaylord Nelson, Cesar Chavez, Ray Marshall, and Eugene McCarthy in and after the 1970s, Barbara Jordan, Michael Lind, and Dick Lamm in and after the 1980s. Isolated individuals from the liberal-left side did not add up to institutional strength. Immigration reduction is inherently a cause bringing important benefits to, among others, workers unskilled and skilled, blacks, Hispanic Americans, and environmentalists. However, the group leadership of those components of America unflaggingly held to the same open border positions they worked their way into in the 1970s, despite the *Wall Street Journal* and business allies that decision puts them into bed with. Given this stubborn and almost religious resistance to pursuing the real interests of the core constituencies of the center-left on the matter of immigration policy out of fear that it could and would be read as hostility to non-whites, a terrifying risk, our reform cause had not been able, at the end of the century, to broaden itself so as to again be, as in the days of Teddy Roosevelt and Henry Cabot Lodge, of Booker T. Washington and Sam Gompers, its own unique blend of left, middle and right.

Not because we had not tried.

Chapter Twenty-Seven:
All For Immigration Reform—
But What Kind?

This issue is the most emotional, most sensitive, most politically charged issue I've seen during my twelve years in Congress.
— Senator Saxby Chambliss (R-Ga.)

Though beaten for a third time in the Sierra Club vote in March, we reformers in early 2005 were heartened by the explosion of local, citizen-led and spontaneous protests generated across the country by illegal immigration. "Immigration is crawling its way back onto the national agenda," wrote *Newsweek* columnist Robert Samuelson in June. "It's the issue that just won't quit," conceded Frank Sharry.

By late spring the Open Border coalition had pushed forward a cluster of three legislative proposals not much changed from 2004. The president's "plan" was still on the table but had no legislative form. It called for "legalization" of all the 11 million illegals who came forward to register for a three-year (perhaps renewable once) period of work with a specified employer, after which they would be asked to return home and apply for re-entry by getting in line. A guestworker program came with this, overseas (and in-country illegal) workers in unlimited numbers able to take jobs that U.S. employers certified as having no American applicants.

This would expose the entire U.S. economy to massive and sustained infusions of foreign labor. Yet many in the Open Border coalition complained that the president's "return home" idea was too restrictive

413

and thus unacceptable. They preferred a second alternative—a legislative proposal getting much attention because of the name-recognition stature of the bipartisan co-sponsors, John McCain and Edward Kennedy. Their bill made the Bush plan seem cautious, and from the undiluted Open Border perspective, unreasonably "harsh." "McCainedy" gestured toward border enforcement promising the usual increase in Border Patrol personnel. Then it got down to the "reform" part—a new visa (H-5A) for 400,000 low-skill foreign guestworkers upon securing a job offer not in agriculture or "high-skill" occupations, all of these guests to be given permanent resident status after four years. Huge expansions of old and new visa programs were authorized, and even the analysts at FAIR could not easily determine the size of the numerical expansion of annual legal immigration and the legalization of illegals. McCain-Kennedy was a radical, unprecedented expansion of incoming foreign worker numbers along with their families and the usual chains to the families married to those amnestied families. It proposed a Herculean new bureaucratic effort by thinly-stretched and overworked American immigration and Labor Department officials who were not up to their daily tasks even without the additional assignment of processing millions of applications to remain in or enter the U.S. Massive fraud was inevitable, with terrorist penetration only one of the likely problems.

"McCainedy" was Open Borders heavy, and while it was prominent in the news, it did not seem to be moving as spring 2005 became summer, for reasons best known in the inner circles of the White House and the Republican leadership in the senate. Hearings on the bill were finally held in July, and the White House decided to keep its distance in this volatile political climate, declining to send anyone from the administration to testify. "There's momentum for this [Open Border reform]" asserted Lisa Navarrete, vice president of La Raza, in April. Maybe not, thought Thomas Mann, a congressional analyst at the Brookings Institution: "The odds are less than 50-50" that Open Border reform would happen in 2005. "The momentum has undeniably shifted in our favor," Tom Tancredo said in April. He and Mann were right, and she was wrong.

* * *

To my astonishment, our side scored first. Congressman Sensenbrenner had been promised by the GOP leadership at the end of 2004 that he would get a clear channel for serious consideration of his REAL ID bill, which required all states to adopt uniform standards for issuing drivers' licenses and non-driver IDs, tightened political asylum rules, cleared the way for completion of a fence on the border near San Diego, and added detention space and enforcement agents. These steps had been recommended by the 9/11 Commission, and were stalled through 2004. The promise of a place on the legislative calendar was kept, and in February, 2005, President Bush, surely hoping to make some friends among his party's Secure the Border members, said that he "strongly supports" Sensebrenner's bill to prevent terrorists from entering and moving undetected about in the U.S. The REAL ID Act was signed by Bush on May 11. At last (and a case can be made that it was a first), a real, national interest immigration reform measure had passed one house of Congress, and it moved a small distance in our direction.

* * *

While the Open Borders lobby may not have been unified behind any one legislative proposal, they continued to present a unified argument, almost as if they met weekly to rehearse—which, at breakfast with Grover Norquist, perhaps they did. They insisted that tougher enforcement of the law at borders and interior, did not amount to "comprehensive" immigration reform, and therefore "wouldn't work," since we had already tried tougher border controls. Over the past twenty years, they argued, there had been a tenfold increase in funding for enforcement, and a three-fold increase in Border Patrol manpower. Foreign workers armed with an undiminished work ethic were irresistibly drawn to a growing "immigration labor market" inside the U.S., and they cannot be stopped, and need not be.

What more was needed to "fix the broken system?" "Comprehensive reform," which meant action on the supply side to meet the basic problem of shortages of workers inside America. The U. S. should admit more foreign labor annually, and legalize the eleven million illegals already doing our national work. Some border tightening should be added to these essential expansions of legal immigration, without which the border could not be defended.

Americans hearing this argument had been bombarded for at least two decades with a foundational background message about an allegedly deepening national problem and worry to which Open Borders was the answer. Americans could no longer run their own country without foreign help, lots of it and on a sustained basis. Our own citizens "don't want to work out in the fields or up on roofs in the hot sun," and "employers can't pay them enough to make that kind of job worthwhile," Tamar Jacoby of the Manhattan Institute argued, without a shred of evidence offered. "America has a shortage of unskilled workers," pronounced Grover Norquist, without proof. Endlessly one heard that if the foreign labor supply were cut off, entire sectors and regions "would collapse." The movie version of this came in 2005, as the California-based "A Day Without Mexicans," in which the state's economy ground to a halt when illegal entry was impeded. Once we face this reality, the solution is obvious. Expand the legal channels for unskilled and semi-skilled immigrant labor through an economy-wide guest worker program and earned legalization of the eleven million illegals already here. Do this, and we enter a new era in which even larger immigration solves every American employer's problem—eager labor at rock-bottom prices and no lip. And no illegal immigration, as all wanting to come will come legally, leaving only terrorists to sneak in and making them easy to catch (don't question that last part; we are still working on it).

There it was—a two-tiered America, on top the citizens who wouldn't do the low-pay low-status jobs and weren't expected to, on the bottom the imported foreigners who would—replenished continuously by more foreigners, as the children of each wave would grow up into Americans hanging out at the mall and refusing to do menial work.

* * *

Our Case for Real Immigration Reform

In policy battles the war of ideas is crucial, and while all sides need experts operating out of credible and respected institutions, the central need, especially on a subject as complex as immigration, is for generalists who can engage and drive the ongoing public debate through Op-Eds, essays, and congressional testimony. When the legislative showdowns came in 2005, our reductionist angle of vision on immigration matters, frozen out by the nation's research universities and the major think tanks such as Brookings and the Urban Institute, had built an impressive cadre of specialists who could hold forth on past and present guestworker programs (Phil Martin, Norman Matloff), labor market impacts of immigration flows (George Borjas, Vernon Briggs), national security implications (Janice Kephart, Rosemary Jenks, Jessica Vaughan), IDs for illegals (Marti Dinerstein), state and local law enforcement and immigration control (James Edwards, Kris Kobach), and just about any aspect of the demographics and economics of immigration (Steve Camarota, Edwin Rubenstein). CIS alone published sixteen Backgrounders in 2005 written by twelve authors, each now a certified expert ready to testify or talk to the media on some aspect of the immigration issue if they had not been before (most had been).

But generalists? There were intellectuals with the basic skills, such as Peter Brimelow, and the seasoned directors of the two top reductionist-reform groups, Dan Stein and Roy Beck. The media also wanted think tank or university credentials suggesting a research-based expertise yet not confined to one specialty. Fortunately, CIS had nurtured one—Mark Krikorian.

* * *

We had not known this when our search committee hired him back in 1995. However, Mark had a remarkable ability to write quickly, clearly, with striking phrases and examples, and in debate settings he was resourceful, sure footed, and had perfect pitch for these difficult issues. CIS publications were research reports by experts, and Mark recruited, edited and publicized them. In 2000 and after he increasingly found his own voice and outlets. He had developed a rapport with the editors of *National Review*, *National Review Online*, and *The National Interest* which, along with frequent congressional testimony that CIS made available online, allowed him to engage ongoing legislative and policy issues immediately, within a week or two. Or more quickly than that. Mark became a favorite for appearances on Lou Dobbs's news hour, and at O'Reilly's news program on Fox. In 2003 and after, Mark shaped an influential critique of the Open Borderist's argument, and his arguments and phrases had a considerable resonance.

* * *

A crucial underpinning of the amnesty component of the Open Border version of "immigration reform" was the insistence that the 11-20 million illegals in the country must be legalized because "mass deportation" of entire families seemed the only alternative but was no alternative since the public wouldn't support it. Mark attacked such a capitulation to acts of illegality, calling it "declaring surrender," and presented a compelling conception of how sustained strict enforcement of the law could in time resolve the problem of a huge illegal population through "attrition" and self-deportation. Amnesty as against mass deportation was "a false choice." In his CIS Backgrounder, "Downsizing Illegal Immigration: A Strategy for Attrition through Enforcement," a paper called by *Immigration Daily* "probably the best overall blueprint articulating the anti-immigrationist big picture viewpoint," Mark wrote that we should:

> *Shrink the illegal population through consistent, across-the-board enforcement of the immigration law. By deterring the settlement of new illegals, by increasing deportations to the extent possible,… by increasing the number of illegals already here who give up and deport themselves, the U.S. can bring about an annual decrease in the illegal-alien population.*

This "strategy of attrition…would drain down the illegal population to a manageable nuisance, rather than today's looming crisis." What of the argument that we have already proven, in the years after the law of 1986, that we cannot control the border? Mark made a strong rebuttal: we hadn't really tried. IRCA had no teeth because of the rot of document fraud, the INS entirely gave up on interior enforcement in the latter 1990s, and promising enforcement provisions (such as the 3/10 bar) for actual punishment of illegal entry creating a brand new deterrent were never put into practice. So fatalism on illegal immigration control had no historical foundation, since the years of failed trying had not been years of trying—except by the Border Patrol professionals in the trenches, who were backed up by no serious deterrents.

As for ambitious proposals for legalizing eleven (twenty?) million illegals and then searching their backgrounds for criminal and terrorist records, while also performing the same scrutiny of as well as keeping track of untold thousands of incoming foreign guestworkers, Mark drenched the idea in scorn. Does the Department of Homeland Security have the administrative capacity to do the job proposed?

> *The Department…would have to determine that the person was, in fact, an illegal alien on the date of the bill's introduction… that he was employed in the U.S. at the time, that he has remained so employed [or] was a full-time student, that he has not ordered, incited, assisted, or otherwise participated in the persecution of any person on account of race, religion, nationality, membership in a particular social group, or political opinion, and that he is not a security threat, a criminal, a polygamist, or a child abductor.*

And do this "expeditiously! This in addition to the usual workload of the agency within DHS, which in the description of director Eduardo Aguirre in 2004, "in a typical work day…will process 140,000 national security background checks…take 50,000 calls at our customer service centers, adjudicate 30,000 applications for immigration benefits…issue 20,000 green cards, and capture 8,000 sets of fingerprints and digital photos" while doing what we can to reduce the backlog of four million immigration applications. This was "bureaucratic utopianism," John O'Sullivan wrote. Mark's prediction: "The result of placing the huge additional demands of a guestworker program (and also amnesty) onto an already overwhelmed and confused bureaucracy" can be described in two words: "fraud" and "paralysis." We have seen it before—in carrying out the amnesty and agricultural guestworker program launched in 1986, when fraud was omnipresent. IRCA in 1986 was founded upon the idea of "a grand bargain," amnesty and guestworkers in return for promises of control of illegal immigration. It was being proposed again, twenty years later. Fool me once, shame on you. Fool me twice, shame on me.

In testimony before the Senate Committee on the Judiciary, Mark directly challenged (as he did in other writings) the central assumption of both amnesty and guestworker programs—that America needs mass unskilled immigration, that "our vast...300-million-person continent-spanning economy can't function properly without a steady stream of high school dropouts from abroad." This is "economic gibberish." (Economics without the price mechanism, economist Thomas Sowell called it.) If the supply of cheap foreign labor were reduced, Mark noted, employers would increase wages and benefits to attract the labor still available and look for ways of increasing productivity. Steve Camarota later in the year summarized for a House committee the findings on the labor market impacts of current immigration by the National Research Council, the Rand Corporation and various economists including George Borjas and Steve himself: immigration lowered the wages and discouraged labor market participation of native workers without a high school degree. There are no low-skill sectors of the economy where natives don't work and experience competition with immigrants, and (a point strongly made in a report, "Dropping Out," in early 2006), there *is* no low-skilled labor shortage in place or in prospect. There *is* an employer preference for illegal Central Americans and Mexicans, and the government in deciding immigration policy faces a choice between American citizens, workers versus employers.

In a May cover story for *National Review* in the form of a memo to Bill Frist, Rudy Giuliani and other GOP presidential hopefuls, Mark offered a ten-point immigration agenda—including "unambiguous commitment to enforcement," "take amnesty off the table...until *after* we regain control of the immigration system, no illegal workers, document security and tracking for all foreign visitors, and pledge a bottom-up reexamination of the rationale and functioning of the entire visa system. Immigration enforcement is "a sure winner," and the real risk for Republicans is in letting Hillary's statement, "I am, you know, adamantly against illegal immigrants" wedge off Republican voters on this issue.

* * *

By early summer, 2005, the Expansionist offensive, composed of variously packaged amnesty/guestworker deals with "this time we really mean it" enforcement gestures, had run into mounting opposition and was stalled.

This was the work of thousands of aroused Americans around the country, mobilized by a growing number of grassroots and regional immigration reform groups and assisted by the D.C.-based organizations. The intellectual battle was the work of a smaller group, and I have been tracing the influence of one of them—Mark Krikorian.

Of course there were many creative people involved in the "battle of ideas" over immigration reform, a variety of voices doing the work of critique and advocacy, some of them either sounding like or known to be Republicans breaking with their president. In June, former Reagan Attorney General Edwin Meese headed a Heritage Foundation team that produced the Backgrounder, "Alternatives to Amnesty: Proposals for Fair and Effective Immigration Reform." They wrote: "For the sake of national security and the rule of law," the number of "individuals who are unlawfully present in the U.S. must be reduced. But this must be done without any form of amnesty, which despite denials is the core element in all legislative proposals now before Congress. Lawbreakers must leave the U.S. and re-enter through legal means. Programs of aid "to assist undocumented workers in returning to their host countries" should be considered, possibly including a national voluntary trust fund. The report's footnotes were well fortified by citations to the research and analysis of CIS and FAIR.

* * *

Why was the Expansionist legislative fleet becalmed on the D.C. ocean in 2005? Part of the answer is the skill and energy that we have already seen mobilized in the Washington lobbying efforts of several groups, primarily Roy Beck's NumbersUSA and FAIR. Roy's operation continued to combine a prodigious and responsive number of FAX-activists across

America informed by the lobbying work of Rosemary and Jim Edwards on the Hill. By 2005, FAIR was a considerably stronger force than it had been in the 1990s, both in Washington and outside. Dan Stein, at times visibly tired in the late 1990s by twenty years of institution building in one of the most emotionally draining policy struggles in Washington, had been relieved of day-to-day managerial duties by the hiring of a COO, allowing Dan to concentrate on strategy, major statements and fundraising. A new Government Relations Director invigorated FAIR's Capitol Hill lobbying effort by retaining as consultant former Congressman Brian Bilbray and hiring several new staff including two lawyers who happened to be young, attractive, and female--a nod to the achievements of Rosemary Jenks. Backed by this on-the-Hill presence, FAIR installed its own version of NumbersUSA's FAX network of activists, and presented a newly designed and intellectually heftier newsletter edited by veteran writer and long-time staffer, Ira Mehlman.

* * *

This said, the most important action and energy in 2005 was not in Washington, but was firing up around the country. In my years on the FAIR board, Dan and the staff field directors told us at practically every meeting through the 1980s and 1990s that "the field" was growing and energizing and we should spend more money there. They presented evidence of growing grassroots activism—e-mail, letters, and media reports of local group activities. But then field staff always want more money for field activities. By 2004 and 2005, they weren't exaggerating. The media attention to the Minutemen on the Arizona border seemed to have fanned the brushfires of citizen reform activism across the country that we had been watching and encouraging for several years. New groups sprang up in states like Utah (two, in that sparsely populated state), Oregon, Indiana, and Pennsylvania. Established groups in Connecticut, Georgia, and California made national news with their picketing of day laborer sites and appearances before legislative hearings on drivers' licenses or college tuition. Every time I looked at lists of immigration reform web sites, there were more of them—ninety-four by the count of The American Resistance Foundation in early 2005.

FAIR hired a national field director for the first time, and Susan Tully made a convincing case in early 2005 that it was time not only for another "bring the field volunteers to Washington" spring meeting (called IRAW since the first one in 1996), but a larger one built around the offer of Roger Hedgecock, top rated radio talk show host in San Diego, to "lead an immigration reform army" to D.C. in April. This grew into a gathering of 500 activists from around the country for "Hold Their Feet to the Fire," a week of lobbying and speeches kicked off by a rally in Lafayette Park across the street from the White House, with Hedgecock and other talk radio hosts broadcasting on eighteen radio programs at all hours of the day. "The Spring of 2005," announced William Gheen, head of a North Carolina group Americans for Legal Immigration, "will be seen as the time when the tide turned against rampant illegal immigration in America." "We have reached the turning point," said Congressman Dana Rohrabacher to thunderous applause. Two young California activists told me they were fired up by the meeting but regretted that everybody there seemed to be a Republican.

There was considerable evidence justifying the hope that a turning point had finally been reached. Within a month, the REAL-ID passed Congress by a resounding vote. On the evening news, Bill O'Reilly on Fox and, especially, Lou Dobbs at CNN continued their frequent coverage of immigration issues with a bias new to us, since it was a bias toward our view of the problem. A Zogby poll showed 81 percent of respondents in favor of stationing the American military on the border. Some of those in attendance at "Hold Their Feet to the Fire" imagined that this growing social movement could use more than one national umbrella organization. Representatives from over thirty immigration reform groups held a "summit" in Las Vegas a month later, and heard speeches by the movement's emerging stars—Tancredo, Peter Gadiel[6] of 9/11 Families for a Secure America, Jim Gilchrist and Chris Simcox

---

[6] One May evening on Lou Dobbs' news show, Peter Gadiel told Dobbs that he had easily obtained from the Mexican government a Matricula Consular, the identity document provided to Mexican citizens in the U.S. Dobbs was shocked at this easily procured false documentation—especially when Gadiel said he had also purchased one for Dobbs, and he held it up on national TV, with Dobbs' name and photo. Dobbs was visibly uneasy seeing his own fake ID on the screen. The point was well made.

of the Minuteman Project, Bay Buchanan of Tancredo's Team America PAC, Barbara Coe, and D. A. King of Georgia's American Resistance Foundation. No national organization emerged from this meeting, apparently. They had not yet found their John Tanton.

* * *

9/11 Commission Leadership Defects to Open Border Ranks

I found the 9/11 Commission's Report in 2004 in a local bookstore, and, thumbing the pages quickly, found support for our immigration policy reforms. Beginning at p. 383 there were seven to eight pages on immigration matters with some welcomed language: "Secure identification should begin in the U.S. The federal government should set standards for the issuance of...sources of identification;" a "biometric entry-exit screening system" was needed. "Travel documents are as important as weapons." "There is a growing role for state and local law enforcement agencies." The Commission had also authorized a staff report on "Terrorist Travel" which was posted on the web and given virtually no notice. It presented a 276-page terrorist travel narrative of a shockingly easy exploitation by terrorists of our system of visas, drivers license issuance and customs inspections. It reported little progress from 2001 to 2004, in addressing these problems in order to make border security "the cornerstone of national security policy."

Upon the termination of the 9/11 Commission's authority in August, 2004, the two chairs, Hamilton and Kean, accepted private funding that allowed them to continue for a year as a lobbying force pressing for implementation of their recommendations—which seemed like a good idea, but led to a shocking and never explained betrayal. They became a private, independent group known as the 9/11 Public Discourse Project, funded (this was not initially disclosed) by the Ford, Carnegie, John S. and James L. Knight, Smith Richardson and Hewlett foundations. Each of these foundations (with the exception of Hewlett) has a long track record of support for La Raza, American Immigration Lawyers Association, MALDEF, and National Immigration Forum. Miraculously,

Hamilton and Kean suddenly lost interest in the immigration-reform features of their 9/11 report. In May, a task force on Immigration and America's Future was formed, Hamilton yoked together as co-chair with Open Borderite (and recently defeated) former Senator Spencer Abraham. The director was Doris Meissner, Bill Clinton's incompetent and irresolute INS Director and now affiliated with the Open Border Migration Policy Institute.

Hamilton soon took the prestige of the 9/11 Commission leadership into congressional lobbying against immigration tightening. In September, two rival pieces of legislation known as "9/11 Commission Implementation Bills" emerged in Congress— a senate version authored by Senators Collins and Lieberman, which had nothing to say about border security, visas, terrorist travel, or security IDs, and a House version, HR 10, with extensive provisions in all these areas. Hamilton and Kean appeared at a press conference with the two senators to endorse their bill, and vigorously opposed HR 10. On the Discourse Project web site one could find this statement: "Whether illegal aliens should be able to get driver's licenses is a valid question for debate." Later, Hamilton and Kean said not a word in support of Congressman Sensebrenner's REAL ID act as it moved slowly toward passage. "Betrayal!" charged the 9/11 Families for a Secure America when they learned from a December *Congressional Quarterly* story of Discourse Project's secret funding and lobbying tilt against a more secure border.

Also outraged at Kean and Hamilton's betrayal was Commission staff lawyer Janice Kephart, the lead author of the ignored and now betrayed staff report, *9/11 and Terrorist Travel*, which was finally published to little fanfare in August 2005 after a disappointing year of neglect of its findings and recommendations. How could she call attention to what was not getting done after 9/11 on immigration policy issues? A call came from Mark Krikorian, who had read the report on terrorist travel, and in September Kephart authored CIS Paper 24, *Immigration and Terrorism: Moving Beyond the 9/11 Staff Report on Terrorist Travel*. It drew on new data about ninety-four terrorists operating in the U.S. in the 1990s to 2004, and in an accessible twenty-four pages of text (the *Terrorist Travel* report had been a formidable 276 pages). It presented an unnerving story of successful immigration fraud, undetected violations, reception of immigration benefits, and multiple false ID documents.

"Fraud was rampant" was one of her phrases that might have served as a better title for a report that "highlights the danger of our lax immigration system."

* * *

Stalemate

Autumn came, and it was clear that we reformers, and America, had for another year fended off all versions of the radical Bush-McCain-Kennedy bipartisan amnesty/guestworker "comprehensive reform" formulation that had emerged in 2001 and been backed by a president, large parts of both political parties, and a formidable Open Border lobby. But stalemates on volatile issues are fragile. Which way was the momentum running?

The year 2005 harbored both possibilities. The rending of the social fabric at the southwestern border and the political backlash it created finally drove two Democratic governors with long histories of denial—Bill Richardson of New Mexico and Janet Napolitano of Arizona—to declare in August "a state of emergency" on their borders with Mexico. Tom Tancredo's Immigration Caucus grew to ninety-one members by November. More important, House Majority Leader Tom Delay continued to distance himself from the president's strategy. In June, he told Bush that a guestworker program ought to wait until "we actually enforce the law" we pass on border security. In late summer, Delay endorsed Tancredo's REAL GUEST Act which took up enforcement first and postponed guestworker measures. Half of the Republican House and Senate members responding in July to a *National Journal* poll named immigration as the issue "most on the minds of your constituents these days," one of them calling it "the highest-octane issue in America."

There were only scattered elections in the fall of 2005, and only a handful in which different views on immigration seemed likely to decide the issue. A seat in California's forty-eighth congressional district was opened when the incumbent moved to head the Securities and Exchange

Commission, and Jim Gilchrist, co-founder of the Minuteman Project, entered the race on the ticket of the marginal American Independent Party with border control his main issue. He polled 25 percent, second in a field of five, holding the winner, a well-known state senator, to 45 percent of the vote in a district in which the Republican incumbent had last won by 65 percent. In Virginia's race for governor, the Republicans took a tough stance on illegal immigration, yet the Democrats narrowly won. Analysts thought the race hinged on other factors, chiefly the popularity of the departing Democratic governor. Races in California, Idaho and Arizona featured strong immigration policy positions. Voters in 2005 gave a muted, scattered, and inconclusive message as to whether they were beginning to vote on the immigration issue, and which position would hurt which party the most.

In time, the historians will give us their views on why George Bush interpreted all of this as a signal to persist in his immigration stance. We already know that his poll results on the public's approval ratings had been sliding downward through 2005, pushed by the mounting costs and uncertain results of the war in Iraq, the administration's dismal, television-told performance after the Katrina hurricane struck the Louisiana-Mississippi coast late in August, and the fumbling nomination as Supreme Court nominee of marginally-qualified Bush aide Harriet Miers. A *USA Today*/CNN/Gallup Poll found that 65 percent of the public disapproved of Bush's handling of the immigration issue, a NBC/*Wall Street Journal* poll found that 58 percent disapproved of Bush's amnesty plan, and a Fox News poll found that 79 percent favored putting troops on the border.

* * *

The Republican Party was now deeply split, and the legislative momentum seemed to have shifted to strengthen the party's "enforcement first" wing—a shift among not only politicians, but conservative intellectuals and pundits. Pat Buchanan in the 1990s had seemed quite alone on the fringe of the conservative tent as he tried to reinforce his unsuccessful political forays with writing about the need for immigration reduction. By 2005-2006, however, the conservative case for tighter borders was being made in many places—the pages of *National Review*,

The American Conservative, www.Vdare.com, and by people like Reagan's Attorney General Ed Meese, and veteran conservative strategist Paul Weyrich in a comprehensive sentence written to columnist Cal Thomas late in the year: "As conservatives, we need to make it clear that we will not vote for any candidate who refuses to close our borders to illegal immigration and cut back on legal immigration, at least until we can acculturate the immigrants we already have."

* * *

Still it surprised me and, I think, people both informed and uninformed, when the House on December 16, after only two days of debate (and many near escapes from derailment), passed by a vote of 239-182 a border security bill (H. R. 4437) which, among other things, would make "illegal presence" a felony crime, end catch-and-release, mandate the "Basic Pilot" program by which companies check job applicants' immigration status, authorize a multi-layered fence along 700 miles of the U.S.-Mexico border, require immigration authorities to complete background checks before granting an immigration benefit, and end the notorious diversity visa lottery—the first reduction in overall immigration voted by Congress in eighty years. FAIR helpfully released a statement saying that the bill "should have been stronger," reminding the public of the still-unaddressed agenda. As a leading example, an amendment ending birthright citizenship was blocked at the eleventh hour, as was Rep. J. D. Hayworth's proposal to delay any legislation on amnesty or guestworkers until enforcement had been found effective.

* * *

With this remarkable legislative achievement in one House, a turbulent, unpredictable year of center-stage immigration politics was over. I agreed with a leftist writer assessing the immigration debate, Tom Barry of the New Mexico-based International Relations Center, when, in a 2005 paper entitled "Politics of Class and Corporations," he conceded that "right-wing critics of U.S. immigration and border control policies" had in recent months "pushed their way" from being "voices in the political wilderness, consigned to the far margins of both political parties" to "the center of a heated political debate about immigration policy." How? They have focused not on "nativist" appeals, but "positioned themselves as the champions of U.S. labor" and critics of corporate America, leaving "pro-immigration groups…fumbling for credible arguments to counter the rising backlash against immigrants." Further, "nowhere do the pro-immigration groups and unions deal with immigration policy as an issue of numbers. How many immigrants can be integrated into U.S. society?" Astonishing—someone on the left conceding that population-growth and assimilation issues were legitimate topics rather than "fears."

This was a remarkable and unprecedented piece of clear thinking on the left. But it was only one leftist, isolated out in New Mexico. What we had on the national policy scene was a stalemate—a House bill which moved in our direction but was stalled along with Expansionist plans. Even if a sharp policy turn against illegal immigration could be legislated and administered, this still left legal immigration roaring along at more than a million a year, flawed by much-criticized features such as the visa lottery, anchor babies making up nearly one out of every ten births in the U. S., large-scale guestworker numbers in the several "H" visa programs for skilled workers, and gaping holes in the visa issuance and foreigner-tracking systems. These and other flaws in legal immigration were hardly on the serious congressional calendar.

At one meeting on the Hill, Roy and Rosemary offered a hopeful observation for which I had no rebuttal. Aren't folks on our side reaching a wider audience, and enjoying in the new century a great deal more influence than in the last two decades of the twentieth? The Expansionists don't contemptuously brush us aside as once they did, and they don't even get to call illegals "undocumented," which must gall them. The media concedes the issue of our broken system a place right at the top of urgent issues needing attention.

I had no answer to that. Professional politics-watchers confidently predicted that our 2005 counter-offensive would continue in 2006. The Congress-watching publication *Roll Call* announced that "Immigration is Poised to Become a Hot Topic for 2006," and an Arizona Republican lobbyist went further. You can put "immigration at the top of the list" of "dominating issues in play next year," he wrote. We had long wanted it at the top, and there it was, after thirty-five years of effort. However, as

Roy said to me in June, with that success came the absolute necessity to win. For if our reform was now high on the national agenda, so was the Open Border's White Flag, which would mean an official, not merely an unofficial, Open Door.

Chapter Twenty-Eight:
Stalemate Settles In—2006-08

Nothing ever gets settled in this town. — George P. Schulz
former Secretary of State

It seemed in early 2006 that the senators were nervous, inclined to pursue the same combination of mass amnesty and large-scale guestworker program, but not eager to risk the amnesty hammering of the year before. McCaineddy came forward again, along with two tortured alternatives that required illegals to (1) return to their home countries and await clearance, or (2) return to a U. S. port of entry and spend a few nights in a motel awaiting permission to re-enter on a citizenship track. These were new dodges, but not new ideas, nor was the continued rationale provided by *The New York Times* on May 7: "The problem is…an overwhelming gap between demand and supply. "The backlog" of 3 million people wanting to move to the U.S., requires that America "adjust its formulas for immigrant visas to eliminate the backlogs." This meant opening up the legal doors until the problem of "backlogs" disappeared. This was "comprehensive" reform, dealing with the *real* problem—that the U.S. didn't admit as many foreigners as wanted to come here.

The cannonade of criticism of the basic rationale of the Senate-White House "comprehensive reformers" if anything was more intense and spiced with ridicule than the year before—from George Borjas, Steve Camarota, Heather MacDonald, John O'Sullivan, and the Vdare authors. Mark Krikorian seemed to write an Op-Ed piece each week— on why every "reform" version coming out of the senate was still built

431

around an amnesty, on the dismal history of guestworker programs, on the massive fraud that could be absolutely predicted within any new guestworker program in view of the administrative incapacity of the Homeland Security Department. This was not just Krikorian's opinion. In March, the Government Accounting Office (GAO) issued a report which documented massive corruption and pervasive administrative failure in the immigration benefits performance of the new U. S. Citizenship and Immigration Services, ("benefit fraud was pervasive and significant") which would have the job of administering the Bush/Senate proposed massive amnesties and guestworker programs.

The familiar critics were joined by converts, and people who had not been heard from since the 1980s. "I used to favor a program to allow in guest workers," wrote *The New York Times* editorial writer Nicholas Kristof, "but I've changed my mind…because of growing evidence that low-wage immigration hurts America's own poor." Former California Governor Pete Wilson wrote in *Investor Business Daily* in May that proposals in the senate are "tantamount to repeal of our immigration laws and throwing open our borders." What we need, Wilson concluded, is "a physical barrier like that in Israel," and no amnesty. Heritage Foundation's Ed Meese that same month wrote in *The New York Times* that "the situation today bears uncanny similarities to what we went through" in the debate over the Immigration Reform and Control Act of 1986. It was indeed an amnesty (as Ronald Reagan had conceded privately to his staff), there was widespread document fraud in the implementation, and it didn't even solve the problem. This time, let those here illegally correct their status by "returning to their country of origin and getting in line with everyone else." Also weighing in for the first time as open critics of Bush-Senate immigration plans were conservative writers Charles Krauthammer ("serious border enforcement is missing") and former Bush speech writer David Frum, who in March wrote a piece in the apparent hope of convincing the president that "the Republican rank-and-file are seething over immigration."

* * *

Clearly a tipping point was being reached in many American communities, a landslide of anger at the seemingly endless augmentation of an illegal and mostly low-skilled foreign population pressing into their educational, social welfare and criminal justice systems. The change in political climate in American communities was striking. "So far this year," the *New York Times* learned from the National Conference of State Legislatures in early May, "no fewer than 461 bills related to immigration have been offered in the forty-three states where legislatures have been in session." The proposed legislation was overwhelmingly aimed at unwelcoming the illegal population through measures such as denial of in-state tuition and non-emergency health benefits, tighter measures excluding illegals from driver's licenses, ending or reducing Medicaid and other welfare eligibility, punishment for employers who employed illegals, and explicit authorization for local policy agencies to enforce federal immigration laws.

A growing citizens mobilization could be seen in another place. The influential e-magazine VDARE compiled a list of Minuteman groups, which had multiplied and also splintered as Jim Gilchrist led the Minuteman Project and Chris Simcox founded the Minuteman Civil Defense Corps, and other groups affiliated with neither one. VDARE's list in late 2007 counted eighty-eight groups spread across the country. Border states were strongly represented but Minuteman groups operated in states like Pennsylvania, Tennessee, and New Jersey.

The churning over immigration spread to (or up from?) local communities, producing what one journalist called "a raging fire of ordinances" in places like Valley Park, Missouri, Farmers Branch, Texas., Manassas, Virginia, and Hazelton, Pennsylvania. There was (as far as I could discern) no reliable estimate of local immigration control ordinances proposed or passed, and many of them were challenged in court after passage and thus of uncertain permanence or effect. In my own state of North Carolina, some examples: Gaston County Commissioners ordered that illegals be denied social services, and the town of Landis made English the official language. Some local law enforcement officials moved into immigration enforcement without ordinances, sensing a changed political climate before it was evident to city or county elected politicians. In Mecklenburg County (Charlotte), Sheriff James Pendergraph, elected by the people and not hired or fired by the city council or board of supervisors, made his department a partner for the first time of ICE, and in 2006 deported 960 illegal aliens from the Mecklenburg jail population.

The national spotlight lingered on a few such communities, among them Herndon, Virginia, a suburb of Washington, D. C., scene of a long-running battle over whether the town should fund, or prohibit, a hiring hall for illegals who were clustered in large numbers on the edge of town. In May, 2006, voters threw out Mayor Michael O'Reilly who had backed a taxpayer-funded day-laborer center in 2004. He paid the ultimate political price for mis-reading the voters' mood, and the D.C. metropolitan news media took note.

* * *

To me, the most engaging as well as legally important ongoing story of local government veering away from the Sanctuary to the Run Them Out of Town strategy on illegal immigrants was taking place that year in Hazelton, Pennsylvania. I heard Mayor Louis Barletta speak in September, 2006. Hazelton had been in the national news as a town which in July "passed an ordinance aimed at making it one of the most difficult places in America for illegal immigrants." Hazelton? Where was it, and what was it? This former coal-mining town northwest of Philadelphia absorbed 7-11,000 Hispanic immigrants in the 1990s, and experienced unprecedented crime rates, gangs in public schools, and escalating demands on social services. Mayor Barletta declared that "illegal immigrants are destroying the city," and led the City Council in passage of an "Illegal Alien Relief Act," suspending the license of any business employing illegal aliens to do business with the city, requiring people renting in the city to apply for licenses conditional on citizenship, and suspending the license and fining any business that "employs, retains, aids or abets" immigrants without valid documents. The law was immediately challenged by a well-funded coalition, and defended by FAIR's legal staff, organized in a subsidiary named Immigration Reform Law Institute (IRLI). Whatever the eventual legal outcome, a degree of success came at once. "We have literally seen people loading up mattresses and furniture and leaving the city en masse," Barletta said at our September meeting. "This was our goal, to have a city of legal immigrants who are all paying taxes." Several other cities were said to be ready to follow the Hazelton model. A certain newspaper in New York lamented this as "immigration reform in pieces" and "demagoguery," but I had met and heard the demagogue and his wife, and found him the most gifted and persuasive political figure since, well, the early 1960s.

* * *

There was much evidence that the political mobilization of citizens ran deeper than resentment of the local costs imposed by otherwise desirable cheap foreign labor. Intellectuals in our reform movement had been warning since the 1980s that what was ultimately at stake in the effort to contain immigration was the cohesion of the nation itself. This deeper level of concern became visible at one particular meeting in 2005. I have heard Governor Dick Lamm speak fifteen or twenty times since the early 1980s, and he rarely fails to warn that unchecked immigration threatened the ecological and social foundations of the America our grandchildren will inherit. Audiences nodded consent. In 2005, something different happened. In October, Dick was scheduled to give a talk entitled "How to Destroy a Nation" to a FAIR Advisory Board meeting of over a hundred people. Unexpectedly he spoke for only ten minutes or so, and sat down, after saying something like this:

> *I have a secret plan to destroy America. Here is my plan: make America a bilingual-bicultural country.... Invent "multiculturalism" and encourage immigrants to maintain their own culture...Celebrate diversity rather than unity...Add a second underclass—unassimilated, undereducated, and antagonistic to our population. Then I would place all these subjects off limits—make it taboo to talk about. Next, make it impossible to enforce our immigration laws.*

Dick then strode the length of the aisle and took his seat. The audience was stunned, and silent for what seemed an awkward interval. Then came waves of applause, most in the audience standing and shouting approval. Somebody put his talk on the internet, and it was e-mailed and blogged around the country for months. An important part of the public mood of 2005-2006 on the immigration issue was captured in that revealing episode.

* * *

With the senate cautiously dallying during that spring of 2005, and public opinion continuing to tilt against the amnesty and guestworker versions of reform, the Open Border lobbying coalition decided that it was time for direct political pressure from the streets.

Who was managing this vast campaign? News stories identified a corporate consortium named the Essential Worker Immigration Coalition as well as several ethnic, religious, labor, and immigrant-aid groups behind the spring demonstrations promoting "comprehensive reform," their preferred phrase for the White Flag amnesty and guestworker legislation moving through the Senatesenate. A series of three street demonstrations in several cities began on March 25 and were repeated on April 10 and then on May 1 or "May Day"—an established international leftist and working class political calendar event. The street turnouts in March were sizeable. In April, the numbers grew, and in May, police in Los Angeles estimated a crowd of 400,000 walking down Wilshire Boulevard. Organizers in most places seemed to have learned that American flags should be carried, and not upside down (this seemed difficult for the march organizers to control), and that the stars and stripes were better PR than Mexican and Guatemalan flags, though those flags were always part of the banner parade. The marchers when filmed or interviewed did not always look or sound like average Americans but as "a sea of mostly Latino marchers," in the words of a *New York Times* story on May 4. Many signs were in Spanish—"*Si, Se Puede*" (we can do it), "*Amnistia*"— but speeches and signs in English conveyed the basic ideology that motivated the demonstrators: "No Human Is Illegal." "We are not criminals." Orators were displayed on the evening news repeating the mantra that only "comprehensive immigration reform" was acceptable, and that the "jobs that Americans won't do" had to be done by foreigners. Some demonstrators were photographed and filmed (usually on Lou Dobbs or Fox News) in angry outbursts against the racists and Nazis who disagreed with them. In some cities "immigrants" were urged to leave work or school and join the rallies, though the leadership was split on this, and there was some talk but no real follow-through of a nationwide "boycott" of companies who were insufficiently supportive of La Causa. Voter registration drives were promised.

The New York Times after the May 1 rallies in Los Angeles, Las Vegas, Chicago, Denver, New York, Atlanta and other cities saw them as "extraordinarily positive...a joyous outpouring." Most of the media in March designated the demonstrators as "civil rights marchers," and did not seem concerned that they were asserting a new civil right to break into a nearby country and then successfully demand that the laws against this be set aside. This comparison of thousands of illegals walking unmolested through many American cities to the black and white marches famously led by Martin Luther King, Jr. in favor of civil rights already in the Constitution and statutory law was preposterous and especially offensive to some blacks who complained of it in the print media.

After May 1 the media began to report and concede a different public perception of these marches. The Prop. 187 experience seemed to have been repeated. The much-televised scenes of Latino crowds and Mexican flags demanding the repeal of the core of U. S. immigration law seemed to have produced the same sort of backlash as similar scenes in 1994 in California. "By the end of today," Mark Krikorian boldly predicted in the *Wall Street Journal* on May 1, "any possibility of a bill reaching the president's desk will be dead." In his view, the media pictures of thousands in the streets with Spanish-language signs and some foreign flags was producing a backlash that would injure more than it helped the Open Border cause. This view was shared by a few march organizers, according to press accounts, and was confirmed by comments from some prominent legislators. Congressman J. D. Hayworth saw "an incredible backlash," and Rep. Steve King reported that "his office had been flooded with angry calls" complaining of the marches. Senator Trent Lott said "they lost me" when he saw so many Mexican flags.

* * *

That the senate's amnesty-guestworker idea was taking months to foal reflected among other things a searching critique coming from all points on the political spectrum. Two unexpected blows to the senate's approach

437

came in May from Heritage Foundation analyst Robert Rector, who published in May an estimate that the proposed S.2611 in its latest form (a compromise measure offered by Republican Senators Chuck Hagel and Mel Martinez would result in admitting 103 million immigrants (S.2611's increases added to those already built into the system) into the U.S. over the next twenty years, "the most dramatic change in immigration law in eighty years." Rector's paper had an immediate impact on the senate, which just days after the appearance of his report passed Senator Jeff Bingaman's amendment to cut the number of legal immigrants to be admitted under S. 2611. Rector quickly calculated that the senate had moved from adding 103 million to "only" 66 million over the next twenty years. In a *National Review Online* essay Rector in that same month estimated that the 10+ million amnestied illegals and their parents (eligible for immediate entry) would cost $50 billion, "the largest expansion of the welfare state in thirty-five years."

For those shocked by the forecast that "comprehensive reform" would result in adding 103 million new foreign arrivals in twenty years, a trimmed down expansion of 56 to 66 million new Americans was surely still a dismaying idea. No senator, no White House voice stepped forward to defend these huge numbers. All I could find in the media was a remark by K-Street corporate lobbyist Grover Norquist, who did not have to run for office. "We need more people in the U.S. to remain a world power and simply function as an economy," he was quoted as saying to a reporter. "We need 500,000 more people [annually] than we let in." Did anyone else hold such grotesque views of the purpose of immigration policy?

We reductionists had a discouraging track record on promoting serious discussion of this fundamental national choice—population size. However, 2006 brought us what seemed to be a teaching moment. The Census Bureau reported that the U.S. population would reach 300 million some day in October. "U. S. Population Nears 300 Million," was the headline of an associated Press story of June 26. "Milestones will be reached in the fall, with Latinos Driving Growth." We hoped this October landmark would be an opportunity, again, to connect immigration to national population to energy issues to global warming to everything else it was connected to.

* * *

Cracks in the Expansionist Front?

The immigration policy standoff might have seemed entirely a quarrel within Republican ranks, but at this point in 2006 a subdued debate, or at least some hitherto unspoken doubts about the Bush-senate strategy, could be heard on the Democratic side. In April, Howard Dean, Chair of the Democratic National Committee, was quoted in late May as saying that border security would be his party's top priority in the midterm elections and that a guestworker program was "indentured servitude" that threatens American workers' wages. AFL-CIO President John Sweeney agreed that guestworker programs "were a bad idea and harm all workers." Liberal columnists such as Paul Krugman and Nicholas Kristof expressed concern about the impact of continued large-scale immigration on working-class wages. FAIR helped organized a new committee of black leaders, Choose Black America, and a parallel Hispanic group, You Don't Speak For Me, both urging curbs on immigration. It seemed that parts of the Expansionist alliance were becoming shaky.

* * *

White Flag Reform Rejected Again—2006

At the end of May the senate finally passed its stone. The McCain-Kennedy formula, now smothered in amnesty labels, gave way to the Hagel-Martinez "compromise" approach to the same ends. There was opposition in the senate, but not much. Senator Bryan Dorgan was a rare Democrat who denounced the whole guestworker idea as a strategy of "corporate America," to bring in "low-wage replacement workers." Senator Jeff Sessions declared that the legislation "is unworthy of the United States Senate and that it should never pass," and Senator Diane Feinstein declared the three-tiered system of Hagel-Martinez "a bureaucratic nightmare sure to encourage document fraud." Still, S.

2611 passed the senate by a vote of 62-36. The 600-plus page monster underwent so many last minute changes and amendments that even its supporters were not sure of all the details. Never mind the details, among celebrating supporters. *The New York Times* on May 27 ran a lead editorial announcing that "Americans should be proud of what the U. S. Senate did this week," passing "a flexible and sensible policy" after "months of thoughtful debate." This came from the nation's leading newspaper.

S. 2611 was loaded with other mistakes beyond the amnesties, such as a new unskilled guest worker program, new foreign student visa programs, and a 400 percent increase in the program of "H" category employment-based visas. A June paper by Steve Camarota of CIS, using the text of the bill and the experience of the amnesties of 1986, estimated that S.2611 if enacted would legalize 10 million illegals, one-fourth of them fraudulently, and add to them an expected 4.5 million family members.

The tone of the immediate commentary by Republicans in the House forecast trouble in a House-Senate conference committee, if there ever was to be one.

James Sensenbrenner: "The senate is not where the American people are at."

Lamar Smith: "The senate bill…is not good for America and American workers."

J. D. Hayworth: "The 1986 amnesty law had a similar approach and that was a catastrophe."

Tom Tancredo: "It's bad for our national security, and it's bad for American workers."

The *Washington Post* found that Republican House members "facing the toughest races this fall are overwhelmingly opposed to any deal that provides illegal immigrants a path to citizenship," and such members reported 80 to 90 percent of the feedback from constituents was negative toward what Bush and the senate were pushing. Leading conservative intellectual and political leaders, including William Bennett, Robert Bork, William F. Buckley, Ward Connerly, Newt Gingrich, Phyllis Schlafly and Thomas Sowell on June 19 signed an open letter to the president and congressional leaders asking that full and successful implementation of enforcement come first, after which "we can debate" whether either amnesty or guest worker programs were needed.

Apart from the widening rift in his own party, May and June of 2006 was not a good time for the president to ask voters to trust the government to competently administer a massive amnesty and guestworker adventure, as well as fix the porous border. Bush's approval ratings, pulled downward by the floundering military intervention in Iraq, the fiasco of the government's response to Hurricane Katrina, lobbyist corruption scandals, runaway spending, and rising gas prices, reached the lowest point (33 percent) in his presidency in May, and the percentage of voters who thought the nation on the wrong track rose sharply.

* * *

No Conference, No Compromise

The House Republican leadership, a group of overweight elderly white guys who had never been close enough to a major national policy debate to have national reputations, displayed in June and after an unexpected degree of backbone and political savvy. Perhaps they were emboldened by the victory in an early June California House election by former congressman and outspoken critic of illegal immigration, Brian Bilbray, who bested eighteen opponents. There would be, the leadership announced, no conference on what they called the "Reid-Kennedy bill" hatched in the senate. Instead, there would be a "time out" for field hearings around the country to learn more about the implications of Reid-Kennedy and to assess the mood and hear the views of the public.

"We want to make sure," said House Speaker Dennis Hastert, "before we send our chairmen into that [conference with the senate] room, that they have heard from the American people."

July and August were to be devoted to more than twenty such public hearings in places like San Diego, Philadelphia, Phoenix, Houston, and El Paso. They ranged widely across the likely costs and results of the legislation. What would Reid-Kennedy's amnesty proposal cost? The CBO estimated $127 billion in the first ten years, admitting the costs would then become higher.

House Republicans understood that they could not go to the voters in November bragging only about twenty-one field hearings, and after a policy conference in mid-September they announced that the hearings had confirmed that "the Reid-Kennedy Democrat bill would undermine, rather than strengthen, our border security."

"We found through these hearings, said Speaker Hastert, "that every state is a border state, and almost every city is a border city."

Instead of taking up the senate's Expansionist, amnesty-infected proposals, House leaders recognized that the first step must be border security. Nine pieces of the original House bill were quickly passed by large margins, dealing with matters such as expedited deportation, detention space, even a measure to criminalize the building of cross-border tunnels. Attracting most attention was a provision to build a "big fence" along a large part or even all of the border, augmented by sensors, cameras, and unmanned aerial vehicles. The senate retreated, and in early October passed the Secure Fence Act of 2006 by a 80-19 vote. President Bush signed it into law in October, and almost nobody gave a big cheer. House Republicans said it was a good start. We reductionists knew and said that even if the fencing and other border defenses were seriously installed, illegal immigration control required interior enforcement that imposed serious costs on both employers and illegals.

Never mind. The fence authorization meant that the only immigration policy change in 2006 would reflect the philosophy of enforcement first, however inadequate the first step. There would be no other steps until enforcement was assessed. The fence vote was no big victory for us. The victory was that 2006 turned out to be a year in which our defense not only shut the Expansionists out, but put on the scoreboard some modest, even if entirely inadequate gains in the border control effort.

* * *

Television loves a vivid picture, and the news shows by Lou Dobbs, O'Reilly and others began in 2005-2006 to frequently present border scenes—young males climbing fences or wading through rivers at sundown—far more often than alien arrests at Iowa pork factories or Central American gang members' tattoos as they were loaded into ICE vans in Los Angeles. The border now meant, overwhelmingly, Arizona and Texas rather than south of San Diego. The border story was also laced by the shadowy presence of drug cartels, and rumors of Mexican Army incursions onto U. S. soil. A FAIR-sponsored meeting of border-interested people in Sierra Vista, Arizona in October 2006 gave me a chance to see the combat zone for myself and assess Arizona's immigration politics.

At a Saturday morning meeting we heard from several locals, among them Roger Barrett, the soft-spoken Douglas, Arizona rancher who had first received national news coverage for mobilizing his neighbors for an armed resistance to flows of illegals across his property; and Sheriff Larry Dever of Cochise County, who explained to us that we would find law enforcement officials sharply divided between popularly-elected sheriffs (like himself) who would take whatever measures were required to curb illegal immigration, and police chiefs who, because they answered to city councils cowed by ethnic activists, meekly went along with sanctuary laws and refused to cooperate with the Border Patrol or ICE.

Our meeting attracted about sixty people, Caucasian but for one black and two Hispanics. They were educated, articulate, angry at both political parties, and as always almost entirely middle-aged or older. Most intended to go Sunday morning to Benson to give a send-off cheer to a group called the Southern Arizona Harley Riders and Friends of the Border Patrol who intended to have a little breakfast, music and speeches before riding their cycles along the border and finishing at Tombstone. Locals told us that Arizonans were complaining more than ever about the border invasion, even when they employed, and usually got along well with, the illegals. T. J. Bonner, head of the BP union, told us that the size of the invasion was still growing. Arrests of aliens in the Arizona sector were 10 percent higher than last year, and researchers in the San Diego sector, where the increase was 30 percent, found that 60 percent of those entering had heard of Bush's amnesty/guestworker programs for those who managed to get inside the U.S. The Tucson paper that weekend quoted a pollster from Northern Arizona University saying that "immigration unquestionably is the top issue in this election." Political consultant Wes Gullet said that one had to ask what are the top four issues in Cochise County south of Tucson, "because the first three are immigration."

We then rode two buses down the flanks of the Huachuca Mountains, turned east on Highway 92 to parallel the border with Mexico until we met it at the little town of Naco, the center of one of the busiest sectors for illegal human traffic along the entire U.S.-Mexican border. There, the border was marked by a formidable fifteen-foot fence that the U. S. Marines had recently built out of World War II corrugated steel landing mats, paralleled by a line of electronic detectors and lights, as well as a road patrolled by BP vehicles. Was this fortification effective? So much so, the BP officer told us, that the drug cartels on the other side had spent much money and time digging a well-lit tunnel that opened into an inconspicuous house on the U.S. side. From Naco to Douglas we bumped along a pot-holed road that followed the border for several miles before veering northeast a bit to enter Douglas. It was dusk, and some illegals had begun to move north, when we saw two small groups of arrested males seated next to a BP van, surely disappointed that this time all they got for their coyote fees and efforts would be a sandwich and a bus ride back south of the border at Agua Prieta. In this stretch of brush and breathtaking vistas across the San Pedro River valley, the "fence" was a puny, rusted three-foot barbed wire gesture over which only a cow could (probably) not jump. The gringos, one could conclude, were sometimes semi-serious about border protection, and sometimes not even that. In Douglas the larger fence reappeared, with a deep and summer-dry drainage canal under which the cartels had laboriously dug another tunnel through which thousands of pounds of narcotics had been carried before the BP became suspicious of the foot and vehicular traffic. The Tucson *Arizona Daily Star* happened to run a front page story that weekend on the 1,950 National Guard troops now deployed along the Arizona border. They reported that border deaths and apprehensions were down 46 percent and 27 percent from a year ago. We saw no National Guardsmen that night.

* * *

There was also mounting energy on our side of the book-writing part of the debate. That year saw the publication of Tom Tancredo, *In Mortal*

Danger, J. D. Hayworth, *Whatever It Takes: Illegal Immigration, Border Security, and the War on Terror*, Jim Gilchrist and Jerome R. Corsi, *Minutemen: The Battle to Secure America's Borders*, Frosty Wooldridge, *Immigration's Unarmed Invasion*, Lance Sjogren, *Immigration Politics*, and Pat Buchanan, *State of Emergency: The Third World Invasion and Conquest of America*. Buchanan's book spent several weeks on *The New York Times* best-seller list, and stood apart for its historical sweep and relentless argument that, as harmful were the immigrant-borne labor market impacts, contributions of tropical diseases and organized crime, immigration on the current scale and composition put national identity and cohesion at serious risk. And because his astute research efforts resulted in citing my *Unguarded Gates* eight times.

Other footnotes in the books I just mentioned displayed the influence of the research base and conclusions that CIS, and to a lesser extent, FAIR, had established. CIS staff and Senior Fellows in the first half of 2006, when the senate's disastrous legislation teetered on the edge of success, testified before congressional committees twenty-one times, and made thirty-three television appearances on FOX News and CNN. Mark made a presentation on his "Attrition Through Enforcement" proposal to the American Legion, and that group, long on the sidelines in the modern immigration debate, endorsed his plan by name in a May 10 resolution. FAIR's web site coverage of legislative developments now compared with NumbersUSA, no small achievement, and FAIR's legal counsel Mike Hethmon was deeply involved in drafting the enforcement legislation in Georgia, Colorado, and Hazelton.

* * *

As the summer ended, even the Open Borderists were conceding that the dream of unlimited immigration would not happen that year and that the Enforcement First and Only strategy was in place, at least for the moment. "It looks dismal," said La Raza President Janet Murguia in mid-summer.

"Any hope of an immigration overhaul is dead for the year," editorialized the big New York newspaper in late July, "except in the states," which "veer toward harshness," and in the federal vacuum, "localities [are] running wild."

The Open Border coalition tried to revive the marches over Labor Day weekend, but the crowds in Washington, Chicago, Los Angeles and Phoenix had shriveled from the numbers in the spring. Los Angeles saw between 400 to 1,500 marchers, compared to 400,000 in May. Voter registration was to have been the marchers' next phase, but an Associated Press review of several large urban areas reported no surge in voter registration among Hispanics, or any other group. The exhausted contending armies on Capitol Hill reminded me of the armies of Lee and Meade at Gettysburg on July 2, at the end of that bloody, inconclusive second day. Both sides, resting in their encampments, sensed that after the overnight lull there would be a great re-engagement—a decisive one, when the third day came.

* * *

Sometime in October, 2006, the Census Bureau announced, the 300 millionth American would be born, or would immigrate here. In 1967, when the 200 million population number had been reached, President Lyndon Johnson led a national celebration. We should have learned enough since that time about the costs of population growth to mark the 300 million mark in a different spirit—with dismay, and a determination to cap the growth and welcome a drift downward for a while. All the major immigration reform groups, hoping to make this 300 million mark a teaching moment, filled our newsletters with that message about the need for population stabilization, and the immigration reduction connection.

In some quarters, predictably, there was celebration anyway. Giant baby product corporations like Gerber and Johnson & Johnson spent heavily on ads expressing optimism and joy at all the diapers and baby food to be sold. News magazines like *Time* and *U. S. News and World Report* ran feature stories, but the tone was a combination of boasting with salutes to the inevitability of growth, which was the American way.

"In America, we have always done Big well," said *Time* in a letter to readers.

No need to alter course. "Growth and vitality are the same thing," celebrationally opined the *New York Times*.

The *U. S. News and World Report* ran a cover story headlined, "Where Will Everybody Live?," and answered blandly: in larger cities and suburbs.

Media discussion stubbornly continued to use the same old language to describe the arrival of the 300 millionth American and the shifting patterns of state growth. Rhode Island and Michigan "suffered losses" of population in recent census counts, whereas North Carolina "delivered an indignity to New Jersey" by growing faster and replacing it in the top ten "biggest" states. "Gain," don't "lose;" climb up the list of "biggest" states; move "up." The elites who edited and wrote for our popular news media were cheerfully raising no questions about the growth trajectory, though some demographers were quoted as worried about problems on the way to the next milestone, the tally of 400 million by 2040. I saw no serious discussion of the need to curb this growth monster now rather than later, and how. The only encouraging sign of rationality was, oddly enough, found in *The New York Times*, which ran five letters to the Editor responding to the paper's coverage of the 300 million milestone, and all five denounced the paper for its ignorant and outdated optimism about population growth.

Another opportunity for public education on the high costs of high immigration also surfaced that year, and it, too, fizzled. Media coverage of the onset of global warming and its likely disruptions had been substantial for a decade, and seemed to intensify in 2006. On April 3, *Time* ran a cover story, "Special Report on Global Warming: Be Worried. Be Very Worried," and other news media described melting glaciers, shrinking arctic ice caps, and upward curving recent temperature charts. On the fact of warming, environmental writer and one-time skeptic Greg Easterbrook wrote in May, "The science has changed from ambiguous to near-unanimous." Then in June, Al Gore's documentary on global warming, "An Inconvenient Truth," reached movie theatres and had a surprisingly large audience and favorable reception.

I had argued in *Unguarded Gates* (2004) that the inevitable international bargain on greenhouse gas emissions will lead to national and then to per capita emission limits, and difficult cuts in fossil fuel use in many if not most countries, including most importantly the largest polluting country, the U.S. Every immigrant to America would under those circumstances shrink each U.S. citizen's allowable allocation, and an irresistibly powerful rationale for immigration reduction would suddenly surge into American politics. Gore's movie (and a companion book) came and went, and there seemed every month more worriers about climate change and the other urgent reason to reduce fossil fuel consumption—the impending peak in oil production. Yet one heard almost nothing on the obvious implications for U. S. immigration policy of the arrival of global warming and peak oil—which were, we must shrink immigration to net replacement levels, around 300,000 a year or lower, so that the nation could wrestle with these new emergencies without the additional burdens of a daily increase in population.

* * *

2006 Congressional Elections

In the balloting on Tuesday, November 7, the Democrats gained twenty-eight seats in the House and six in the Senate, taking over leadership in both chambers. What were the implications for immigration politics?

What was certain was the shift of the House Majority to the Democrats, which took the House Judiciary chairmanship from James Sensenbrenner and gave it to an Open Border Democrat. In 2007-2008, the leadership of both houses of Congress would apparently be aligned in broad agreement with the president's amnesty-guestworker plan for immigration policy reform. Still, for most issues, the new Democratic control of Congress, combined with a lame duck and unpopular president, meant that "all the elements of gridlock are in place," in the view of Stephen Hess of the Brookings Institution. Yet some speculated that, if there was an issue on which party cooperation might materialize, it could be immigration. "The chances of comprehensive immigration reform being enacted in the next Congress [now] go up significantly," Frank Sharry said and hoped. Doubtless he knew that just after the elections, 900 companies sent a letter to the Hill saying they desperately needed skilled workers and wanted action at least on Senator Cornyn's bill to double H-1B visas. This possibility was raised within hours of the election, when President Bush invited new House Speaker Nancy Pelosi to lunch at the White House and promised to explore common ground on immigration and minimum wage measures.

Friends in our movement who e-mailed me after the election agreed that Democrats coming into Hill leadership was unwelcome, but the prospects ahead were not hopeless. Dan Stein went on the Lou Dobbs show the day after the election and predicted that the new Democratic House delegation, their ranks enlarged by moderates like Heath Shuler, , who denounced porous borders and took the North Carolina seat of an eight-term Republican, would back away from an open border immigration deal with Bush. He pointed out that no Democrat in any House race campaigned on a promise to back amnesty and guestworkers. Mark noted in *National Review Online* that all six state ballot initiatives making life harder for illegal immigrants had passed; four of them in Arizona and passing by majorities in the 70-80 percent range. "Its still a long way from a deal," Roberto Suro of the Pew Latino Center agreed.

* * *

Still, at the end of 2006, one uncontested result of the November election was the removal of the Republican House leadership's blocking position against senate-presidential gate-opening. If a new blocking position could be fashioned it would have to include more Democrats who were willing to resist their own leadership. Thomas Edsall argued in late November that the election had strengthened "the protectionist wing" of the party, and that the mood of Democratic voters generally was now "populist with a lot of nativism" and that there was "a solid block" of Democrats in Congress, encouraged by labor unions, who are now "inclined to put the brakes on all cross-border activity." Not long after, CNN ran full page newspaper ads hailing Lou Dobbs's news hour for being "up 73 percent" over some unspecified point in the past. Dobbs' growing audience could surely be described as "populist with a lot of nativism."

Speaker Nancy Pelosi was cautious when she issued a post-election "Six for 06" list of her party's immediate goals, and immigration reform was not on the list.

* * *

2007: Another Nerve-Wracking Year of Playing Defense

For another year, we had held off the Expansionists, blocking plans to admit 60 million additional immigrants by 2020 and sending another amnesty signal to those poised to break their way into America if the legal slots were inadequate. Yet still this was defense, leaving the existing mass immigration policies in place. What next?

The Expansionists would surely come at us again, this time with the Democrats formally controlling both Houses. They held no hearings on specific legislation, using the spring to meet and tinker with the 2007 version of their basic goal—more cheap labor and forgiveness for those who had broken in. Tom Tancredo confessed some pessimism.

"We will fight it," he told the *Washington Times*, and "we will lose.... It will pass...the president will sign it."

That was not unreasonable pessimism, considering that the president and the party leaders in both Houses were in general agreement on Expansionism. The media reported that the negotiations among senators was difficult, but in April a "grand bargain" was reached across party lines. On May 17, the president endorsed a package of measures announced that day in a press conference held by senators of both parties and two Cabinet secretaries. The details had been rearranged and need not be reviewed here. There were signs of strain inside the coalition. The process alone stirred up resentment, which Frank Sharry conceded to an AP reporter: "It's been hatched in the backroom at the eleventh hour." Still, the 2007 version was now hatched. We knew that our side was united and very apprehensive, but we heard from our sources that their side was divided and also apprehensive—that their large coalition might not hold together.

It didn't hold together, because we reformers, and a sizable part of the American public, were ready.

The membership of Roy Beck's NumbersUSA surged from nearly a quarter-million to a half-million in 2007, and FAIR also reported a spurt of growth. These new member/activists were not passive well-wishers, but angry, aroused, and remarkably informed citizens. They were a part of a twenty-first century surge of citizens who took advantage in large numbers of the policy updates, FAX and phone call campaigns sustained by the two large national reform organizations in D.C., as well as groups such as the Eagle Forum, CAPS in California, and newer groups like Grassfire.org springing up around the country as recently as 2006. The anti-amnesty faxes and phone calls reached a volume congressional staff had never experienced. Beck's members alone sent one million faxes in the May-June period. Thirty-seven talk radio hosts were rallied by FAIR in April for three days of continuous air time in another "Hold Their Feet to the Fire" event headquartered in the Phoenix Park Hotel on Capitol Hill. In addition, talk show hosts across the country, led by Rush Limbaugh, Sean Hannity, and Michael Savage with 34 million listeners, stayed with the audience-arousing "amnesty bill" issue as it started its legislative journey in May.

"Talk radio is running America," Senator Trent Lott complained to the print media.

Or was it Lou Dobbs, who devoted 27 percent of his airtime to immigration in the second quarter of the year? Or all of them together?

It was not just talk show callers and Roy Beck's incensed members who were in full revolt over a 400-page bill on which no hearings had been held. Some prominent Republicans who had said little or nothing on Bush-style immigration reform in the past began in 2007 to express opposition in respectable channels—Newt Gingrich in conservative blogs, journalist and George Bush speech writer Peggy Noonan in the *Wall Street Journal*, and Heritage Foundation President Ed Fuelner in his own newsletter.

Then on Thursday evening, June 7, "the grassroots roared," conceded *The New York Times*. The bill's managers moved to cut off further debate so that a vote could be held on the bill. They needed sixty votes, and fell fifteen votes short. Majority Leader Harry Reid glumly announced that the bill would be pulled off the senate floor. In a few days he had reconsidered and promised another try, and debate was renewed amid a flurry of confusing amendments. On the last Thursday in June, the senate's convoluted procedures reached a decision point that only members and a few Capitol Hill watchers understood, when fifty-three senators voted against closing debate. That was it. The bill had failed—

again, and finally, for 2007, and perhaps longer. Mark Krikorian called in from an airport in Canada to ask where the victory party would be tomorrow, and was told it was already joyously cranked up in Roy Beck's Hill offices.

* * *

How to explain the collapse of warm-sounding "comprehensive immigration reform" when everyone acknowledged that the system was broken? The nation's political and media elites offered Monday morning blames, usually of the other political party's performance, undergirded by the main theme, that America's many nativist bigots had unfortunately been out in unprecedented numbers to destroy a promising solution.

Such rubbish actually leads us to the starting point for understanding this startling legislative implosion. America's elites had for some time been profoundly out of touch with reality and also with public opinion on immigration (and other issues). The editorial boards of every national newspaper but the *Washington Times* spoke for the leadership of both political parties, corporate America, organized labor and organized religion, philanthropy, and the universities when they endorsed as a promising policy package a grotesque combination of a mass amnesty, an unprecedented expansion of legal immigration with a guestworker enlargement at its core, and more promises of border control. If public opinion polls were worded cleverly, about half of the public seemed to acquiesce in this package. When polls bluntly asked about amnesty for all illegals, the response was overwhelmingly negative, and registered something more important—public contempt for the federal government's promises to follow through on enforcement.

Still, public opinion, alone, did not dictate this outcome. It has to show up for the fight, but must be formed and channeled. As Tip O'Neill taught us, immigration reduction once had no constituency—in the 1980s.

What was new in the Expansionist campaigns during the George Bush presidency was the organizational muscle on the reductionist side, exploiting what Colin Hanna of the conservative organization Let Freedom Ring described for *The New York Times* in June: "Technologically enhanced grassroots activism is what turned this around, people empowered by the Internet and talk radio."

Yes, Tip, there is now a constituency out there. Instead of 20 million illegals, "The American people came out of the shadows," wrote the editors of *National Review*.

Plus the fact that the visible immigrant community, much of it illegal, had rapidly spread from five to six states to thirty to forty, to Hazelton and Raleigh, Storm Lake and Atlanta. "Every state is now a border state," said Susan Tully, field director for FAIR.

Plus President Bush, after 2005, sank hopelessly to the lowest approval ratings of any modern president.

Plus the federal government that promised to control the borders as part of the package deal was the same government that did not enforce IRCA, that displayed its natural disaster rescue skills when New Orleans and the Mississippi coast were hit by Hurricane Katrina, and that could not clear a growing backlog in the renewal of passports. The legislation proposed a deal "with a fatal flaw," Harvard's Christopher Jencks wrote in August:

"Employers get what they want right away, while opponents of illegal immigration have to wait. In view of the federal government's miserable record on enforcement, no sensible...person of any political persuasion... would now accept mere promises."

* * *

So "Comprehensive Immigration Reform" had another bad year in 2007. The Expansionist version inviting sixty million additional immigrants and their children to become Americans by 2020 had been blocked and sidelined until the presidential election year was over—the pundits seemed to agree. This was the good half of the whole picture. The discouraging reality was that there was zero interest in Congress to take up our reductionist version of immigration reform built around the Jordan Commission recommendations to end illegal and greatly reduce legal immigration. There was indeed some legal immigration policy reform taking place in 2007 and likely to extend into 2008, but it was taking place within state and local governments which were increasingly active on the enforcement side with results nobody could see clearly.

* * *

2008: At Last—A Presidential Race With an Immigration Dimension

The American political system tends toward policy gridlock, and when the nation needs a course correction we have come to look to the president, more often than Congress or the courts, to supply the catalytic leadership. Immigration policy was last reformed in a major way in 1965 when John Kennedy and then Lyndon Johnson provided the impetus. We reductionist reformers who wanted those misguided changes corrected had been trying for thirty years and seven presidential elections to thrust the immigration question into the bully pulpits of presidential contests, and from there to the White House. Our success at this over these years amounted to one or two rare questions in televised presidential debates, with the candidates mumbling their way past the unwelcome question. Presidential candidates were never asked their immigration positions in campaigning among the public or in media interviews.

The campaigning of 2008 proved vastly different, a stunning turnaround. Our issue swarmed all over the intense presidential campaigning beginning in late 2007. The first sign that immigration choices would be aired came when Congressmen Tom Tancredo and Duncan Hunter, both Republicans, entered the race and claimed a place in the debates in order to highlight the immigration problem. By autumn, 2007, with the New Hampshire and Iowa primaries just ahead, polls and fundraising success had established six candidates (Democrats Hillary Clinton, Barack Obama, and John Edwards, Republicans Mitt Romney, John McCain, and Rudy Giuliani) as front-runners—expanded to seven late in the year when Tennessee former senator and movie actor Fred Thompson was persuaded by favorable public opinion polls to enter. Nobody knew what Thompson thought about immigration or much else, but, as the campaigning cranked up, it was at once clear that the immigration issue was prominent in the public mind. In early December, 2007, the *Los Angeles Times* was proclaiming immigration "a hot issue" in Iowa. The *The New York Times* called it "a relentless issue" there, and an Iowa state poll showed 2.4 percent of voters regarded immigration as "most important," but 85 percent said a candidate's position on it was "important" or "very important."

The candidates suddenly found their Expansionist records on the issue an acute embarrassment. On the Republican side, Rudy Giuliani could not deny that he had proclaimed New York a "sanctuary city" when mayor, and had said of illegals: "You're one of the people we want in this city." Governor Mitt Romney of Massachusetts was charged with employing illegals as gardeners at his estate. Arkansas Governor Mike Huckabee had offered drivers' licenses to illegals, favored "a path to citizenship" for them and said those who objected were prejudiced. Senator McCain had been a spear carrier along with Ted Kennedy for the notorious McCaineddy amnesty bills. Among Democrats, every presidential candidate who was a senator (Hillary Clinton, Barak Obama, Joseph Biden, and Christopher Dodd) had voted for every version of McCaineddy—that is, for amnesty for twelve million illegals and for more guestworkers.

The good news was that, under sustained questioning about their positions on immigration, all of them, especially the Republicans, stumbled over each other in a scramble to retreat from open border views earlier held and votes earlier recorded, while criticizing the rest for the sins of Open Borderism. Romney chided Giuliani for presiding over "Sanctuary City," and Giuliani denounced Romney's "Sanctuary Mansion" where illegals cut the grass. McCain sank for months in the polls as Republicans remembered his "with Kennedy" open borderism, and he conceded in January, 2008 that finally "I got the message" from voters that the border must be made secure before any other changes would be considered. *The New York Times'* summary of positions on major issues such as Iraq and health care now included a focus on illegal immigration—do you favor "a path to legalization" or not? The most dramatic shift of position must have been that of a second-tier candidate fast rising in the polls, Arkansas Governor Mike Huckabee, who in early December, embarrassed by opponents' exposure of his early deeds and words protective of illegal aliens, proposed a tough "no amnesty" enforcement plan which he conceded to have come from a 2005 article in the *National Review* by Mark Krikorian. All the Democrats squirmed to align themselves with border control and steer discussion away from their votes for "comprehensive" border-opening legislation, with Hillary Clinton floundering under the extra burden of explaining her support for New York Governor Eliot Spitzer's proposal to issue drivers' licenses to illegal aliens.

* * *

Our issue was for the first time front and center in a presidential campaign—or, a piece of our issue—the illegal component. How much progress did that represent? Much, and far from enough.

To start with the much, it was clear before the election year was half over that there would not be a massive "Comprehensive Reform" amnesty that year, nor probably in 2009 or 2010. As columnist Froma Harrop wrote late in 2007, The American public, or a huge piece of it, had rejected the proposed "grand bargain" of another huge amnesty in return for promises of enforcement, because "no one believed in the sales pitch. . . . They won't go for a "Yes" until they've heard a "No." Senator McCain, whose successful run for the GOP nomination had very nearly been derailed early on by Republican grassroots anger at his Open Borders/amnesty proposals, conceded this in February, 2008: "Only after we achieved widespread consensus that our borders are secure would we address other aspects of the problem."

Further, Mark Krikorian's concept of "attrition through enforcement" offered an alternative strategic framework that seemed to be working. Federal enforcement efforts mounted through the election year, with large raids on employers of illegals, while USICS reported that in the year from September, 2007-2008 it had tripled the number of deported illegal alien convicted felons to 164,000. State and local governments, once bastions of a variety of sanctuary practices, had veered toward tough enforcement. The National Conference of State Legislatures reported that states considered 1,404 measures to curb illegal immigration by summer, 2007, and enacted 170 of them. This was two and a half times the legislative activity of the year before, and the trend ran through 2008. By April, 1, one hundred immigration enforcement bills had been introduced in forty-four states. The toughest state law was passed in Arizona, pulling the license of any employer knowingly employing one of the state's estimated 500,000 illegals. The liberals who wrote *The*

New York Times' editorials were distraught, lamenting in March, 2008 that "The harsh enforcement virus has spread far beyond the Capitol—to Oklahoma, Arizona, Virginia..." San Francisco stood out as the only major city still openly bragging that it was a sanctuary for illegals.

As enforcement toughened, interior communities as well as in the workplace and at the border, there was parallel evidence, soft but widespread, of what Mark had predicted—self-deportation as illegal status became ever more vulnerable. "Arizona Seeing Signs of Flight by Immigrants," was the headline and substance of a front page *New York Times* article in February. Schools in Latino districts reported a decline in enrollment, businesses catering to Hispanics complained of a falloff of business, and "a consensus is developing among economists, business people and immigration groups" that recent increases in enforcement efforts was combining with a national economic slump that began in 2007 to create, in the words of one immigrant organizer, "a disincentive to stay in the state."

Were the unwelcoming policy and economic changes also contributing to attrition of the illegal population in another way, convincing many below the border and abroad that perhaps they would not migrate to El Norte at all, at least for a while? Some anecdotal evidence of this flitted across the media, and border arrests in both 2007 and 2008 were half the 1.64 million apprehensions in 2000, the peak year.

* * *

Despite these signs of progress toward building a political majority able to block more border opening, and the unprecedented penetration into 2008 presidential politics of the public's strong reductionist leanings on immigration issues, our gains had their limits. We reductionists had a reform agenda (going back three decades) aimed at fundamental changes in legal immigration policy, reducing numbers and shifting selection away from extended family kinship. This agenda was still being pushed off stage by the intense focus on illegal immigration. Our full message was not yet out there in the forefront of American public life—that it was time to end mass immigration, legal and illegal, and aim for population and ecological sustainability. The mass media journalists who had such an important role in thrusting the illegal immigration mess into national discussion—Lou Dobbs, Rush Limbaugh, Bill O'Reilly, and Glenn Beck—had only a dim and intermittent understanding that the entire legal immigration strategy of the United States was indefensibly based on demographic and economic assumptions totally out of fit with modern reality.

And we had to be disappointed in the performance of the two presidential candidates whose central issue was immigration reform. Little has been written about the campaigns of Duncan Hunter, never more than a marginal figure of considerable decency, and of the more visible chairman of the House Immigration Reform Caucus, Tom Tancredo, that deeply committed junior congressman who stood alone at the House podium for so many late nights beginning in 1999, explaining why America had a serious immigration problem. Tancredo's campaign did not educate or ignite the public, as he (like Hunter) somehow was isolated as a "one issue" figure, though immigration is connected to just about everything else—jobs, public services, education, organized crime, rapid population growth, and security from terrorists within. He failed to argue for the political advantages to Republicans of opposing illegal immigration on the grounds, among others, that illegals competed with American Latinos in his Colorado district for jobs as well as scarce educational and housing resources. Tancredo's decency and total absence of any animosity against the individual foreigners breaking into America were a contribution to a slow-building public understanding that reductionist reformers turned out when you met them in person to be, like most everybody else, likeable and patriotic people. However, Tancredo could not frame the entire immigration issue to become an integral part of an appealing larger vision of what America, and Americans of all ethnicities and races, needed. He dropped out of the race at the end of December, and in early 2008 announced his decision not to run for his seat again. When he showed up at an October meeting of the Writers Workshop in Roslyn, Virginia, the audience stood for several minutes in heartfelt applause.

If Tancredo and Hunter failed to master the chemistry and architecture of a new populist politics that included a commitment to smaller-scale immigration, who in modern American politics had ever done so—other than Pete Wilson, once? Republican voters punished Senator McCain for his amnesty stance, but seemed to ignore the conversion to a tough line of Massachusetts Governor Romney, an attractive former businessman who had led the government of a large state. He embraced a very strong enforcement position on illegal immigration after floundering a bit on the issue, but voters did not rally to him and he ended his campaign late in 2007 and faded into vice- presidential hopefulness on the sidelines. Governor Huckabee veered from sympathy and amnesty for illegals to tough enforcement, and his standing in the polls seemed unaffected. A CIS poll in early 2008 found, in Mark Krikorian's summary, that "most voters have little knowledge of their candidate's stance on immigration." Close to half were unaware that the three finalists McCain, Obama and Clinton favored citizenship for illegals, a position repudiated by 75 percent of Rrepublicans and 50 percent of Democrats.

Thus in the first presidential election in the four decades of the modern mass immigration era in which immigration was a top issue across the numerous televised debates and media interviews, the large majority of the candidates for the presidency who continued to favor amnesty and guestworker expansions somehow managed to obfuscate their way past an irritated, poorly informed electorate leaning strongly the other way. When I grumped about this at a CIS board meeting in June, fellow board member and D.C. lawyer Bill Chip reminded me that while the eight Members of Congress running for the White House through late 2007 and all of 2008 had managed to obscure and thus pay no political price for their votes and support for one version or another of Comprehensive Amnesty-Guestworker Reform, they had also uttered no complaint when the legislation was shelved during the pre-election year. They had been frightened away from the Open Border legislating that came so close to success from 2004 to mid-2007, and that was no small achievement by those who frightened them. Perhaps they will stay frightened for a while.

Which, even if I had to concede to Bill that this was good news for those of us who had joined in the frightening, it still left the United States with the largest immigration intake of any country and a higher rate than in any period in American history—one-third of it illegal, a large proportion low-skilled workers without a high school education, all of them transiting our leaky borders by paths terrorists could readily use. The unreformed status quo, a CIS paper concluded, was adding 1.6 million immigrants a year, thus adding 106 million people to U. S.

population by 2060, reaching a total of 468 million—or half a billion, rounded up.

* * *

On the bright side, at the end of 2008, America's indefensible immigration policy was not immediately going to be made worse by our leaders in Washington, despite the pleas of employers like Bill Gates and also by the Congressional Hispanic Caucus. Subdued Latino activists staged a few puny rallies on "May Day." Our movement, by contrast, kept adding strength. The FAX-active membership of Roy's NumbersUSA sent a million faxes to Congress in the spring, 2008. The membership of CAPS in California grew by 320 percent in 2008. FAIR's "Hold Their Feet to the Fire" telecast in September featured Lou Dobbs and fifty radio talk show hosts appearing on national television, the organization's lawyers won a large victory in a California suit against a state law giving in-state tuition rates to illegal aliens, and FAIR moved into larger office space at the foot of Capitol Hill.

On another front, Mark Krikorian in July published *The New Case Against Immigration* (2008), arguing that fundamental changes in American society made mass immigration, legal or illegal, no longer compatible with the national interest. David Frum of AEI called the book "superbly researched and brilliantly argued...This short book may save a great nation."

* * *

"Lou Dobbs is winning," David Brooks of *The New York Times* wrote mid-way through 2008, "not winning personally...but his message is winning." Brooks was acknowledging Dobbs' relentless and audience-expanding critical coverage of the many costs of globalization—the factory closings, unemployment, and streams of illegal immigrants brought by the globalization gospel that the free and ever-expanding movement of people, goods and ideas across national borders was the path to universal social progress. True enough, Dobbs' newscasts wove a protest against illegal immigration into a suspicion of "free trade" and especially toward our major trade partner, China, the core of a populist, "defend the middle class" package that steadily increased his ratings.

None of my reductionist friends regarded Dobbs as a deep thinker on international economics or a fully adequate critic of the immigration mess. Neither did Brooks, who was recognizing a real achievement, that Dobbs had found, and was trying to shape and expand, a populist audience built around meshed themes including immigration reduction. Our social movement had been working at this task of education and political mobilization around immigration reform for four decades. Our intellectual and educational work had been superb, though always beating into the prevailing winds. The political leadership that could connect reduced immigration to a winning coalition of constituencies had never come forward.

* * *

U. S. immigration policy, "broken" from every viewpoint, drifted in 2008 toward a presidential election repeatedly marked by the disruptive presence of the immigration issue with no clarity on choices or candidates' positions. Since both candidates had long been supporters of "Comprehensive," i.e., amnesty and Expansionist reforms, it seemed possible that the election would create a political opening for making things worse. It did not. There was much evidence in polls and local contests that the public insisted on enforcement first, and still was negative about amnesty. Reflecting this, both party platforms veered toward the enforcement emphasis. The GOP platform took up immigration as a first item, rejected amnesty and defined immigration as "a national security issue." The Democrats also hardened their platform, with language requiring illegal immigrants to "go to the back of the line' and "we need to secure our borders." The infrequent and brief campaign comments on immigration by John McCain and Barack Obama in the autumn were hard to distinguish, except that McCain had made statements that the border must be secured before enacting amnesty and expansion of legal numbers, "reforms" to which he and Obama were both dedicated. Obama had nothing to say on immigration before general audiences, though in his Berlin speech he used the word "walls" sixteen times to deliver the message that "the walls between races and tribes, natives and immigrants, Christian and Muslim and Jew, must come down."

Of course, the coalition bent upon admitting all who wish to come was still in place—the president, large majorities in both houses of congress, all of the business community large and small, all ethnic lobbies, the headquarters bureaucracies of religious denominations and labor unions, all universities, the refugee industry, the immigration bar, all major newspaper editorial staffs except the *Washington Times*, and you and I when we want the toddlers watched or want relief from tiresome yard work. Even so, the circumstances under which President Obama will take office in 2009 weigh heavily against an early and successful push for Open Borderist reform. A recession and rising unemployment are forecast for that year and perhaps longer, while the country faces an urgent, crowded and difficult agenda of financial reform, federal deficits, two wars in the Middle East, health care reforms, and much else. Immigration reform seems situated for the sidelines and an extended stalemate.

Of course, politics can deliver surprises. Recall the infrequent but sometimes decisive role of disasters in breaking policy logjams and redirecting policy currents. "Walls would go up everywhere" against immigrants, columnist Tom Friedman wrote in his book, *The World is Flat*, if Islamist terrorists exploit porous borders and spotty interior controls in order to detonate conventional or nuclear bombs or launch anthrax attacks. Officials at airports and ports would also turn back many foreigners if a global flu or other disease pandemic breached our borders. Americans might then demand an historic and radical shift over to a new, small and controlled immigration regime, appropriate for modern conditions. I would acclaim this outcome, but not the route to it through some catastrophic event. It is a sad and deeply flawed political system and policy apparatus that can be moved to decisive and necessary change not by majority opinion and known vulnerabilities, but only by disaster, which in any event we must hope to be remote.

Chapter Twenty-Nine:
Immigration and America's Unchosen Future

Those who stay and struggle to change things for the better—the Lech Walesas of the world—are the real heroes. — John Tanton

> *It is possible that things will not get better*
> *Than they are now, or have been known to be.*
> *It is possible we are past the middle now...Now*
> *we are being given tickets, and they are not*
> *tickets to the show we had been thinking of,*
> *but to a different show, clearly inferior.*
> — Robyn Sarah, "Riveted"

> *And gentlemen in England, now a-bed*
> *Shall think themselves accurs'd they were not here*
> *And hold their manhoods cheap whiles any speaks*
> *That fought with us upon Saint Crispin's Day.*
> — William Shakespeare, <u>Henry V</u>

America Headed in the Wrong Direction

The first decade of the twenty-first century brought the United States a mix of conflicting and mostly unsettling indicators of where the nation was headed, and public opinion polls registered a steady increase in pessimism. Presidential candidates in 2008 encountered a public telling pollsters that 81 percent of them "say the nation is headed on the wrong track," reported *The New York Times* in April, 2008, the highest level of dissatisfaction with the country's direction since polls asked this question in the early 1990s. Public loss of confidence had plenty of sources—a stalled economy further weakened in the autumn, 2008, by a collapse of financial institutions, a widening gap between lower/middle and elite classes, a mounting public debt, surging petroleum prices with predictions of an historic peaking of global production as demand insatiably grew, predictions of disruptive climate warming atop pre-existing environmental troubles from agriculture to oceans, repeated evidence of governmental incompetence including a misguided and costly war in Iraq as the main response to the terrorist threat.

Was another major cause of public worry the four decades of ever-larger runaway immigration invited by the 1965 Act, one-third of that influx now illegal? This took time to work its way up the "it's broken" list. Mainly negative public responses to polls about large-scale immigration, especially the illegal sort, persisted on the edges of public discourse through the last three decades of the twentieth century. Yet the issue was politically contained, making no appearance in the presidential elections of 1968, 1972, 1976, 1980, 1984, 1988, 1992, 1996, 2000, or 2004. Then, late in 2007 as the 2008 presidential campaigns geared up, there it was in the large—immigration as one of the top five issues agitating the public and discomfiting the presidential candidates.

How did it get there? The expansionist 1965 Act and subsequent liberalizations rode on the wings of a myth about our national immigration experience—that, however large and however composed, immigration had brought and always would bring only good things, Einsteins and Gershwins and boatloads of nation-building workers and settlers, taking English and civics classes at night. That myth about the costless impacts of immigration eras far back in the national story joined with a new multiculturalist ideology to stifle public criticism when it began to mount in and after the 1980s. Criticism escalated because the myths were no guide to modern America as it absorbed post-1965 mass immigration. The sustained arrival of foreigners, invited and uninvited, brought rising costs felt acutely in the middle and working class layers of American life—labor market competition, fiscal costs to local and state governments. While elites happily employed cheap immigrant labor in suburban homes and watering holes, in agribusiness and meat factories, most Americans over four decades of mass immigration experienced escalating costs in their neighborhoods, schools, hospitals and other social infrastructure. These costs were felt first in the four southwestern border states, but by the end of the twentieth century had expanded across the south and midwest, deep into New England and the pacific northwest. Daily life in neighborhoods and communities was the incubator of social resentment.

Our multi-voiced social movement to change immigration policy and patterns worked to accelerate this social learning, generating a now-bulging shelf of books, reports, articles and organizational newsletters, lectures, conferences and meetings small and large, information-filled e-mails, and blogs and letters to editors.

The daily experience in American communities combined with gales of critical fact and analysis from our reduction movement's verbalizers and communicators taught a growing majority of the public to understand that our era's mass intake, almost half of it in violation of law, is not a welcome repeat of the familiar nation-building formula that led us to global pre-eminence. Instead, it is now a major current carrying our communities and nation to a place we and our children do not want to go—and thus deserves its place high on the national "worry and must change" list. Reductionist energies broke through in California and elsewhere in the 1990s. Then 9/11 came, and our porous border vulnerabilities increased the pressure of public dissatisfaction with the decades-long bipartisan laxity in immigration law enforcement. The immigration issue reached presidential politics within both parties in 1907-08 as a small-sized gorilla that no candidate was willing or able to dodge or turn to advantage.

This was half of the story of modern immigration politics, the half I have tried in this book to reconstruct as I saw it. As John Tanton and others had predicted in the 1970s, decades of large-scale immigration, especially when it came disproportionately from nearby Mexico, would in time generate mounting demands for a very different sort of "reform"—moving from a regime of very porous borders to essentially no borders at all.

So there has emerged, in time for the 2008 presidential election and sure to extend beyond it, two sharply different reform efforts. Perhaps both should be called social movements—one of them unlike all other American social movements, in that its foot soldiers when summoned into the streets were mostly illegal foreigners whose basic loyalties were suggested by the Mexican and Central American banners they carried.

The battle is now fully joined, at last. In 1978, founding FAIR, we did not think it would take so long for most Americans to see that this immigration era was a mistake. And I cannot recall any of us warning that the alliance responsible for mass immigration would never rest until all borders were down and immigration had no limits.

* * *

Where is this four-decade Big Immigration era taking us? In the debate over the expansionist reforms of 1965, its sponsors assured us that the proposed new system would not make immigration flows larger, but it did and does. It would not change American unwelcome ways, but it did and does.

in

* * *

Where Immigration is Taking America

As to population size, the Immigration Act of 1965 and subsequent expansionist laws and lax administration diverted the U. S. from the demographic path it was on toward a stabilized population—probably at 240 million, demographer Leon Bouvier estimates, if immigration had remained at pre-1965 levels. Instead, expanding immigration made this nation the fastest-growing developed society, likely to reach 500 million by 2040 and still robustly expanding. Foreigners, at congressional invitation, have cancelled the growth stabilization path chosen by American citizens. A CIS paper in 2007 calculated from Census Bureau data that the current level of immigration (1.25 million a year) will add 105 million to the nation's population by 2060. Immigrants and their children account for more than 80 percent of U. S. population growth. Average citizens intuitively understand that a policy producing half a billion Americans, and rising, means more traffic, urban congestion, environmental degradation, extinction of species of wildlife, and resource shortages from petroleum to fresh and potable water. Continued population growth in a country of our size had become, as the Rockefeller Commission said a generation ago, "an intensifier or multiplier of many problems impairing the quality of life in the U. S."

* * *

These and other costs of population growth must now be framed within a larger new context established by the warming of the planet. The most recent calculations of the Intergovernmental Panel on Climate Change foresee a warming of 3.5-7 degrees Fahrenheit, producing among other things melting glaciers and the Arctic ice cap, inundating coastal areas where one-sixth of humanity now lives; fiercer hurricanes; an increase of the geographical range of tropical diseases; expanded desertification; radical alterations of agricultural economies bringing more painful disruptions than benefits; the possibility of a collapse of the gulf stream resulting in radical changes in European climate; and the possibility of oceanic acidification with unknown results.

The effort to curb the increase and if possible reduce greenhouse gases in the atmosphere proceeds now at the level of feel-good gestures from individuals who are "helping the environment" by buying a hybrid car or cycling to work; of brags from corporations claiming "greener" products and processes; of pledges from towns, cities and states that by a date certain they will somehow reduce their "carbon footprint" to this or that target in order to solve the problem. The price of the decarbonization of our society will be much higher (and also the benefits) than these newly-greened Americans imagine. Americans, their political leaders coming last, will soon figure out that the necessity of reducing carbon emissions will require painful reductions and shifts in energy use. Then, inevitably, the realization will spread that such sacrifices grow a bit larger every time an immigrant or immigrant's baby enlarges the American population base that is trying to stay within acceptable emission limits. All future immigrants and their children, and all babies born to American families over 2.1 fertility per woman, move the goalposts back. Immigration reduction is an essential policy tool in all environmental policy efforts, including sharply curbing the emission of greenhouse gases. Policymakers and the public did not yet make the connection between growing environmental and resource problems and the expanding population that immigration brought, and a series of prominent ads in print media in mid-2008, posted by a coalition of four of our reductionist groups, drew no rebuttals or any other public comment.

This slowly emerging perspective on the collateral damage inflicted on the global environment by America's high and rising population levels cannot be confined only to our citizens. The prospect of more heavy-footprint Americans is one in which foreigners have some stake that cannot indefinitely escape them. In a recent best-selling book, *Collapse*, UCLA geographer Jared Diamond pointed out that we affluent, high consumption Americans consume thirty-two times the resources, and produce thirty-two times the wastes as inhabitants of the Third World. This huge American footprint grows even more crushing and costly as we add Americans to the total, which is one of the contributions of the immigration policy in place since 1965.

* * *

As these troubles intensify, the world's population is projected to rise from today's near-7 billion to 9-10 billion, worsening global ecological degradation and resource stringency. Rising numbers will be dislodged and turned into environmental and/or political refugees from failed states plagued by civil wars over ethnic divisions or water. Global warming will accelerate this human flight from homelands, especially where coastal regions are inundated and agricultural patterns disrupted. The pressure on the West of swelling numbers of migrating refugees will intensify, and the basic scenario of *Golden Venture* and even *Camp of the Saints* will be repeated many times. "How many should go where?," two Indian economists writing in *The New York Times* in May, 2005, asked about the fate of the 200 million "climate exiles" expected to be driven from their homes by rising ocean levels. They calculated that, based on national emissions of greenhouse gases, the U.S. should absorb 21 percent of these, or up to half a million annually "for seventy years or so" until all are relocated. Their estimates may have been vastly low. In April 2007, a panel of eleven retired admirals and generals issued a report on climate change as a "threat multiplier." They estimated that rising ocean levels threatened to dislodge many of the four *billion* Asians living within forty-five miles of the coast.

Thus the future holds ever more massive pressures from foreigners wishing, demanding, to come to America. Some of them would be Islamist terrorists or potential recruits. As a body, whatever the mixture of "hardworking and law abiding" and the smaller number of actual and potential recruits for Jihad, they expand the national population and make more difficult the nation's efforts to cope with global warming and other environmental and resource problems. It is increasingly clear that we enter this future with our national immune system down. We have been on a sustained diet of large-scale immigration, the wrong way to prepare for this new future.

As we have learned, immigration is not an individual and isolated act, but a collective process that develops momentum, especially in countries like our own whose selection policies give greatest weight to kinship ties. When very large numbers come over many decades, networks of information and kinship strengthen, ethnic lobbies in the new homeland develop political skills and audacity as they manipulate a growing diaspora, refugee agencies using government funds siphon in their clients, and employers demand endlessly replenished cheap foreign labor. To prepare for a world in which global warming not only demands a lighter American population footprint but also expands the range of ecological harms and joins with civil wars and failed states to dislodge unprecedented millions, the last thing the globe's chief carbon producer nation should do is to schedule four to five decades of million-plus annual influx, augmenting immigration momentum and foreign-born diaspora populations to a peak that continues to rise. Population stabilization, the *sine qua non* of sustainability, is incessantly pushed farther out of reach.

* * *

Mass immigration is re-shaping America in another way as it joins forces with other social developments tending to fragment the nation.

John Tanton once said of a particular legislative battle over immigration that it was "only a skirmish in a wider war" over American identity and cohesion. He was in good company in perceiving this. What Arthur Schlesinger, Jr. called *The Disuniting of America* in his 1991 book has been a major theme in our intellectual life as the twentieth century yielded to the twenty-first.

Social fragmentation has many sources, and Schlesinger joined many "disuniting writers" in avoiding the immigration issue. His main concern was the trend among the new generation of historians of emphasizing celebratory treatment of various ethno-racial minorities in place of a common story. He had little to say about the incoming waves of newcomers bringing foreign allegiances, cultures and languages, instead indicting as the major nation-divider the new cultural force called multiculturalism. It was initially a welcoming spirit toward ethnic and racial diversity but grew into a critique of assimilation and denial of a shared national history. Robert Pickus of the Bay Area World Without War Council helpfully enlarged this list, attributing "the profound erosion of common ground in America" to several "separatist realities in American life...Duke's English Department, corporate America, religious decay or religious assertiveness, Hollywood, and the media."

"The balance," Schlesinger concluded his book, "is shifting from Unum to Pluribus."

Have we become, asked Richard E. Morgan in *Disabling America* (1999), "simply a collection of ethnics huddled around a standard of living?"

Time asked, "Who Are We?" on the cover of the July 8, 1991 issue, and asked a group of intellectuals, "What Do We Have in Common?"

Most gave the politically correct and entirely unconvincing answer: "Diversity."

Historian John Higham noted in 1997 that "ethno-racial tensions are acute and in some ways growing. Are we witnessing an approaching end of nation-building itself?...an erosion of the nation-state, as its capacity to maintain national borders and an effective national center weakens?"

These and other commentators on societal fragmentation at the end of the twentieth century tended to locate the causes in the cultural divides opened in the Sixties and in globalization's sapping of the powers of the nation state. They dodged the immigration issue as Schlesinger had done—warned by friends that they would be "called bad names." But others—Peter Brimelow, Georgie Anne Geyer, Brent Nelson, Laurence Auster, Pat Buchanan, Robert Kaplan, Samuel Huntington and Juan Enriquez, to mention only a few—had the courage to address this fundamental source of the apparent unwinding of social bonds in contemporary America. In their books and essays they found assimilation of incoming foreigners faltering as the incoming numbers increased and the host culture lost its confidence. The national print media also weighed in. *Newsweek* offered a major story on demographic trends in January, 1997, and saw ahead an America "crowded, mean-spirited and glum—a balkanized nation increasingly split between have's and have-nots, old and young, and immigrants and the native-born," with a population rising by 2050 to "more than 500 million persons" in which whites are a minority.

President Clinton joined this conversation in 1998—or, perhaps future research in his presidential papers will require us to say, the president's speechwriters prepared a commentary for him on what a century earlier had been called, "The National Question." In a speech at Portland State University in Oregon, Clinton noted that "a new wave of immigration, larger than any in a century, far more diverse than any in our history," means that there will be "no majority race" in California in five years and in the U. S. in fifty. "Unless we handle this well, immigration of this sweep and scope could threaten the bonds of our union."

Clinton dropped the subject, but had he been serious about the issue or less timid he might have appointed a National Commission on Bonds of Our Union. Then there would have come under scrutiny many worrisome trends to assess along with "a new wave of immigration." The Commission would surely have pondered historic lows reached in poll-measured public trust in government and society's major institutions; the growth of the underground off-the-books economy; the shift in the generation and consumption of news from three television channels and one or two local newspapers in every metropolis to the information-splintering of hundreds of television channels and an expanding universe of four million internet blogs; the growth of gated communities; public school systems losing students to private schools and homeschooling. Such an inquiry would have strongly suggested that the bonds of union were weakening, and the end of the twentieth century had been a poor time to admit the largest immigrant streams in our history.

Nations, after all, are not eternal, but can unravel, which seemed to be "the tendency of our time," wrote British-born American immigrant and historian Niall Ferguson in 2001. The drift of contemporary history "is for existing political units to fragment." The consolidation of nation-states that multiplied the number of independent countries in the world in 1871 (excluding sub-Saharan Africa) from sixty-four to fifty-nine was reversed after World War II, with eighty-nine counted by 1950 and 102 by 1995. As the twenty-first century began, 200 territories or ethnic groups were seeking secession from larger units, providing much of the international news due to conflicts in places like Serbia-Kosovo, Iraq, Russia, Tibetan China, Sierra Leone, Sudan, Belgium, Scotland, Spain, and Canada.

* * *

What about the United States? Senator Daniel Patrick Moynihan noted in his 1993 book, *Pandemonium*, that the splintering of nations would perhaps lead to the formation of fifty to 150 new nations in the next fifty years. "Some of them in North America? Possibly." Was he thinking of Canada? Perhaps Quebec is a secessionist possibility, but surely one need not take seriously the strong support in Hawaii and even in the U. S. Senate for a proposed Native Hawaiian Reorganization Act which would create a sovereign government for 400,000 "native Hawaiians" and "allow for the complete legal and territorial independence from the United States." Or the convening in Burlington, Vermont in November, 2006, of the First North American Secessionist Convention?

What of our own Southwest, a region taken from Mexico by force only six generations earlier and receiving a sustained flow of Mexicans, a unique population of immigrants from a country with a 2,000 mile common border and whose numbers accounted for one-third of all immigrants to the U.S. and 60 percent of legal ones. This northward flow of Mexicans was not tapering off, but had sustained momentum into the future. The Mexican government estimated thirty more years of immigration flow at 400,000 or more a year.

Was this in effect a "peaceful invasion" aiming at irredentism—in Spanish, a *Reconquista* of territory lost a century and a half ago?

Some Mexican and Mexican-American politicians as well as tenured professors of Chicano Studies at American universities openly and proudly call it just that. Mexican President Ernesto Zedillo in 1995 said to a rally in Chicago: "I have proudly proclaimed that the Mexican nation extends beyond the territory enclosed by its borders and that Mexican migrants are an important, a very important part of it." (Translated from the Spanish) "California is going to be a Hispanic state, and if you don't like it you should leave," said Mario Obledo of the Mexican-American Legal Defense and Education Fund in the early 1990s. "*Somos Mexicanos!*" shouted the Speaker of the California Assembly (now Mayor of Los Angeles) Antonio Villaraigosa at a 1997 rally: "The question is not whether *reconquista* will take place, but how and with what consequences?" Mexican writer Carlos Loret de Mola wrote in the Mexico City newspaper, *Excelsior*:

> *A peaceful mass of people, hardworking, carries out slowly and patiently an unstoppable invasion, the most important in human history…a large migratory wave by an ant-like multitude, stubborn, unarmed, and carried on in the face of the most powerful and best-armed nation on earth.*

Can this chauvinism be dismissed as merely over-heated posturing and blather from politicians who sense a cheap way to appeal to their ethnic flock and who know the rest of America will meekly ignore contemptuous political speeches of this sort? Well, there is more than just rhetoric here. The Mexican government has an aggressive policy pursued since 1990 under three presidents—"*acercamiento*," or getting closer to "Mexican communities abroad." Programs run out of Mexican consulates in American cities promote national ties, solidarity and language maintenance among Mexicans and Mexican-Americans north of the border. Presidente Vicente Fox said he was president of 125 million Mexicans—one hundred in Mexico, and 25 million in the U. S. who could lobby the American government for whatever Mexico

City wanted. "We feel that in the future, Mexico can use us," said the Chairman of LULAC Eduardo Morga, "as Israel uses American Jews, as Italy uses Italian-Americans." Use us as an ethnic pressure group$ with primary allegiances elsewhere.

These political and cultural activities within the Mexican diaspora in the U. S. are minimized by some, under the assumption that Mexican governments are notoriously incompetent and can hardly hold their own nation together, let alone secure a beachhead in El Norte. Yet undeniably the demographics project unprecedented and unpredictable change in many parts of the U.S. Stanford historian David Kennedy wrote in 1996 that it was the first time in our history that one-third of the immigrants to the U. S. came "flowing into a defined region from a single cultural, linguistic and national source—Mexico. The possibility looms that in the next generation or so we will see a kind of Chicano Quebec take shape in the American Southwest." In 2001, a majority of births in California were Hispanic, as were 72 percent of the students in Los Angeles public schools. "The United States is becoming a Latino nation," Jorge Ramos asserted in *The Latino Wave* (2004), a hybrid; not part of Mexico but decidedly, especially in the Southwest, Latinized. Victor Davis Hanson, California rancher and historian, wrote that his home state of California was becoming a place he called "Mexifornia" in his book of that name, a "hybrid civilization" taking form across the entire southwest in which "Spanish is coequal with English, poverty becomes endemic...schools erode, crime soars, and integration and Americanization falter."

* * *

In these and other areas, the glue seems not to be holding across the American nation. Samuel Huntington reports in *Who Are We?* that nineteen scholars were asked to evaluate the level of "American national integration" over time, and on a scale of one to five, with one the highest, they rated 1930 at 1.71, 1950 at 1.46, 1970 at 2.65, and 1990 at 2.60. Scholars from many disciplines, Huntington reports, perceive "the eclipse of nationhood," "faded patriotism," "the devaluation of American citizenship," and speak of the U. S. in the early twenty-first century as moving into a "transnational era." Historian John Higham, who had become an advocate of immigration restriction despite his reputation of a critic of that persuasion, wrote in 1997: "Ethno-racial tensions are acute and in some ways growing. Are we witnessing an approaching end of nation-building itself? An erosion of the nation-state, as its capacity to maintain national borders and an effective national center weakens?" And in 1999, Higham again wrote:"Nation-building has collapsed both as strategy and concern, particularly in the high culture of the academic world. If so, immigration may prove to be just an aspect of a wider social fragmentation." Aspect and major contributing cause.

* * *

A Future-Aligned Alternative Immigration Policy

The central message of our immigration reductionist social movement over three decades has been making the case that a small immigration regime, with different selection criteria, is in the national interest for multiple reasons, and must replace the costly Expansionist tidal wave authorized in 1965. We have made this case with many voices for thirty years, and have built a social movement organized from tiny grassroots groups upward to several national organizations. We did not turn immigration policy decisively our way; indeed, we saw matters worsen. More of that may lie ahead.

But to me this is not yet a narrative of defeat. When the American feminists met at Seneca Falls in 1848, they did not imagine that the right to vote would come only after seventy-two years of struggle. Social movements to bring fundamental change to this large country have a history that teaches patience driven by determination. Still, it is fair for activists to ask: "What did we get for all the small and large contributions of money, of faxes sent to senators and letters to editors and meetings small and large?" Not yet the turnaround we seek. Yet we have awakened, encouraged and empowered many Americans, have won some small skirmishes, and have recently fought off a disastrous Expansionist campaign, and are well organized, Mainstreet to Washington, for the next stage of the struggle.

Most important, in the historical shadow of an earlier immigration restriction movement, we managed to craft a new language and tone—immigration reform toward lower numbers, again, but this time without the nineteenth century's nativism or xenophobia, without disparaging immigrants or their cultures, reserving condemnation for our own incompetent and shortsighted public officials and ethnocentric lobbyists rather than the immigrants caught in the mighty currents of globalization.

In the language of the civil rights movement, being in "the struggle" was in a sense its own reward. As I served four years in the Navy Reserve and three years on active duty with the U. S. Marines, I thought this met the needs of my patriotic impulses. My professional career led me into the world of research university academics, a world of dedicated and admirable people. But in the contemporary university world, patriotism is a forgotten if not thought to be a distasteful, war-starting term. Immigration reform brought me into association with people who had glimpsed a problem ahead for our nation and our children, and made time in their lives to try to steer the nation in a different and better direction, at the cost of attacks on their character and values. That is patriotism in its best sense, taking hold of a precious out-of-uniform opportunity to pay some of your debt. As Dick Lamm once said, "We are trying to go beyond being Good Citizens, and be also Good Ancestors."

* * *

Most of our energies over these years have gone toward a critique of the mass immigration regime regrettably legitimated in 1965. We were obliged to speak more about what we were against—that half-illegal and badly flawed immigration system in place—than about what we were for. It is my hope that this book has introduced readers to an admirable cohort of re-thinkers and reformers, who have thought deeply about the design and purpose of America's reformed new immigration policy in our vastly changed domestic and global circumstances.

No one to my knowledge has suggested an appealing label for the reformed immigration regime we seek. There is an appealing (to me) movement for Slow Food, and Slow Cities, and even Slow Medicine. Slow Immigration?

* * *

The movement now needs a political leadership that Ross Perot and Pete Wilson could not (for different reasons) give it in the 1990s, nor Tom Tancredo and Duncan Hunter in their runs for the presidency in 2007-2008.

There are constituencies across the left-center-right spectrum for a reduced immigration regime—one that aims at zero-sum or replacement immigration to make possible the goals of environmentalists and energy de-carbonizers; a flow cut down in size so as to pose little labor market competition inside the American workplace; a flow small enough to facilitate assimilation and national security monitoring; and an immigration stream that is entirely legal, bringing firmly to an end the deeply corrupting flaunting of law and the loathsome criminal importation of the foreign and underground component of our two-tiered population.

These components must be politically held together by a vision that other nations might one day adopt, when we offer to the world a model of an appropriately-sized population with altered lifestyles, passing on a sustainable ecology and economy to our posterity. Essential to this vision is public recognition that, whatever your cause, it's a lost cause without population stabilization at sustainable levels. This means a return to small immigration, for our foreseeable future.

The politics of this are there to be pulled together by a leader of superb educational gifts, as Theodore Roosevelt, with the help of a mobilized citizenry, thrust a new crusade, conservation, to the foreground a century ago. Another President Roosevelt gave a new reform vision and national goal a name when campaigning in 1932. The "New Deal," you anticipate? That is the label the press fastened upon FDR's plans, and he was happy with the label. But in another speech that same year he spoke from his environmentalist convictions, calling for changes aimed at the realization of "a Permanent Country." That is a national goal that must replace endless growth, requiring an immigration policy that forwards that goal rather than driving it out of reach.

And in New York harbor a re-named monument: Sustainability Enlightening the World.

Index

Printed in the United States
131674LV00004B/2/P